SUPERMAN

SACRIFICE

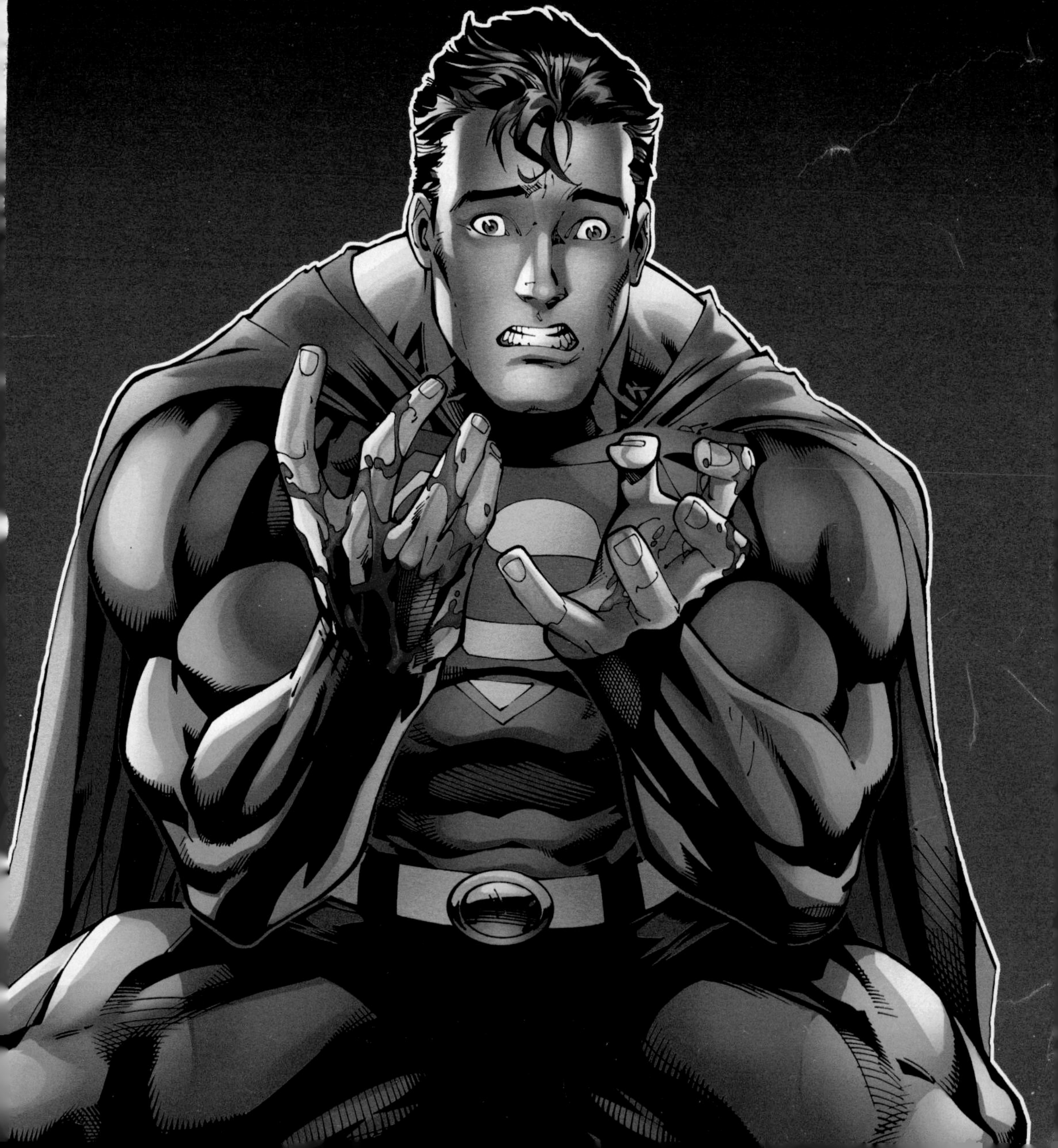

SUPERMAN
SACR

Eddie Berganza Ivan Cohen Editors – Original Series
Tom Palmer, Jr. Associate Editor – Original Series
Jeanine Schaefer Assistant Editor – Original Series
Jeb Woodard Group Editor – Collected Editions
Robert Greenberger Senior Editor – Collected Edition
Steve Cook Design Director – Books
Bob Harras Senior VP – Editor-in-Chief, DC Comics
Diane Nelson President
Dan DiDio and Jim Lee Co-Publishers
Geoff Johns Chief Creative Officer
Amit Desai Senior VP – Marketing & Global Franchise Management
Nairi Gardiner Senior VP – Finance
Sam Ades VP – Digital Marketing
Bobbie Chase VP – Talent Development
Mark Chiarello Senior VP – Art, Design & Collected Editions
John Cunningham VP – Content Strategy
Anne DePies VP – Strategy Planning & Reporting
Don Falletti VP – Manufacturing Operations
Lawrence Ganem VP – Editorial Administration & Talent Relations
Alison Gill Senior VP – Manufacturing & Operations
Hank Kanalz Senior VP – Editorial Strategy & Administration
Jay Kogan VP – Legal Affairs
Derek Maddalena Senior VP – Sales & Business Development
Jack Mahan VP – Business Affairs
Dan Miron VP – Sales Planning & Trade Development
Nick Napolitano VP – Manufacturing Administration
Carol Roeder VP – Marketing
Eddie Scannell VP – Mass Account & Digital Sales
Courtney Simmons Senior VP – Publicity & Communications
Jim (Ski) Sokolowski VP – Comic Book Specialty & Newsstand Sales
Sandy Yi Senior VP – Global Franchise Management

SUPERMAN: SACRIFICE Published by DC Comics. Cover, introduction, and compilation copyright © 2006 DC Comics. All Rights Reserved.

Originally published in single magazine form in SUPERMAN 218, 219, 220, ADVENTURES OF SUPERMAN 442, 443, ACTION COMICS 829, WONDER WOMAN 219, 220. Copyright © 2005 DC Comics. All Rights Reserved. All characters, their distinctive likenesses and related elements featured in this publication are trademarks of DC Comics. The stories, characters and incidents featured in this publication are entirely fictional. DC Comics does not read or accept unsolicited submissions of ideas, stories or artwork.

DC Comics, 2900 W. Alameda Avenue, Burbank, CA 91505
Printed by RR Donnelley, Salem, VA, USA. 3/25/16.
First Printing. ISBN: 978-1-4012-6440-6
Cover illustration by J.G. Jones
Publication design by John J. Hill

PEFC Certified
Printed on paper from
sustainably managed
forests and controlled
sources
PEFC/29-31-75   www.pefc.org

Library of Congress Cataloging-in-Publication Data

Names: Rucka, Greg, author. I Verheiden, Mark, author. I Simone, Gail, author. I Benes, Ed, illustrator. I Byrne, John, 1950- illustrator. I Kerschl, Karl, illustrator. I Morales, Rags, illustrator. I Lopez, David, 1981- illustrator. I Randall, Ron, illustrator. I Lei, Alex, illustrator. I Lea, Rob, illustrator. I Benes, Mariah, illustrator. I DeCastro, Nelson, 1969- illustrator. I Kerschl, Karl, illustrator. I BIT, illustrator. I Propst, Mark, illustrator. I Reis, Rod, illustrator. I Major, Guy, illustrator. I Horie, Tanya, illustrator. I Horie, Richard, illustrator. I Klein, Todd, illustrator. I Leigh, Rob, illustrator. I Napolitano, Nick, illustrator. I Fletcher, Jared K., illustrator. I WildStorm FX (Firm) illustrator.

Title: Superman : sacrifice / Greg Rucka, Mark Verheiden, Gail Simone, writers ; Ed Benes, John Byrne, Karl Kerschl, Rags Morales, David Lopez, Ron Randall, [and four others], pencillers ; Alex Lei, Rob Lea, Mariah Benes, Nelson, Karl Kerschl, Bit, Mark Propst [and five others], inkers ; Rod Reis, Guy Major, Tanya & Richard Horie, WildStorm FX, colorists ; Todd Klein, Rob Leigh, Nick Napolitano, Jared K. Fletcher, letterers.

Other titles: Sacrifice
Description: Burbank, CA : DC Comics, [2016] | "Originally published in single magazine form in SUPERMAN 218, 219, 220, ADVENTURES OF SUPERMAN 442, 443, ACTION COMICS 829, WONDER WOMAN 219, 22."
Identifiers: LCCN 2015049609 I ISBN 9781401264406
Subjects: LCSH: Graphic novels. I Superhero comic books, strips, etc.
Classification: LCC PN6728.S9 S934 2016 I DDC 741.5/973—dc23
LC record available at http://lccn.loc.gov/2015049609

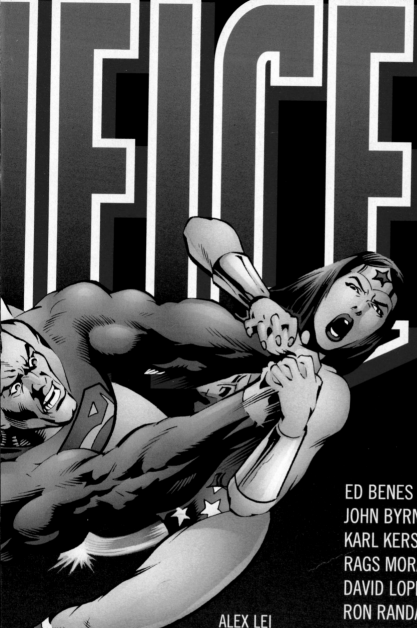

FICE

GREG RUCKA
MARK VERHEIDEN
GAIL SIMONE
Writers

ED BENES
JOHN BYRNE
KARL KERSCHL
RAGS MORALES
DAVID LOPEZ
RON RANDALL
DEREC DONOVAN
GEORGES JEANTY
TOM DERENICK
TONY DANIEL
Pencillers

ALEX LEI
ROB LEA
MARIAH BENES
NELSON
KARL KERSCHL
BIT
MARK PROPST
DEXTER VINES
ROB PETRECCA
CAM SMITH
SEAN PARSONS
MARLO ALQUIZA
Inkers

ROD REIS
GUY MAJOR
TANYA & RICHARD HORIE
WILDSTORM FX
Colorists

TODD KLEIN
ROB LEIGH
NICK NAPOLITANO
JARED K. FLETCHER
Letterers

SUPERMAN created by
JERRY SIEGEL & JOE SHUSTER
By special arrangement with the Jerry Siegel family

WONDER WOMAN created by
WILLIAM MOULTON MARSTON

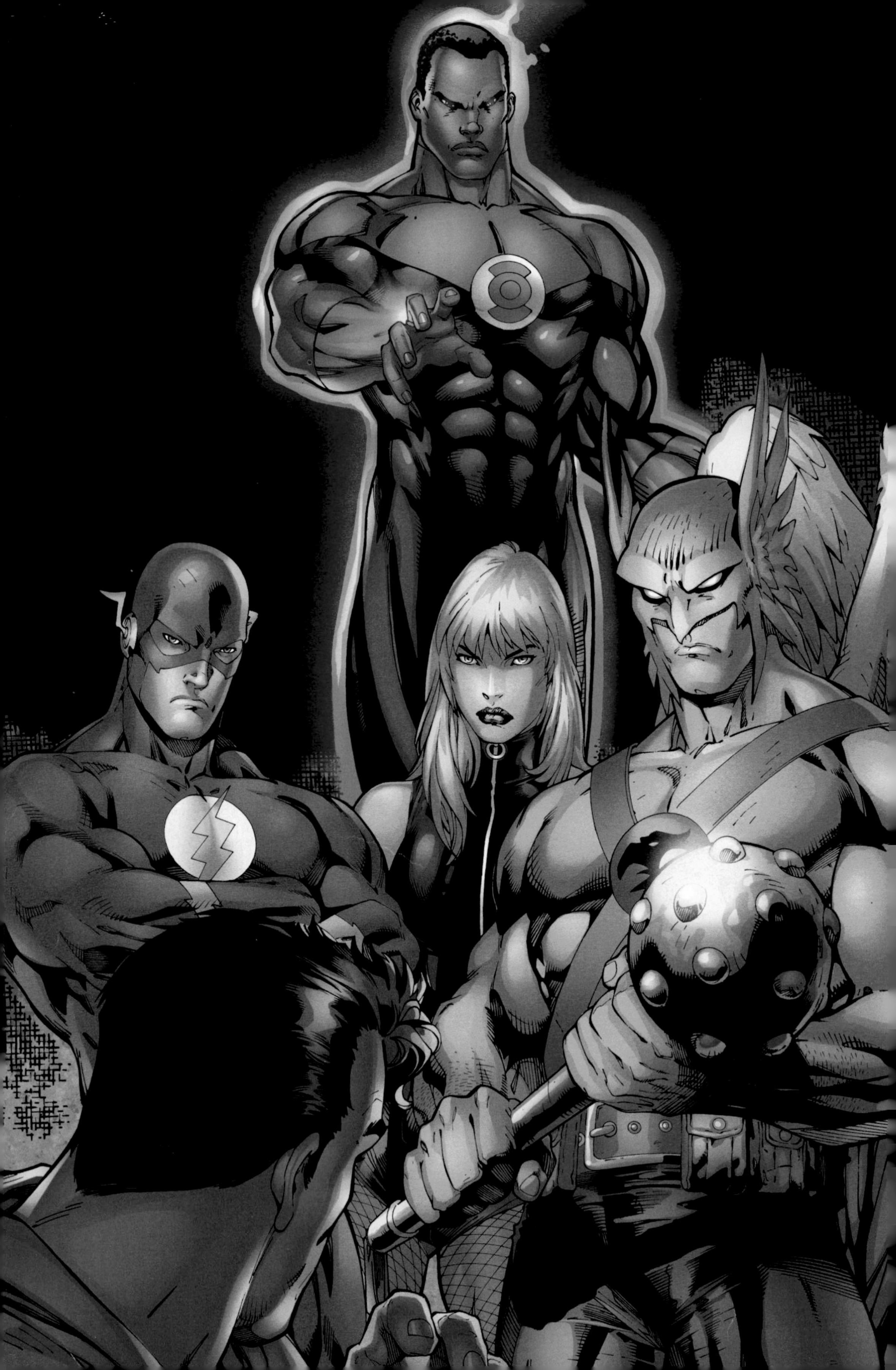

PREVIOUSLY...

Superman believed he had created paradise, a better world beyond ours in the Phantom Zone. Paradise was, instead, corrupted by the essence of the Kryptonian villain Zod, quickly becoming a living hell for the one million people — including his wife Lois Lane — whisked there during the "vanishing." In the real world, as others conspired against him, the Man of Steel found himself at odds with several of his fellow heroes, coming to blows with his dearest friends.

After Superman and Wonder Woman destroyed his Arctic home, the Fortress of Solitude, Superman searched for a new location for a personal refuge. He selected a remote portion of South America, but the peace he sought was shattered by a robotic construct that possessed abilities equal to his own.

His peers have had to cope with the violent death of several comrades, including the Blue Beetle and Sue Dibny, wife of Elongated Man, a burden compounded by a grim development. Knowledge that various heroes have conspired to alter the memories and even the personalities of their criminal opponents is spreading among both the costumed champions and their deadliest foes. The resulting rift among the members of the JLA has led to physical conflict, and the rift is growing.

As a result of this revelation, the villains have been working together to see to it that such affronts never occur again. There have also been other distractions across the stars and on other planes of existence, but the more immediate threats both in the JLA Watchtower and around Earth have prevented Earth's protectors from focusing on these problems.

And in the back of Superman's mind is a warning that a time of darkness is coming, that he will be at the center of a great crisis. But will he be ready? Will he be able to act in time? And will those actions truly be his?

SUPERMAN 218 - ART BY ED BENES

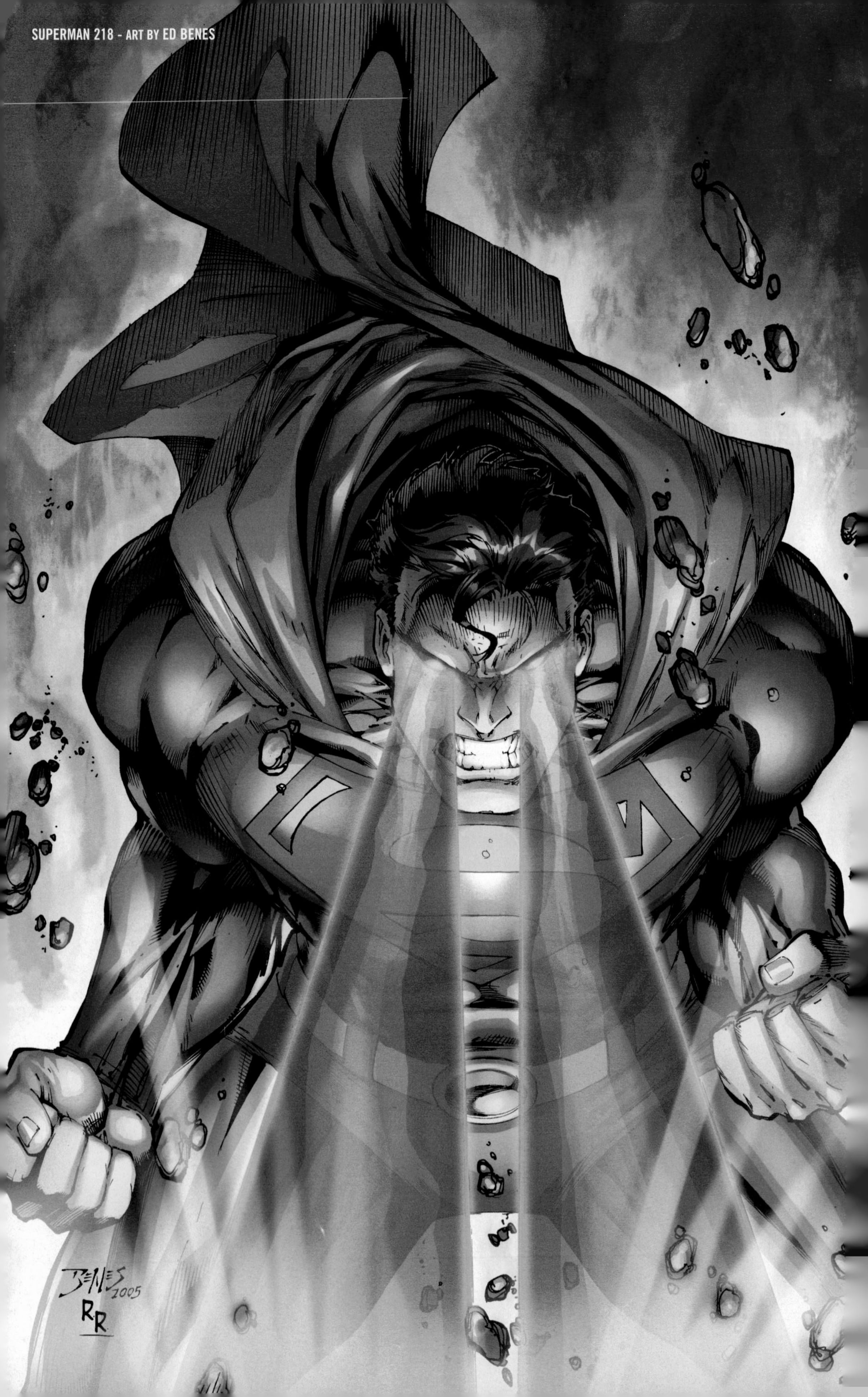
BENES 2005
RR

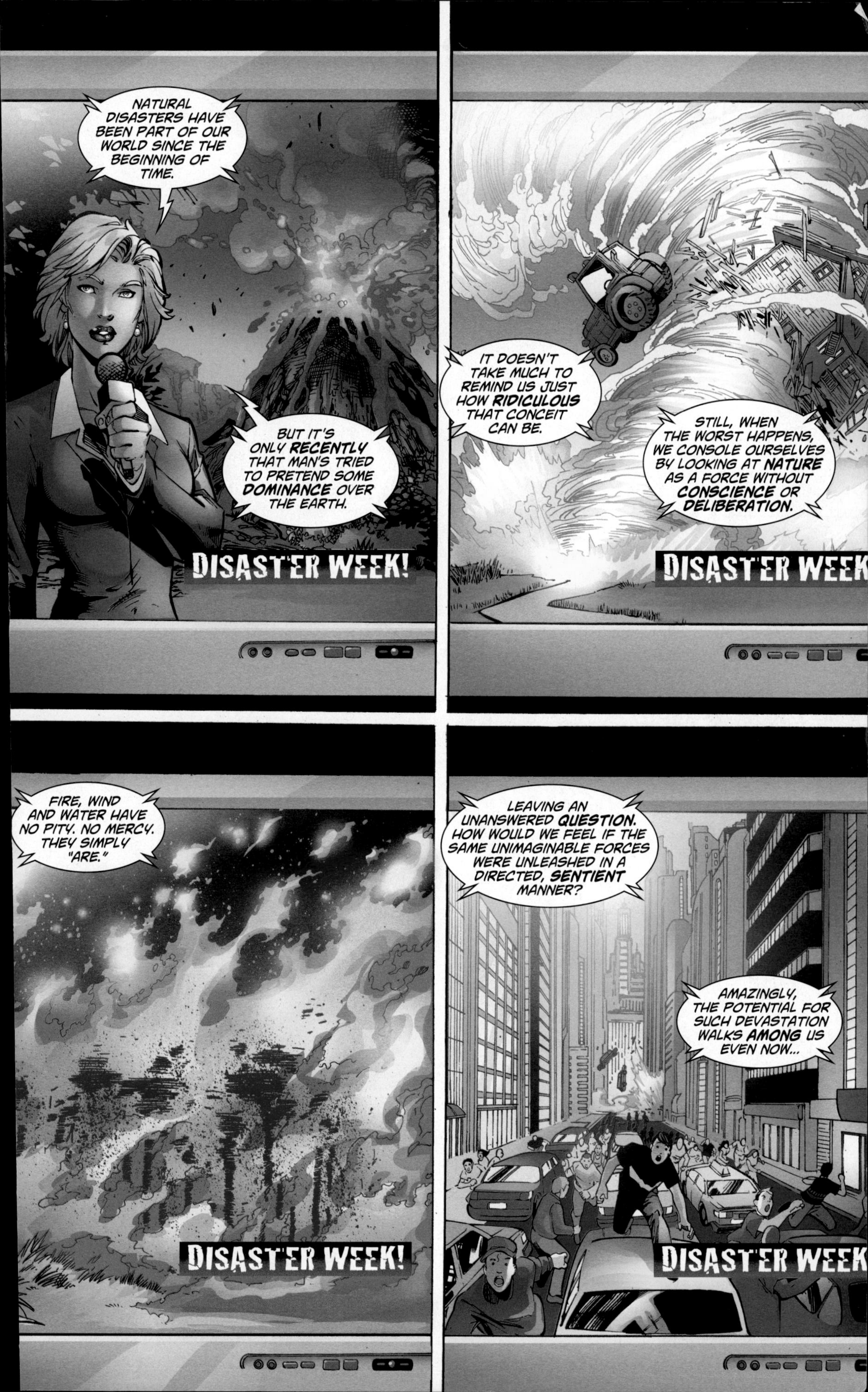
NATURAL DISASTERS HAVE BEEN PART OF OUR WORLD SINCE THE BEGINNING OF TIME.
BUT IT'S ONLY RECENTLY THAT MAN'S TRIED TO PRETEND SOME DOMINANCE OVER THE EARTH.
DISASTER WEEK!
IT DOESN'T TAKE MUCH TO REMIND US JUST HOW RIDICULOUS THAT CONCEIT CAN BE.
STILL, WHEN THE WORST HAPPENS, WE CONSOLE OURSELVES BY LOOKING AT NATURE AS A FORCE WITHOUT CONSCIENCE OR DELIBERATION.
DISASTER WEEK
FIRE, WIND AND WATER HAVE NO PITY. NO MERCY. THEY SIMPLY "ARE."
DISASTER WEEK!
LEAVING AN UNANSWERED QUESTION. HOW WOULD WE FEEL IF THE SAME UNIMAGINABLE FORCES WERE UNLEASHED IN A DIRECTED, SENTIENT MANNER?
AMAZINGLY, THE POTENTIAL FOR SUCH DEVASTATION WALKS AMONG US EVEN NOW...
DISASTER WEEK

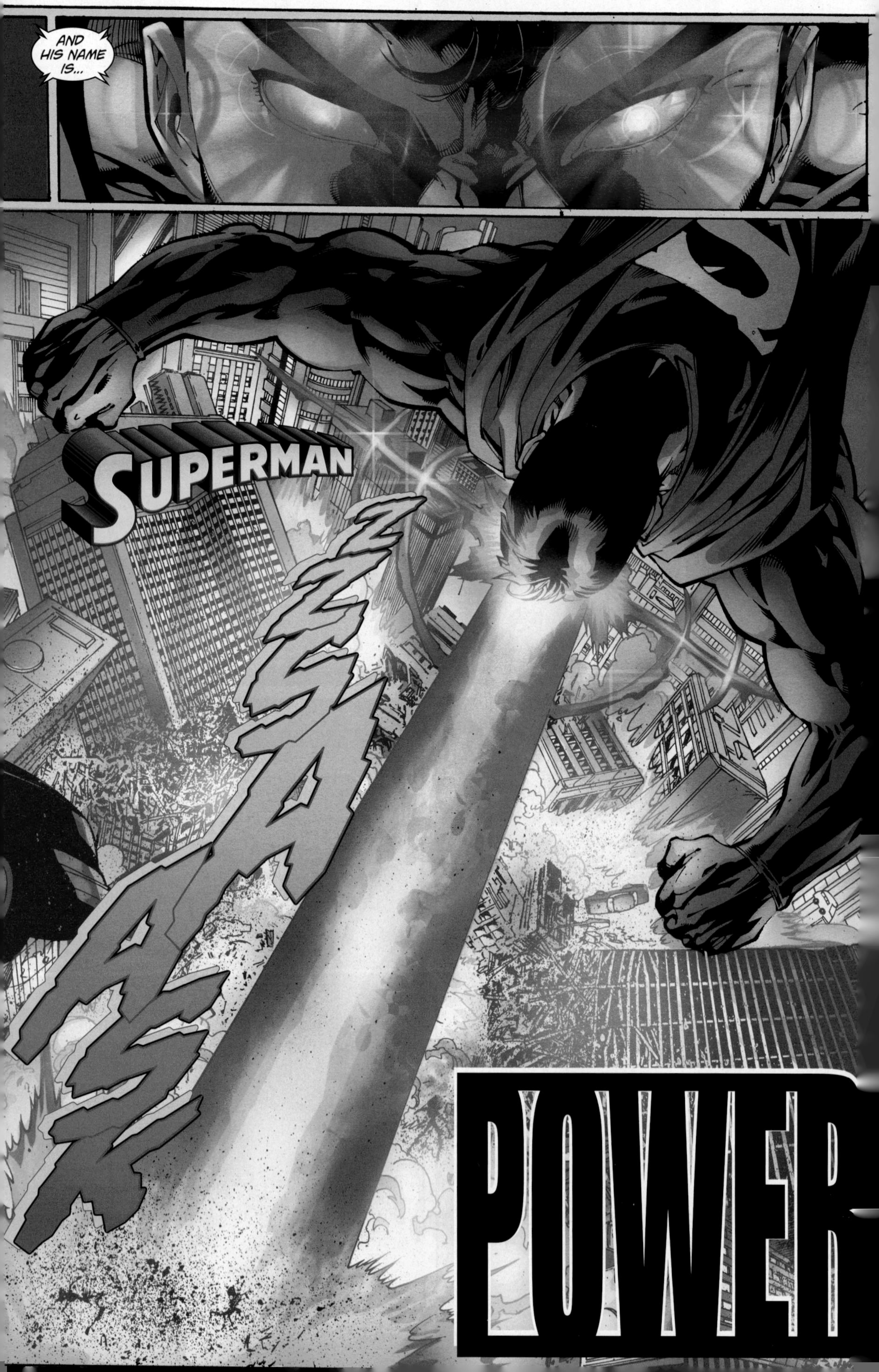
AND HIS NAME IS...
SUPERMAN
POWER

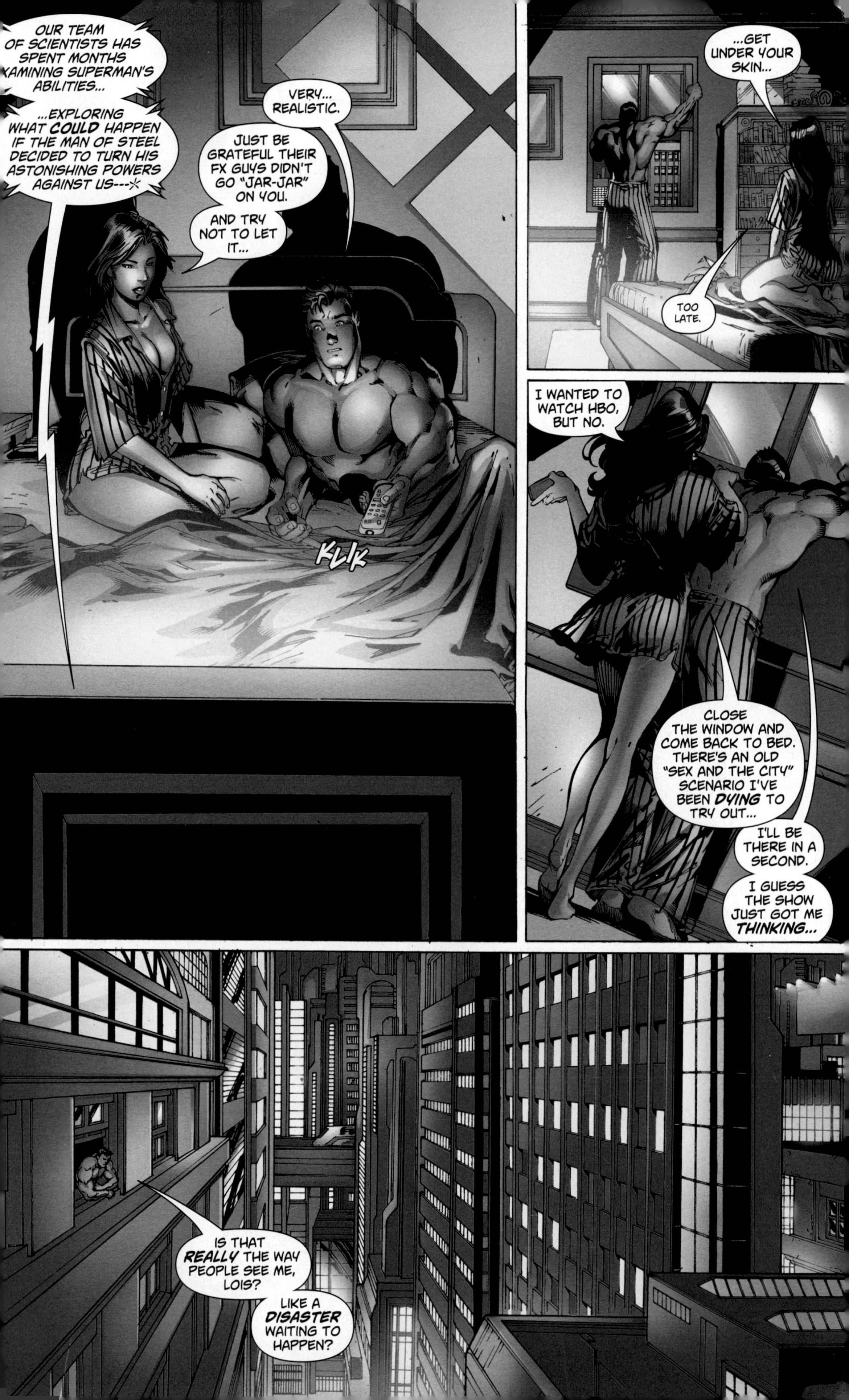

OUR TEAM OF SCIENTISTS HAS SPENT MONTHS XAMINING SUPERMAN'S ABILITIES...
...EXPLORING WHAT COULD HAPPEN IF THE MAN OF STEEL DECIDED TO TURN HIS ASTONISHING POWERS AGAINST US---
VERY... REALISTIC.
JUST BE GRATEFUL THEIR FX GUYS DIDN'T GO "JAR-JAR" ON YOU.
AND TRY NOT TO LET IT...
KLIK
...GET UNDER YOUR SKIN...
TOO LATE.
I WANTED TO WATCH HBO, BUT NO.
CLOSE THE WINDOW AND COME BACK TO BED. THERE'S AN OLD "SEX AND THE CITY" SCENARIO I'VE BEEN DYING TO TRY OUT...
I'LL BE THERE IN A SECOND.
I GUESS THE SHOW JUST GOT ME THINKING...
IS THAT REALLY THE WAY PEOPLE SEE ME, LOIS?
LIKE A DISASTER WAITING TO HAPPEN?

CLARK, *PLEASE*.

IT'S HOW ONE RATINGS-STARVED POP-*SCIENCE* SHOW SEES YOU. I WOULDN'T EXACTLY CALL THAT A REPRESENTATIVE SAMPLE.

MAYBE WE SHOULD POLL THE PEOPLE OF *PUCCALPA*...

AT LEAST THE ONES WHO *SURVIVED* THE RELOCATION OF MY FORTRESS.

HEY. YOU DIDN'T *CAUSE* WHAT WENT DOWN IN SOUTH AMERICA.

AND SUDDENLY THIS ISN'T ABOUT SOME SOON-TO-BE-FORGOTTEN *TV SHOW*.

LOIS, SOMEONE *ATTACKED* ME IN PUCCALPA AND PRACTICALLY FOUGHT ME TO A *STAND-STILL*.

I *PAINT-SHOPPED* HIS IMAGE AND HAD THE FORTRESS *COMPUTERS* CHECK IT AGAINST ALL AVAILABLE DATABASES.

SO FAR THEY'VE DRAWN A *BLANK*.

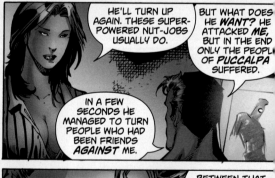

HE'LL TURN UP AGAIN. THESE SUPER-POWERED NUT-JOBS USUALLY DO.

IN A FEW SECONDS HE MANAGED TO TURN PEOPLE WHO HAD BEEN FRIENDS *AGAINST* ME.

BUT WHAT DOES HE *WANT*? HE ATTACKED *ME*, BUT IN THE END ONLY THE PEOPLE OF *PUCCALPA* SUFFERED.

BETWEEN THAT, TAKING A HIT FROM *PETE ROSS* AND NOW DOCUMENTARIES SUGGESTING I'M THE ULTIMATE *W.M.D.*...

I GUESS I'M JUST WONDERING.

WHAT IF THAT WAS THE *POINT*?

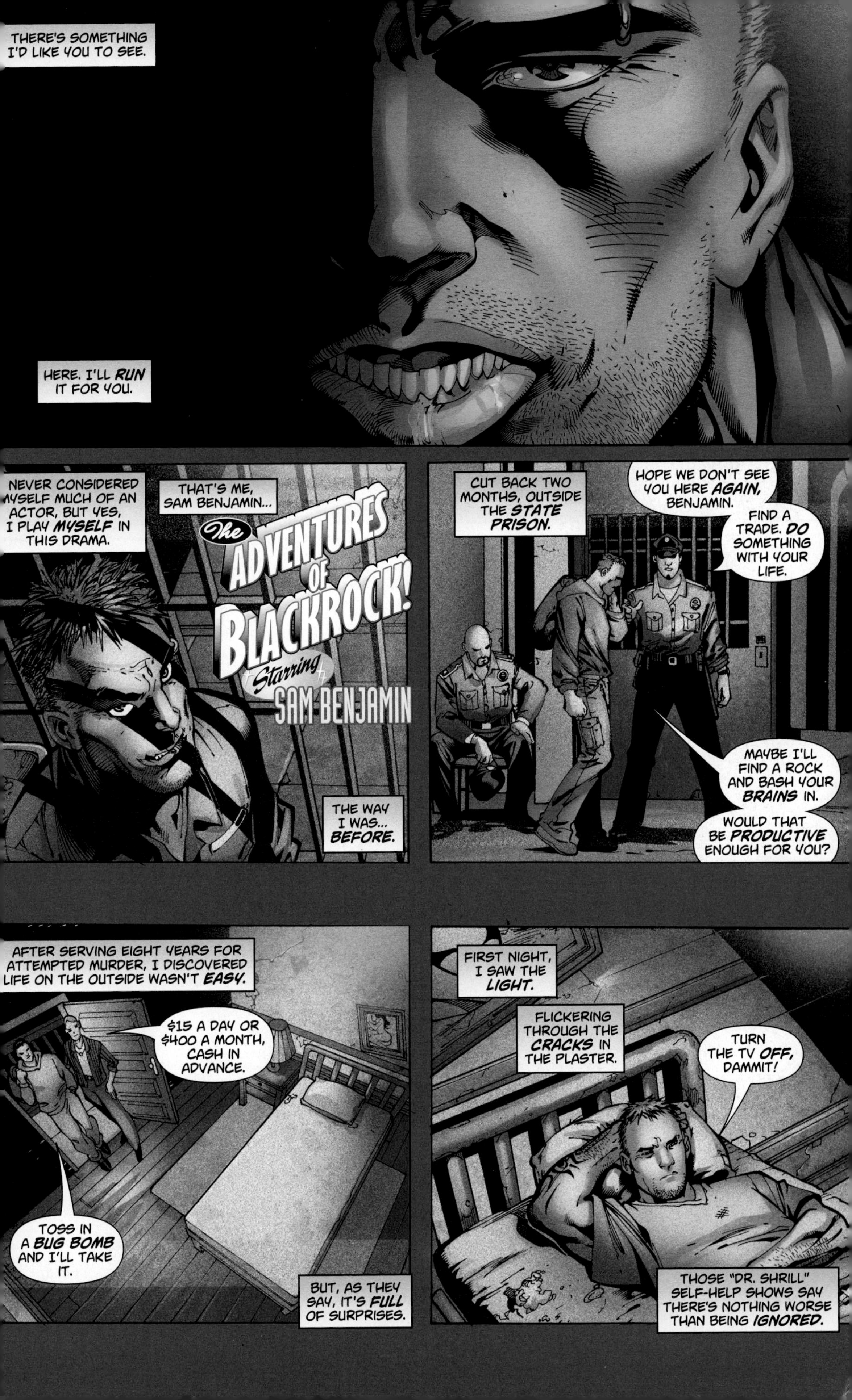

THERE'S SOMETHING I'D LIKE YOU TO SEE.
HERE. I'LL RUN IT FOR YOU.
NEVER CONSIDERED MYSELF MUCH OF AN ACTOR, BUT YES, I PLAY MYSELF IN THIS DRAMA.
THAT'S ME, SAM BENJAMIN...
The ADVENTURES OF BLACKROCK!
Starring SAM BENJAMIN
THE WAY I WAS... BEFORE.
CUT BACK TWO MONTHS, OUTSIDE THE STATE PRISON.
HOPE WE DON'T SEE YOU HERE AGAIN, BENJAMIN.
FIND A TRADE. DO SOMETHING WITH YOUR LIFE.
MAYBE I'LL FIND A ROCK AND BASH YOUR BRAINS IN.
WOULD THAT BE PRODUCTIVE ENOUGH FOR YOU?
AFTER SERVING EIGHT YEARS FOR ATTEMPTED MURDER, I DISCOVERED LIFE ON THE OUTSIDE WASN'T EASY.
$15 A DAY OR $400 A MONTH, CASH IN ADVANCE.
TOSS IN A BUG BOMB AND I'LL TAKE IT.
BUT, AS THEY SAY, IT'S FULL OF SURPRISES.
FIRST NIGHT, I SAW THE LIGHT.
FLICKERING THROUGH THE CRACKS IN THE PLASTER.
TURN THE TV OFF, DAMMIT!
THOSE "DR. SHRILL" SELF-HELP SHOWS SAY THERE'S NOTHING WORSE THAN BEING IGNORED.

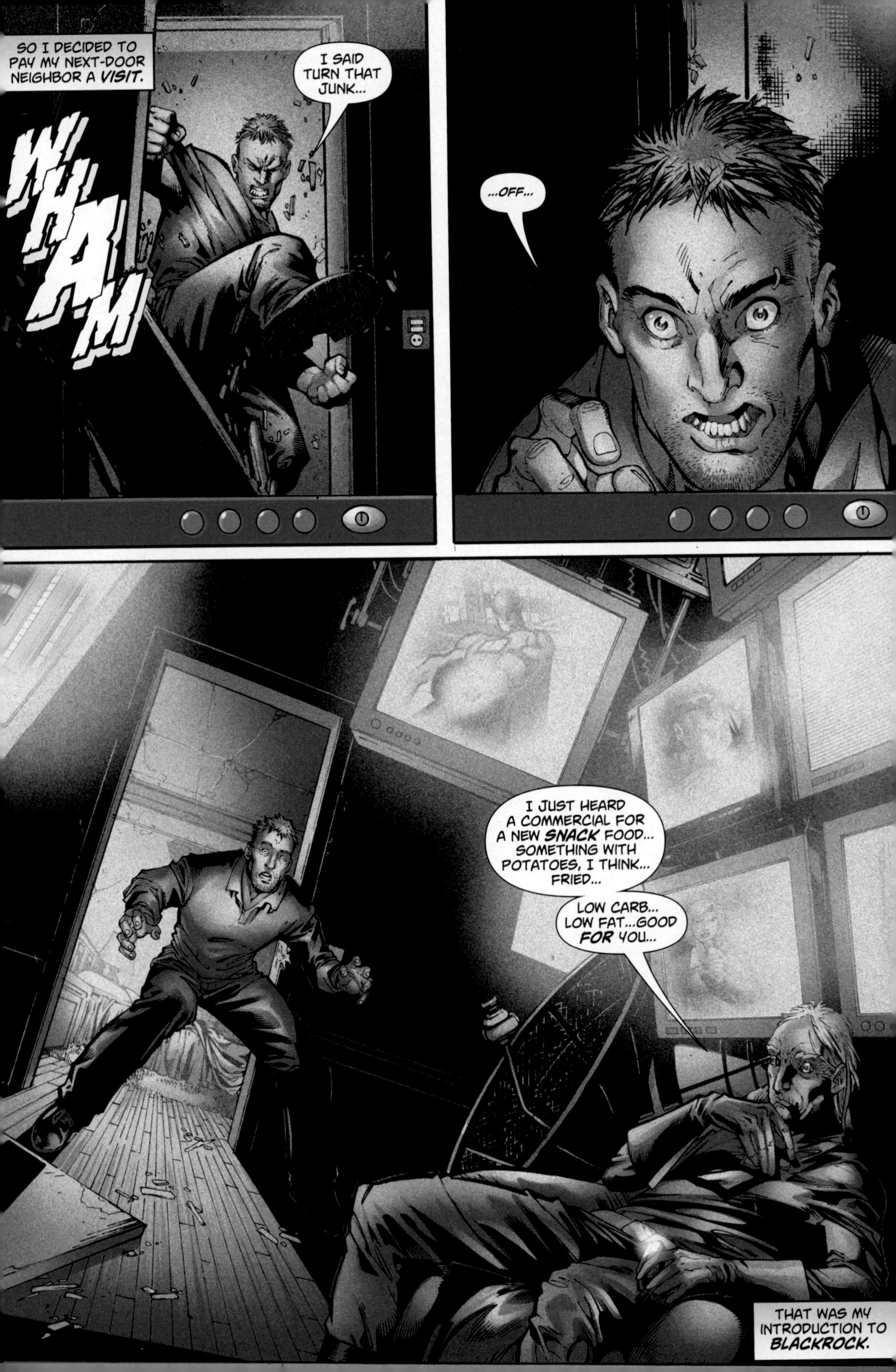
SO I DECIDED TO PAY MY NEXT-DOOR NEIGHBOR A VISIT.
I SAID TURN THAT JUNK...
WHAM
...OFF...
I JUST HEARD A COMMERCIAL FOR A NEW SNACK FOOD... SOMETHING WITH POTATOES, I THINK... FRIED...
LOW CARB... LOW FAT...GOOD FOR YOU...
THAT WAS MY INTRODUCTION TO BLACKROCK.

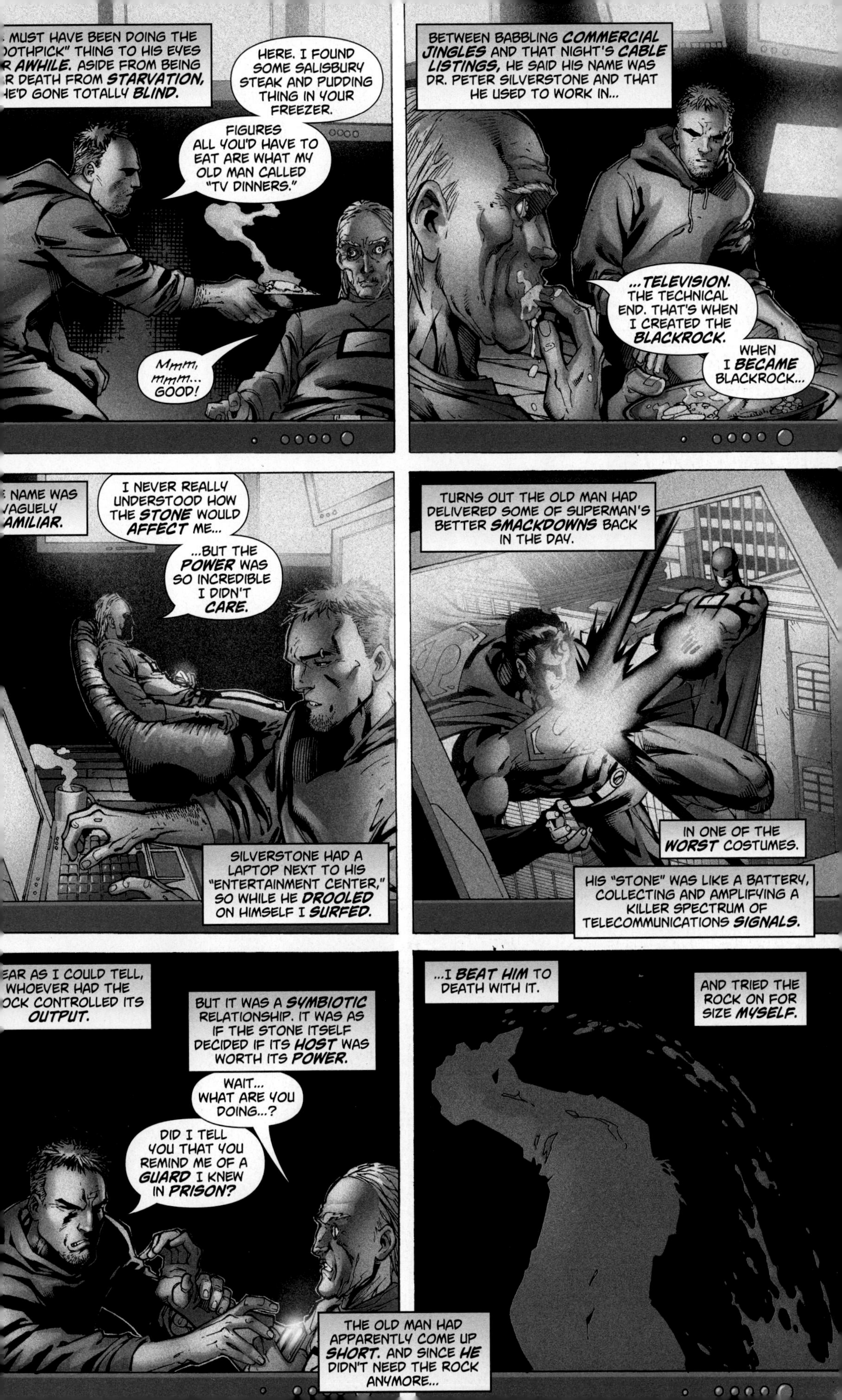

MUST HAVE BEEN DOING THE "OTHPICK" THING TO HIS EYES R AWHILE. ASIDE FROM BEING R DEATH FROM STARVATION, HE'D GONE TOTALLY BLIND.
HERE. I FOUND SOME SALISBURY STEAK AND PUDDING THING IN YOUR FREEZER.
FIGURES ALL YOU'D HAVE TO EAT ARE WHAT MY OLD MAN CALLED "TV DINNERS."
Mmm, mmm... GOOD!
BETWEEN BABBLING COMMERCIAL JINGLES AND THAT NIGHT'S CABLE LISTINGS, HE SAID HIS NAME WAS DR. PETER SILVERSTONE AND THAT HE USED TO WORK IN...
...TELEVISION. THE TECHNICAL END. THAT'S WHEN I CREATED THE BLACKROCK.
WHEN I BECAME BLACKROCK...
NAME WAS VAGUELY AMILIAR.
I NEVER REALLY UNDERSTOOD HOW THE STONE WOULD AFFECT ME...
...BUT THE POWER WAS SO INCREDIBLE I DIDN'T CARE.
SILVERSTONE HAD A LAPTOP NEXT TO HIS "ENTERTAINMENT CENTER," SO WHILE HE DROOLED ON HIMSELF I SURFED.
TURNS OUT THE OLD MAN HAD DELIVERED SOME OF SUPERMAN'S BETTER SMACKDOWNS BACK IN THE DAY.
IN ONE OF THE WORST COSTUMES.
HIS "STONE" WAS LIKE A BATTERY, COLLECTING AND AMPLIFYING A KILLER SPECTRUM OF TELECOMMUNICATIONS SIGNALS.
EAR AS I COULD TELL, WHOEVER HAD THE OCK CONTROLLED ITS OUTPUT.
BUT IT WAS A SYMBIOTIC RELATIONSHIP. IT WAS AS IF THE STONE ITSELF DECIDED IF ITS HOST WAS WORTH ITS POWER.
WAIT... WHAT ARE YOU DOING...?
DID I TELL YOU THAT YOU REMIND ME OF A GUARD I KNEW IN PRISON?
THE OLD MAN HAD APPARENTLY COME UP SHORT. AND SINCE HE DIDN'T NEED THE ROCK ANYMORE...
...I BEAT HIM TO DEATH WITH IT.
AND TRIED THE ROCK ON FOR SIZE MYSELF.

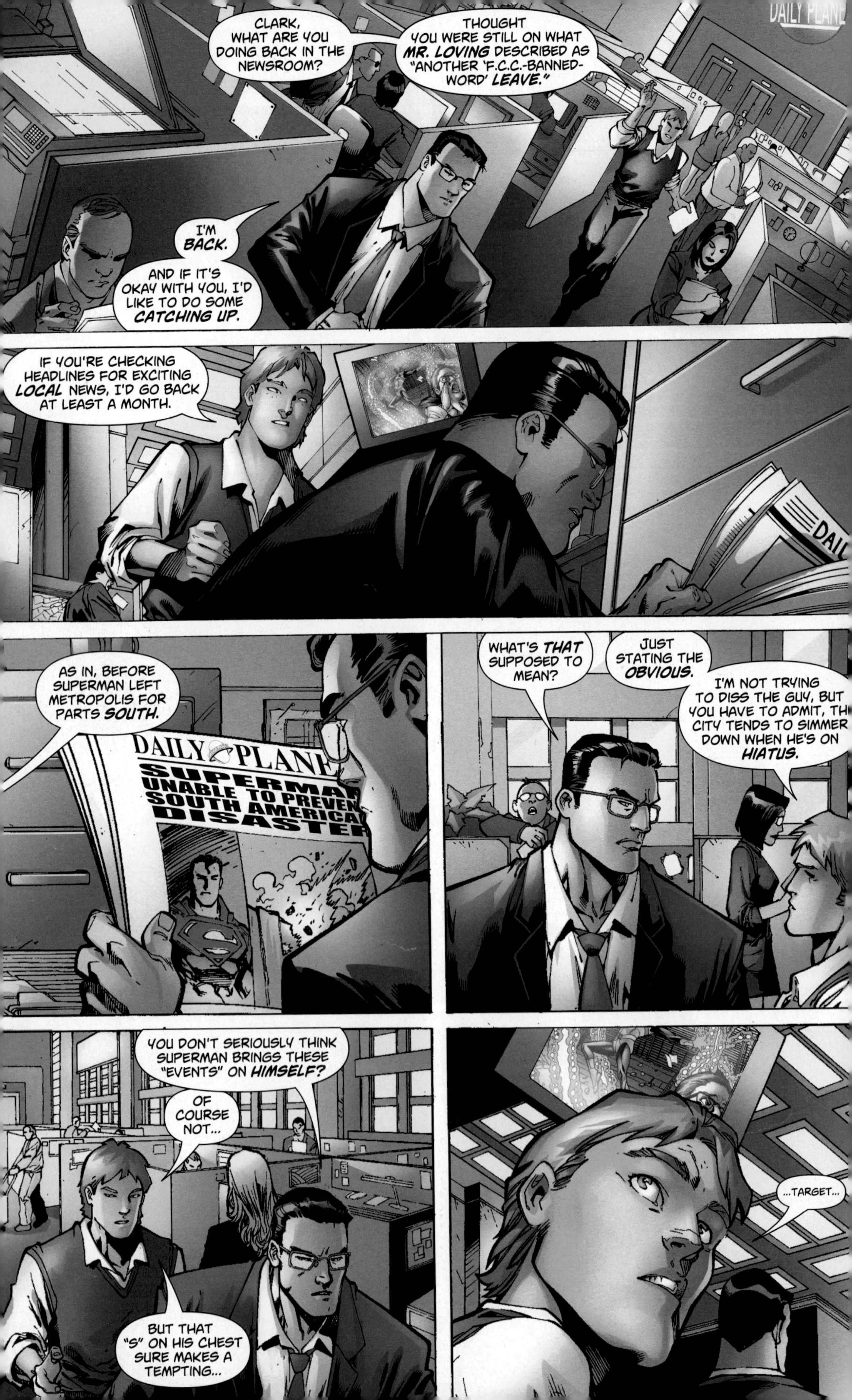
DAILY PLANE
CLARK, WHAT ARE YOU DOING BACK IN THE NEWSROOM?
THOUGHT YOU WERE STILL ON WHAT MR. LOVING DESCRIBED AS "ANOTHER 'F.C.C.-BANNED-WORD' LEAVE."
I'M BACK.
AND IF IT'S OKAY WITH YOU, I'D LIKE TO DO SOME CATCHING UP.
IF YOU'RE CHECKING HEADLINES FOR EXCITING LOCAL NEWS, I'D GO BACK AT LEAST A MONTH.
AS IN, BEFORE SUPERMAN LEFT METROPOLIS FOR PARTS SOUTH.
DAILY PLANE
SUPERMA UNABLE TO PREVEN SOUTH AMERICA DISASTE
WHAT'S THAT SUPPOSED TO MEAN?
JUST STATING THE OBVIOUS.
I'M NOT TRYING TO DISS THE GUY, BUT YOU HAVE TO ADMIT, TH CITY TENDS TO SIMMER DOWN WHEN HE'S ON HIATUS.
YOU DON'T SERIOUSLY THINK SUPERMAN BRINGS THESE "EVENTS" ON HIMSELF?
OF COURSE NOT...
BUT THAT "S" ON HIS CHEST SURE MAKES A TEMPTING...
...TARGET...

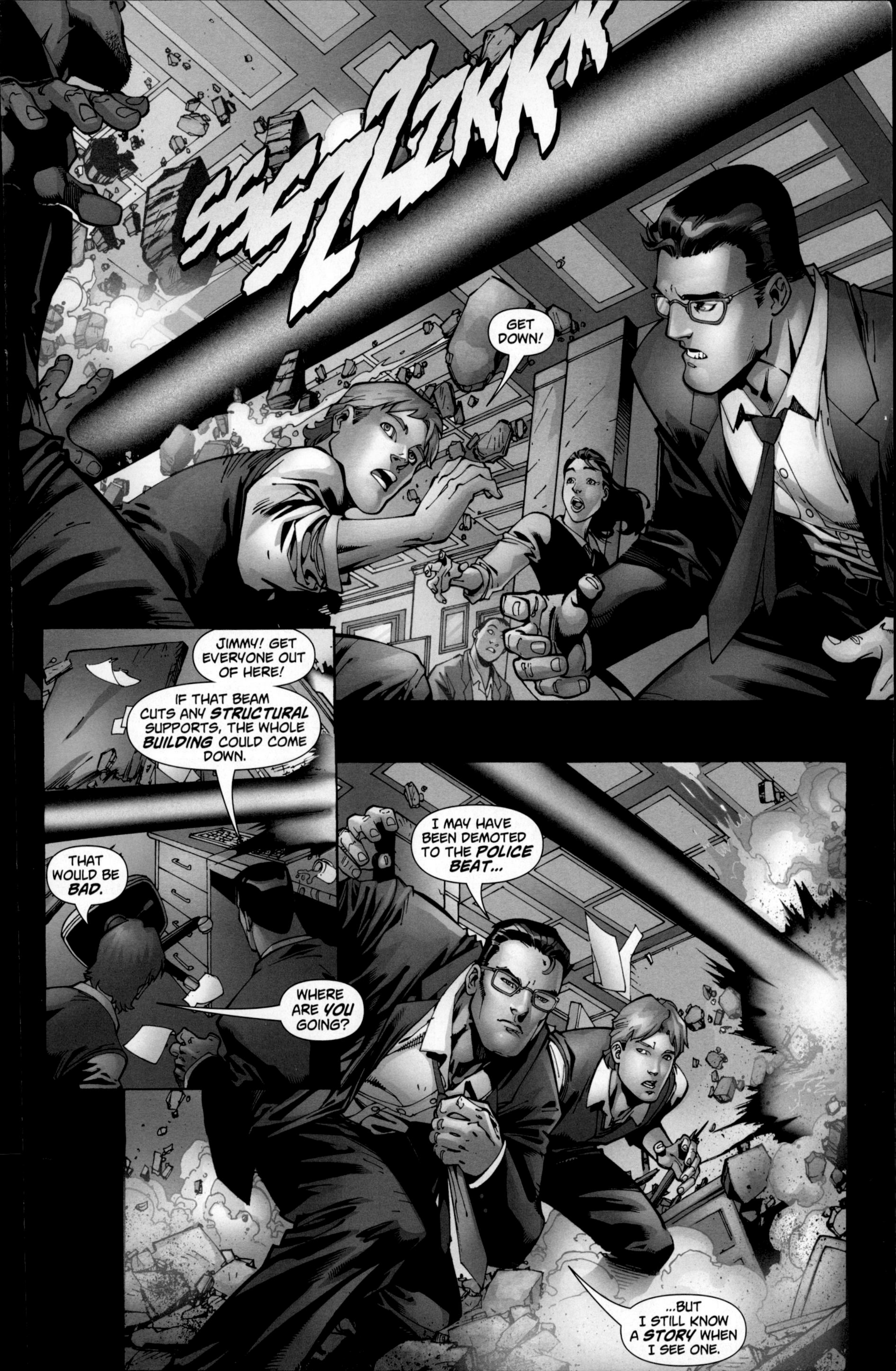
SSSZZZKKK
GET DOWN!
JIMMY! GET EVERYONE OUT OF HERE!
IF THAT BEAM CUTS ANY STRUCTURAL SUPPORTS, THE WHOLE BUILDING COULD COME DOWN.
THAT WOULD BE BAD.
I MAY HAVE BEEN DEMOTED TO THE POLICE BEAT...
WHERE ARE YOU GOING?
...BUT I STILL KNOW A STORY WHEN I SEE ONE.

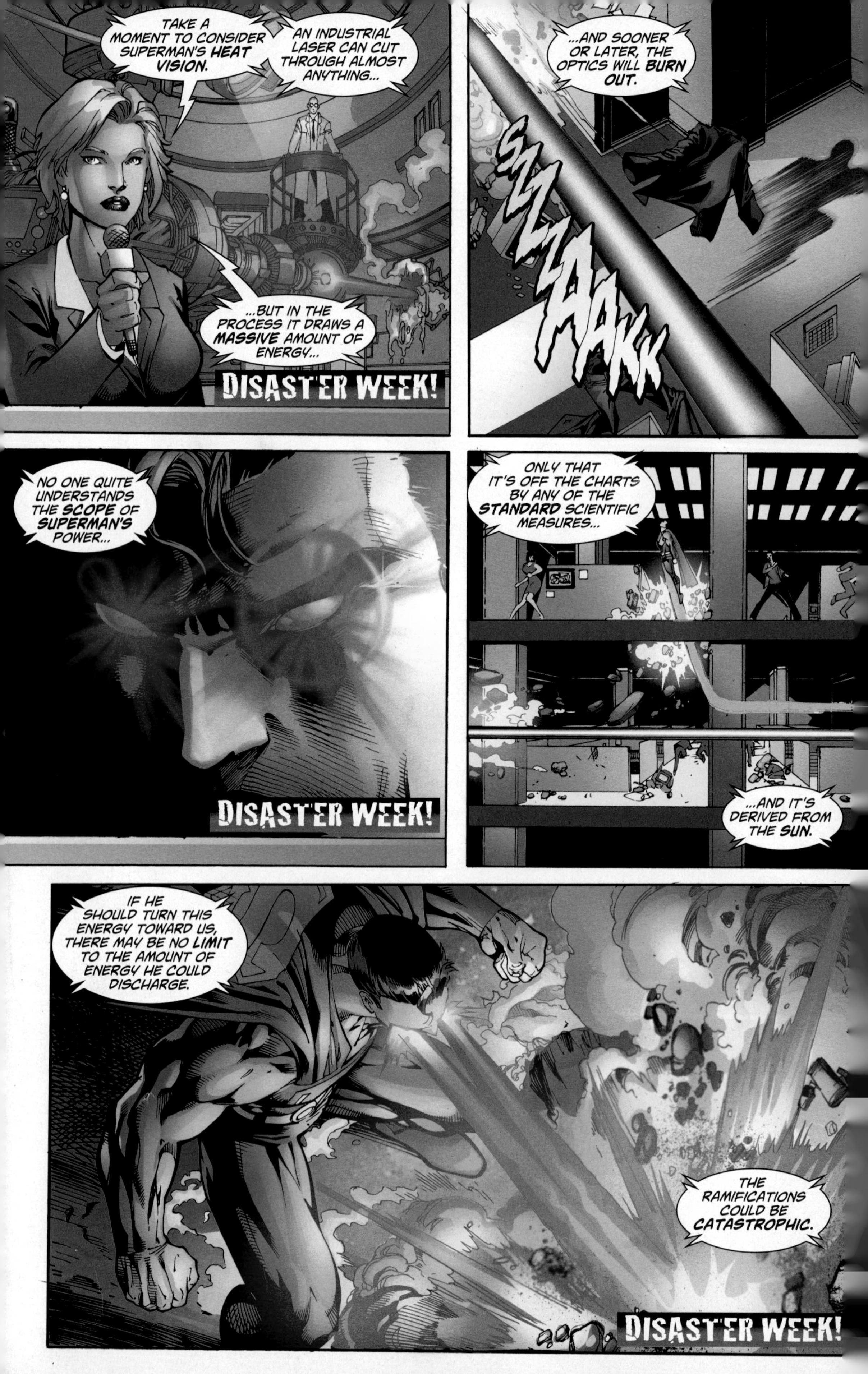
TAKE A MOMENT TO CONSIDER SUPERMAN'S HEAT VISION.
AN INDUSTRIAL LASER CAN CUT THROUGH ALMOST ANYTHING...
...BUT IN THE PROCESS IT DRAWS A MASSIVE AMOUNT OF ENERGY...
DISASTER WEEK!
...AND SOONER OR LATER, THE OPTICS WILL BURN OUT.
SZZZAAKK
NO ONE QUITE UNDERSTANDS THE SCOPE OF SUPERMAN'S POWER...
DISASTER WEEK!
ONLY THAT IT'S OFF THE CHARTS BY ANY OF THE STANDARD SCIENTIFIC MEASURES...
...AND IT'S DERIVED FROM THE SUN.
IF HE SHOULD TURN THIS ENERGY TOWARD US, THERE MAY BE NO LIMIT TO THE AMOUNT OF ENERGY HE COULD DISCHARGE.
THE RAMIFICATIONS COULD BE CATASTROPHIC.
DISASTER WEEK!

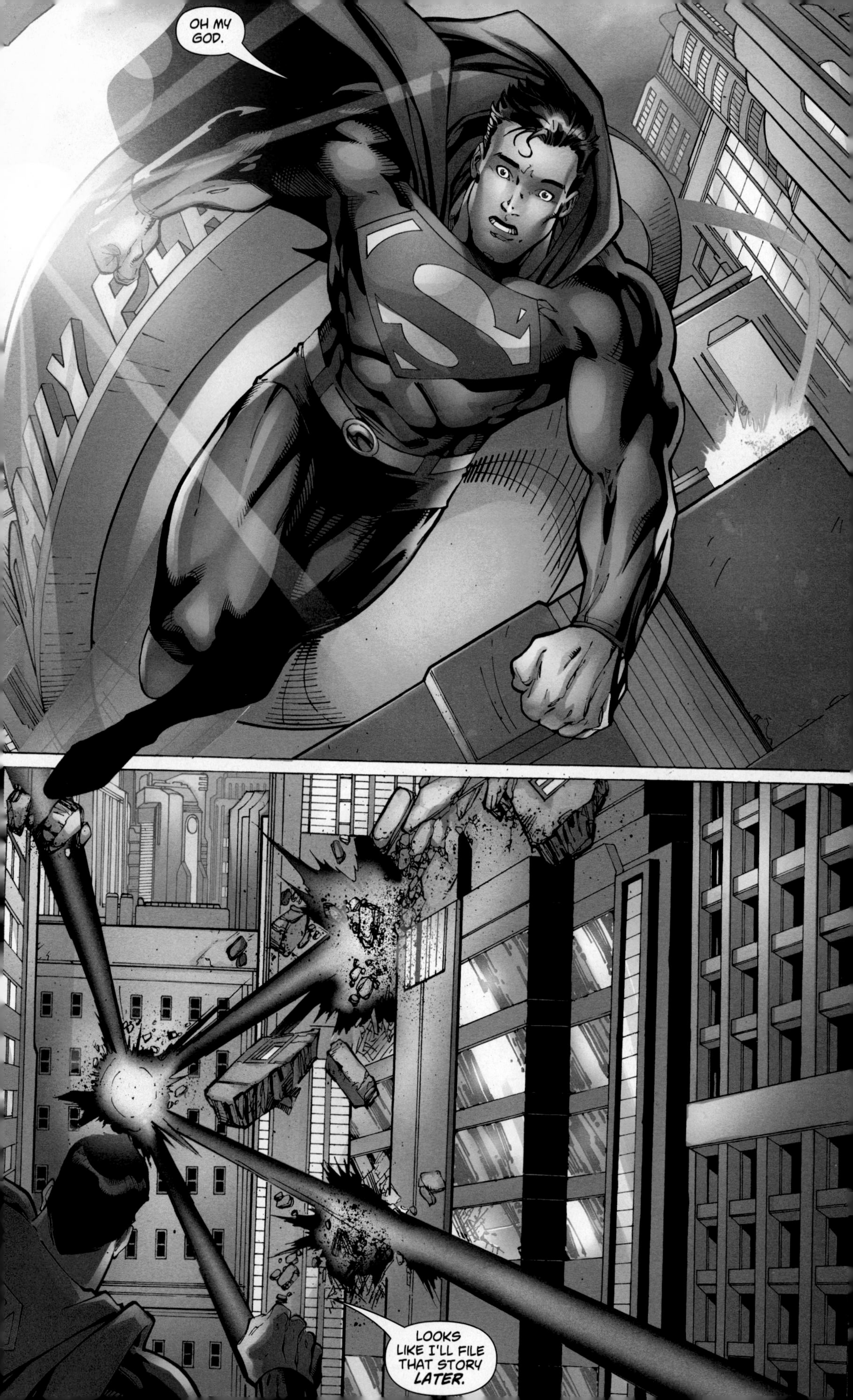
OH MY GOD.
LOOKS LIKE I'LL FILE THAT STORY LATER.

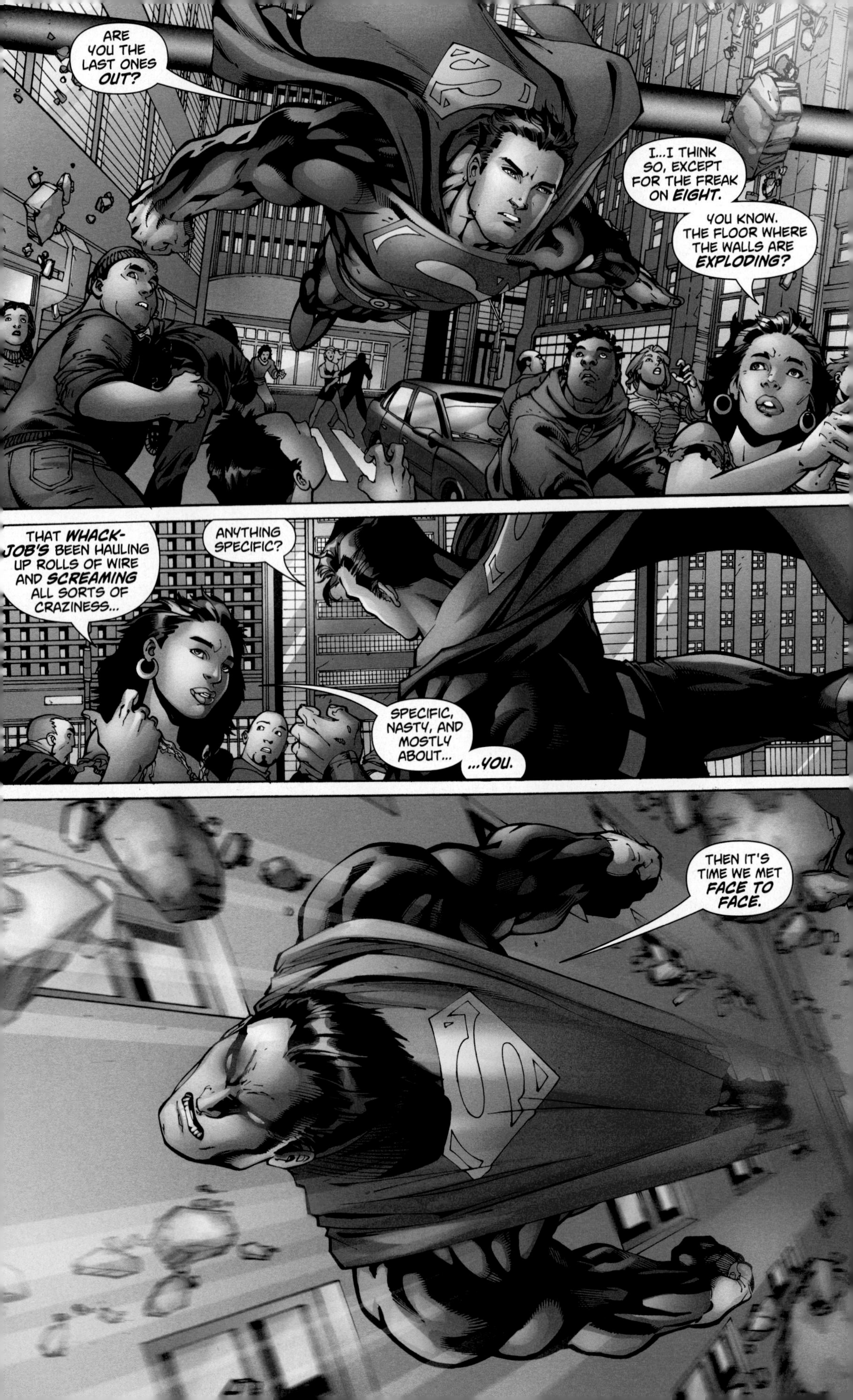
ARE YOU THE LAST ONES OUT?
I...I THINK SO, EXCEPT FOR THE FREAK ON EIGHT.
YOU KNOW. THE FLOOR WHERE THE WALLS ARE EXPLODING?
THAT WHACK-JOB'S BEEN HAULING UP ROLLS OF WIRE AND SCREAMING ALL SORTS OF CRAZINESS...
ANYTHING SPECIFIC?
SPECIFIC, NASTY, AND MOSTLY ABOUT...
...YOU.
THEN IT'S TIME WE MET FACE TO FACE.

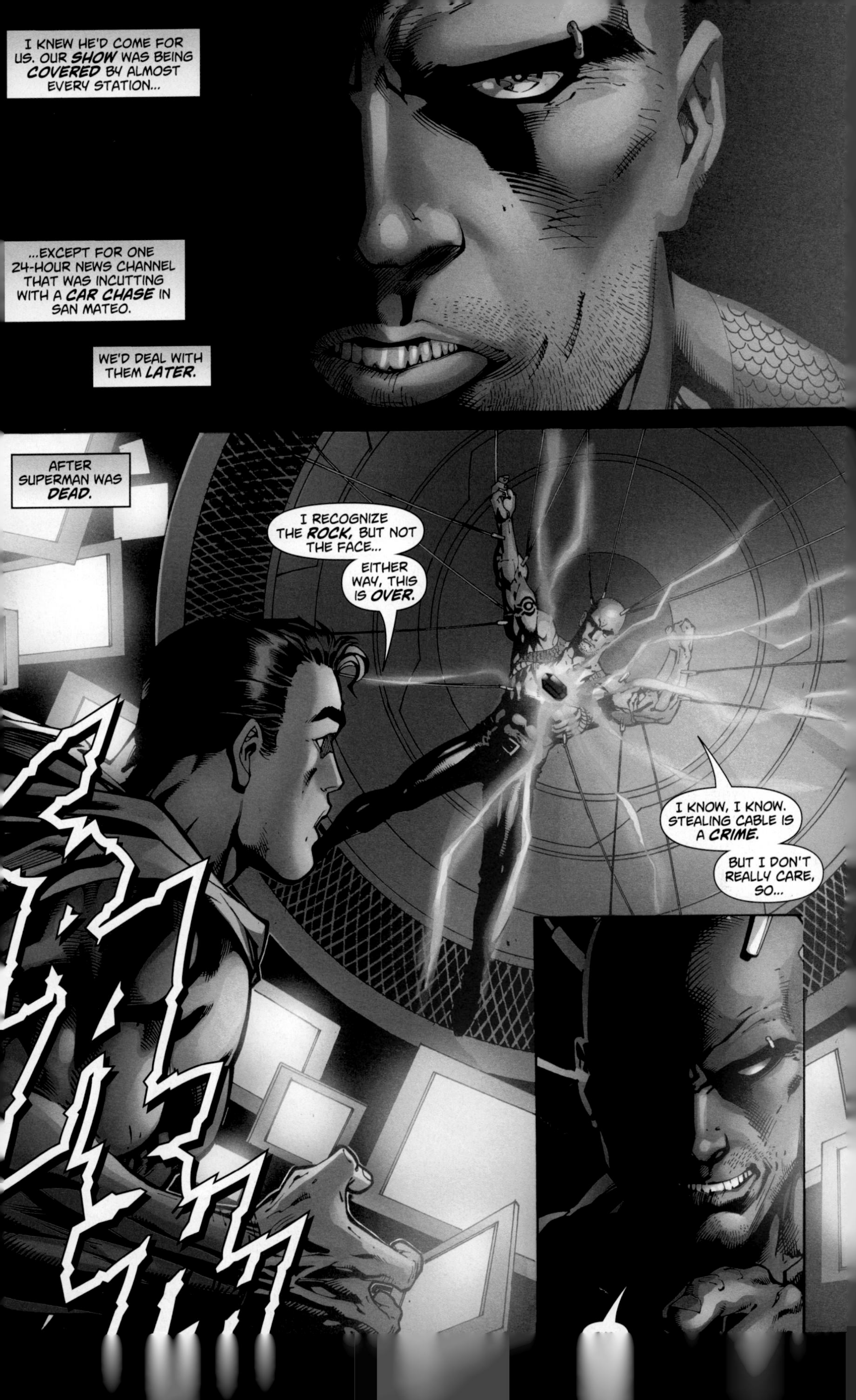
I KNEW HE'D COME FOR US. OUR SHOW WAS BEING COVERED BY ALMOST EVERY STATION...
...EXCEPT FOR ONE 24-HOUR NEWS CHANNEL THAT WAS INCUTTING WITH A CAR CHASE IN SAN MATEO.
WE'D DEAL WITH THEM LATER.
AFTER SUPERMAN WAS DEAD.
I RECOGNIZE THE ROCK, BUT NOT THE FACE...
EITHER WAY, THIS IS OVER.
I KNOW, I KNOW. STEALING CABLE IS A CRIME.
BUT I DON'T REALLY CARE, SO...

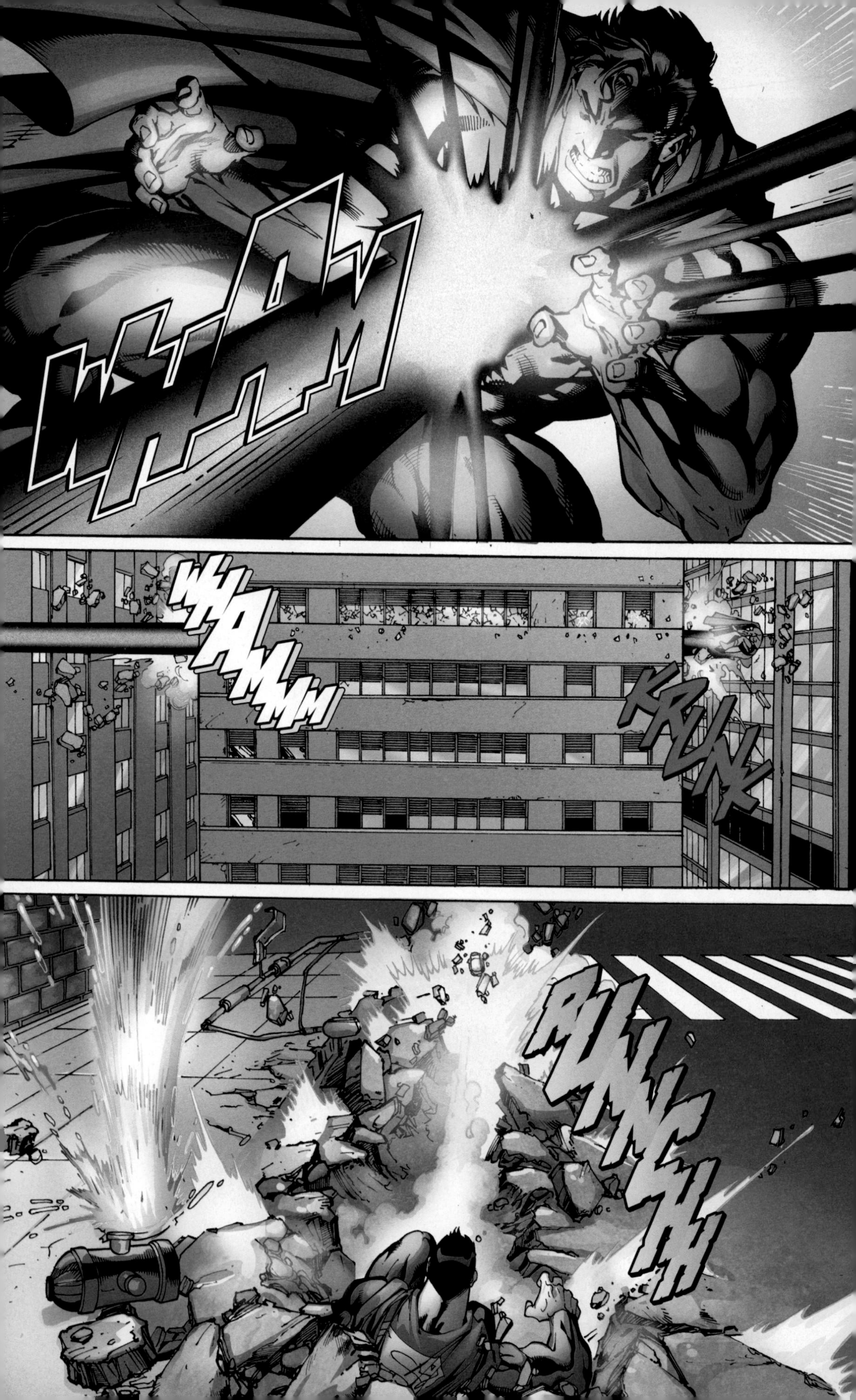
WHAM
WHAMMMM
KRUNK
BUNCHH

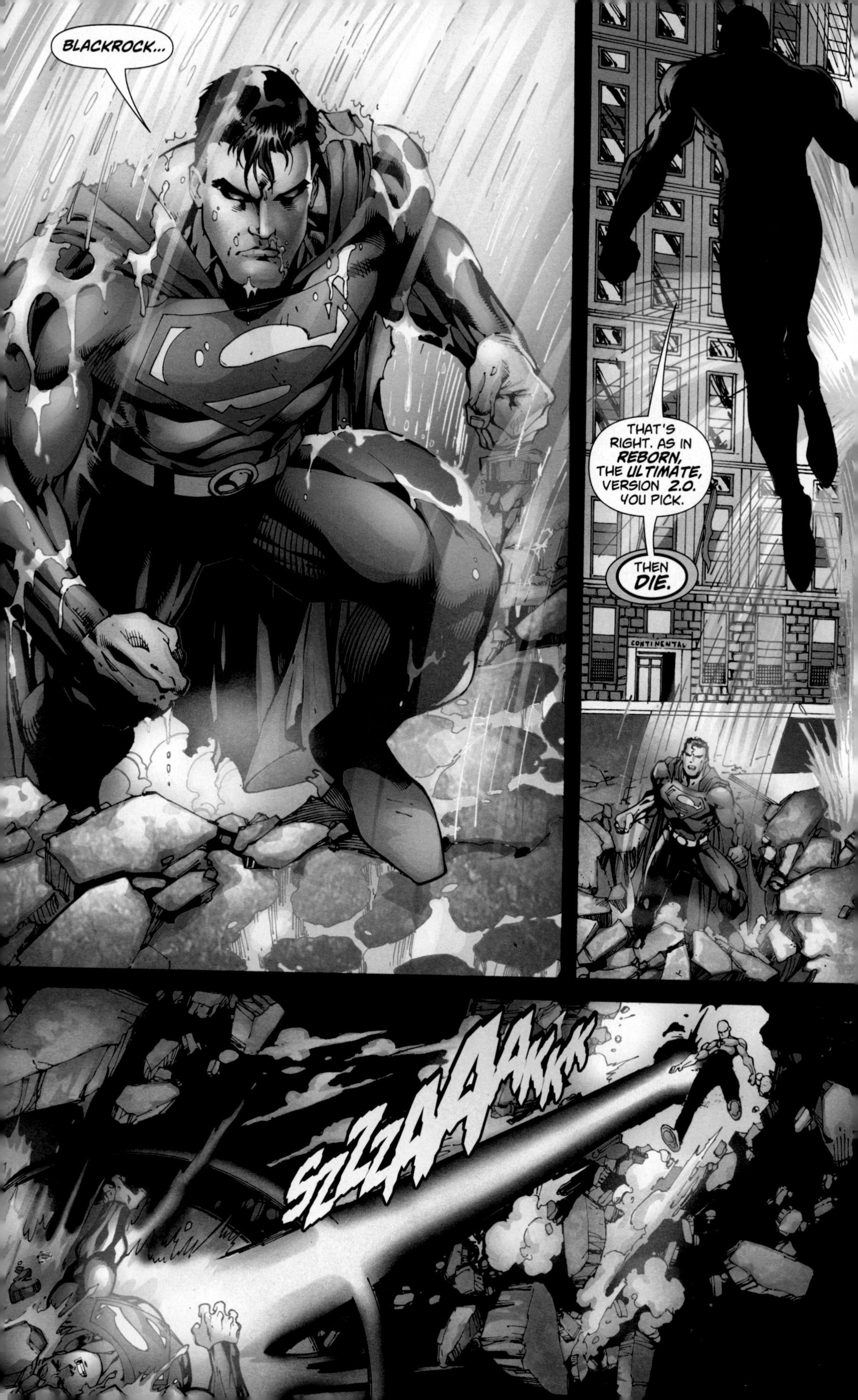
BLACKROCK...
THAT'S RIGHT. AS IN REBORN, THE ULTIMATE, VERSION 2.0. YOU PICK.
THEN DIE.
CONTINENTAL
SZZZAAAAKKK

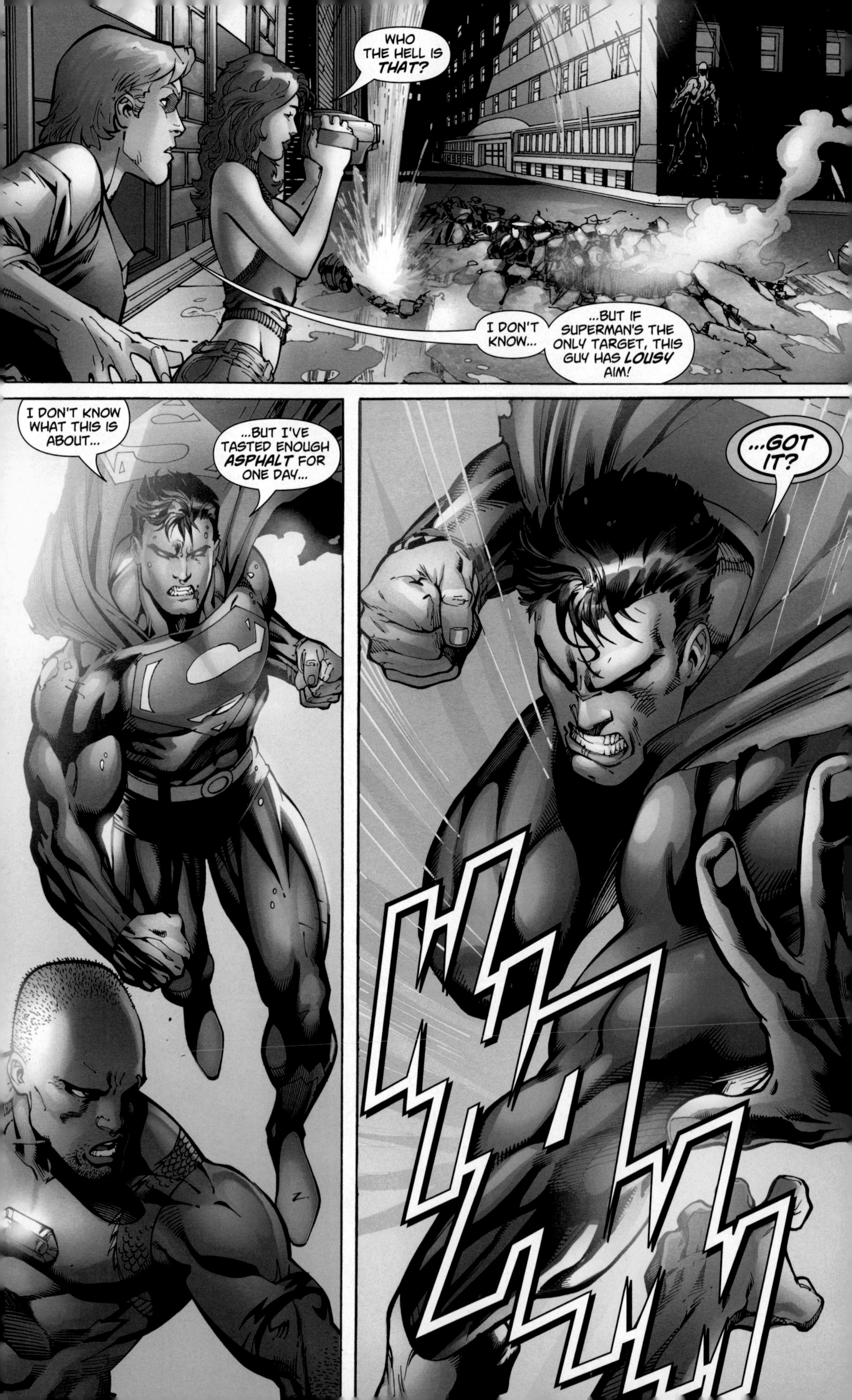
WHO THE HELL IS THAT?
I DON'T KNOW...
...BUT IF SUPERMAN'S THE ONLY TARGET, THIS GUY HAS LOUSY AIM!
I DON'T KNOW WHAT THIS IS ABOUT...
...BUT I'VE TASTED ENOUGH ASPHALT FOR ONE DAY...
...GOT IT?
KLANNG

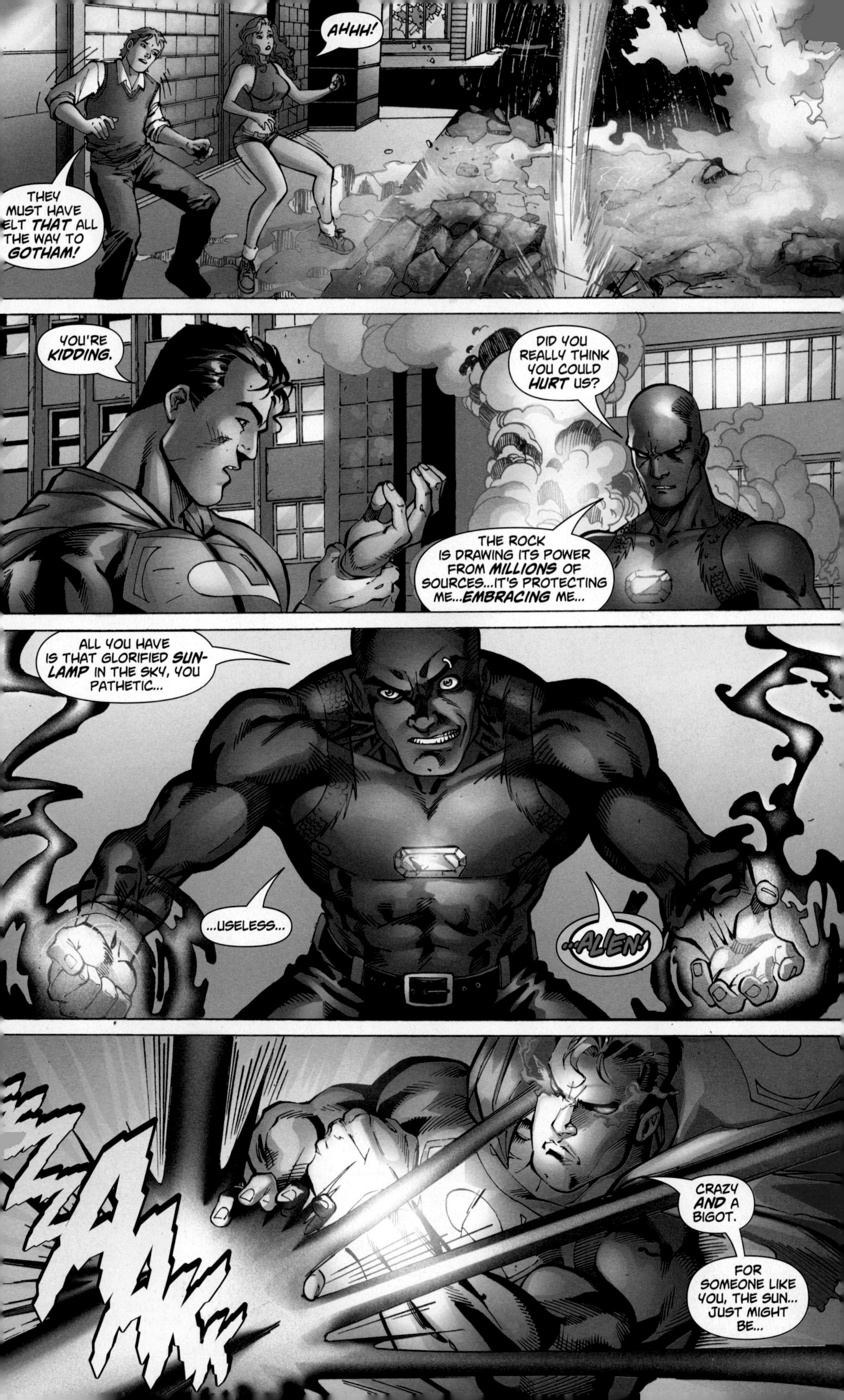
AHHH!
THEY MUST HAVE ELT THAT ALL THE WAY TO GOTHAM!
YOU'RE KIDDING.
DID YOU REALLY THINK YOU COULD HURT US?
THE ROCK IS DRAWING ITS POWER FROM MILLIONS OF SOURCES...IT'S PROTECTING ME...EMBRACING ME...
ALL YOU HAVE IS THAT GLORIFIED SUN-LAMP IN THE SKY, YOU PATHETIC...
...USELESS...
...ALIEN!
ZAAK
CRAZY AND A BIGOT.
FOR SOMEONE LIKE YOU, THE SUN... JUST MIGHT BE...

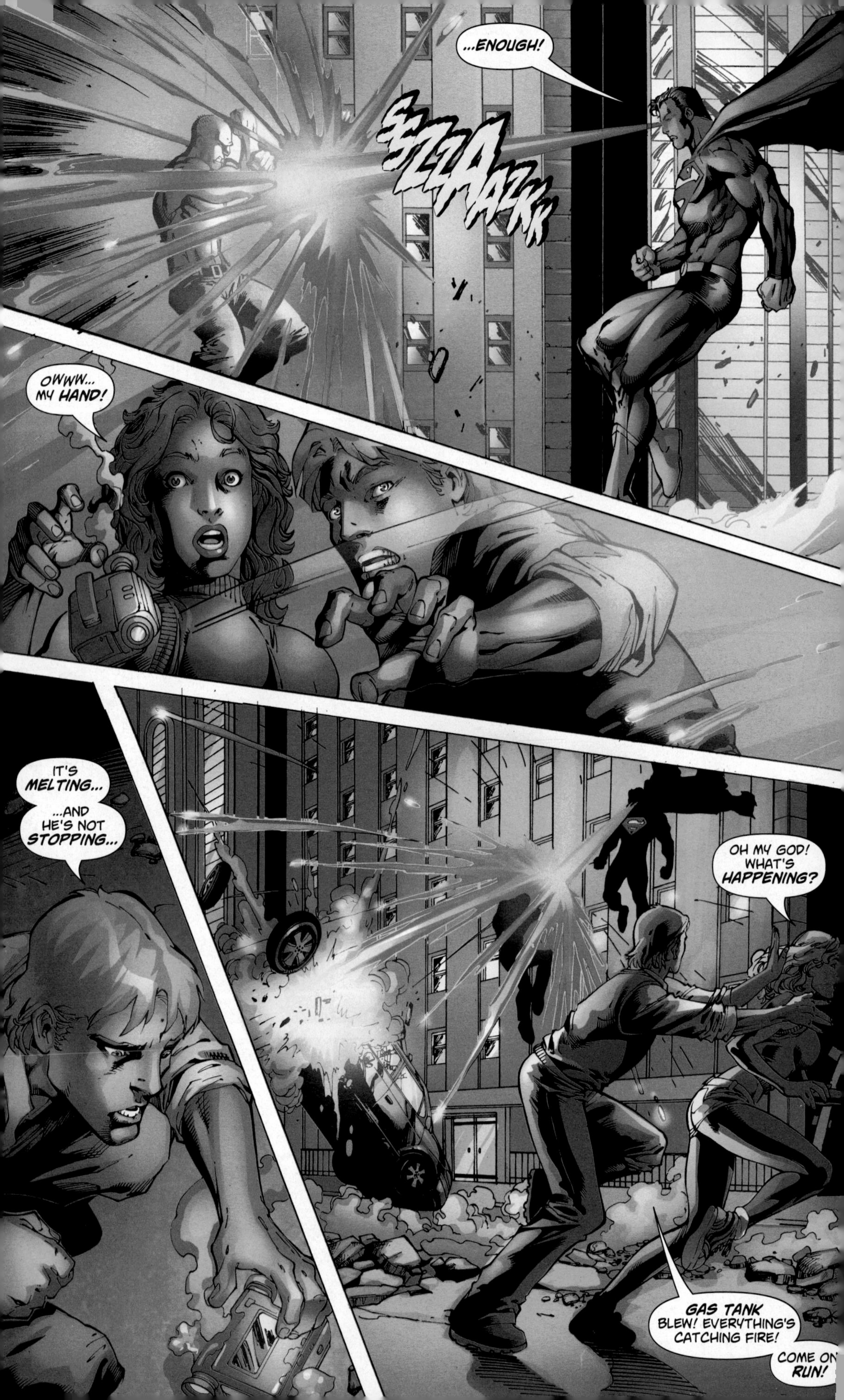
...ENOUGH!
SSZZAAZKK
OWWW... MY HAND!
IT'S MELTING...
...AND HE'S NOT STOPPING...
OH MY GOD! WHAT'S HAPPENING?
GAS TANK BLEW! EVERYTHING'S CATCHING FIRE!
COME ON! RUN!

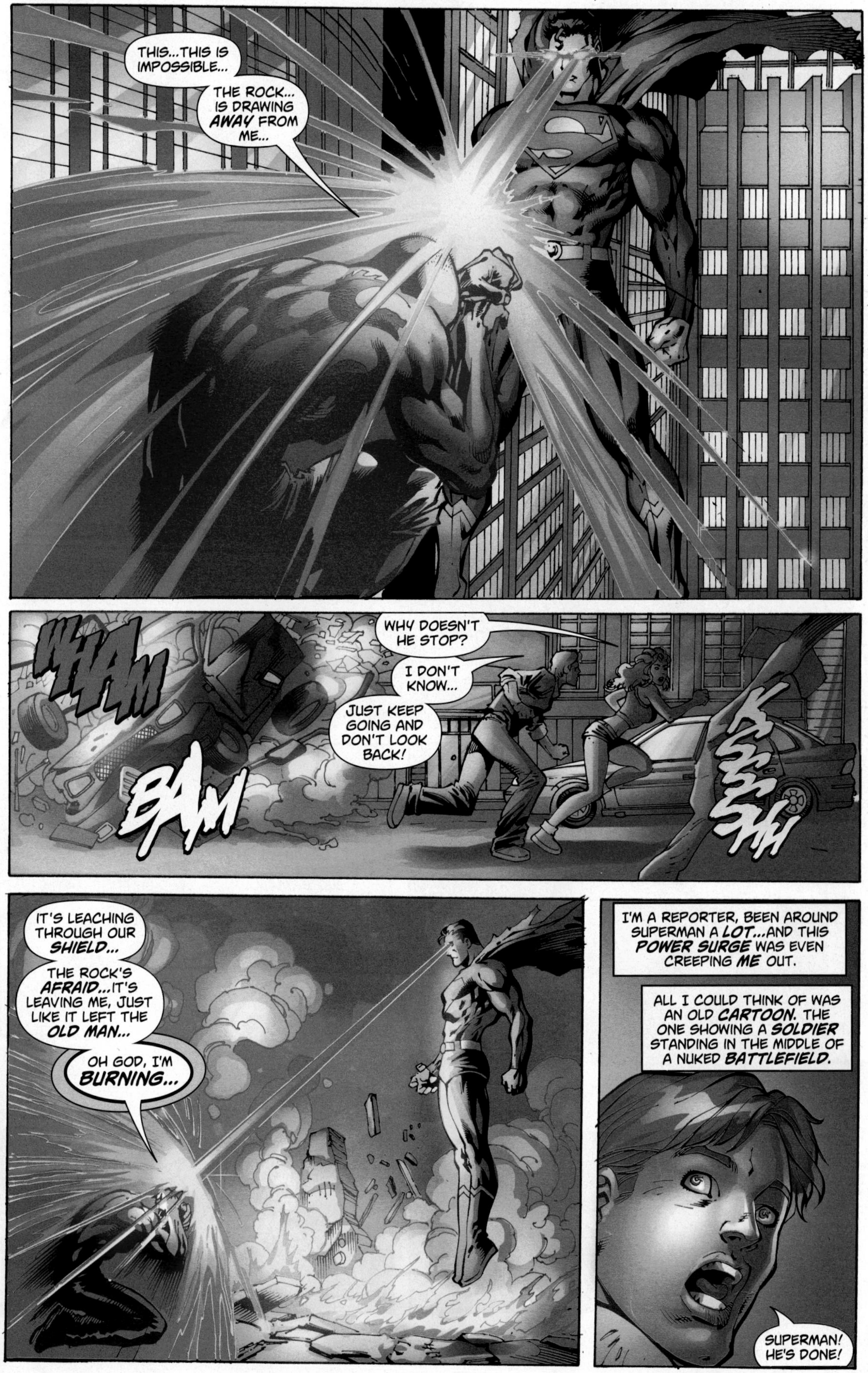
THIS...THIS IS IMPOSSIBLE...
THE ROCK... IS DRAWING AWAY FROM ME...
WHAM
BAM
WHY DOESN'T HE STOP?
I DON'T KNOW...
JUST KEEP GOING AND DON'T LOOK BACK!
IT'S LEACHING THROUGH OUR SHIELD...
THE ROCK'S AFRAID...IT'S LEAVING ME, JUST LIKE IT LEFT THE OLD MAN...
OH GOD, I'M BURNING...
I'M A REPORTER, BEEN AROUND SUPERMAN A LOT...AND THIS POWER SURGE WAS EVEN CREEPING ME OUT.
ALL I COULD THINK OF WAS AN OLD CARTOON. THE ONE SHOWING A SOLDIER STANDING IN THE MIDDLE OF A NUKED BATTLEFIELD.
SUPERMAN! HE'S DONE!

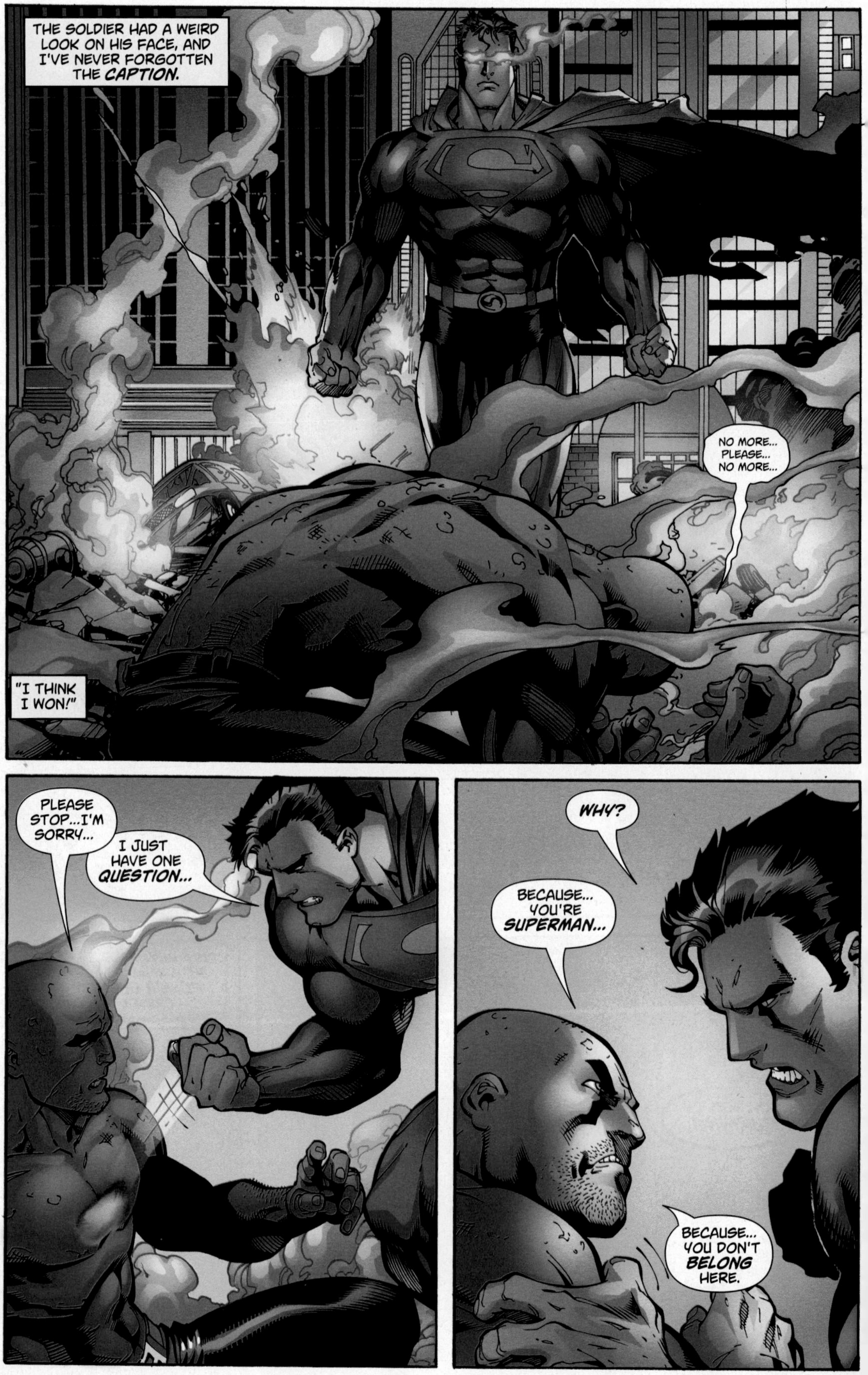
THE SOLDIER HAD A WEIRD LOOK ON HIS FACE, AND I'VE NEVER FORGOTTEN THE CAPTION.
NO MORE... PLEASE... NO MORE...
"I THINK I WON!"
PLEASE STOP...I'M SORRY...
I JUST HAVE ONE QUESTION...
WHY?
BECAUSE... YOU'RE SUPERMAN...
BECAUSE... YOU DON'T BELONG HERE.

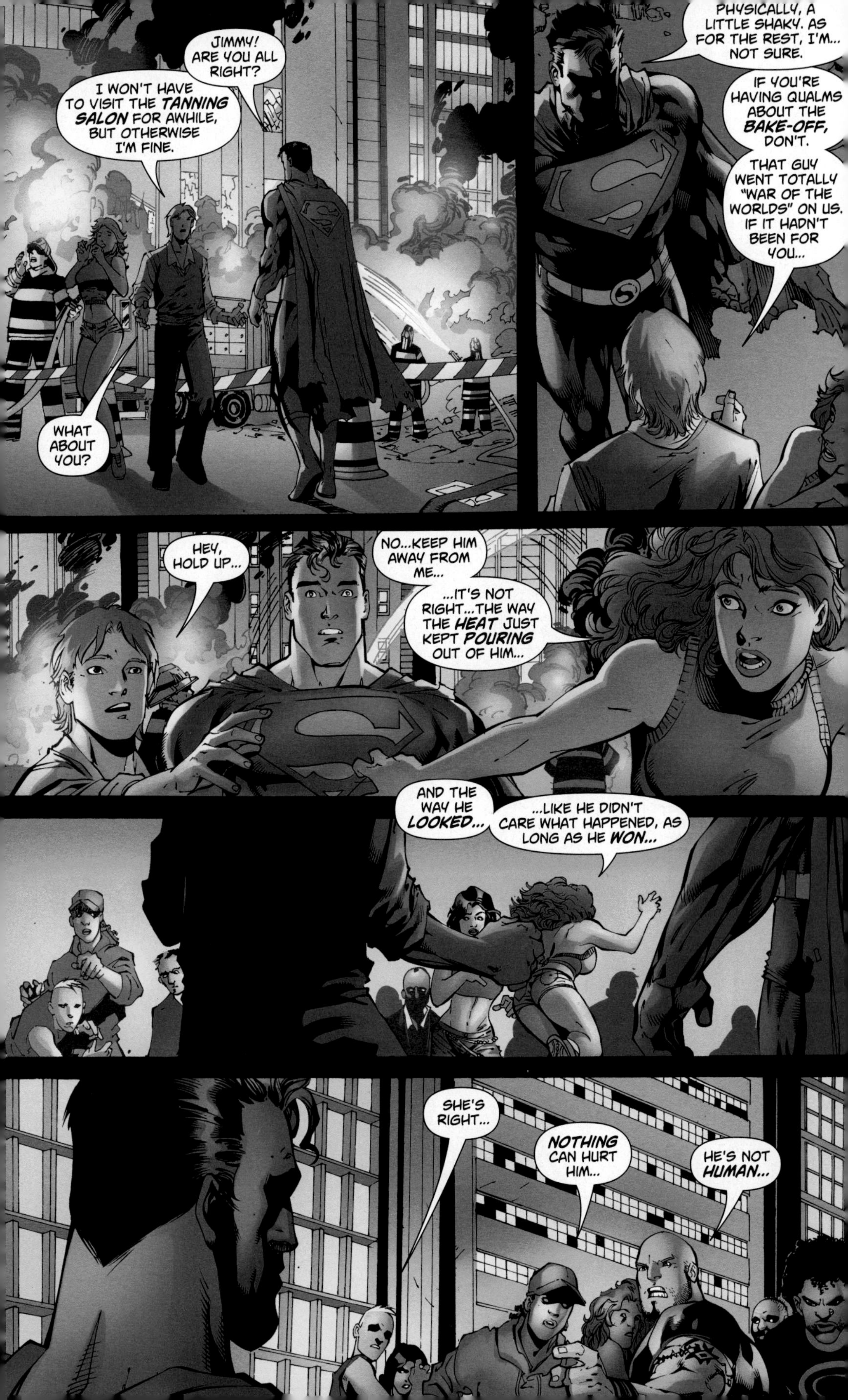
JIMMY! ARE YOU ALL RIGHT?
I WON'T HAVE TO VISIT THE TANNING SALON FOR AWHILE, BUT OTHERWISE I'M FINE.
WHAT ABOUT YOU?
PHYSICALLY, A LITTLE SHAKY. AS FOR THE REST, I'M... NOT SURE.
IF YOU'RE HAVING QUALMS ABOUT THE BAKE-OFF, DON'T.
THAT GUY WENT TOTALLY "WAR OF THE WORLDS" ON US. IF IT HADN'T BEEN FOR YOU...
HEY, HOLD UP...
NO...KEEP HIM AWAY FROM ME...
...IT'S NOT RIGHT...THE WAY THE HEAT JUST KEPT POURING OUT OF HIM...
AND THE WAY HE LOOKED...
...LIKE HE DIDN'T CARE WHAT HAPPENED, AS LONG AS HE WON...
SHE'S RIGHT...
NOTHING CAN HURT HIM...
HE'S NOT HUMAN...

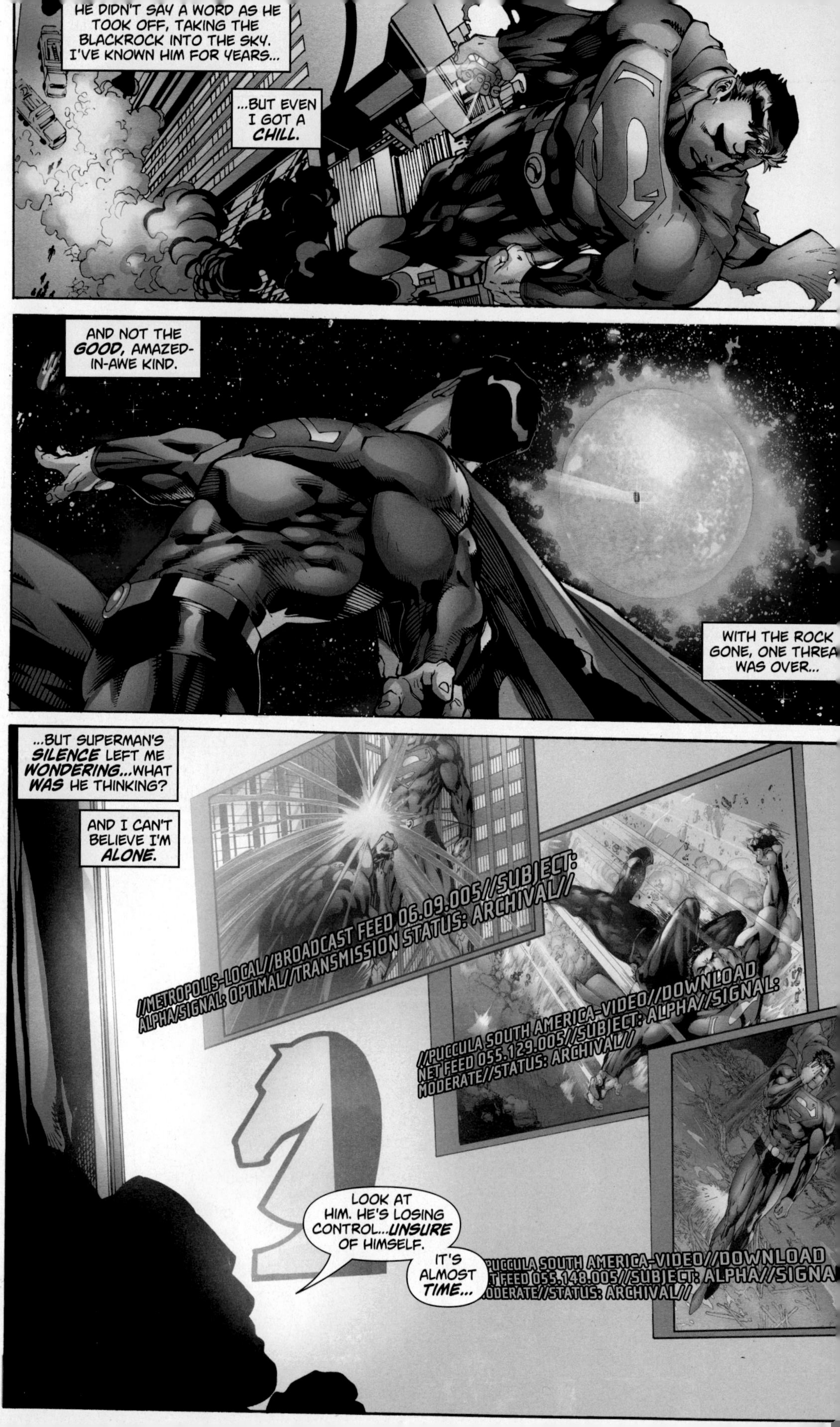
HE DIDN'T SAY A WORD AS HE TOOK OFF, TAKING THE BLACKROCK INTO THE SKY. I'VE KNOWN HIM FOR YEARS...
...BUT EVEN I GOT A **CHILL.**
AND NOT THE **GOOD,** AMAZED-IN-AWE KIND.
WITH THE ROCK GONE, ONE THREA WAS OVER...
...BUT SUPERMAN'S **SILENCE** LEFT ME **WONDERING**...WHAT **WAS** HE THINKING?
AND I CAN'T BELIEVE I'M **ALONE.**
//METROPOLIS-LOCAL//BROADCAST FEED 06.09.005//SUBJECT: ALPHA/SIGNAL: OPTIMAL//TRANSMISSION STATUS: ARCHIVAL//
//PUCCULA SOUTH AMERICA-VIDEO//DOWNLOAD NET FEED 055.129.005//SUBJECT: ALPHA//SIGNAL: MODERATE//STATUS: ARCHIVAL//
LOOK AT HIM. HE'S LOSING CONTROL...**UNSURE** OF HIMSELF.
IT'S ALMOST **TIME...**
PUCCULA SOUTH AMERICA-VIDEO//DOWNLOAD T FEED 055.148.005//SUBJECT: ALPHA//SIGNA ODERATE//STATUS: ARCHIVAL//

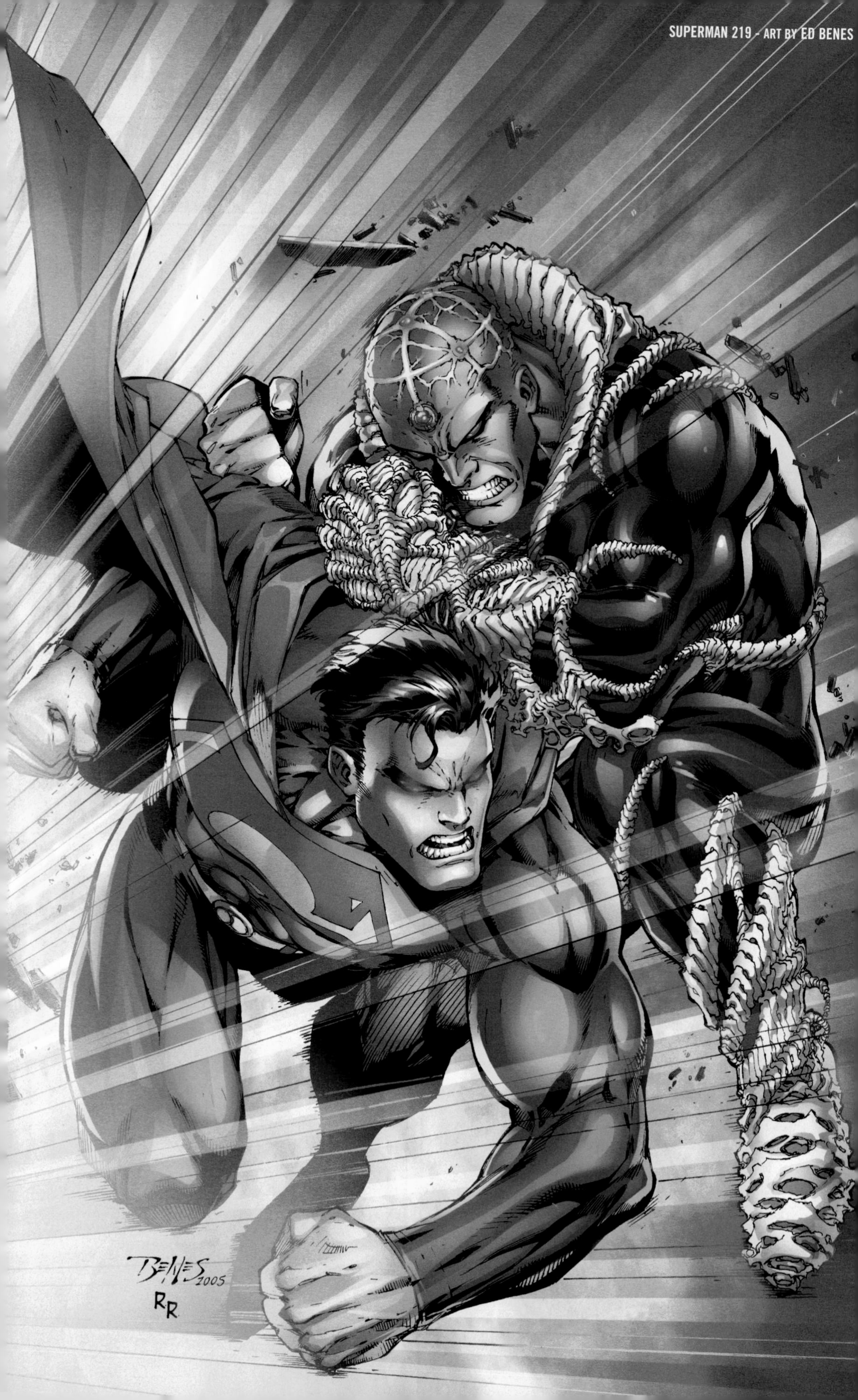
BENES
2005
RR

SUPERMAN 219 - ART BY ED BENES

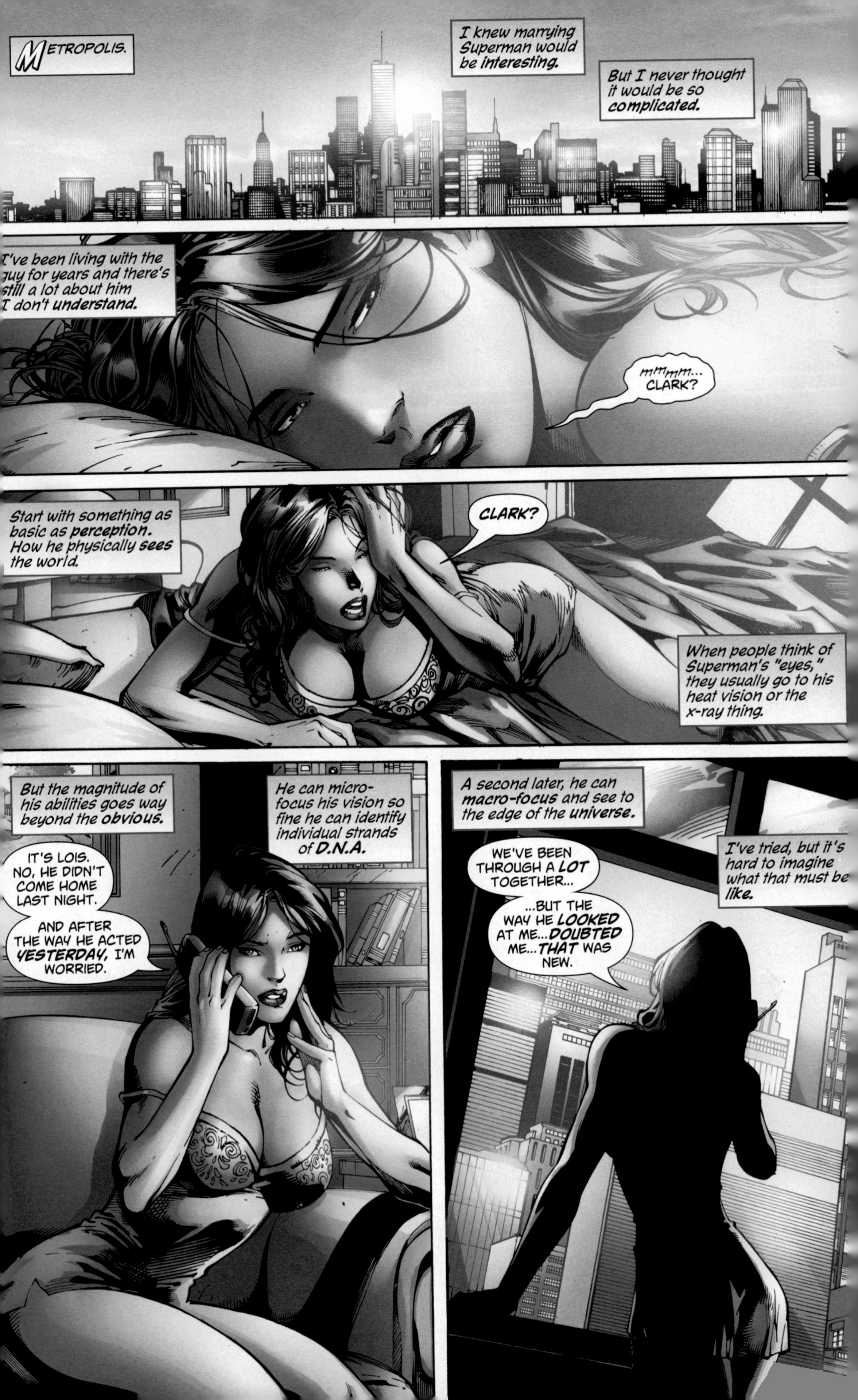

METROPOLIS.
I knew marrying Superman would be interesting.
But I never thought it would be so complicated.
I've been living with the guy for years and there's still a lot about him I don't understand.
mmmmm... CLARK?
Start with something as basic as perception. How he physically sees the world.
CLARK?
When people think of Superman's "eyes," they usually go to his heat vision or the x-ray thing.
But the magnitude of his abilities goes way beyond the obvious.
He can micro-focus his vision so fine he can identify individual strands of D.N.A.
IT'S LOIS. NO, HE DIDN'T COME HOME LAST NIGHT.
AND AFTER THE WAY HE ACTED YESTERDAY, I'M WORRIED.
A second later, he can macro-focus and see to the edge of the universe.
I've tried, but it's hard to imagine what that must be like.
WE'VE BEEN THROUGH A LOT TOGETHER...
...BUT THE WAY HE LOOKED AT ME...DOUBTED ME...THAT WAS NEW.

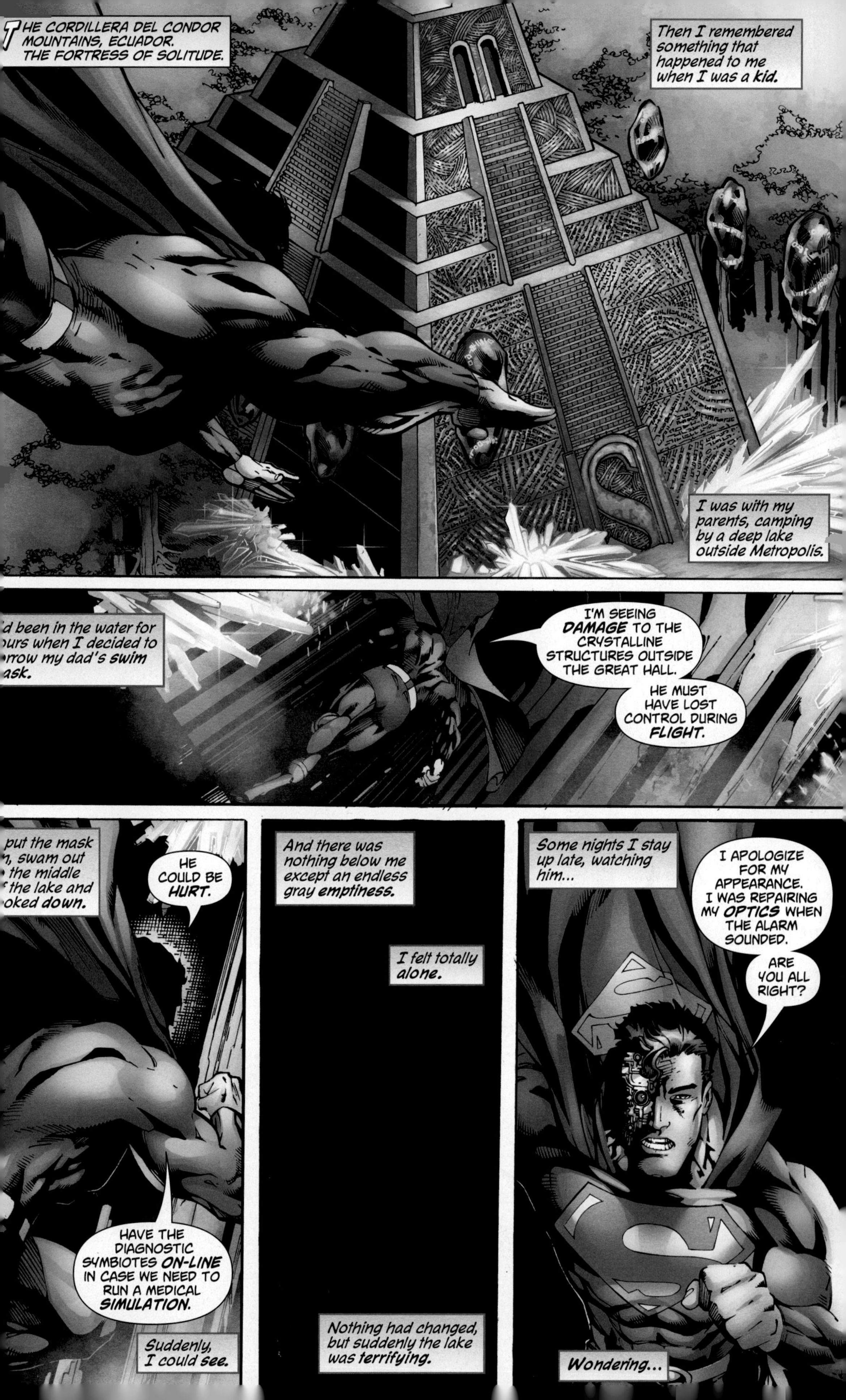
THE CORDILLERA DEL CONDOR MOUNTAINS, ECUADOR. THE FORTRESS OF SOLITUDE.
Then I remembered something that happened to me when I was a **kid.**
I was with my parents, camping by a deep lake outside Metropolis.
'd been in the water for ours when I decided to rrow my dad's **swim** ask.
I'M SEEING **DAMAGE** TO THE CRYSTALLINE STRUCTURES OUTSIDE THE GREAT HALL.
HE MUST HAVE LOST CONTROL DURING **FLIGHT.**
put the mask n, swam out the middle the lake and oked **down.**
HE COULD BE **HURT.**
HAVE THE DIAGNOSTIC SYMBIOTES **ON-LINE** IN CASE WE NEED TO RUN A MEDICAL **SIMULATION.**
Suddenly, I could **see.**
And there was nothing below me except an endless gray **emptiness.**
I felt totally **alone.**
Nothing had changed, but suddenly the lake was **terrifying.**
Some nights I stay up late, watching him...
I APOLOGIZE FOR MY APPEARANCE. I WAS REPAIRING MY **OPTICS** WHEN THE ALARM SOUNDED.
ARE YOU ALL RIGHT?
Wondering...

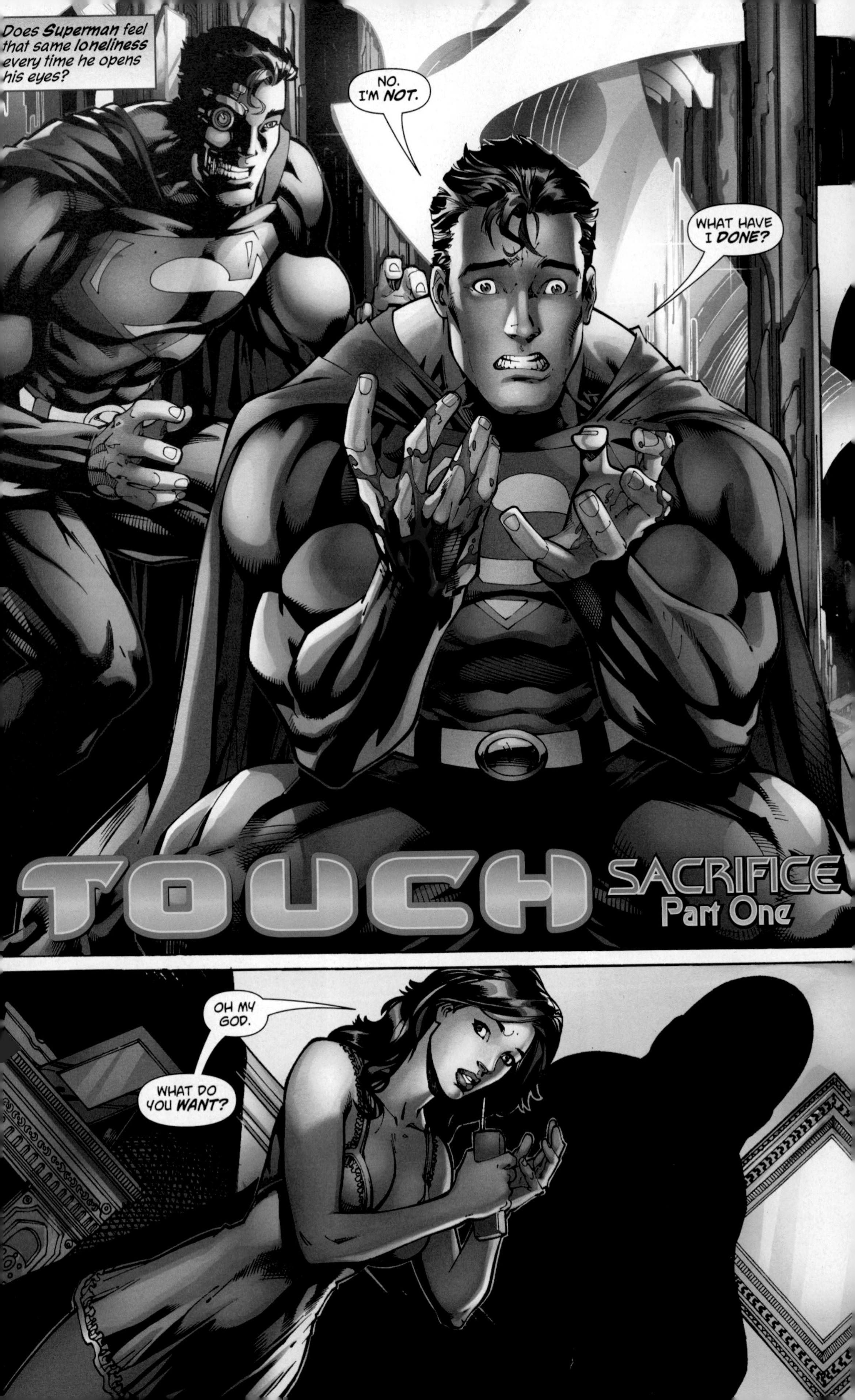
Does Superman feel that same loneliness every time he opens his eyes?
NO. I'M NOT.
WHAT HAVE I DONE?
TOUCH
SACRIFICE Part One
OH MY GOD.
WHAT DO YOU WANT?

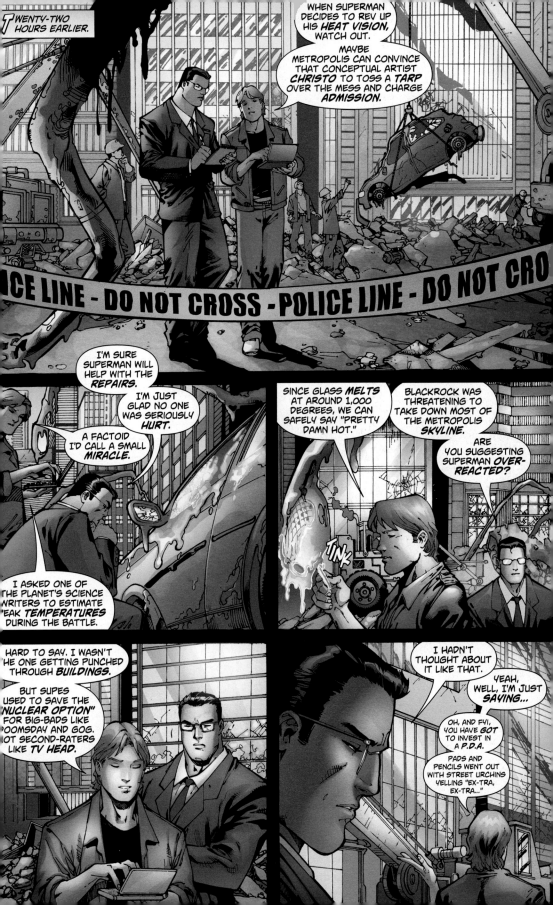

TWENTY-TWO HOURS EARLIER.

WHEN SUPERMAN DECIDES TO REV UP HIS *HEAT VISION*, WATCH OUT.

MAYBE METROPOLIS CAN CONVINCE THAT CONCEPTUAL ARTIST *CHRISTO* TO TOSS A *TARP* OVER THE MESS AND CHARGE *ADMISSION*.

CE LINE - DO NOT CROSS - POLICE LINE - DO NOT CRO

I'M SURE SUPERMAN WILL HELP WITH THE *REPAIRS*.

I'M JUST GLAD NO ONE WAS SERIOUSLY *HURT*.

A FACTOID I'D CALL A SMALL *MIRACLE*.

I ASKED ONE OF THE PLANET'S SCIENCE WRITERS TO ESTIMATE 'EAK *TEMPERATURES* DURING THE BATTLE.

SINCE GLASS *MELTS* AT AROUND 1,000 DEGREES, WE CAN SAFELY SAY "PRETTY DAMN HOT."

BLACKROCK WAS THREATENING TO TAKE DOWN MOST OF THE METROPOLIS SKYLINE.

ARE YOU SUGGESTING SUPERMAN *OVER-REACTED*?

TINK

HARD TO SAY. I WASN'T 'HE ONE GETTING PUNCHED THROUGH *BUILDINGS*.

BUT SUPES USED TO SAVE THE 'NUCLEAR OPTION" FOR BIG-BADS LIKE *OOMSDAY* AND GOG. OT SECOND-RATERS LIKE *TV HEAD*.

I HADN'T THOUGHT ABOUT IT LIKE THAT.

YEAH, WELL, I'M JUST *SAYING*...

OH, AND FYI, YOU HAVE *GOT* TO INVEST IN A *P.D.A.*

PADS AND PENCILS WENT OUT WITH STREET URCHINS YELLING "EX-TRA, EX-TRA..."

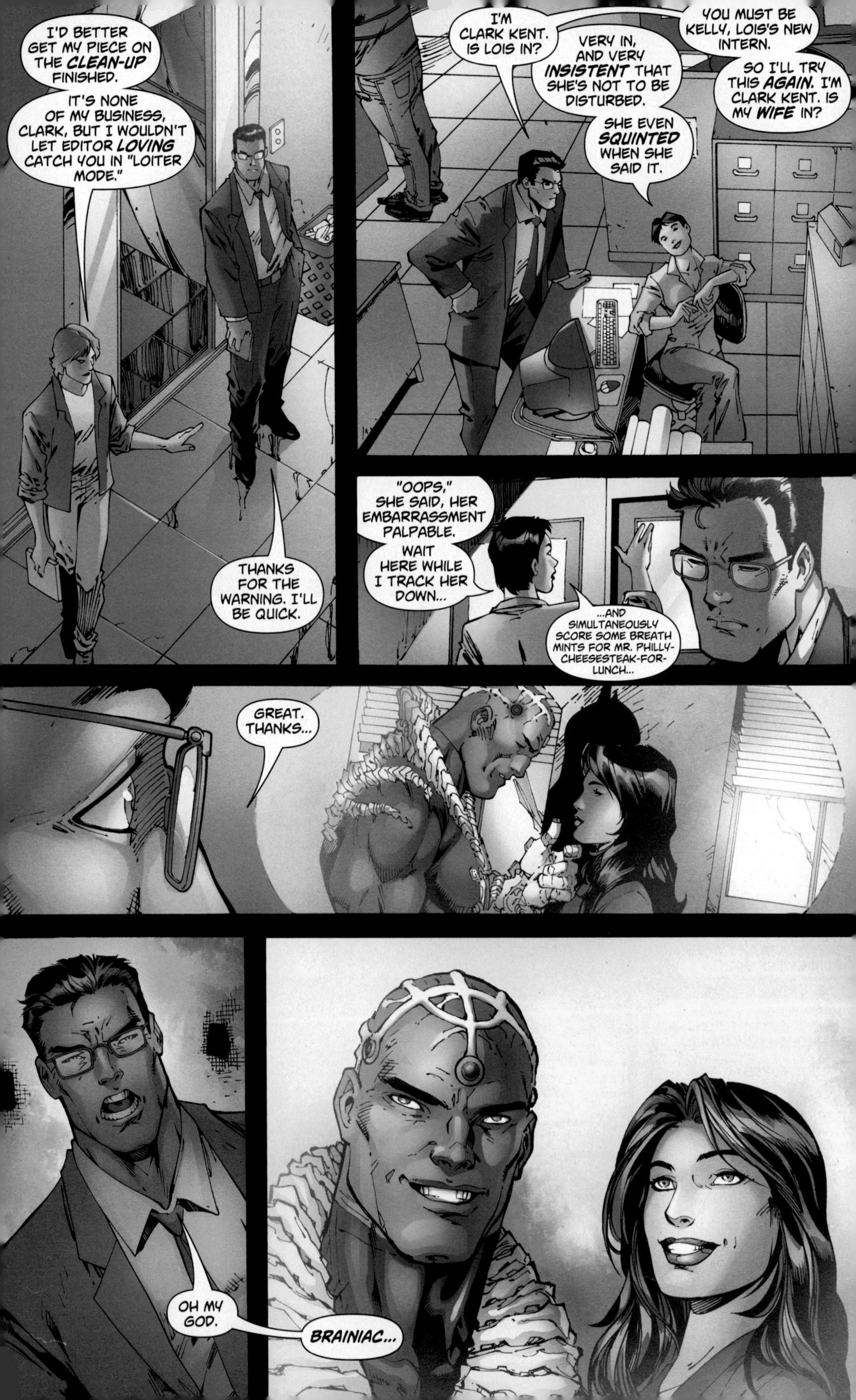
I'D BETTER GET MY PIECE ON THE CLEAN-UP FINISHED.
IT'S NONE OF MY BUSINESS, CLARK, BUT I WOULDN'T LET EDITOR LOVING CATCH YOU IN "LOITER MODE."
THANKS FOR THE WARNING. I'LL BE QUICK.
I'M CLARK KENT. IS LOIS IN?
VERY IN, AND VERY INSISTENT THAT SHE'S NOT TO BE DISTURBED.
SHE EVEN SQUINTED WHEN SHE SAID IT.
YOU MUST BE KELLY, LOIS'S NEW INTERN.
SO I'LL TRY THIS AGAIN. I'M CLARK KENT. IS MY WIFE IN?
"OOPS," SHE SAID, HER EMBARRASSMENT PALPABLE.
WAIT HERE WHILE I TRACK HER DOWN...
...AND SIMULTANEOUSLY SCORE SOME BREATH MINTS FOR MR. PHILLY-CHEESESTEAK-FOR-LUNCH...
GREAT. THANKS...
OH MY GOD.
BRAINIAC...

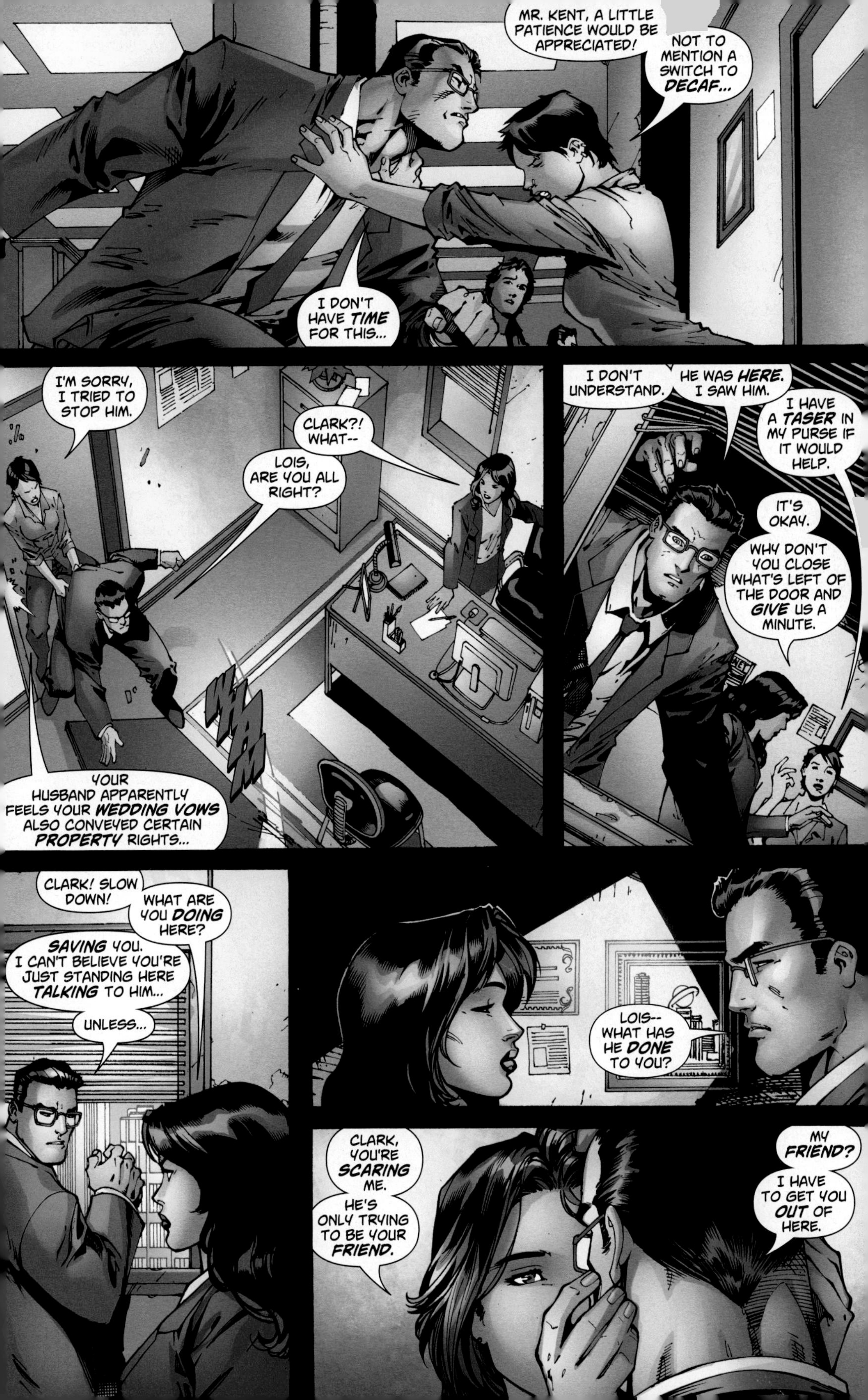

MR. KENT, A LITTLE PATIENCE WOULD BE APPRECIATED!
NOT TO MENTION A SWITCH TO DECAF...
I DON'T HAVE TIME FOR THIS...
I'M SORRY, I TRIED TO STOP HIM.
CLARK?! WHAT--
LOIS, ARE YOU ALL RIGHT?
YOUR HUSBAND APPARENTLY FEELS YOUR WEDDING VOWS ALSO CONVEYED CERTAIN PROPERTY RIGHTS...
WHAM
I DON'T UNDERSTAND.
HE WAS HERE. I SAW HIM.
I HAVE A TASER IN MY PURSE IF IT WOULD HELP.
IT'S OKAY.
WHY DON'T YOU CLOSE WHAT'S LEFT OF THE DOOR AND GIVE US A MINUTE.
CLARK! SLOW DOWN!
WHAT ARE YOU DOING HERE?
SAVING YOU. I CAN'T BELIEVE YOU'RE JUST STANDING HERE TALKING TO HIM...
UNLESS...
LOIS-- WHAT HAS HE DONE TO YOU?
CLARK, YOU'RE SCARING ME.
HE'S ONLY TRYING TO BE YOUR FRIEND.
MY FRIEND?
I HAVE TO GET YOU OUT OF HERE.

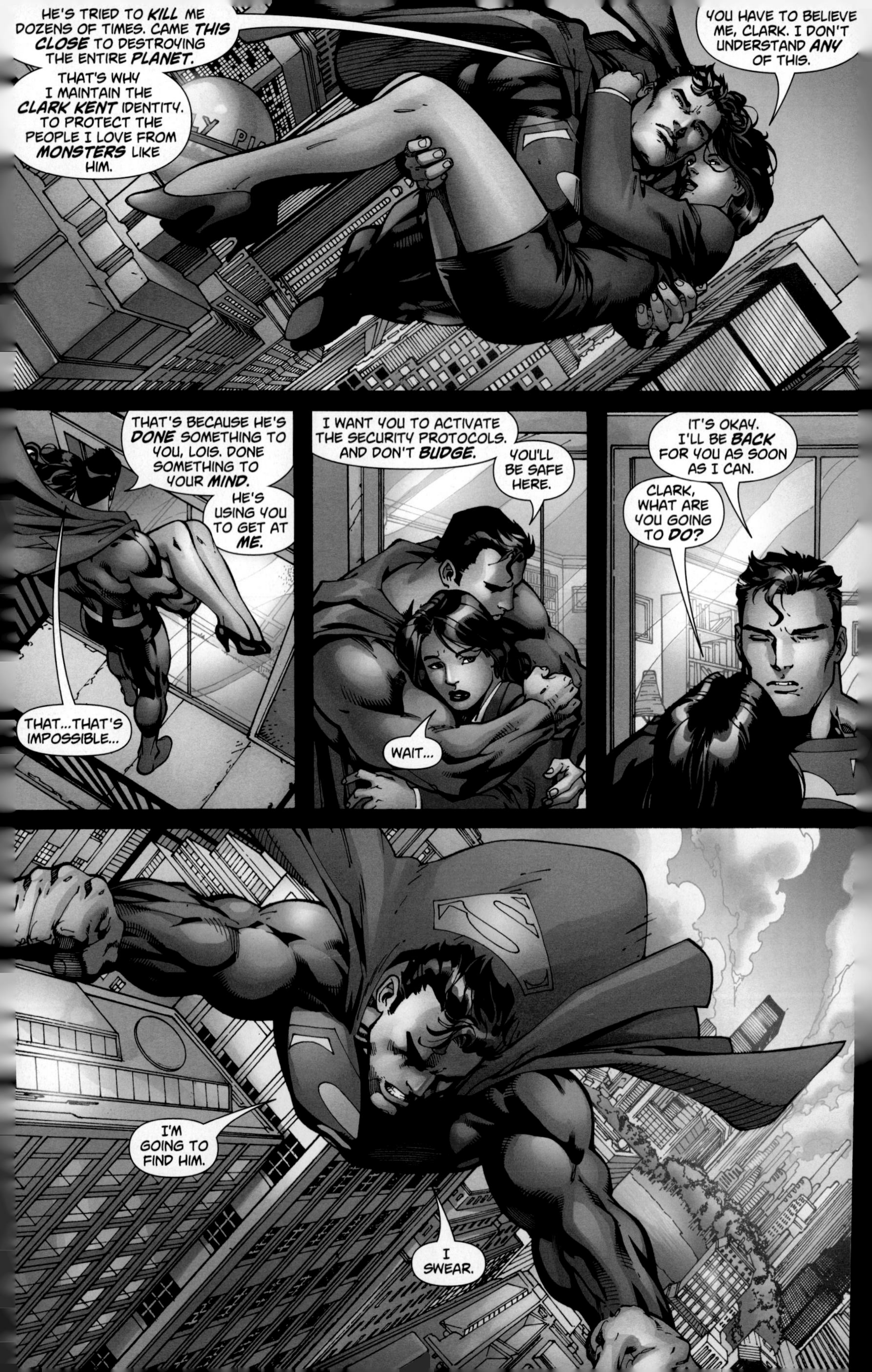
HE'S TRIED TO KILL ME DOZENS OF TIMES. CAME THIS CLOSE TO DESTROYING THE ENTIRE PLANET.
THAT'S WHY I MAINTAIN THE CLARK KENT IDENTITY. TO PROTECT THE PEOPLE I LOVE FROM MONSTERS LIKE HIM.
YOU HAVE TO BELIEVE ME, CLARK. I DON'T UNDERSTAND ANY OF THIS.
THAT'S BECAUSE HE'S DONE SOMETHING TO YOU, LOIS. DONE SOMETHING TO YOUR MIND.
HE'S USING YOU TO GET AT ME.
THAT...THAT'S IMPOSSIBLE...
I WANT YOU TO ACTIVATE THE SECURITY PROTOCOLS. AND DON'T BUDGE.
YOU'LL BE SAFE HERE.
WAIT...
CLARK, WHAT ARE YOU GOING TO DO?
IT'S OKAY. I'LL BE BACK FOR YOU AS SOON AS I CAN.
I'M GOING TO FIND HIM.
I SWEAR.

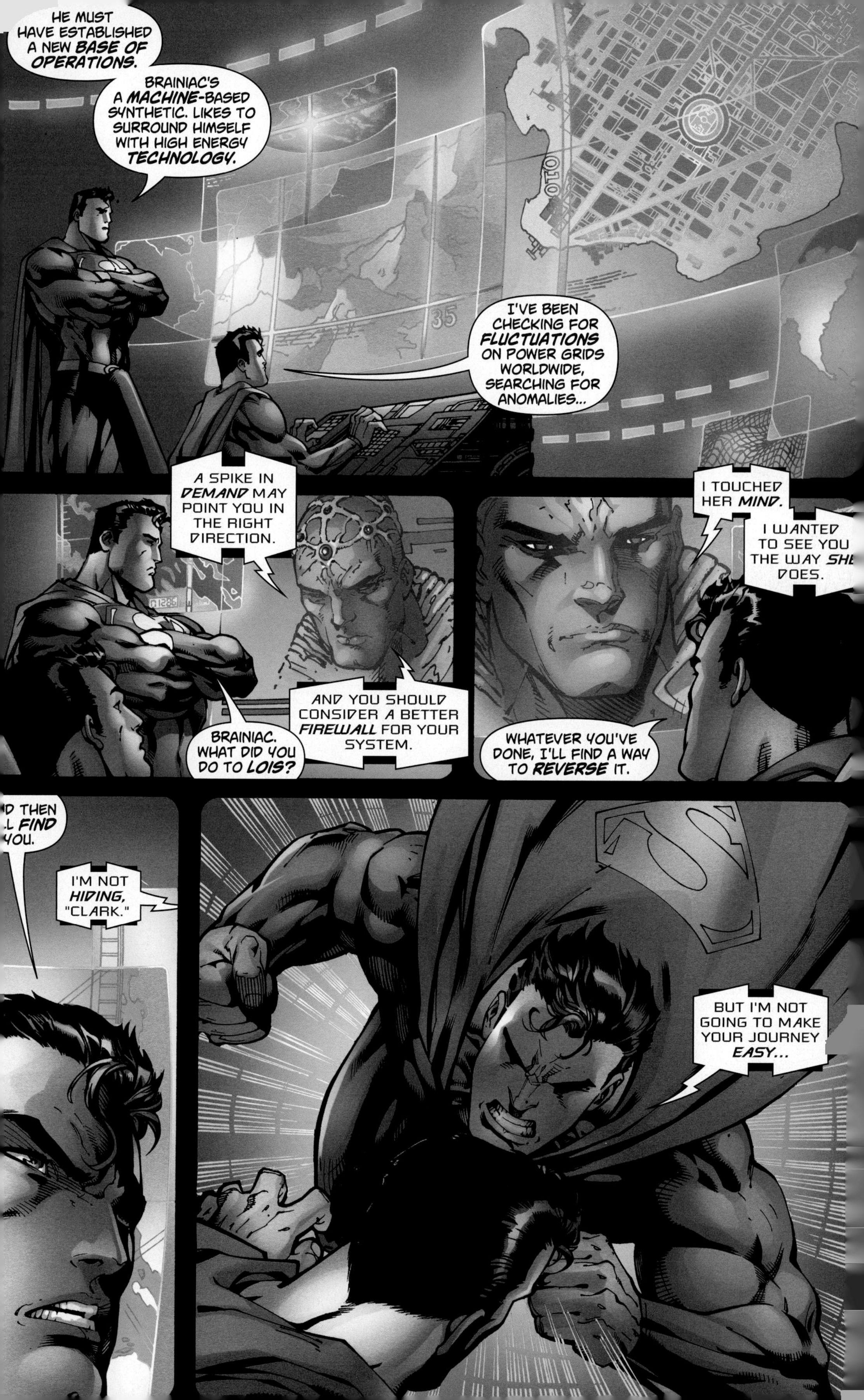

HE MUST HAVE ESTABLISHED A NEW *BASE OF OPERATIONS.*
BRAINIAC'S A *MACHINE*-BASED SYNTHETIC. LIKES TO SURROUND HIMSELF WITH HIGH ENERGY *TECHNOLOGY.*
I'VE BEEN CHECKING FOR *FLUCTUATIONS* ON POWER GRIDS WORLDWIDE, SEARCHING FOR ANOMALIES...
A SPIKE IN *DEMAND* MAY POINT YOU IN THE RIGHT DIRECTION.
AND YOU SHOULD CONSIDER A BETTER *FIREWALL* FOR YOUR SYSTEM.
BRAINIAC. WHAT DID YOU DO TO *LOIS?*
I TOUCHED HER *MIND.*
I WANTED TO SEE YOU THE WAY *SH*
DOES.
WHATEVER YOU'VE DONE, I'LL FIND A WAY TO *REVERSE* IT.
D THEN
FIND
YOU.
I'M NOT *HIDING,* "CLARK."
BUT I'M NOT GOING TO MAKE YOUR JOURNEY *EASY...*

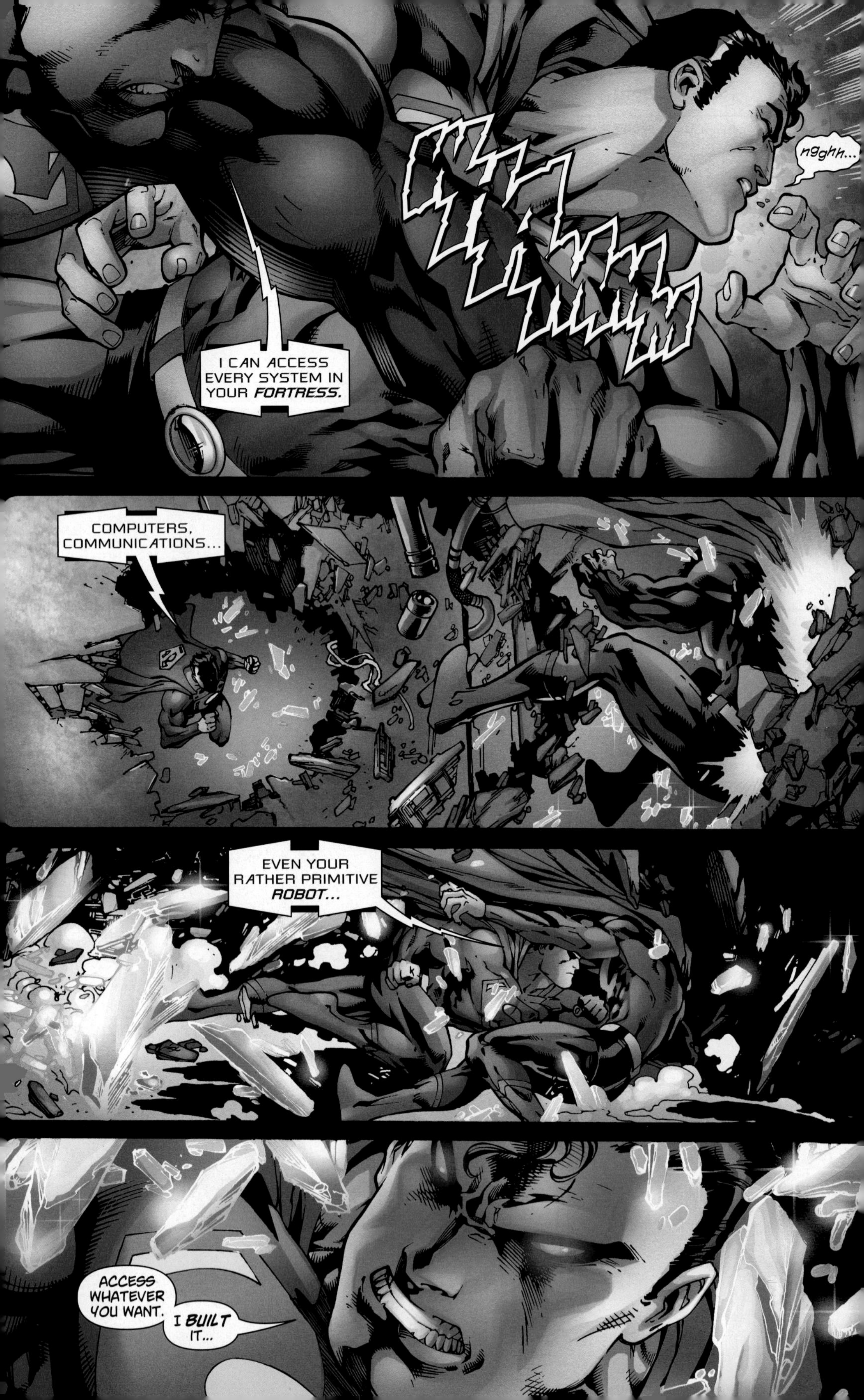
I CAN ACCESS EVERY SYSTEM IN YOUR FORTRESS.
nghh...
COMPUTERS, COMMUNICATIONS...
EVEN YOUR RATHER PRIMITIVE ROBOT...
ACCESS WHATEVER YOU WANT.
I BUILT IT...

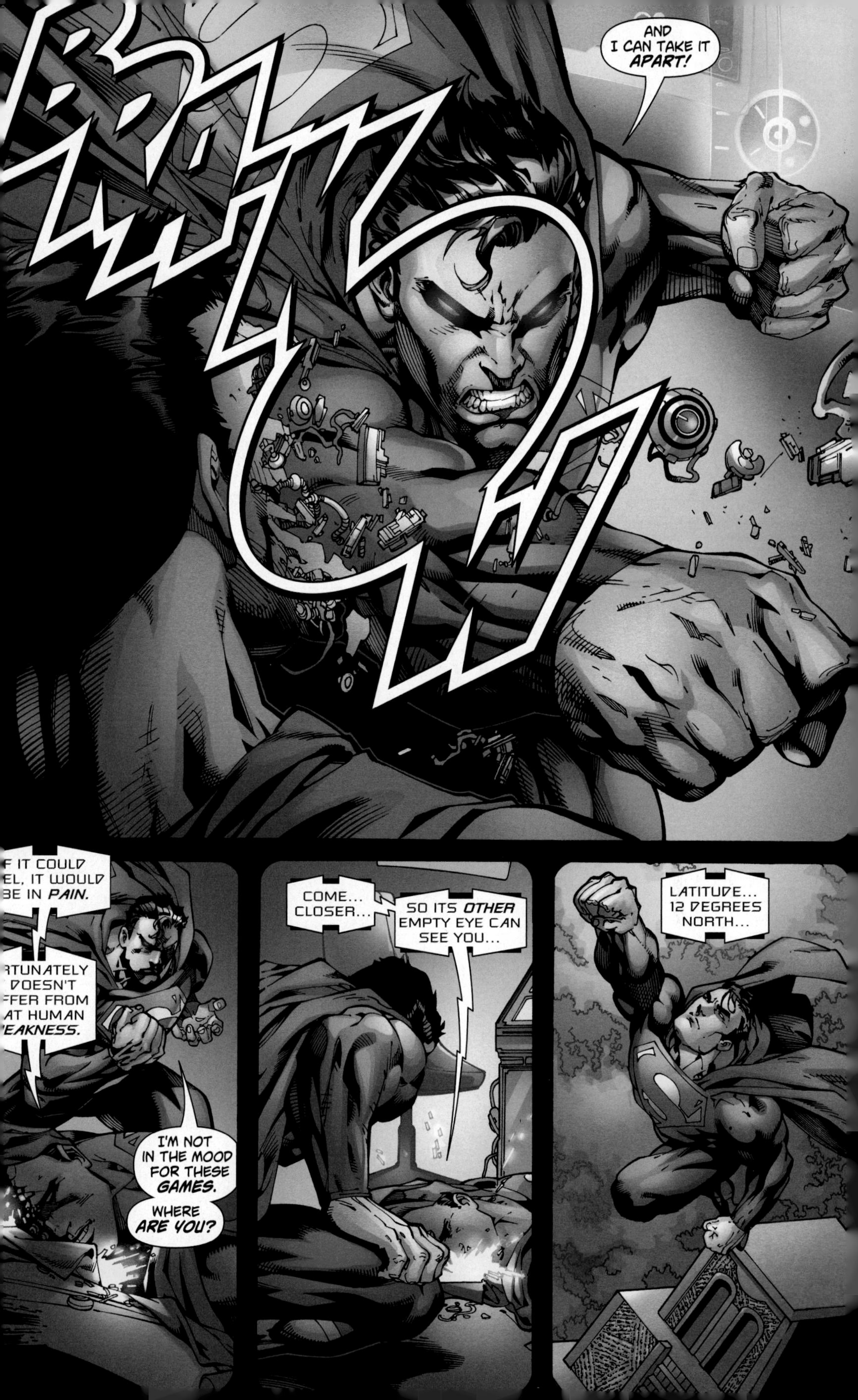
AND I CAN TAKE IT APART!
F IT COULD EL, IT WOULD BE IN PAIN.
RTUNATELY DOESN'T FFER FROM AT HUMAN EAKNESS.
I'M NOT IN THE MOOD FOR THESE GAMES.
WHERE ARE YOU?
COME... CLOSER...
SO ITS OTHER EMPTY EYE CAN SEE YOU...
LATITUDE... 12 DEGREES NORTH...

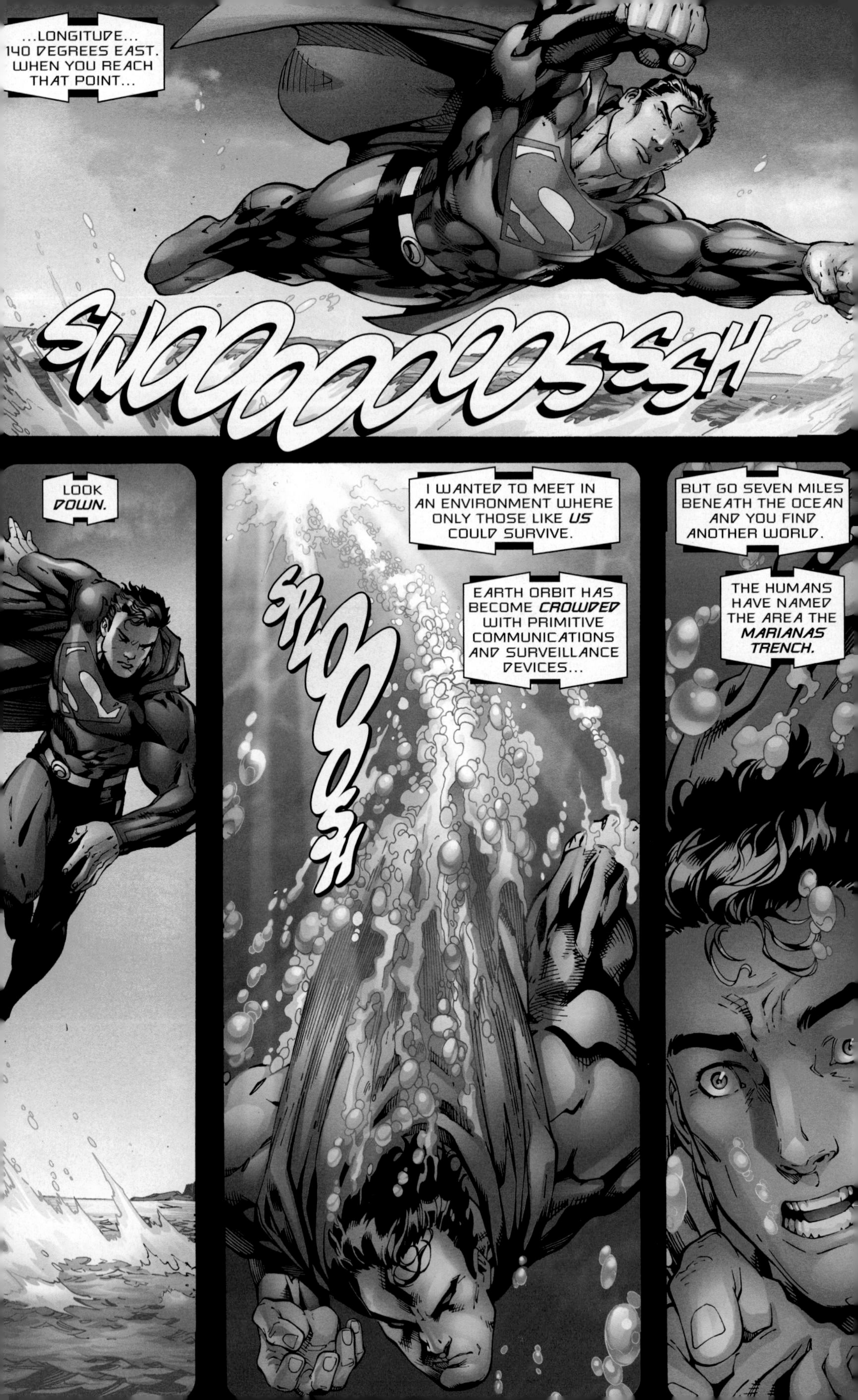
...LONGITUDE... 140 DEGREES EAST. WHEN YOU REACH THAT POINT...
SWOOOOOOSSSH
LOOK *DOWN.*
I WANTED TO MEET IN AN ENVIRONMENT WHERE ONLY THOSE LIKE *US* COULD SURVIVE.
EARTH ORBIT HAS BECOME *CROWDED* WITH PRIMITIVE COMMUNICATIONS AND SURVEILLANCE DEVICES...
BUT GO SEVEN MILES BENEATH THE OCEAN AND YOU FIND ANOTHER WORLD.
THE HUMANS HAVE NAMED THE AREA THE *MARIANAS TRENCH.*

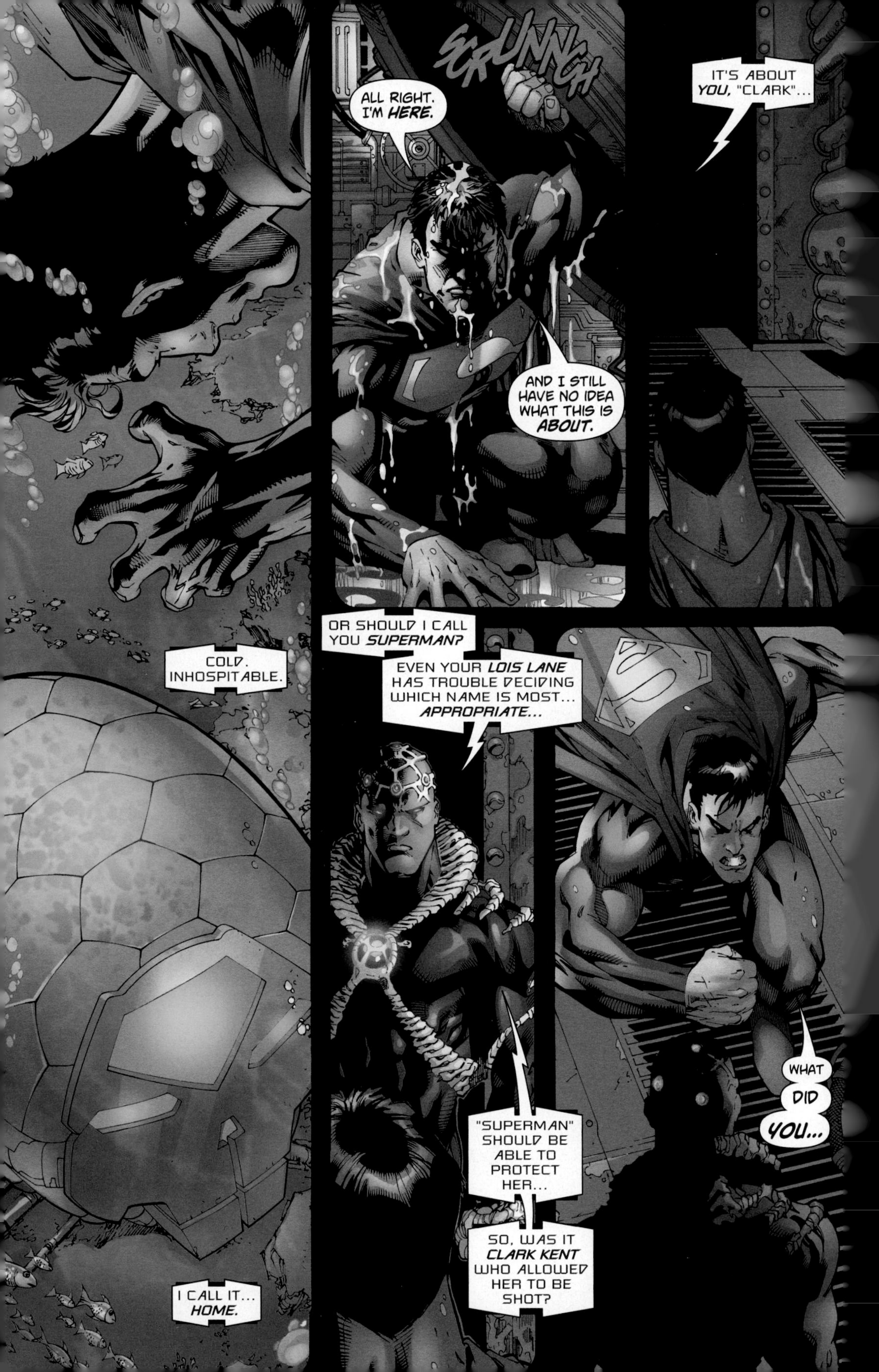

COLD. INHOSPITABLE.
I CALL IT... HOME.
SCRUNNCH
ALL RIGHT. I'M HERE.
AND I STILL HAVE NO IDEA WHAT THIS IS ABOUT.
IT'S ABOUT YOU, "CLARK"...
OR SHOULD I CALL YOU SUPERMAN?
EVEN YOUR LOIS LANE HAS TROUBLE DECIDING WHICH NAME IS MOST... APPROPRIATE...
"SUPERMAN" SHOULD BE ABLE TO PROTECT HER...
SO, WAS IT CLARK KENT WHO ALLOWED HER TO BE SHOT?
WHAT DID YOU...

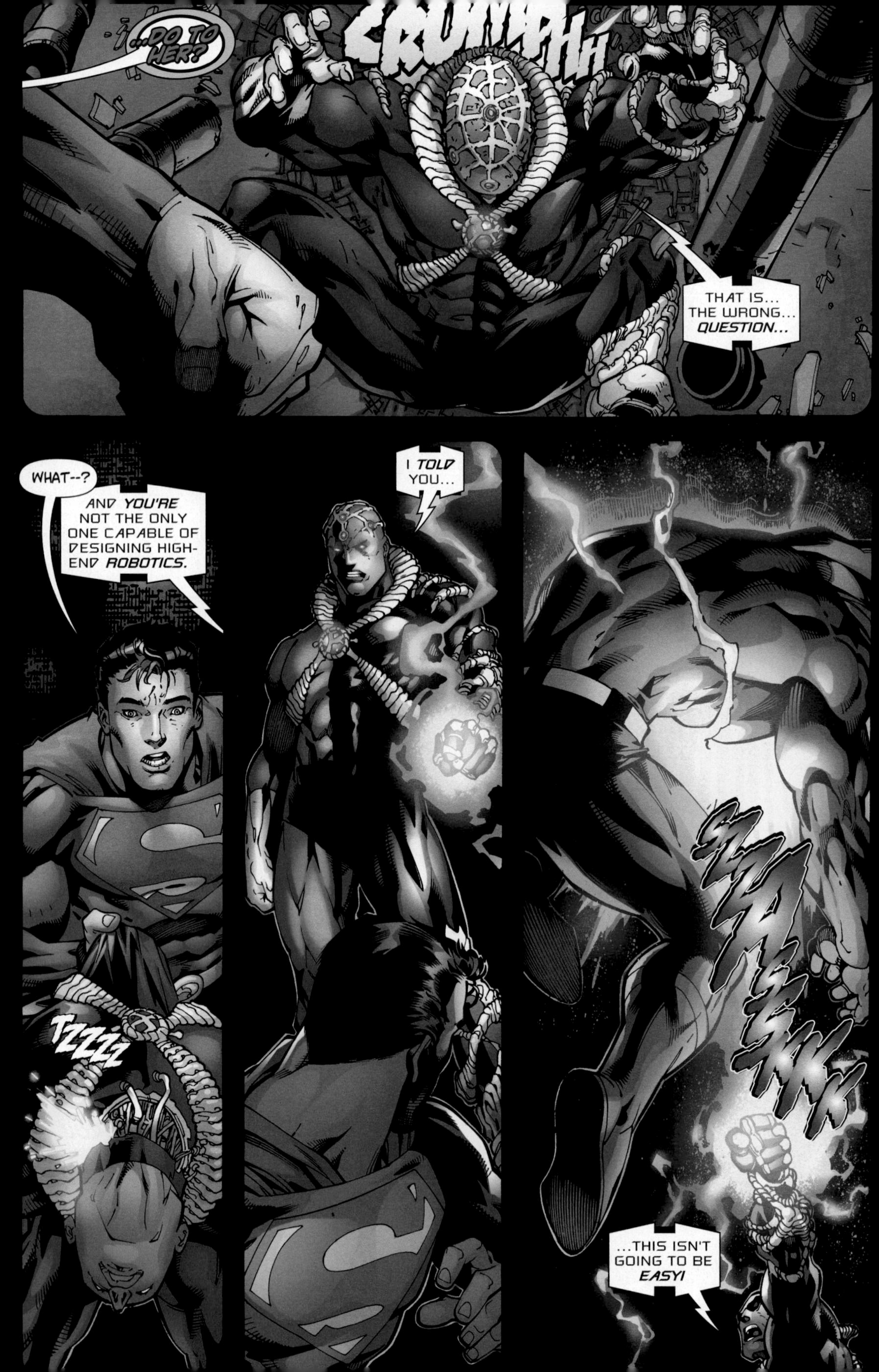
...DO TO HER?
CRUNNNCHH
THAT IS... THE WRONG... QUESTION...
WHAT--?
AND YOU'RE NOT THE ONLY ONE CAPABLE OF DESIGNING HIGH-END ROBOTICS.
TZZZZ
I TOLD YOU...
...THIS ISN'T GOING TO BE EASY!

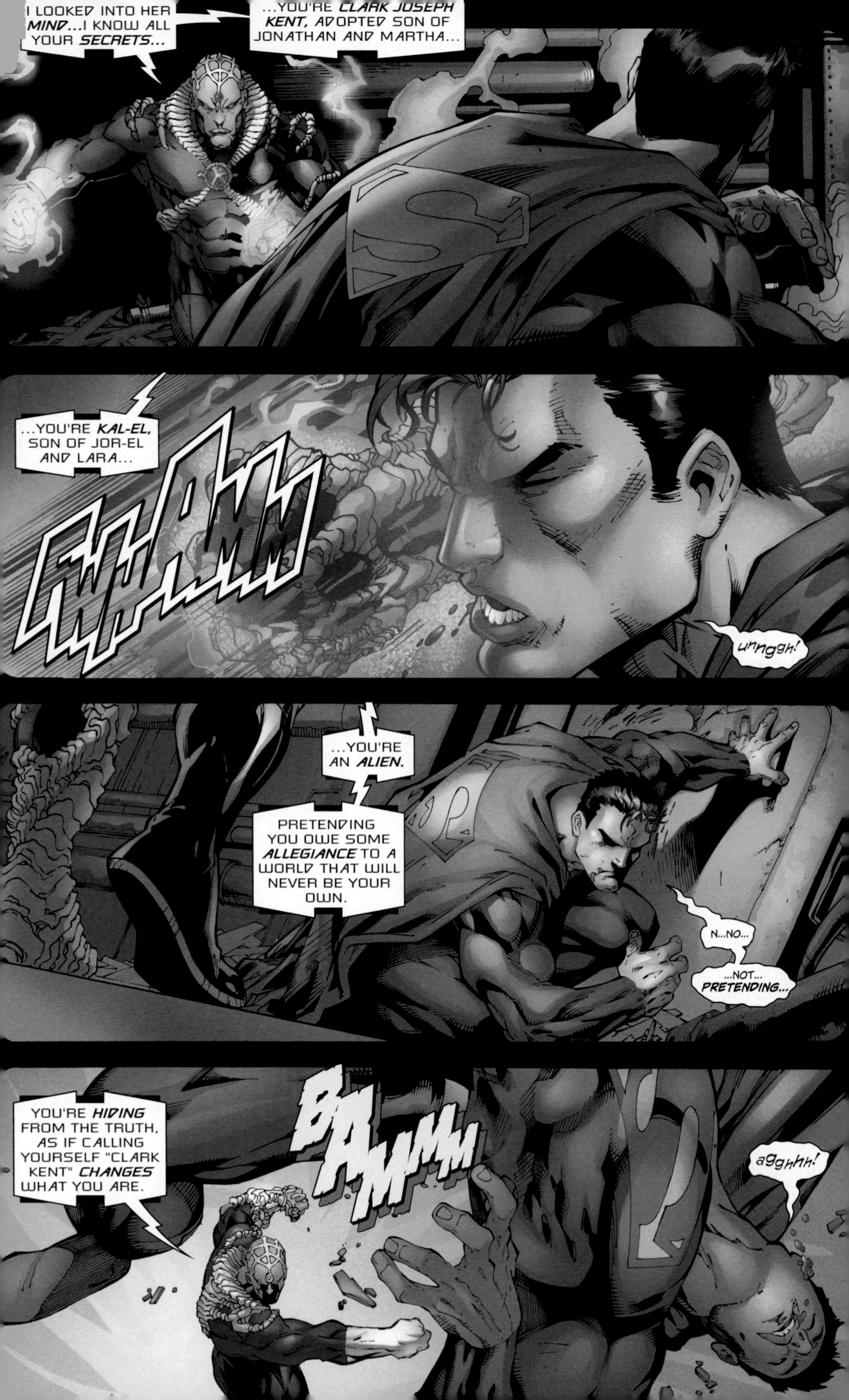
I LOOKED INTO HER MIND...I KNOW ALL YOUR SECRETS...
...YOU'RE CLARK JOSEPH KENT, ADOPTED SON OF JONATHAN AND MARTHA...
...YOU'RE KAL-EL, SON OF JOR-EL AND LARA...
FWHAMM
unnggh!
...YOU'RE AN ALIEN.
PRETENDING YOU OWE SOME ALLEGIANCE TO A WORLD THAT WILL NEVER BE YOUR OWN.
N...NO...
...NOT... PRETENDING...
YOU'RE HIDING FROM THE TRUTH, AS IF CALLING YOURSELF "CLARK KENT" CHANGES WHAT YOU ARE.
BAMMM
agghhh!

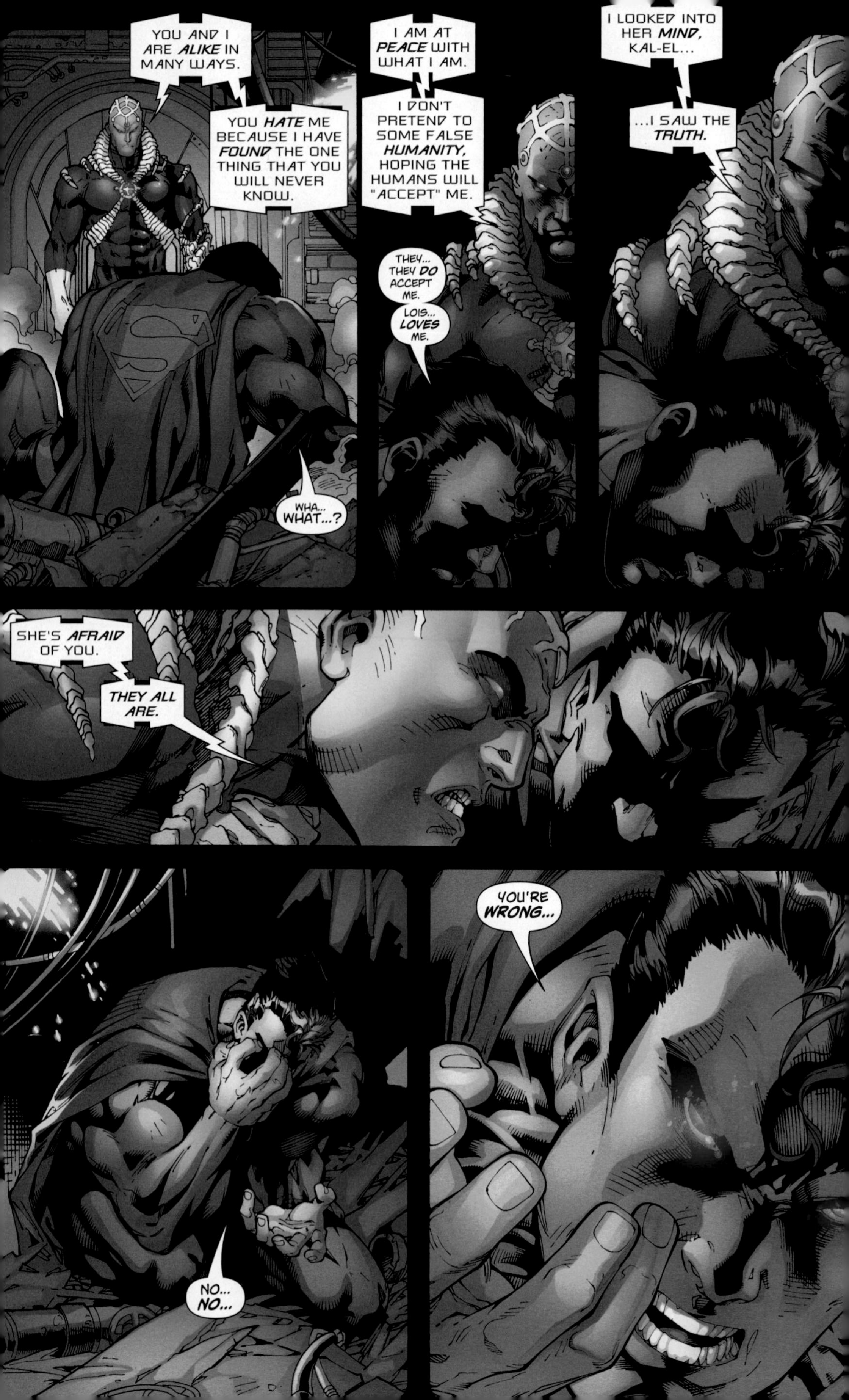
YOU AND I ARE *ALIKE* IN MANY WAYS.
YOU *HATE* ME BECAUSE I HAVE *FOUND* THE ONE THING THAT YOU WILL NEVER KNOW.
WHA... WHAT...?
I AM AT *PEACE* WITH WHAT I AM.
I DON'T PRETEND TO SOME FALSE *HUMANITY,* HOPING THE HUMANS WILL "ACCEPT" ME.
THEY... THEY *DO* ACCEPT ME.
LOIS... *LOVES* ME.
I LOOKED INTO HER *MIND,* KAL-EL...
...I SAW THE *TRUTH.*
SHE'S *AFRAID* OF YOU.
THEY ALL ARE.
NO... *NO...*
YOU'RE *WRONG...*

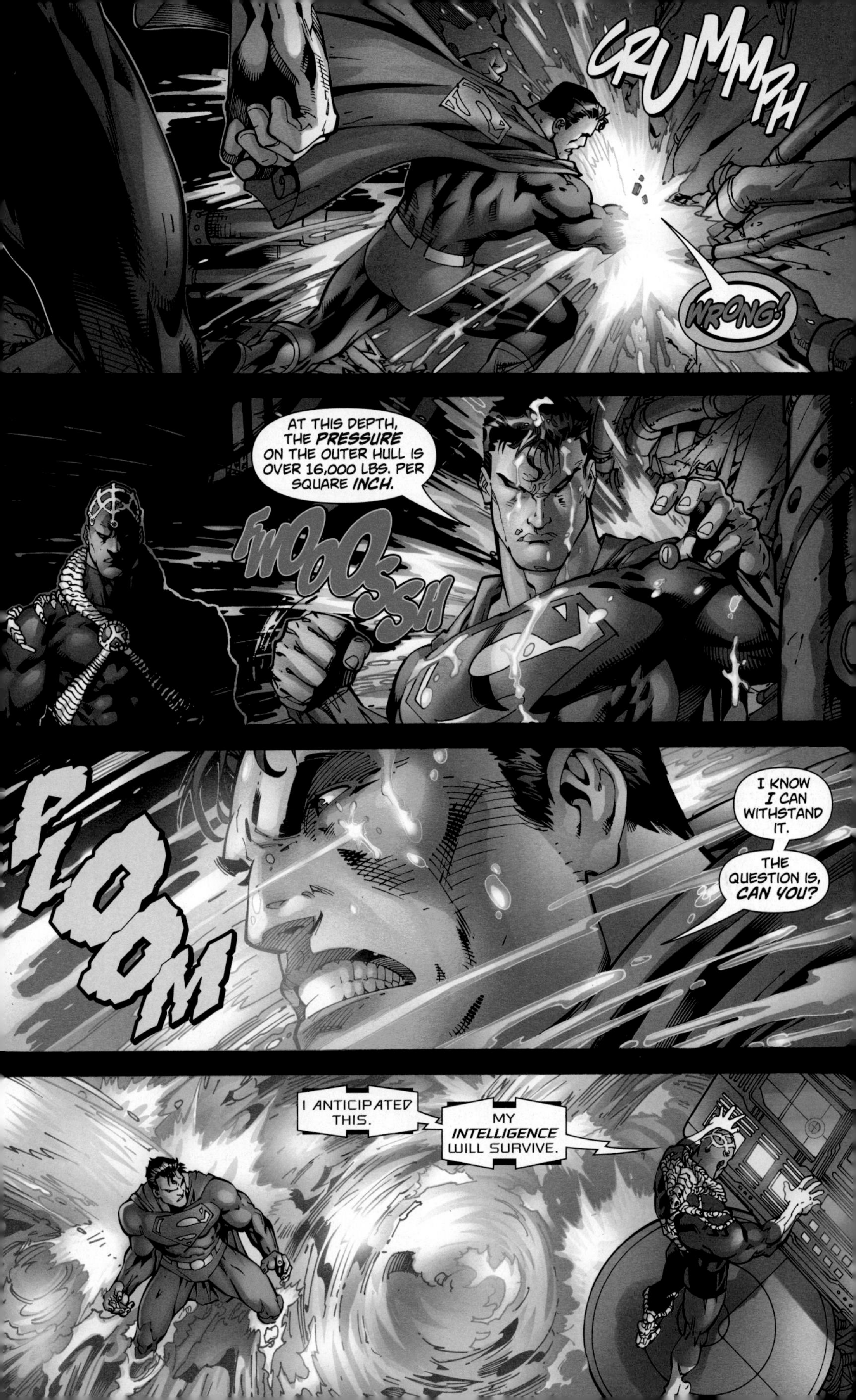
CRUMMMPH
WRONG!
AT THIS DEPTH, THE PRESSURE ON THE OUTER HULL IS OVER 16,000 LBS. PER SQUARE INCH.
FWOOOSSH
PLOOM
I KNOW I CAN WITHSTAND IT.
THE QUESTION IS, CAN YOU?
I ANTICIPATED THIS.
MY INTELLIGENCE WILL SURVIVE.

THEY WILL NOT.

NO... *NO!*

I SAW THEM ALL THROUGH HER *EYES.* SAW HOW *IMPORTANT* THEY WERE TO YOU.

PERRY!

FORGET ABOUT ME, SUPERMAN! HELP THE OTHERS!

I'LL DO ANYTHING!

PLEASE! DON'T LET THEM *DIE!*

THE IRONY IS, THEY WERE *SAFE* UNTIL *YOU* RUPTURED THE HULL.

THE CYLINDERS WERE DESIGNED TO KEEP THE HUMANS *IN.* NOT TO KEEP THE WATER *OUT.*

YOU CAN'T GET THEM TO THE SURFACE. THEIR BLOOD WILL FI WITH *NITROGEN* AND THEY'LL DI

WHEN THE COMPARTMENT IS FULLY FLOODED, THE CYLINDERS WILL *IMPLODE.*

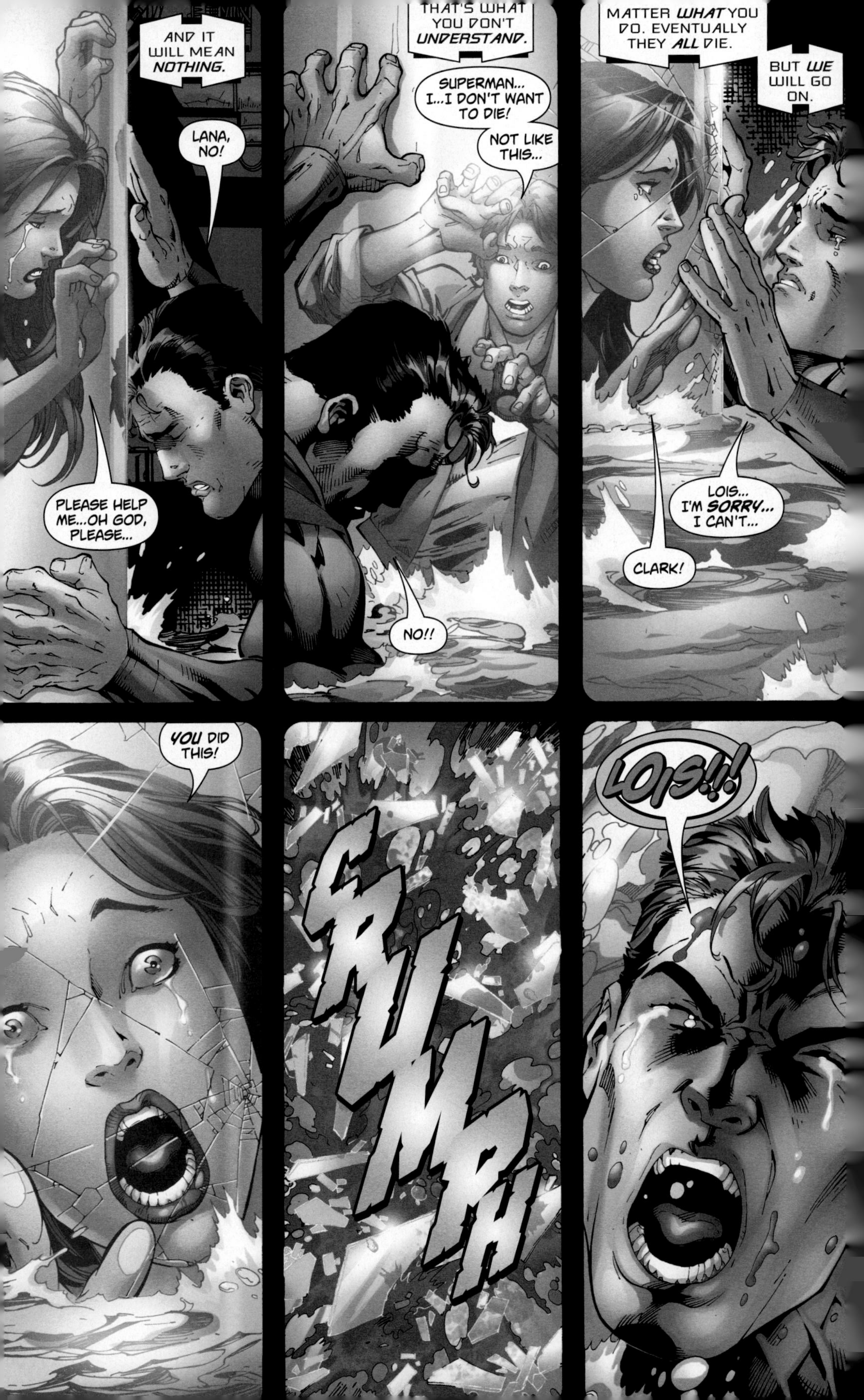
AND IT WILL MEAN *NOTHING*.
LANA, NO!
PLEASE HELP ME...OH GOD, PLEASE...
THAT'S WHAT YOU DON'T *UNDERSTAND*.
SUPERMAN... I...I DON'T WANT TO DIE!
NOT LIKE THIS...
NO!!
MATTER *WHAT* YOU DO. EVENTUALLY THEY *ALL* DIE.
BUT *WE* WILL GO ON.
LOIS... I'M *SORRY*... I CAN'T...
CLARK!
YOU DID THIS!
CRUMPH
LOIS!!!

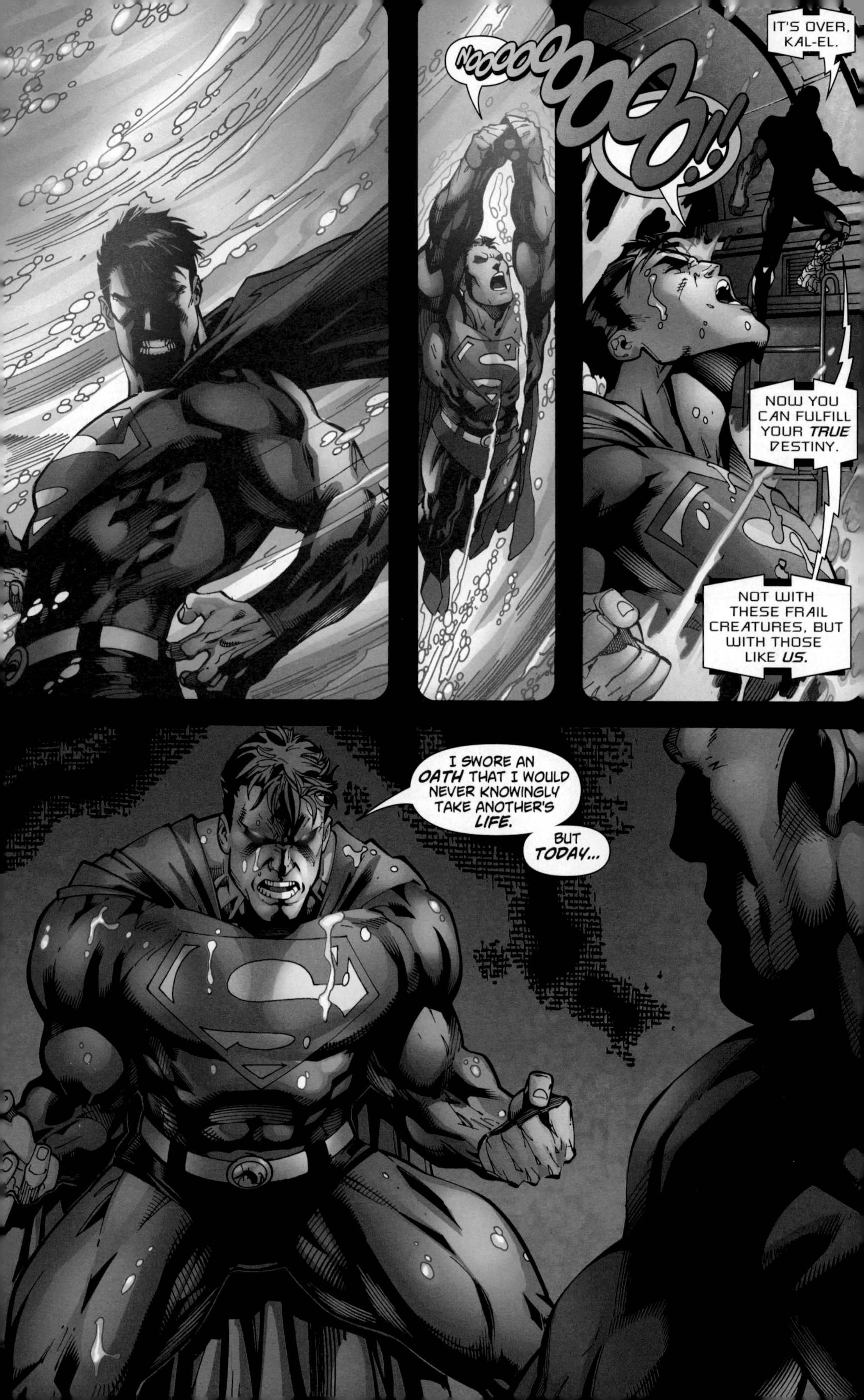
NOOOOOOOOO!!
IT'S OVER, KAL-EL.
NOW YOU CAN FULFILL YOUR TRUE DESTINY.
NOT WITH THESE FRAIL CREATURES, BUT WITH THOSE LIKE US.
I SWORE AN OATH THAT I WOULD NEVER KNOWINGLY TAKE ANOTHER'S LIFE.
BUT TODAY...

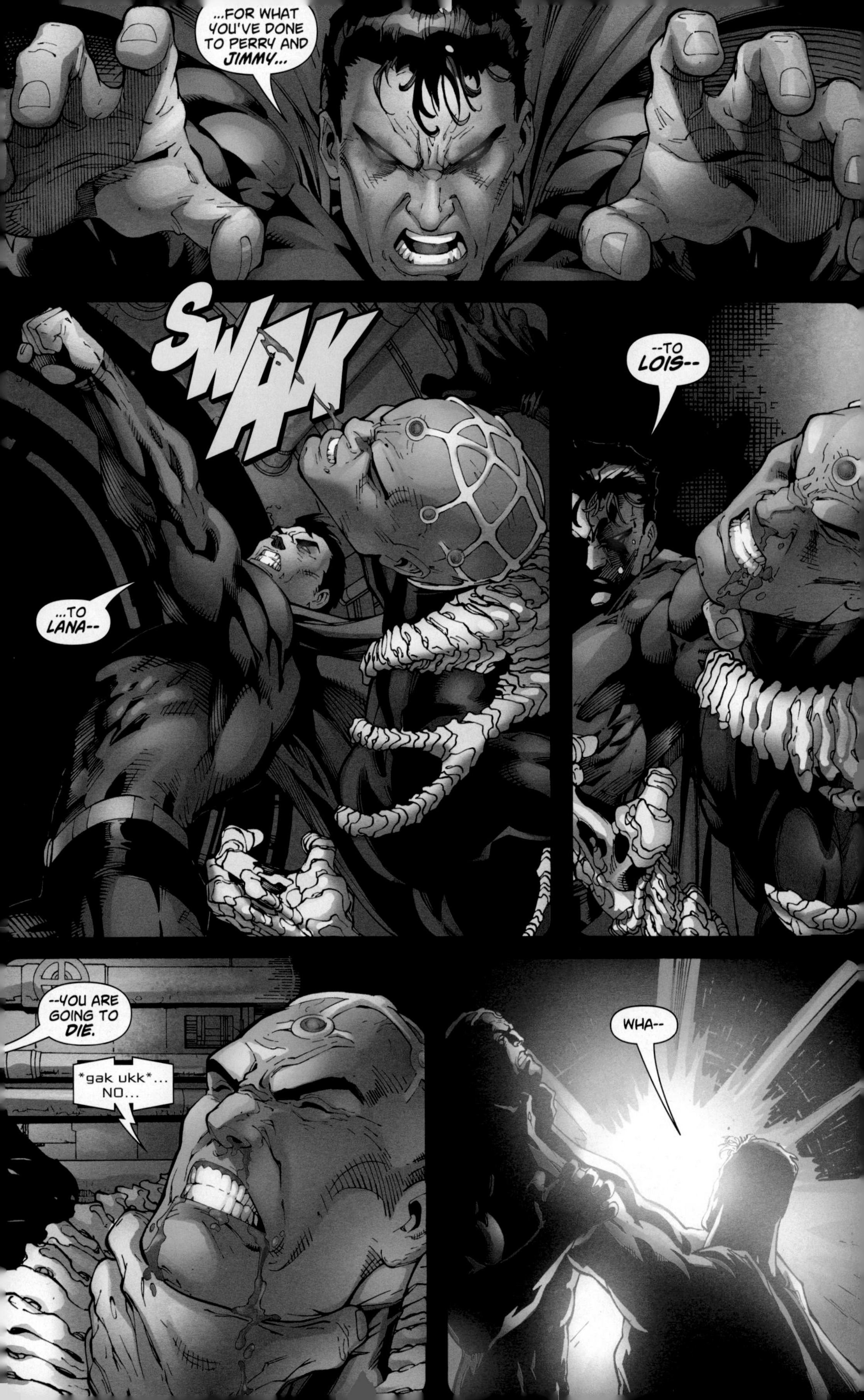
...FOR WHAT YOU'VE DONE TO PERRY AND JIMMY...
SWAK
...TO LANA--
--TO LOIS--
--YOU ARE GOING TO DIE.
gak ukk... NO...
WHA--

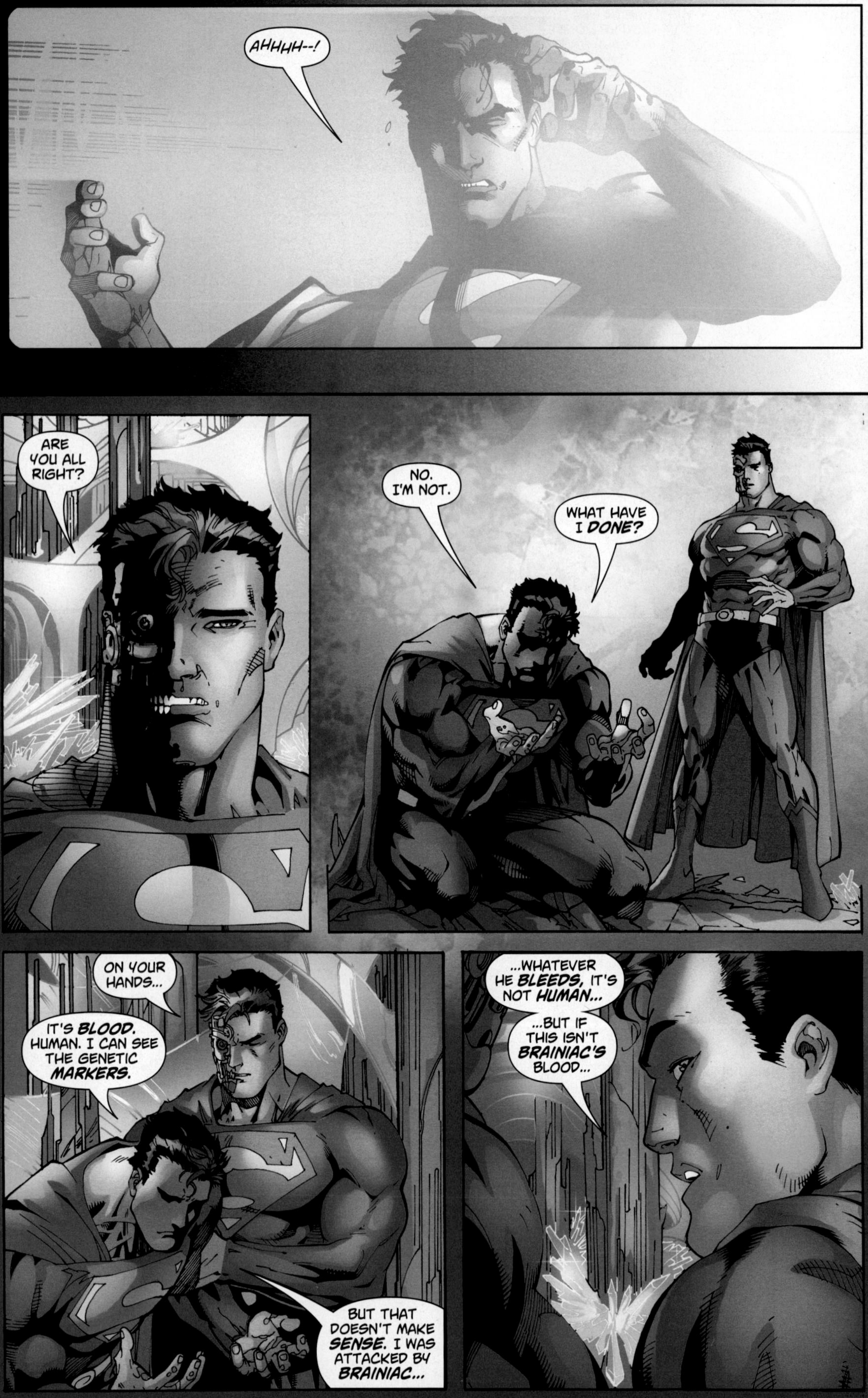
AHHHH--!
ARE YOU ALL RIGHT?
NO. I'M NOT.
WHAT HAVE I DONE?
ON YOUR HANDS...
IT'S BLOOD. HUMAN. I CAN SEE THE GENETIC MARKERS.
BUT THAT DOESN'T MAKE SENSE. I WAS ATTACKED BY BRAINIAC...
...WHATEVER HE BLEEDS, IT'S NOT HUMAN...
...BUT IF THIS ISN'T BRAINIAC'S BLOOD...

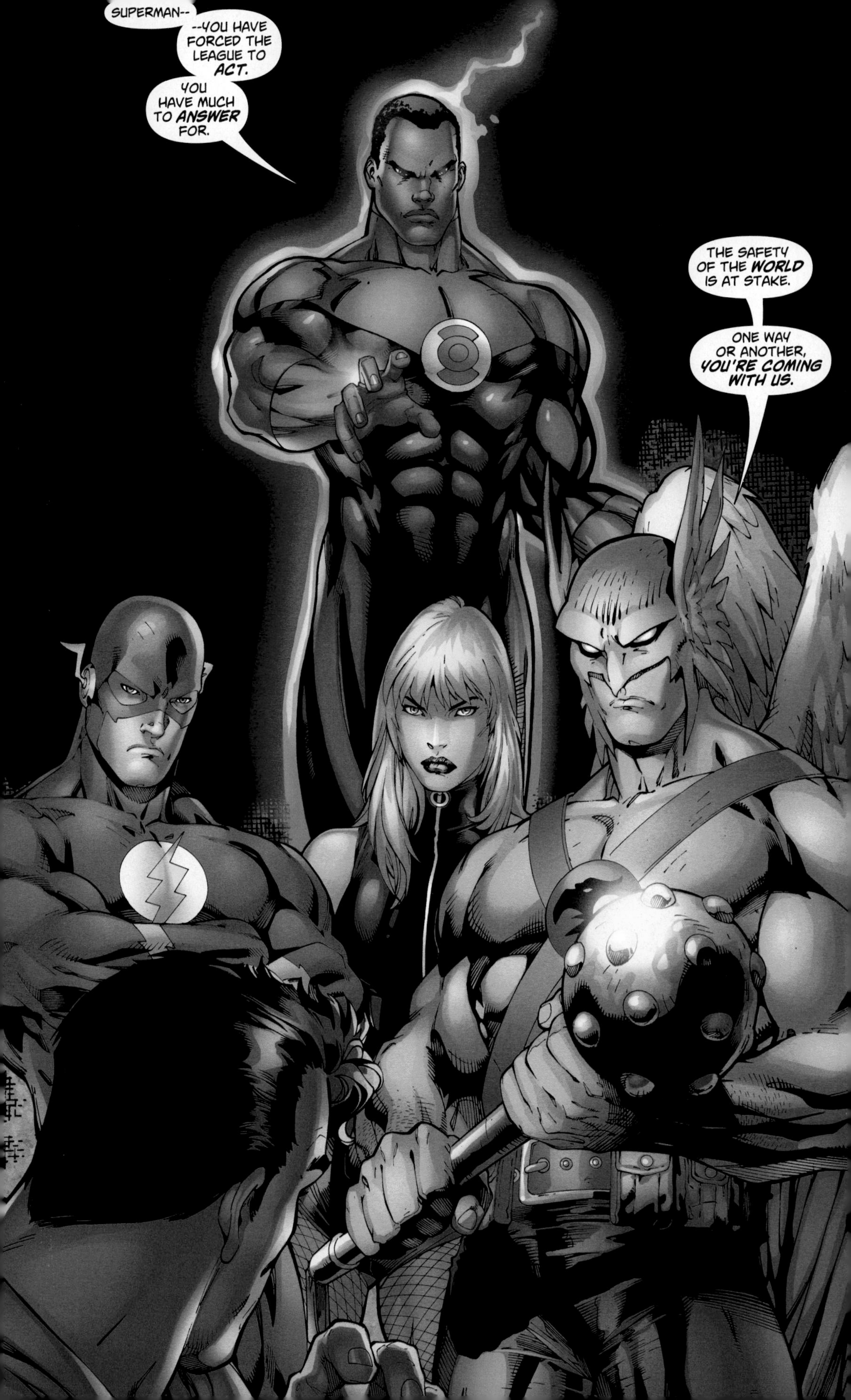
SUPERMAN--
--YOU HAVE FORCED THE LEAGUE TO ACT.
YOU HAVE MUCH TO ANSWER FOR.
THE SAFETY OF THE WORLD IS AT STAKE.
ONE WAY OR ANOTHER, YOU'RE COMING WITH US.

ACTION COMICS 829 - ART BY TONY DANIEL & DEXTER VINES

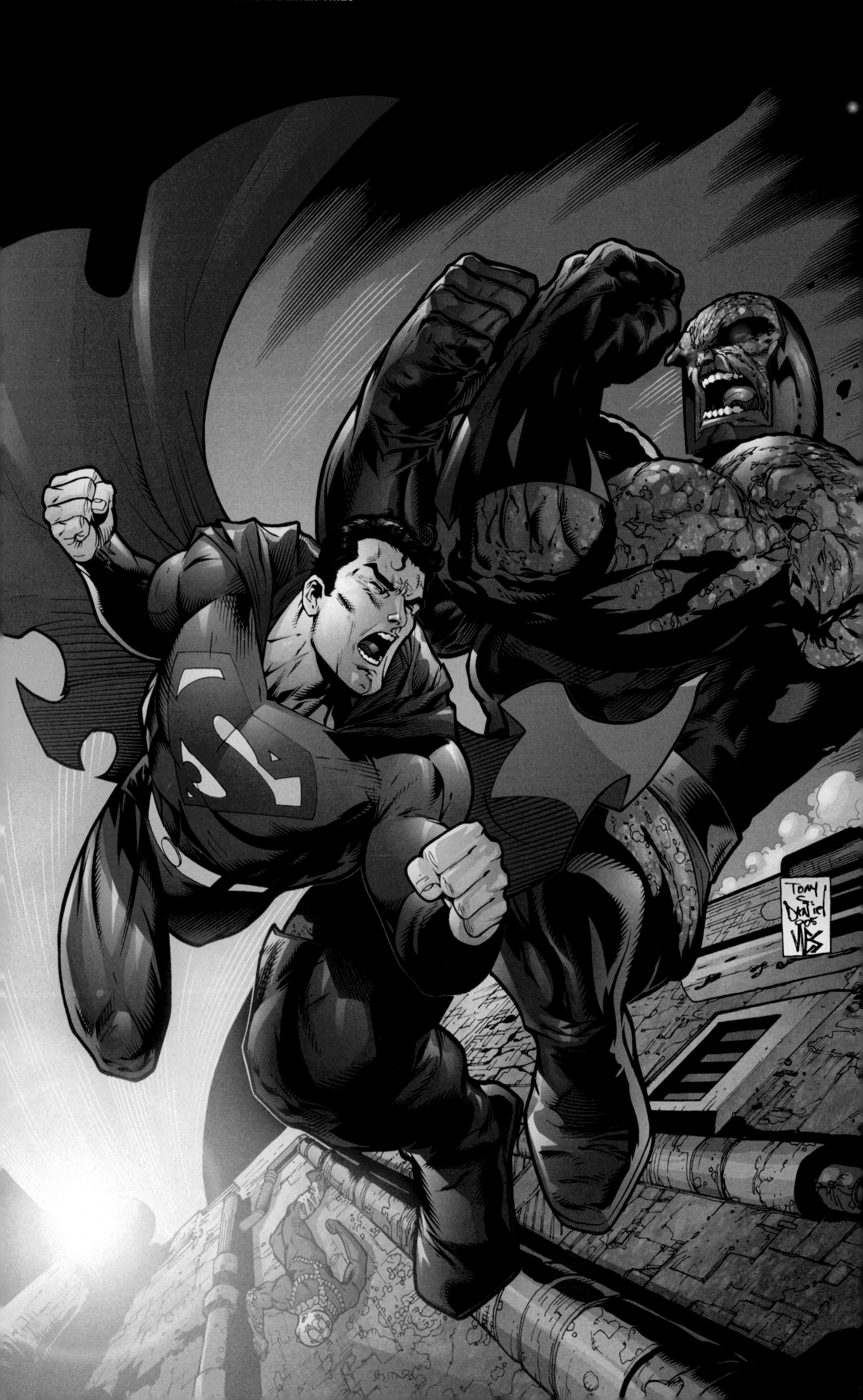

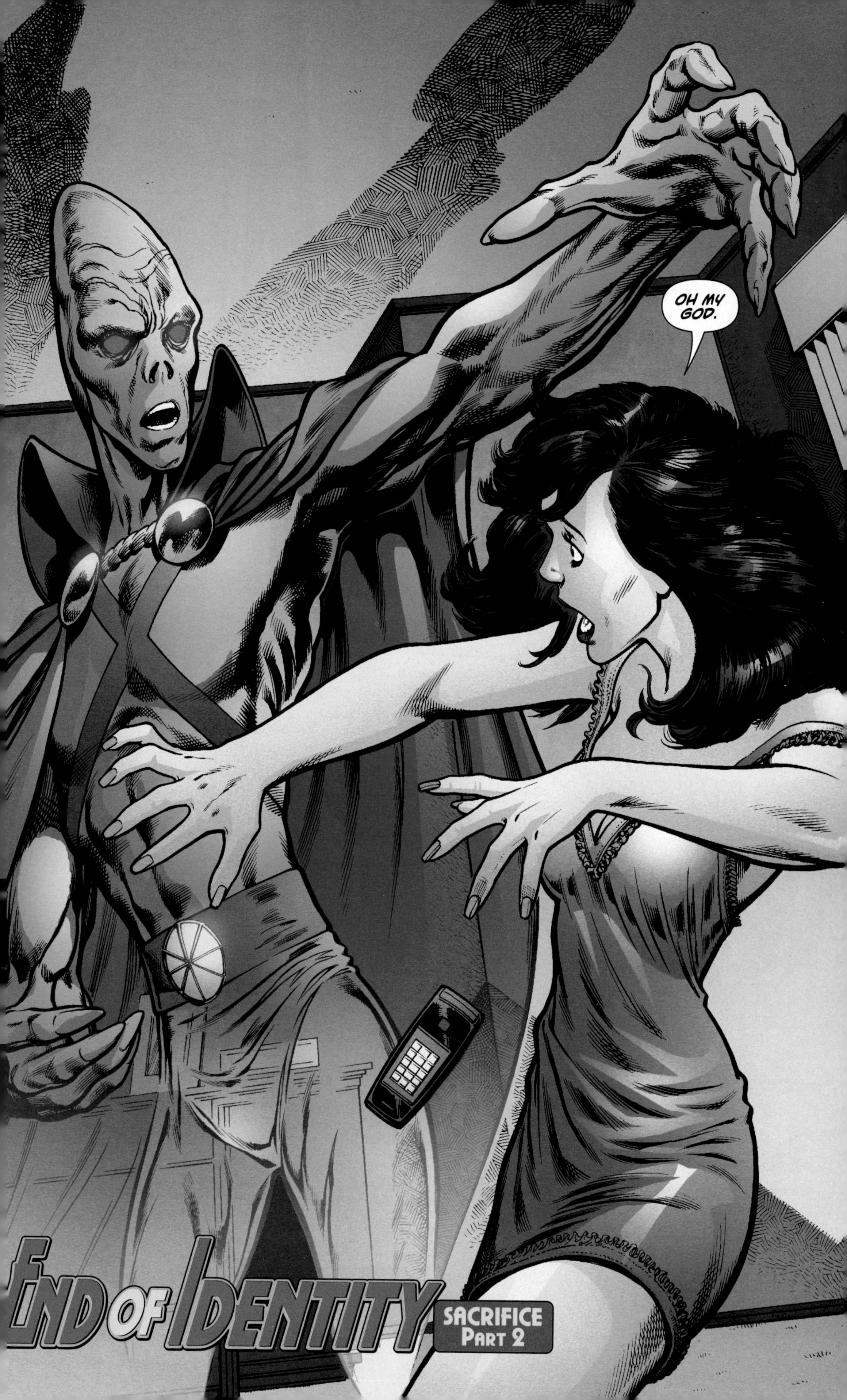
OH MY GOD.
END OF IDENTITY
SACRIFICE PART 2

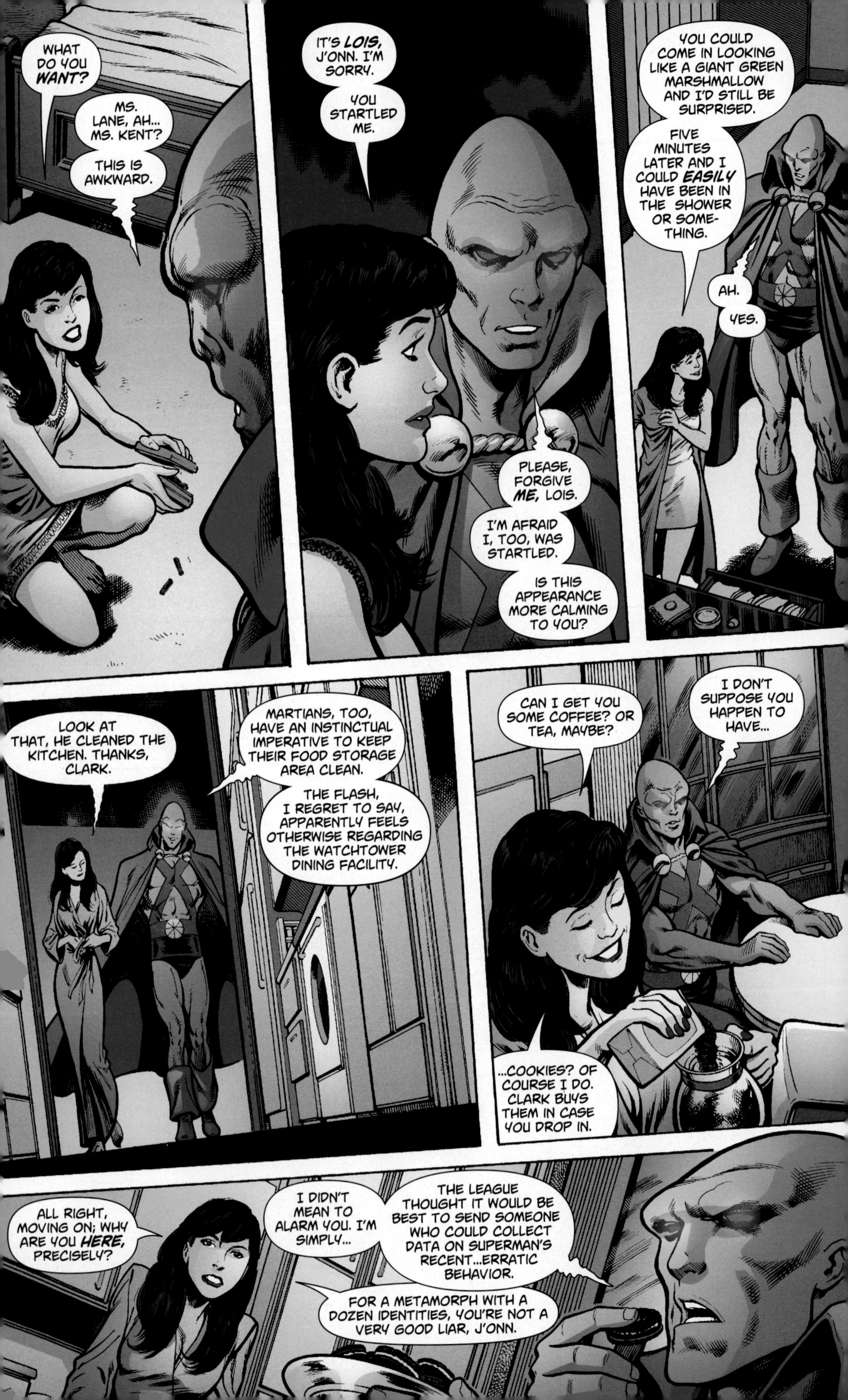
WHAT DO YOU WANT?
MS. LANE, AH... MS. KENT?
THIS IS AWKWARD.
IT'S LOIS, J'ONN. I'M SORRY.
YOU STARTLED ME.
PLEASE, FORGIVE ME, LOIS.
I'M AFRAID I, TOO, WAS STARTLED.
IS THIS APPEARANCE MORE CALMING TO YOU?
YOU COULD COME IN LOOKING LIKE A GIANT GREEN MARSHMALLOW AND I'D STILL BE SURPRISED.
FIVE MINUTES LATER AND I COULD EASILY HAVE BEEN IN THE SHOWER OR SOME-THING.
AH.
YES.
LOOK AT THAT, HE CLEANED THE KITCHEN. THANKS, CLARK.
MARTIANS, TOO, HAVE AN INSTINCTUAL IMPERATIVE TO KEEP THEIR FOOD STORAGE AREA CLEAN.
THE FLASH, I REGRET TO SAY, APPARENTLY FEELS OTHERWISE REGARDING THE WATCHTOWER DINING FACILITY.
CAN I GET YOU SOME COFFEE? OR TEA, MAYBE?
I DON'T SUPPOSE YOU HAPPEN TO HAVE...
...COOKIES? OF COURSE I DO. CLARK BUYS THEM IN CASE YOU DROP IN.
ALL RIGHT, MOVING ON; WHY ARE YOU HERE, PRECISELY?
I DIDN'T MEAN TO ALARM YOU. I'M SIMPLY...
THE LEAGUE THOUGHT IT WOULD BE BEST TO SEND SOMEONE WHO COULD COLLECT DATA ON SUPERMAN'S RECENT...ERRATIC BEHAVIOR.
FOR A METAMORPH WITH A DOZEN IDENTITIES, YOU'RE NOT A VERY GOOD LIAR, J'ONN.

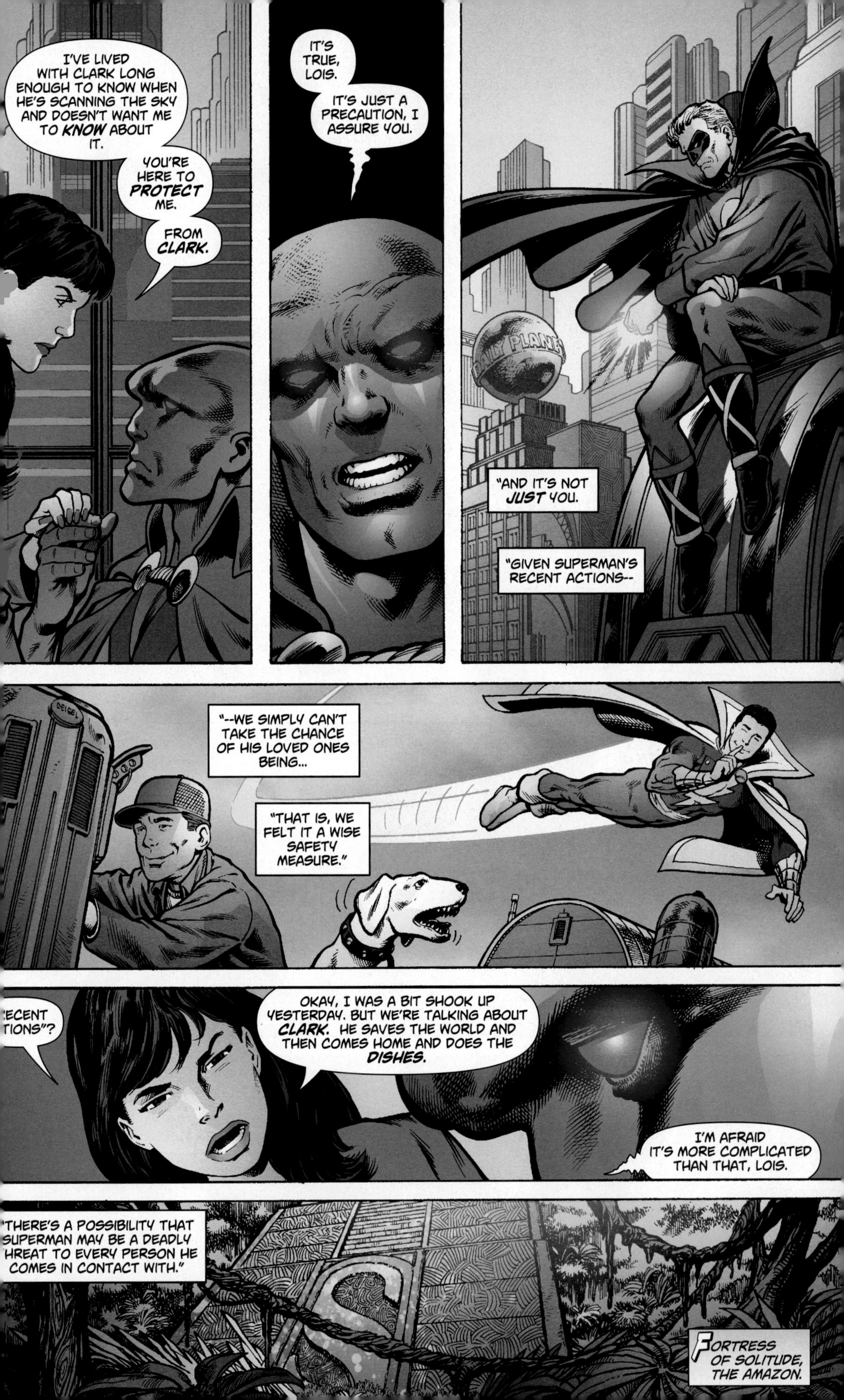
I'VE LIVED WITH CLARK LONG ENOUGH TO KNOW WHEN HE'S SCANNING THE SKY AND DOESN'T WANT ME TO **KNOW** ABOUT IT.
YOU'RE HERE TO **PROTECT** ME.
FROM **CLARK.**
IT'S TRUE, LOIS.
IT'S JUST A PRECAUTION, I ASSURE YOU.
"AND IT'S NOT **JUST** YOU.
"GIVEN SUPERMAN'S RECENT ACTIONS--
DEIGEL
"--WE SIMPLY CAN'T TAKE THE CHANCE OF HIS LOVED ONES BEING...
"THAT IS, WE FELT IT A WISE SAFETY MEASURE."
ECENT TIONS"?
OKAY, I WAS A BIT SHOOK UP YESTERDAY. BUT WE'RE TALKING ABOUT **CLARK.** HE SAVES THE WORLD AND THEN COMES HOME AND DOES THE **DISHES.**
I'M AFRAID IT'S MORE COMPLICATED THAN THAT, LOIS.
"THERE'S A POSSIBILITY THAT SUPERMAN MAY BE A DEADLY HREAT TO EVERY PERSON HE COMES IN CONTACT WITH."
FORTRESS OF SOLITUDE, THE AMAZON.

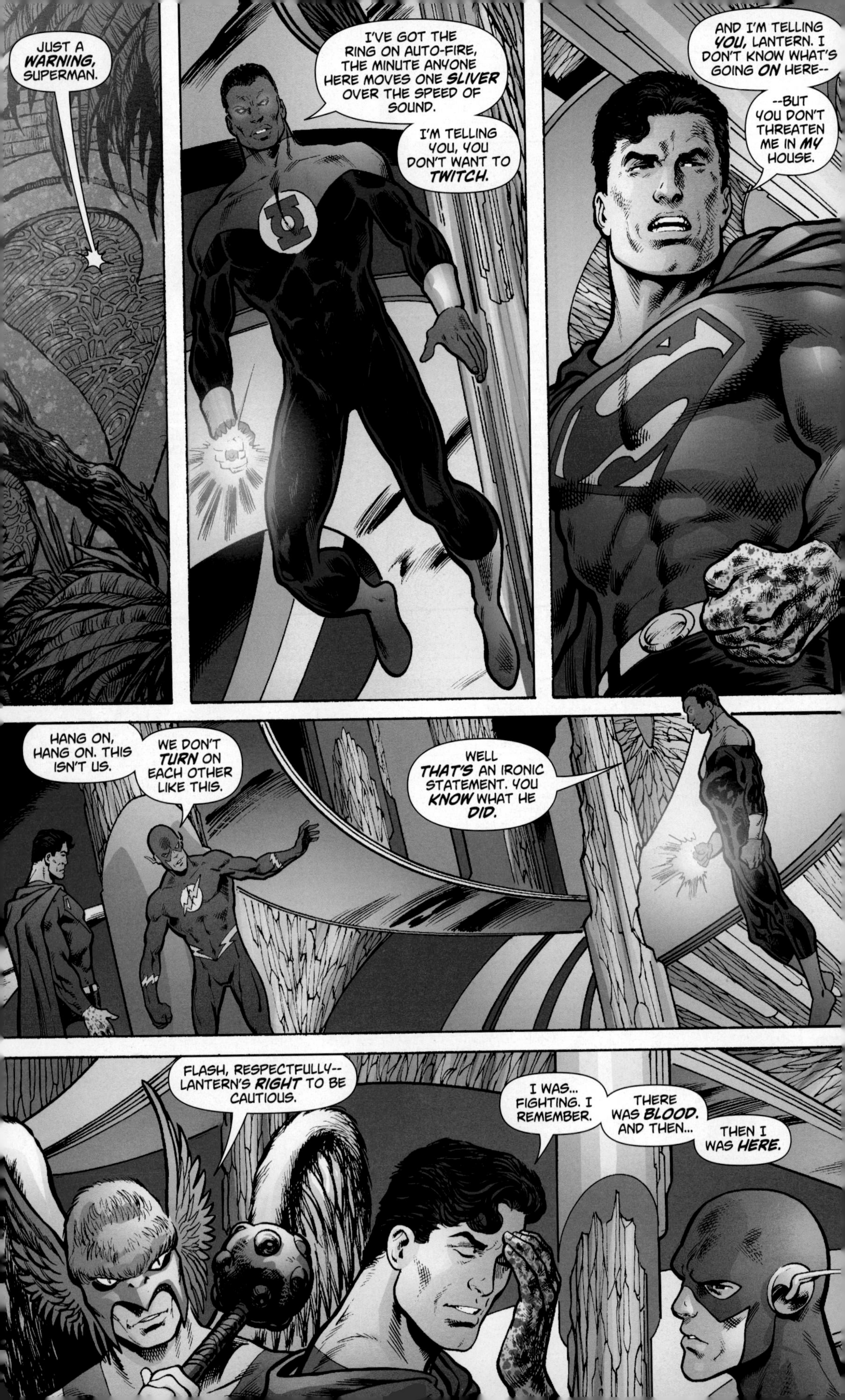
JUST A WARNING, SUPERMAN.
I'VE GOT THE RING ON AUTO-FIRE, THE MINUTE ANYONE HERE MOVES ONE SLIVER OVER THE SPEED OF SOUND.
I'M TELLING YOU, YOU DON'T WANT TO TWITCH.
AND I'M TELLING YOU, LANTERN. I DON'T KNOW WHAT'S GOING ON HERE--
--BUT YOU DON'T THREATEN ME IN MY HOUSE.
HANG ON, HANG ON. THIS ISN'T US.
WE DON'T TURN ON EACH OTHER LIKE THIS.
WELL THAT'S AN IRONIC STATEMENT. YOU KNOW WHAT HE DID.
FLASH, RESPECTFULLY-- LANTERN'S RIGHT TO BE CAUTIOUS.
I WAS... FIGHTING. I REMEMBER.
THERE WAS BLOOD. AND THEN...
THEN I WAS HERE.

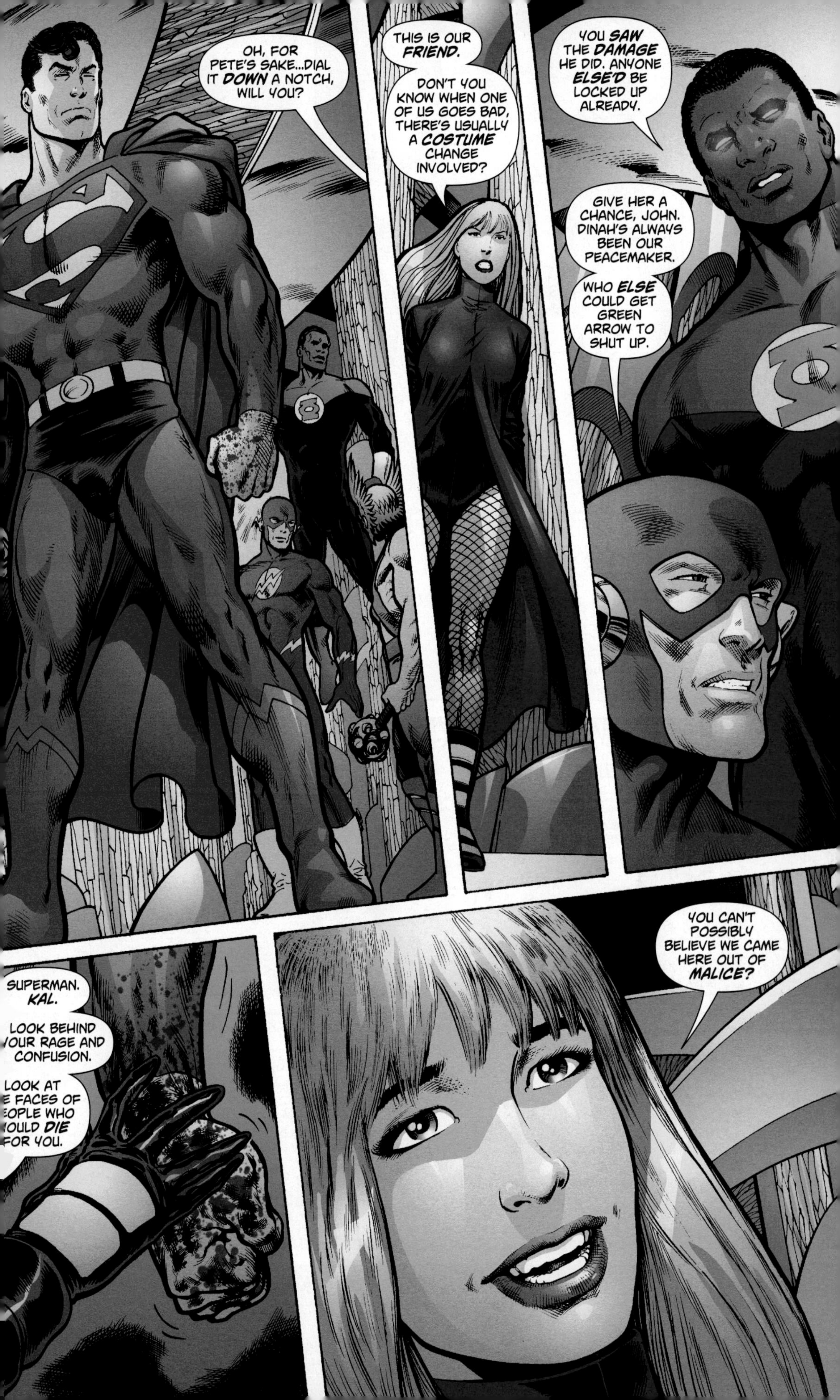

OH, FOR PETE'S SAKE...DIAL IT *DOWN* A NOTCH, WILL YOU?
THIS IS OUR *FRIEND.*
DON'T YOU KNOW WHEN ONE OF US GOES BAD, THERE'S USUALLY A *COSTUME* CHANGE INVOLVED?
YOU *SAW* THE *DAMAGE* HE DID. ANYONE *ELSE'D* BE LOCKED UP ALREADY.
GIVE HER A CHANCE, JOHN. DINAH'S ALWAYS BEEN OUR PEACEMAKER.
WHO *ELSE* COULD GET GREEN ARROW TO SHUT UP.
SUPERMAN. *KAL.*
LOOK BEHIND YOUR RAGE AND CONFUSION.
YOU CAN'T POSSIBLY BELIEVE WE CAME HERE OUT OF *MALICE?*

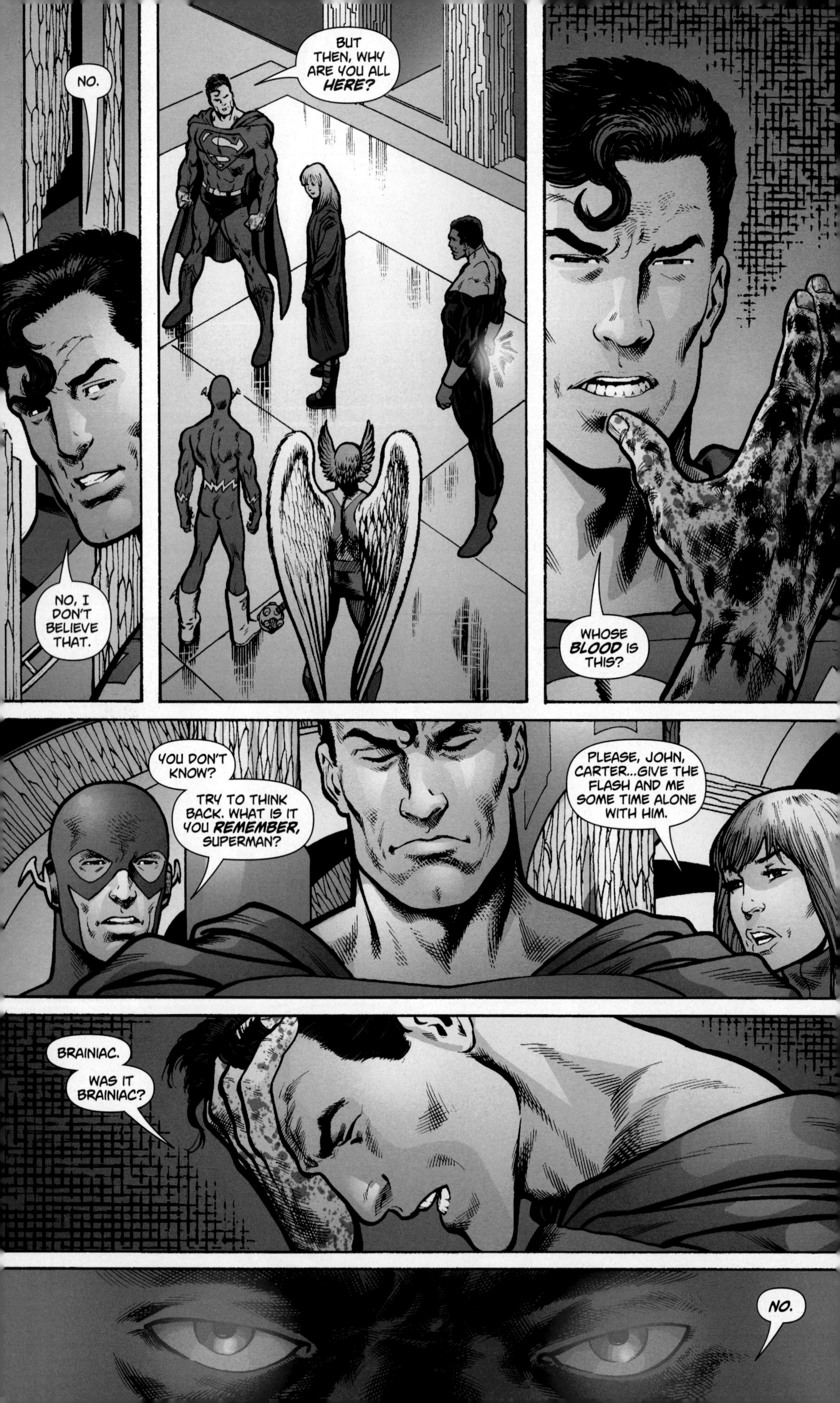
NO.
NO, I DON'T BELIEVE THAT.
BUT THEN, WHY ARE YOU ALL HERE?
WHOSE BLOOD IS THIS?
YOU DON'T KNOW?
TRY TO THINK BACK. WHAT IS IT YOU REMEMBER, SUPERMAN?
PLEASE, JOHN, CARTER...GIVE THE FLASH AND ME SOME TIME ALONE WITH HIM.
BRAINIAC.
WAS IT BRAINIAC?
NO.

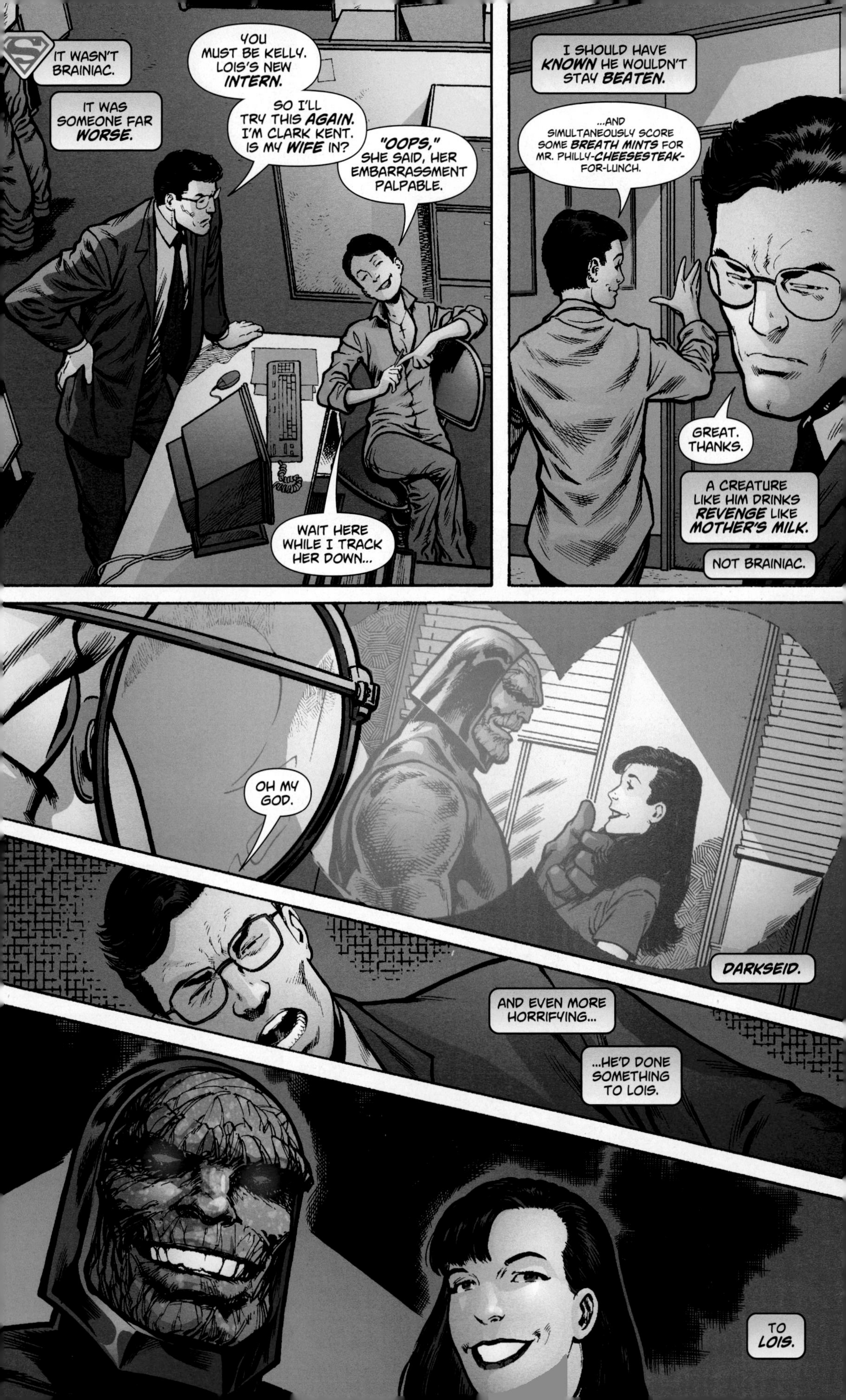
IT WASN'T BRAINIAC.
IT WAS SOMEONE FAR WORSE.
YOU MUST BE KELLY. LOIS'S NEW INTERN.
SO I'LL TRY THIS AGAIN. I'M CLARK KENT. IS MY WIFE IN?
"OOPS," SHE SAID, HER EMBARRASSMENT PALPABLE.
WAIT HERE WHILE I TRACK HER DOWN...
I SHOULD HAVE KNOWN HE WOULDN'T STAY BEATEN.
...AND SIMULTANEOUSLY SCORE SOME BREATH MINTS FOR MR. PHILLY-CHEESESTEAK-FOR-LUNCH.
GREAT. THANKS.
A CREATURE LIKE HIM DRINKS REVENGE LIKE MOTHER'S MILK.
NOT BRAINIAC.
OH MY GOD.
DARKSEID.
AND EVEN MORE HORRIFYING...
...HE'D DONE SOMETHING TO LOIS.
TO LOIS.

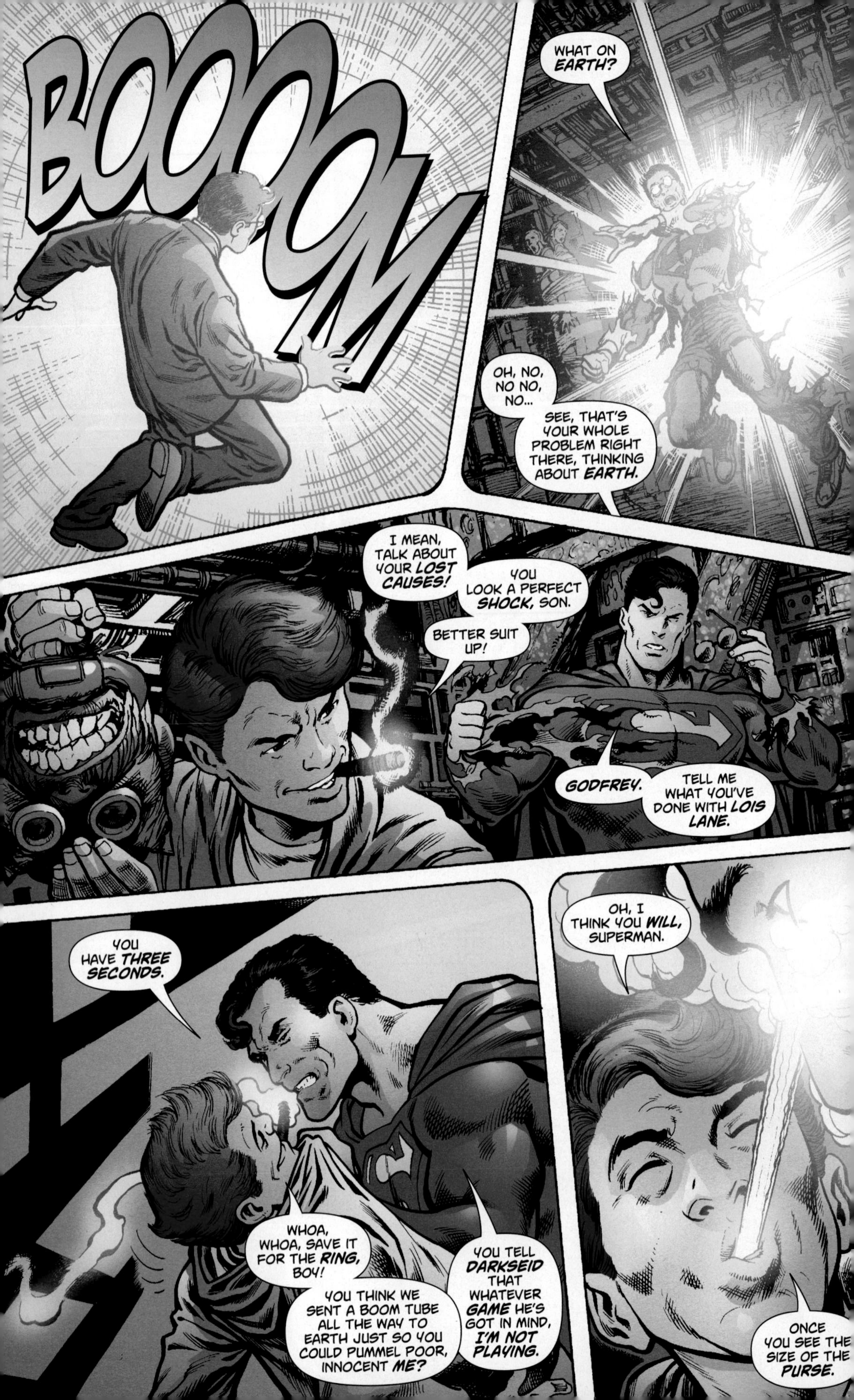
BOOOOM
WHAT ON EARTH?
OH, NO, NO NO, NO...
SEE, THAT'S YOUR WHOLE PROBLEM RIGHT THERE, THINKING ABOUT EARTH.
I MEAN, TALK ABOUT YOUR LOST CAUSES!
YOU LOOK A PERFECT SHOCK, SON.
BETTER SUIT UP!
GODFREY.
TELL ME WHAT YOU'VE DONE WITH LOIS LANE.
YOU HAVE THREE SECONDS.
WHOA, WHOA, SAVE IT FOR THE RING, BOY!
YOU THINK WE SENT A BOOM TUBE ALL THE WAY TO EARTH JUST SO YOU COULD PUMMEL POOR, INNOCENT ME?
YOU TELL DARKSEID THAT WHATEVER GAME HE'S GOT IN MIND, I'M NOT PLAYING.
OH, I THINK YOU WILL, SUPERMAN.
ONCE YOU SEE THE SIZE OF THE PURSE.

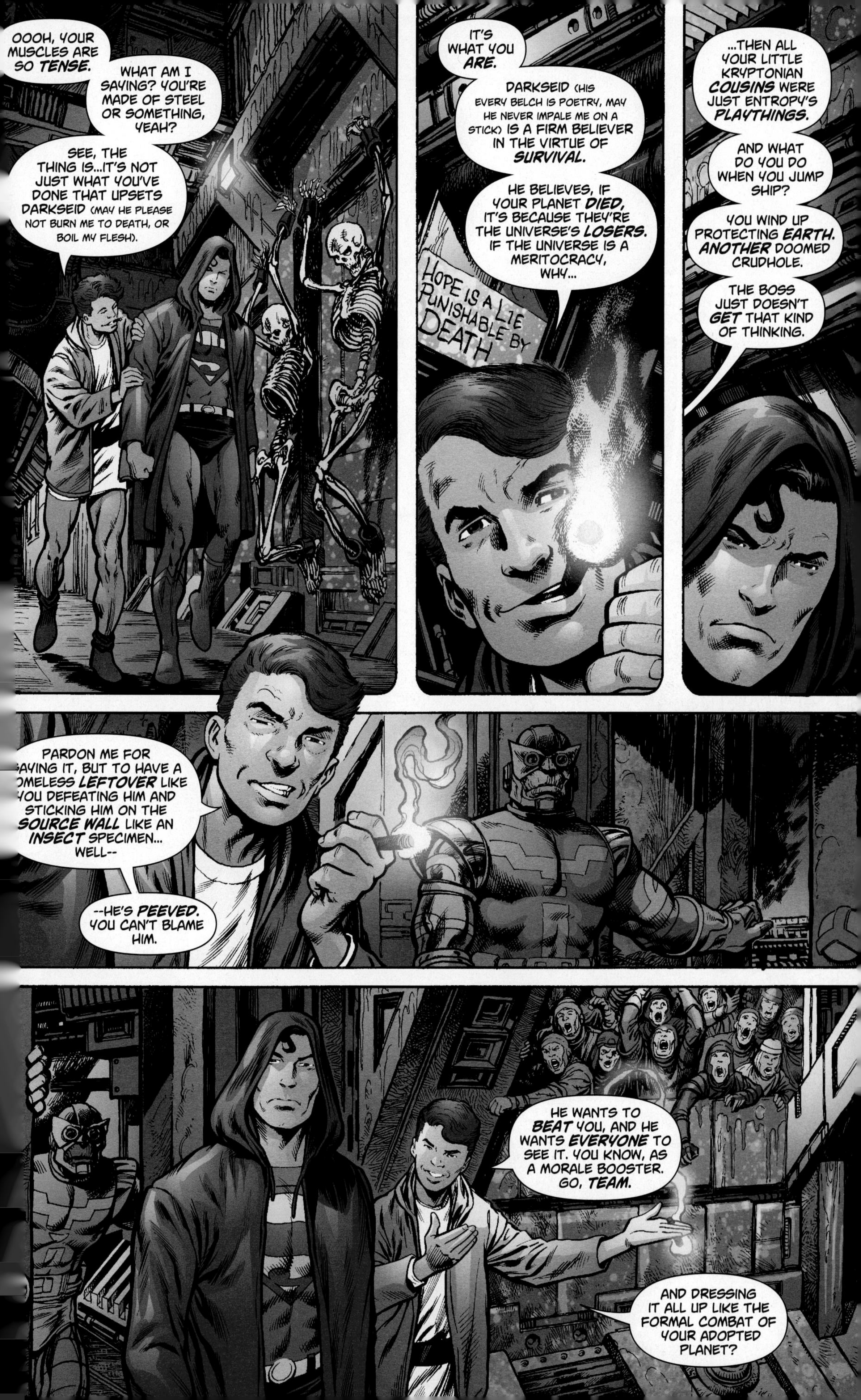
OOOH, YOUR MUSCLES ARE SO TENSE.
WHAT AM I SAYING? YOU'RE MADE OF STEEL OR SOMETHING, YEAH?
SEE, THE THING IS...IT'S NOT JUST WHAT YOU'VE DONE THAT UPSETS DARKSEID (MAY HE PLEASE NOT BURN ME TO DEATH, OR BOIL MY FLESH).
IT'S WHAT YOU ARE.
DARKSEID (HIS EVERY BELCH IS POETRY, MAY HE NEVER IMPALE ME ON A STICK) IS A FIRM BELIEVER IN THE VIRTUE OF SURVIVAL.
HE BELIEVES, IF YOUR PLANET DIED, IT'S BECAUSE THEY'RE THE UNIVERSE'S LOSERS. IF THE UNIVERSE IS A MERITOCRACY, WHY...
HOPE IS A LIE PUNISHABLE BY DEATH
...THEN ALL YOUR LITTLE KRYPTONIAN COUSINS WERE JUST ENTROPY'S PLAYTHINGS.
AND WHAT DO YOU DO WHEN YOU JUMP SHIP?
YOU WIND UP PROTECTING EARTH. ANOTHER DOOMED CRUDHOLE.
THE BOSS JUST DOESN'T GET THAT KIND OF THINKING.
PARDON ME FOR SAYING IT, BUT TO HAVE A HOMELESS LEFTOVER LIKE YOU DEFEATING HIM AND STICKING HIM ON THE SOURCE WALL LIKE AN INSECT SPECIMEN... WELL--
--HE'S PEEVED. YOU CAN'T BLAME HIM.
HE WANTS TO BEAT YOU, AND HE WANTS EVERYONE TO SEE IT. YOU KNOW, AS A MORALE BOOSTER. GO, TEAM.
AND DRESSING IT ALL UP LIKE THE FORMAL COMBAT OF YOUR ADOPTED PLANET?

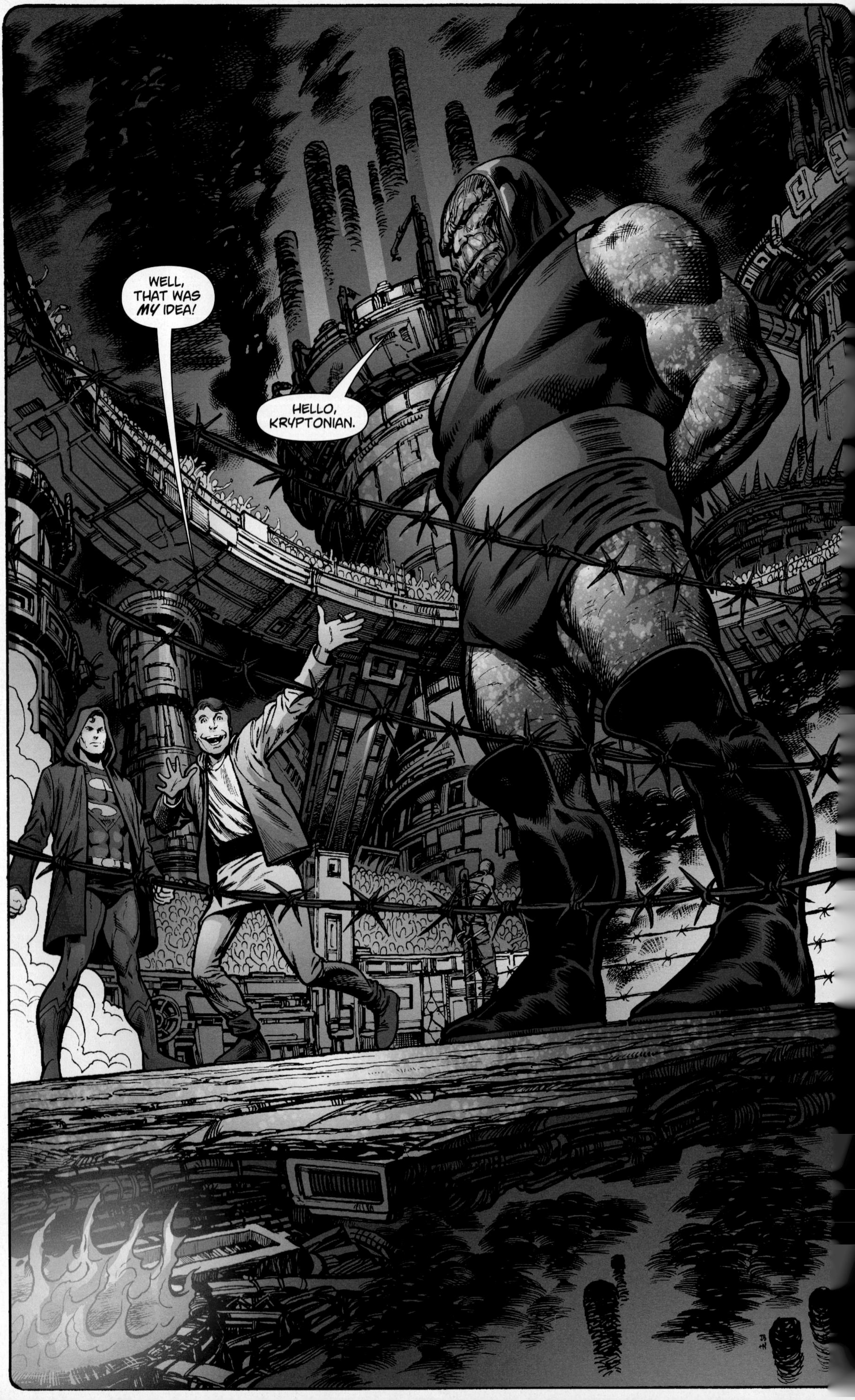
WELL, THAT WAS MY IDEA!
HELLO, KRYPTONIAN.

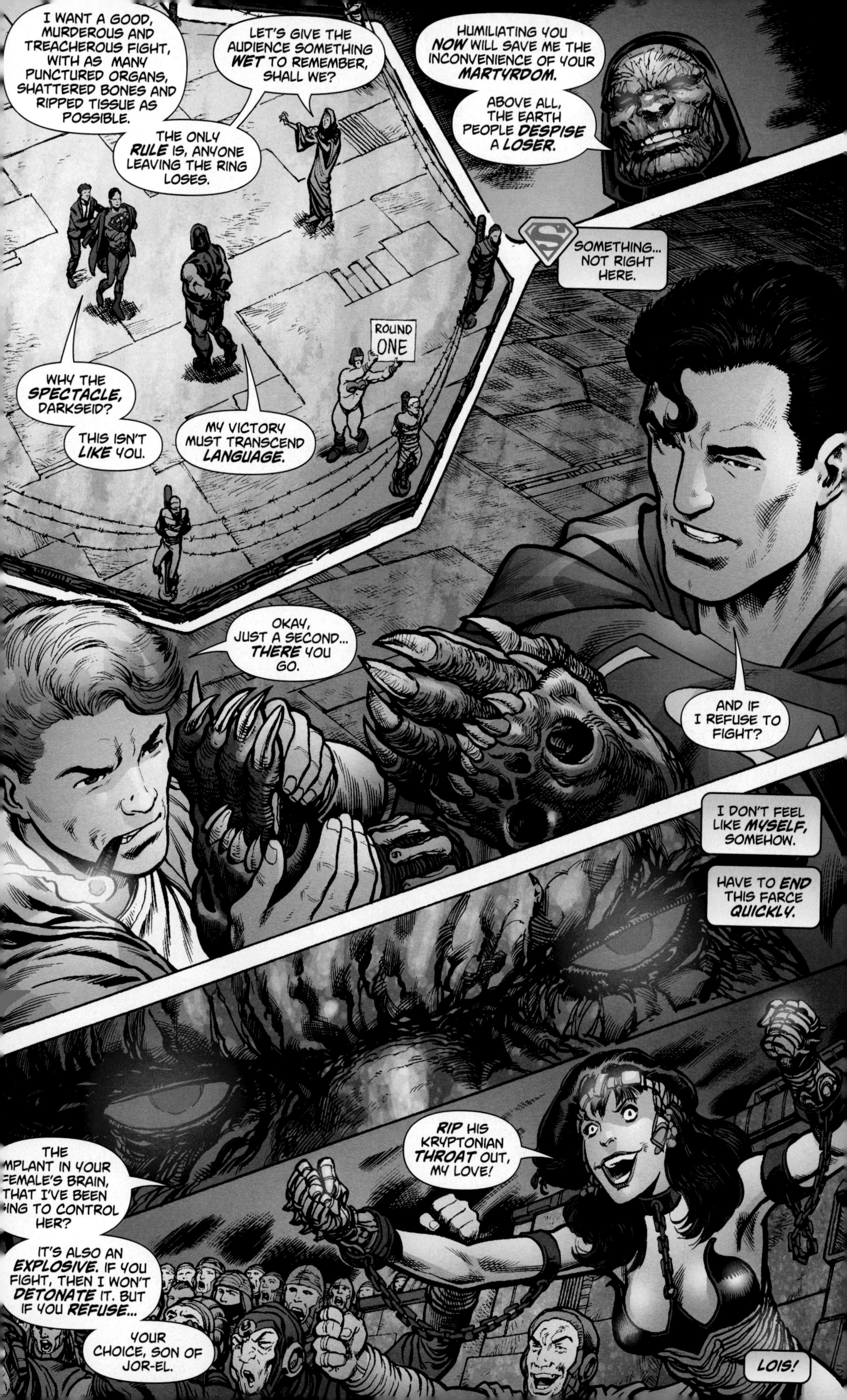
I WANT A GOOD, MURDEROUS AND TREACHEROUS FIGHT, WITH AS MANY PUNCTURED ORGANS, SHATTERED BONES AND RIPPED TISSUE AS POSSIBLE.
LET'S GIVE THE AUDIENCE SOMETHING WET TO REMEMBER, SHALL WE?
THE ONLY RULE IS, ANYONE LEAVING THE RING LOSES.
ROUND ONE
WHY THE SPECTACLE, DARKSEID?
THIS ISN'T LIKE YOU.
MY VICTORY MUST TRANSCEND LANGUAGE.
HUMILIATING YOU NOW WILL SAVE ME THE INCONVENIENCE OF YOUR MARTYRDOM.
ABOVE ALL, THE EARTH PEOPLE DESPISE A LOSER.
SOMETHING... NOT RIGHT HERE.
OKAY, JUST A SECOND... THERE YOU GO.
AND IF I REFUSE TO FIGHT?
I DON'T FEEL LIKE MYSELF, SOMEHOW.
HAVE TO END THIS FARCE QUICKLY.
THE MPLANT IN YOUR FEMALE'S BRAIN, THAT I'VE BEEN ING TO CONTROL HER?
IT'S ALSO AN EXPLOSIVE. IF YOU FIGHT, THEN I WON'T DETONATE IT. BUT IF YOU REFUSE...
YOUR CHOICE, SON OF JOR-EL.
RIP HIS KRYPTONIAN THROAT OUT, MY LOVE!
LOIS!

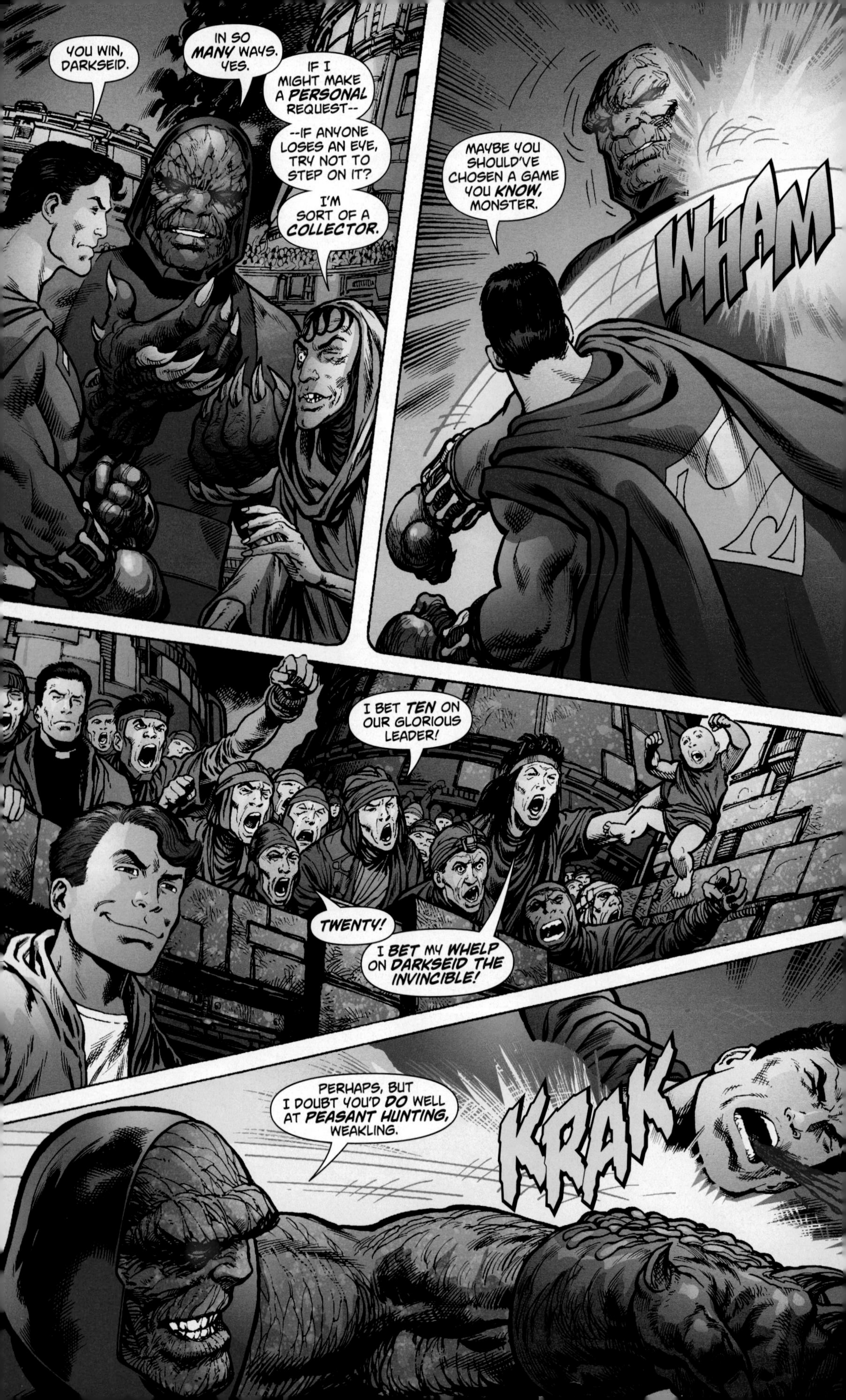
YOU WIN, DARKSEID.
IN SO MANY WAYS. YES.
IF I MIGHT MAKE A PERSONAL REQUEST--
--IF ANYONE LOSES AN EYE, TRY NOT TO STEP ON IT?
I'M SORT OF A COLLECTOR.
MAYBE YOU SHOULD'VE CHOSEN A GAME YOU KNOW, MONSTER.
WHAM
I BET TEN ON OUR GLORIOUS LEADER!
TWENTY!
I BET MY WHELP ON DARKSEID THE INVINCIBLE!
PERHAPS, BUT I DOUBT YOU'D DO WELL AT PEASANT HUNTING, WEAKLING.
KRAK

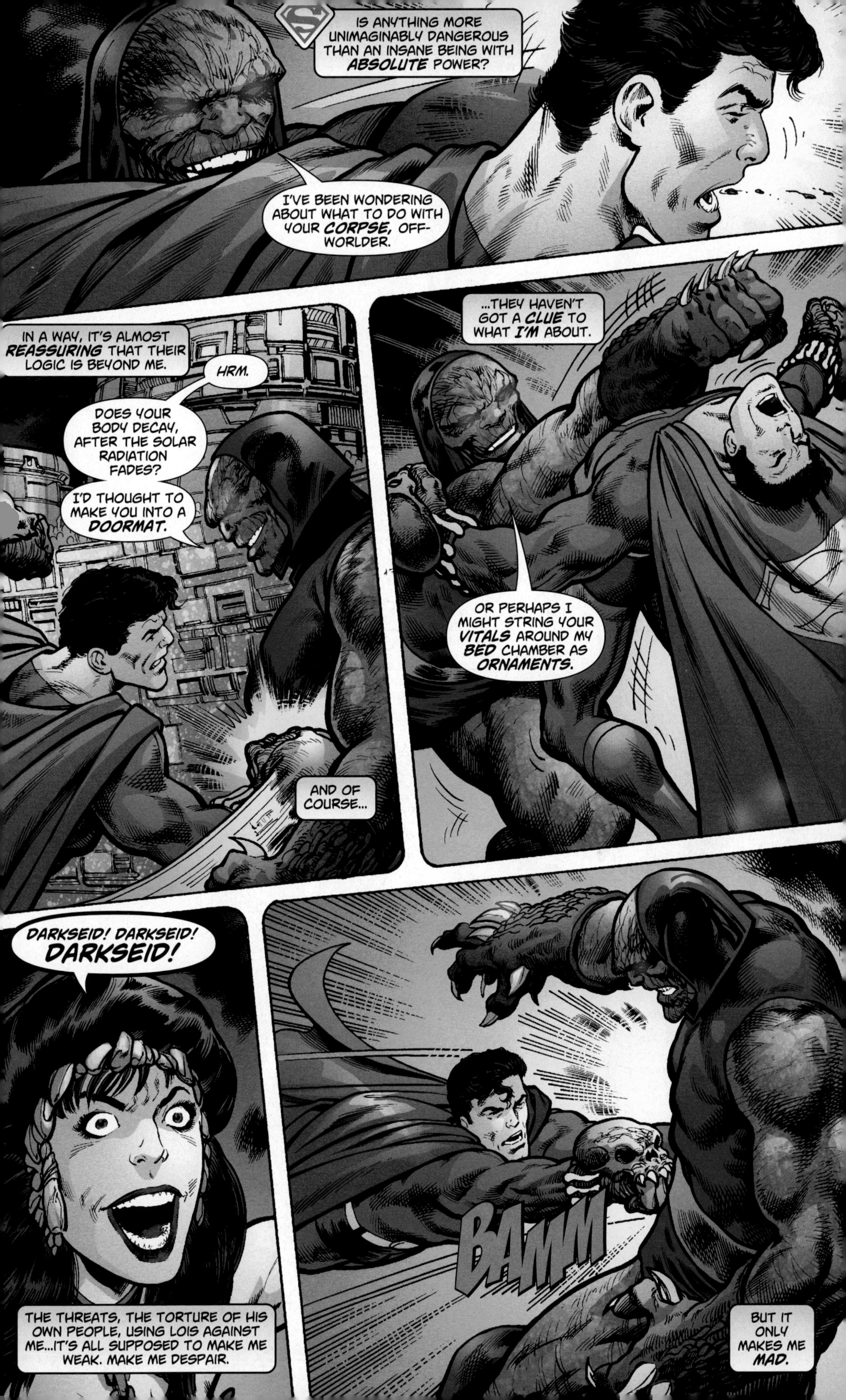
IS ANYTHING MORE UNIMAGINABLY DANGEROUS THAN AN INSANE BEING WITH ABSOLUTE POWER?
I'VE BEEN WONDERING ABOUT WHAT TO DO WITH YOUR CORPSE, OFF-WORLDER.
IN A WAY, IT'S ALMOST REASSURING THAT THEIR LOGIC IS BEYOND ME.
HRM.
DOES YOUR BODY DECAY, AFTER THE SOLAR RADIATION FADES?
I'D THOUGHT TO MAKE YOU INTO A DOORMAT.
...THEY HAVEN'T GOT A CLUE TO WHAT I'M ABOUT.
OR PERHAPS I MIGHT STRING YOUR VITALS AROUND MY BED CHAMBER AS ORNAMENTS.
AND OF COURSE...
DARKSEID! DARKSEID! DARKSEID!
BAMM
THE THREATS, THE TORTURE OF HIS OWN PEOPLE, USING LOIS AGAINST ME...IT'S ALL SUPPOSED TO MAKE ME WEAK. MAKE ME DESPAIR.
BUT IT ONLY MAKES ME MAD.

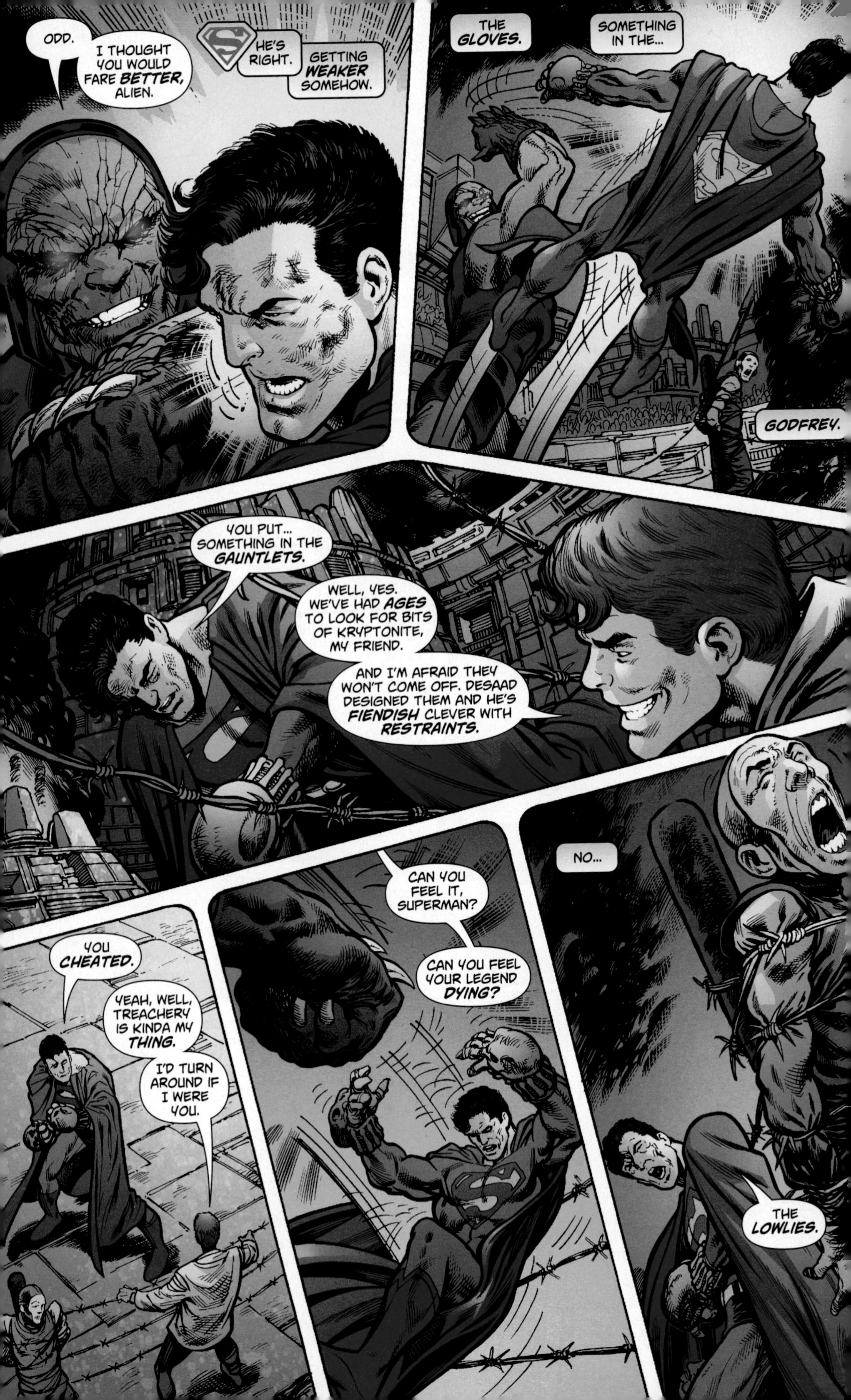

ODD.
I THOUGHT YOU WOULD FARE BETTER, ALIEN.
HE'S RIGHT.
GETTING WEAKER SOMEHOW.
THE GLOVES.
SOMETHING IN THE...
GODFREY.
YOU PUT... SOMETHING IN THE GAUNTLETS.
WELL, YES. WE'VE HAD AGES TO LOOK FOR BITS OF KRYPTONITE, MY FRIEND.
AND I'M AFRAID THEY WON'T COME OFF. DESAAD DESIGNED THEM AND HE'S FIENDISH CLEVER WITH RESTRAINTS.
YOU CHEATED.
YEAH, WELL, TREACHERY IS KINDA MY THING.
I'D TURN AROUND IF I WERE YOU.
CAN YOU FEEL IT, SUPERMAN?
CAN YOU FEEL YOUR LEGEND DYING?
NO...
THE LOWLIES.

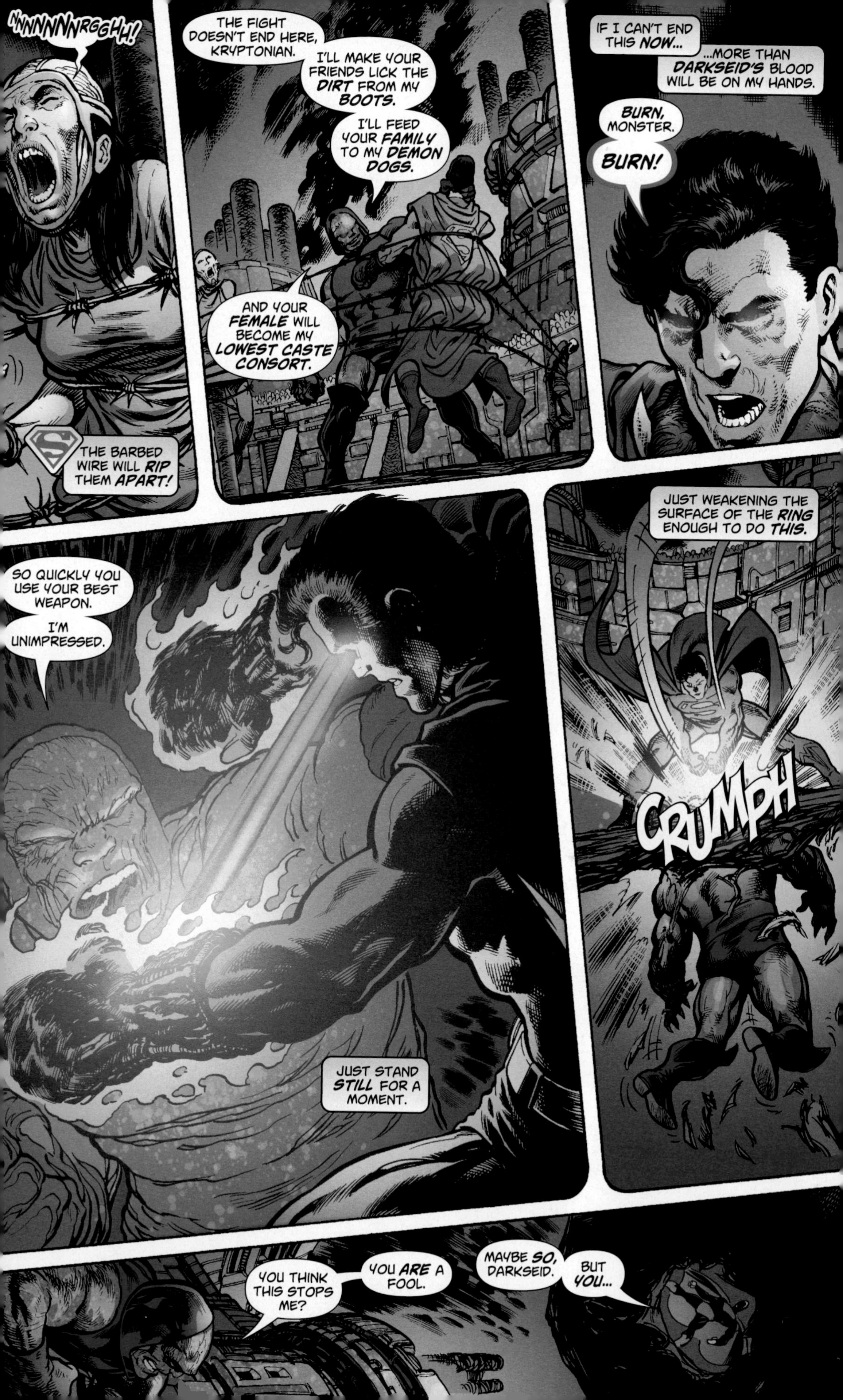
NNNNNNNRGGHH!
THE BARBED WIRE WILL RIP THEM APART!
THE FIGHT DOESN'T END HERE, KRYPTONIAN.
I'LL MAKE YOUR FRIENDS LICK THE DIRT FROM MY BOOTS.
I'LL FEED YOUR FAMILY TO MY DEMON DOGS.
AND YOUR FEMALE WILL BECOME MY LOWEST CASTE CONSORT.
IF I CAN'T END THIS NOW...
...MORE THAN DARKSEID'S BLOOD WILL BE ON MY HANDS.
BURN, MONSTER.
BURN!
SO QUICKLY YOU USE YOUR BEST WEAPON.
I'M UNIMPRESSED.
JUST STAND STILL FOR A MOMENT.
JUST WEAKENING THE SURFACE OF THE RING ENOUGH TO DO THIS.
CRUMPH
YOU THINK THIS STOPS ME?
YOU ARE A FOOL.
MAYBE SO, DARKSEID.
BUT YOU...

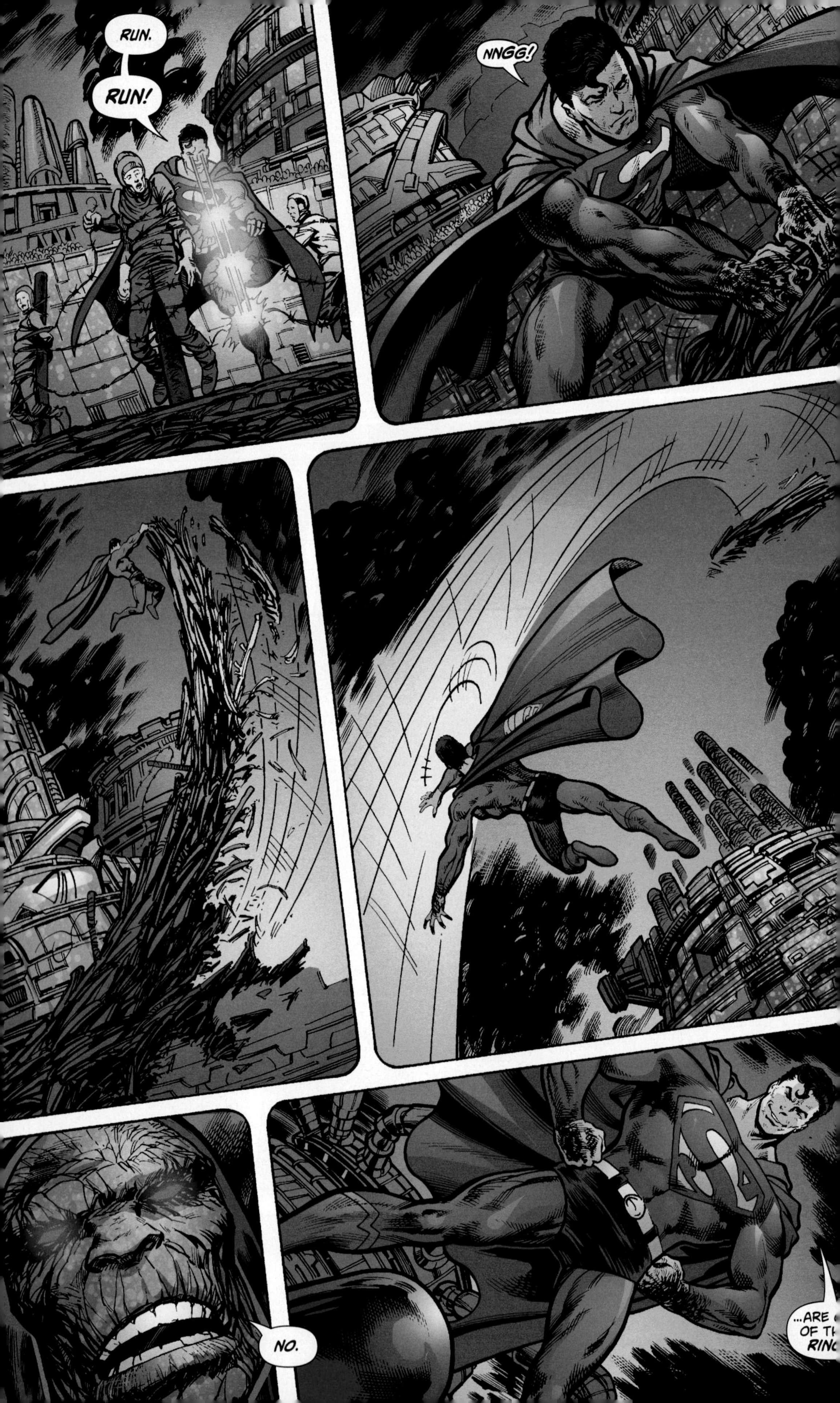
RUN.
RUN!
NNGG!
NO.
...ARE

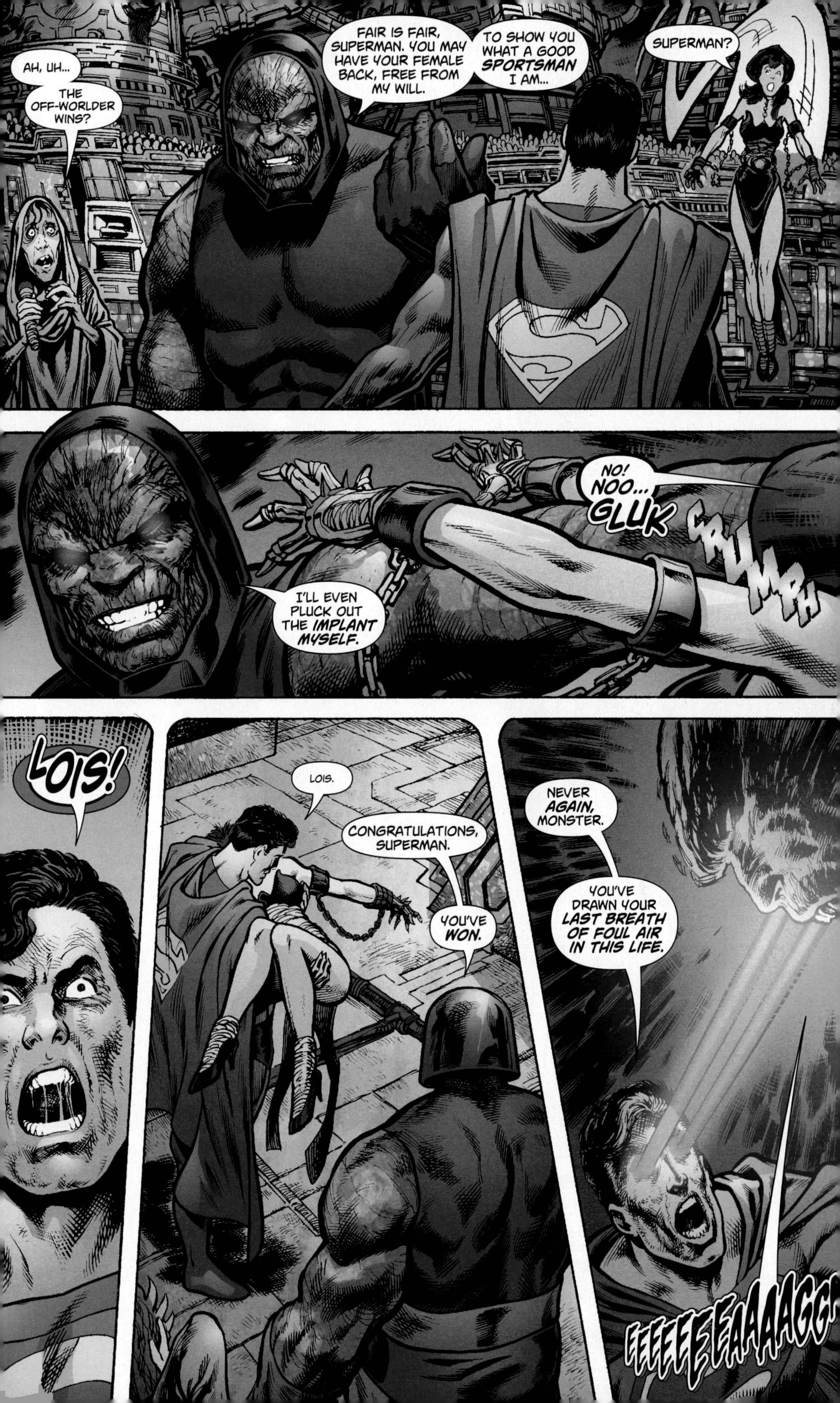
AH, UH...
THE OFF-WORLDER WINS?
FAIR IS FAIR, SUPERMAN. YOU MAY HAVE YOUR FEMALE BACK, FREE FROM MY WILL.
TO SHOW YOU WHAT A GOOD SPORTSMAN I AM...
SUPERMAN?
I'LL EVEN PLUCK OUT THE IMPLANT MYSELF.
NO! NOO... GLUK
CRUMPH
LOIS!
LOIS.
CONGRATULATIONS, SUPERMAN.
YOU'VE WON.
NEVER AGAIN, MONSTER.
YOU'VE DRAWN YOUR LAST BREATH OF FOUL AIR IN THIS LIFE.
EEEEEEEAAAAGG

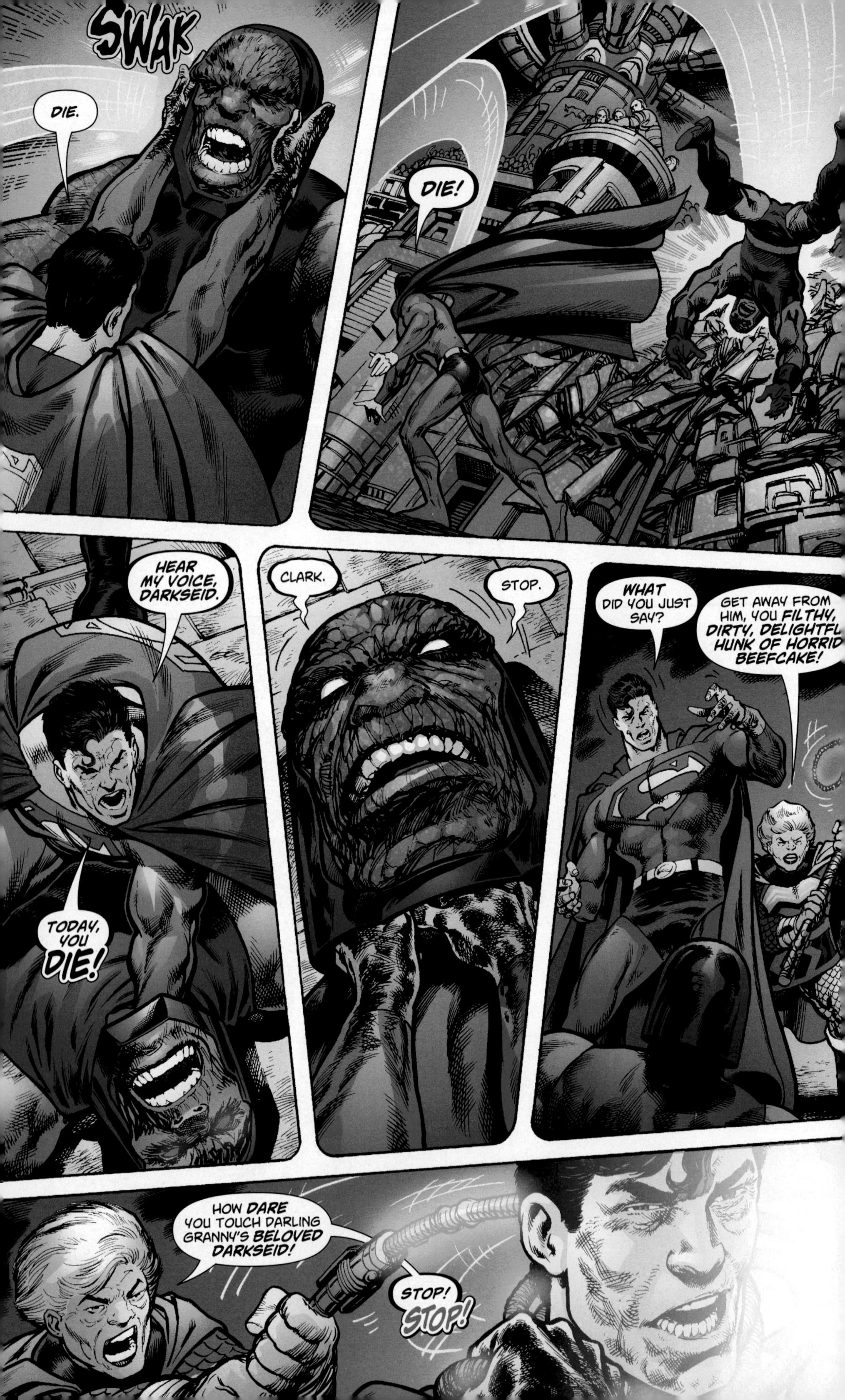
SWAK
DIE.
DIE!
HEAR MY VOICE, DARKSEID.
TODAY, YOU DIE!
CLARK.
STOP.
WHAT DID YOU JUST SAY?
GET AWAY FROM HIM, YOU FILTHY, DIRTY, DELIGHTFU HUNK OF HORRID BEEFCAKE!
HOW DARE YOU TOUCH DARLING GRANNY'S BELOVED DARKSEID!
STOP! STOP!

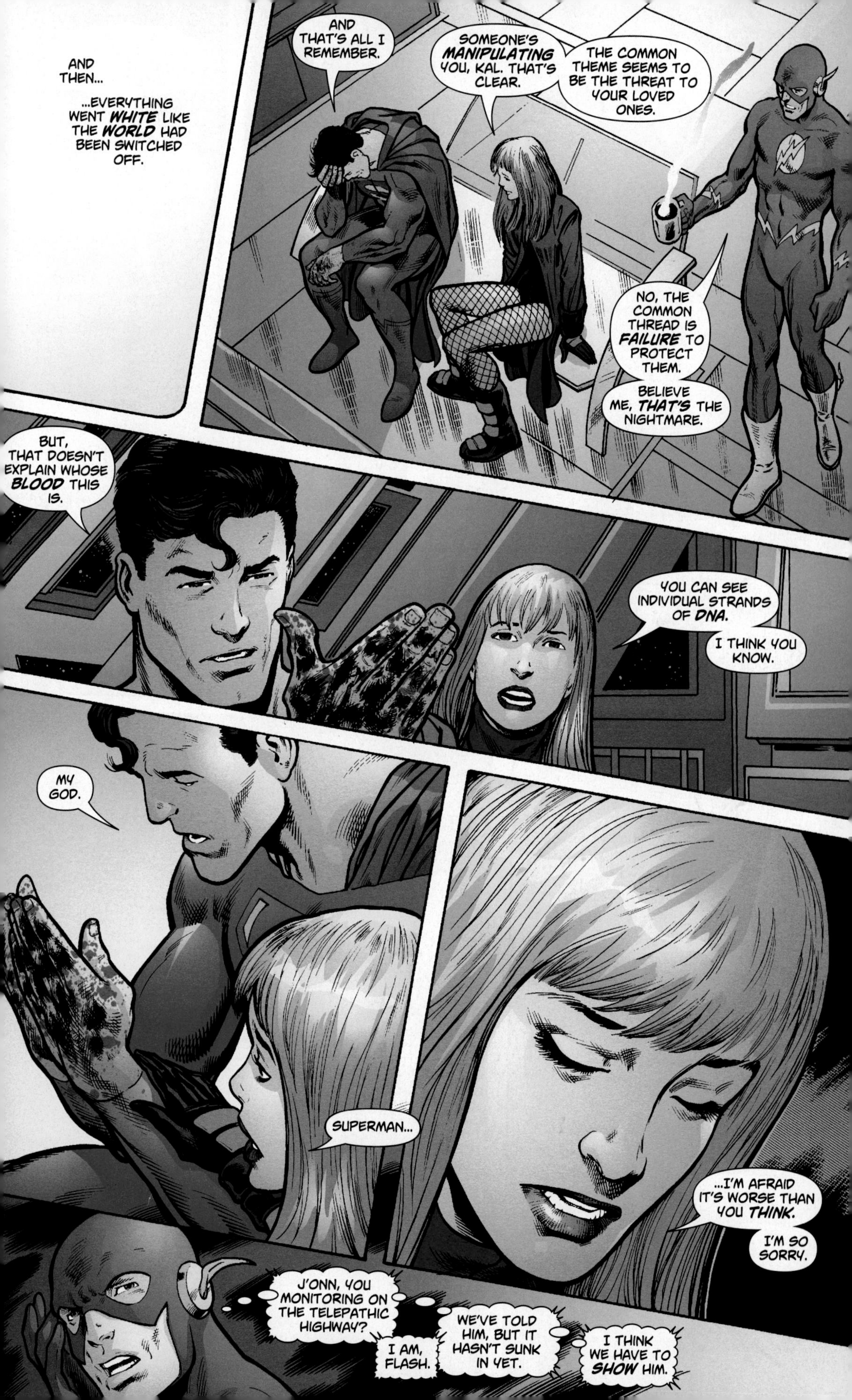
AND THEN...
...EVERYTHING WENT WHITE LIKE THE WORLD HAD BEEN SWITCHED OFF.
AND THAT'S ALL I REMEMBER.
SOMEONE'S MANIPULATING YOU, KAL. THAT'S CLEAR.
THE COMMON THEME SEEMS TO BE THE THREAT TO YOUR LOVED ONES.
NO, THE COMMON THREAD IS FAILURE TO PROTECT THEM.
BELIEVE ME, THAT'S THE NIGHTMARE.
BUT, THAT DOESN'T EXPLAIN WHOSE BLOOD THIS IS.
YOU CAN SEE INDIVIDUAL STRANDS OF DNA.
I THINK YOU KNOW.
MY GOD.
SUPERMAN...
...I'M AFRAID IT'S WORSE THAN YOU THINK.
I'M SO SORRY.
J'ONN, YOU MONITORING ON THE TELEPATHIC HIGHWAY?
I AM, FLASH.
WE'VE TOLD HIM, BUT IT HASN'T SUNK IN YET.
I THINK WE HAVE TO SHOW HIM.

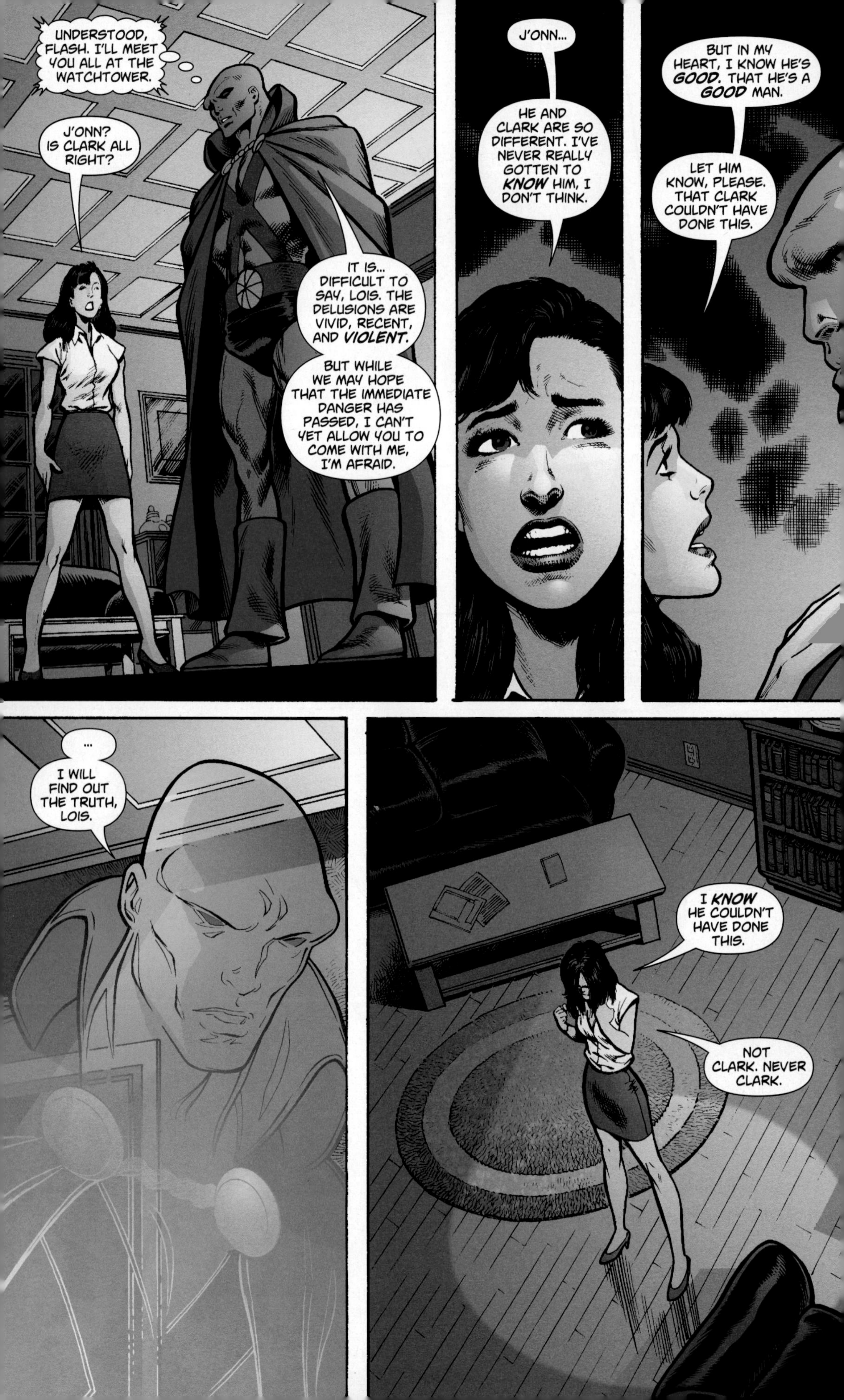
UNDERSTOOD, FLASH. I'LL MEET YOU ALL AT THE WATCHTOWER.
J'ONN? IS CLARK ALL RIGHT?
IT IS... DIFFICULT TO SAY, LOIS. THE DELUSIONS ARE VIVID, RECENT, AND *VIOLENT*.
BUT WHILE WE MAY HOPE THAT THE IMMEDIATE DANGER HAS PASSED, I CAN'T YET ALLOW YOU TO COME WITH ME, I'M AFRAID.
J'ONN...
HE AND CLARK ARE SO DIFFERENT. I'VE NEVER REALLY GOTTEN TO *KNOW* HIM, I DON'T THINK.
BUT IN MY HEART, I KNOW HE'S *GOOD*. THAT HE'S A *GOOD* MAN.
LET HIM KNOW, PLEASE. THAT CLARK COULDN'T HAVE DONE THIS.
...
I WILL FIND OUT THE TRUTH, LOIS.
I *KNOW* HE COULDN'T HAVE DONE THIS.
NOT CLARK. NEVER CLARK.

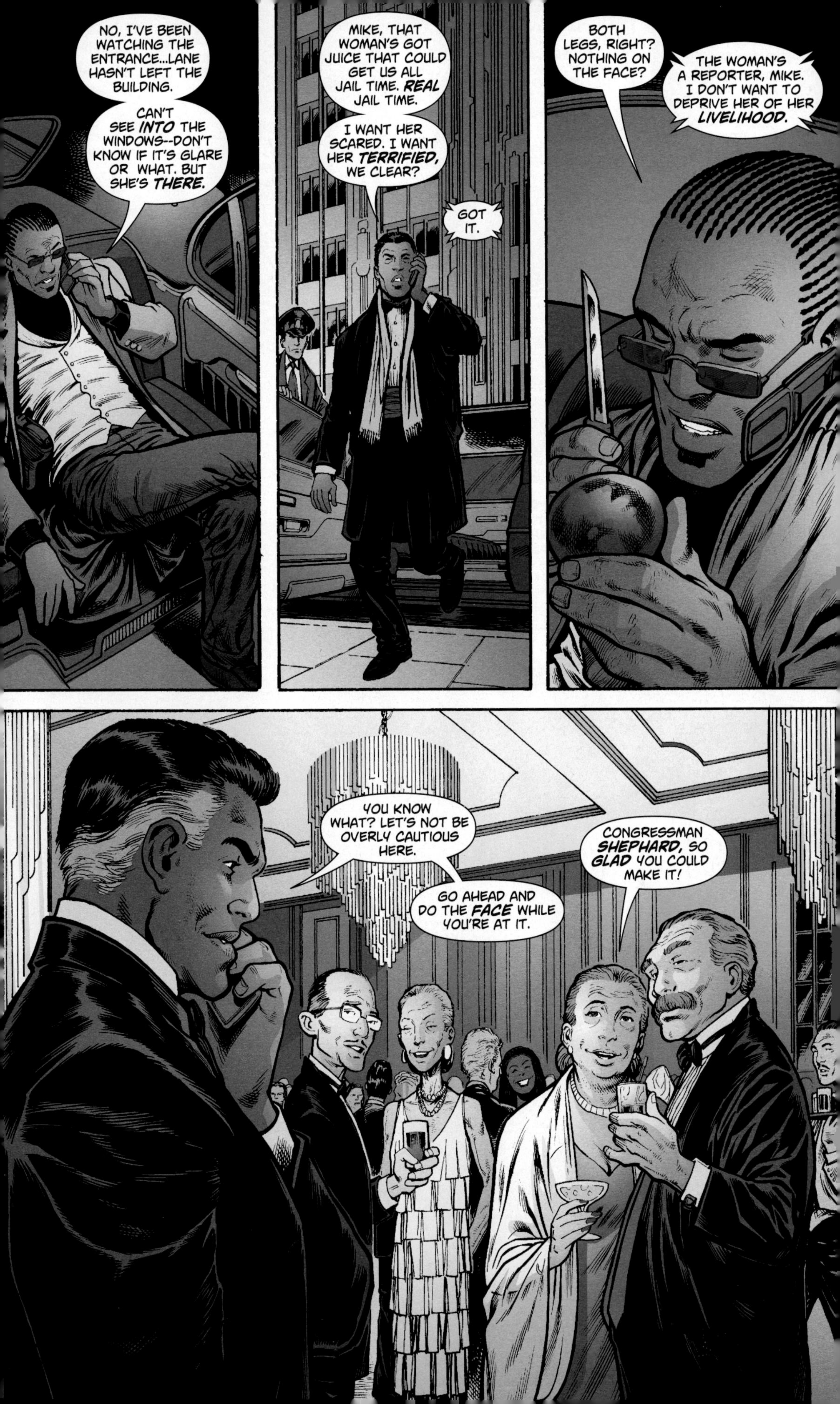

NO, I'VE BEEN WATCHING THE ENTRANCE...LANE HASN'T LEFT THE BUILDING.
CAN'T SEE INTO THE WINDOWS--DON'T KNOW IF IT'S GLARE OR WHAT. BUT SHE'S THERE.
MIKE, THAT WOMAN'S GOT JUICE THAT COULD GET US ALL JAIL TIME. REAL JAIL TIME.
I WANT HER SCARED. I WANT HER TERRIFIED, WE CLEAR?
GOT IT.
BOTH LEGS, RIGHT? NOTHING ON THE FACE?
THE WOMAN'S A REPORTER, MIKE. I DON'T WANT TO DEPRIVE HER OF HER LIVELIHOOD.
YOU KNOW WHAT? LET'S NOT BE OVERLY CAUTIOUS HERE.
GO AHEAD AND DO THE FACE WHILE YOU'RE AT IT.
CONGRESSMAN SHEPHARD, SO GLAD YOU COULD MAKE IT!

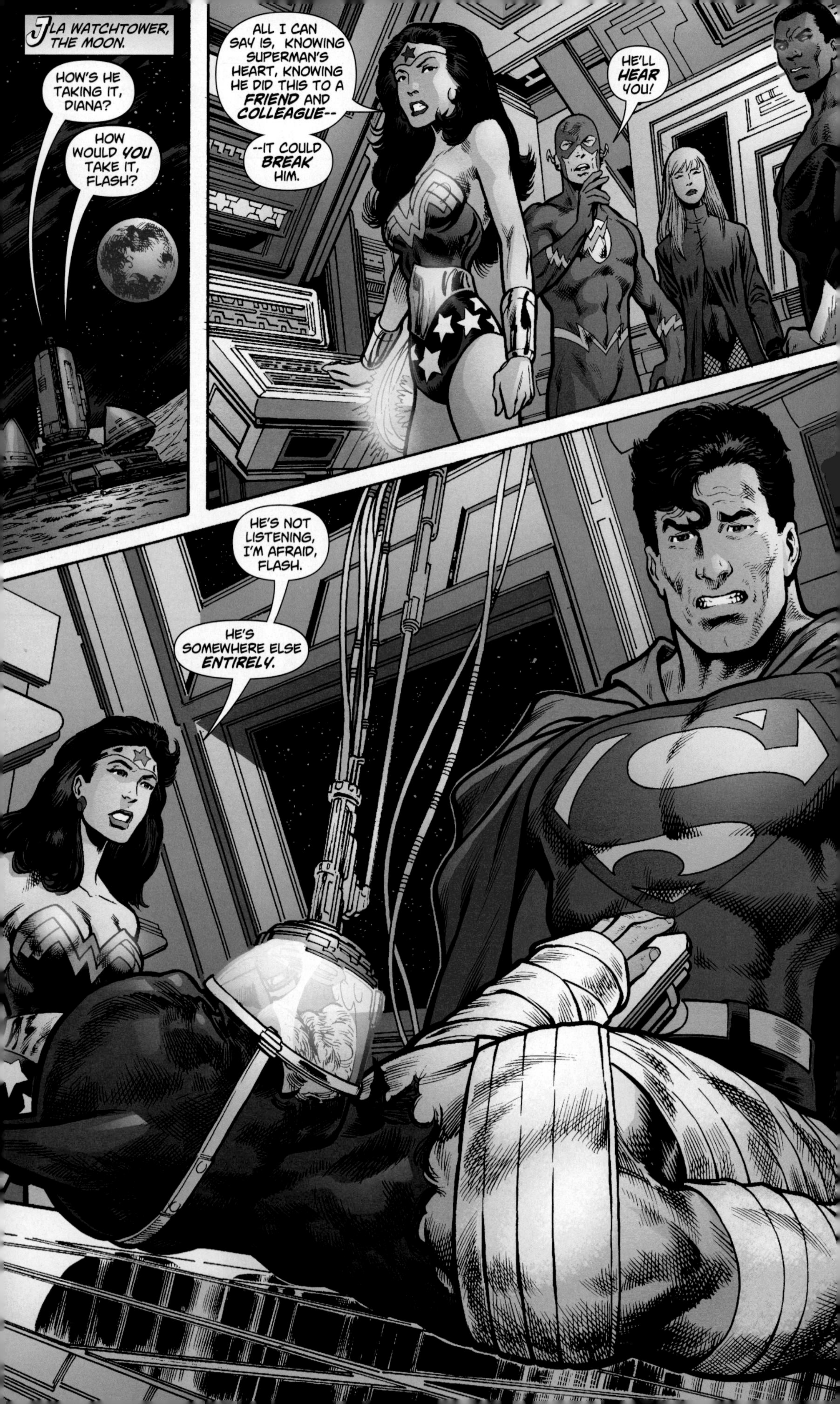
JLA WATCHTOWER, THE MOON.
HOW'S HE TAKING IT, DIANA?
HOW WOULD YOU TAKE IT, FLASH?
ALL I CAN SAY IS, KNOWING SUPERMAN'S HEART, KNOWING HE DID THIS TO A FRIEND AND COLLEAGUE--
--IT COULD BREAK HIM.
HE'LL HEAR YOU!
HE'S NOT LISTENING, I'M AFRAID, FLASH.
HE'S SOMEWHERE ELSE ENTIRELY.

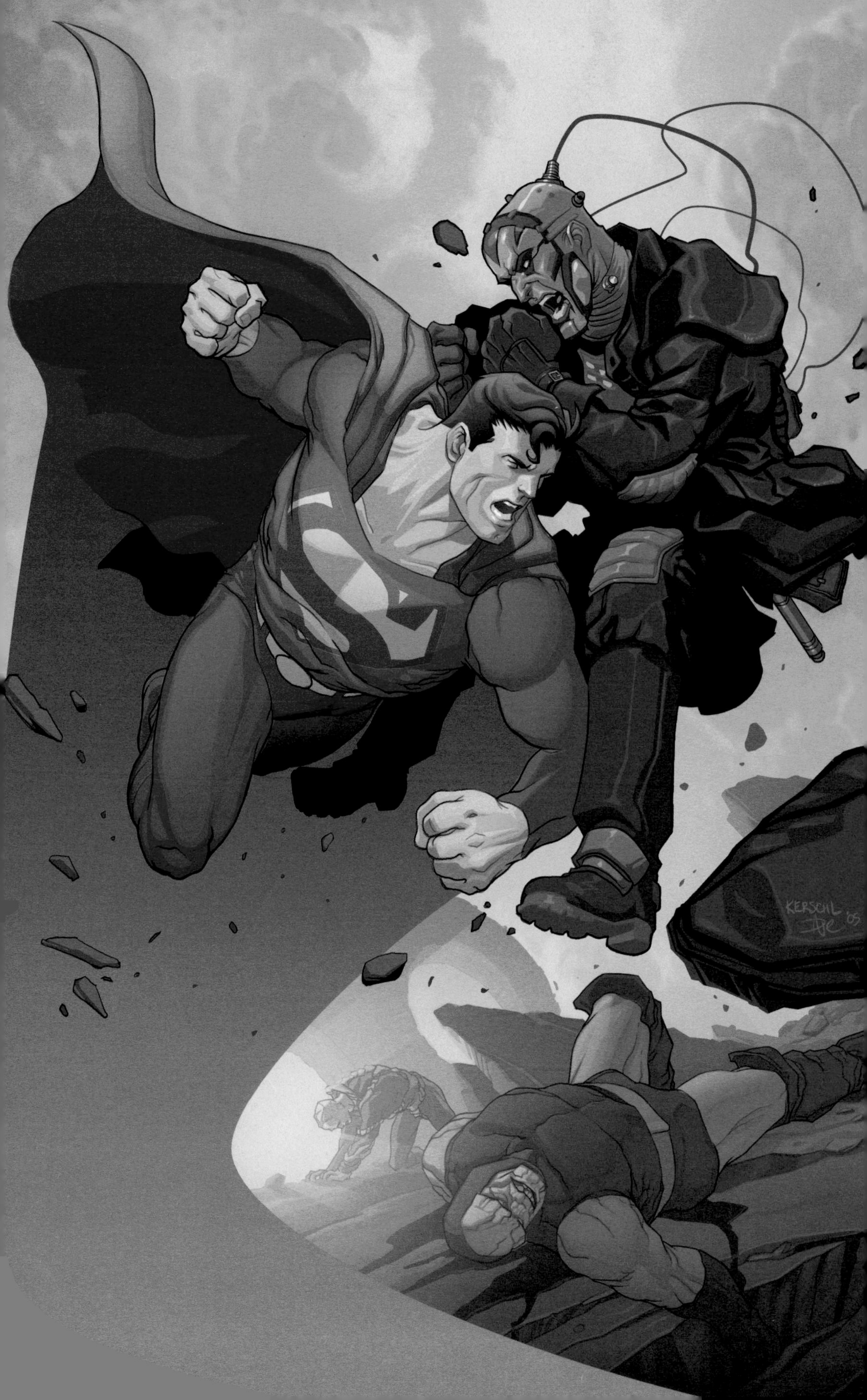
KERSCHL
'05

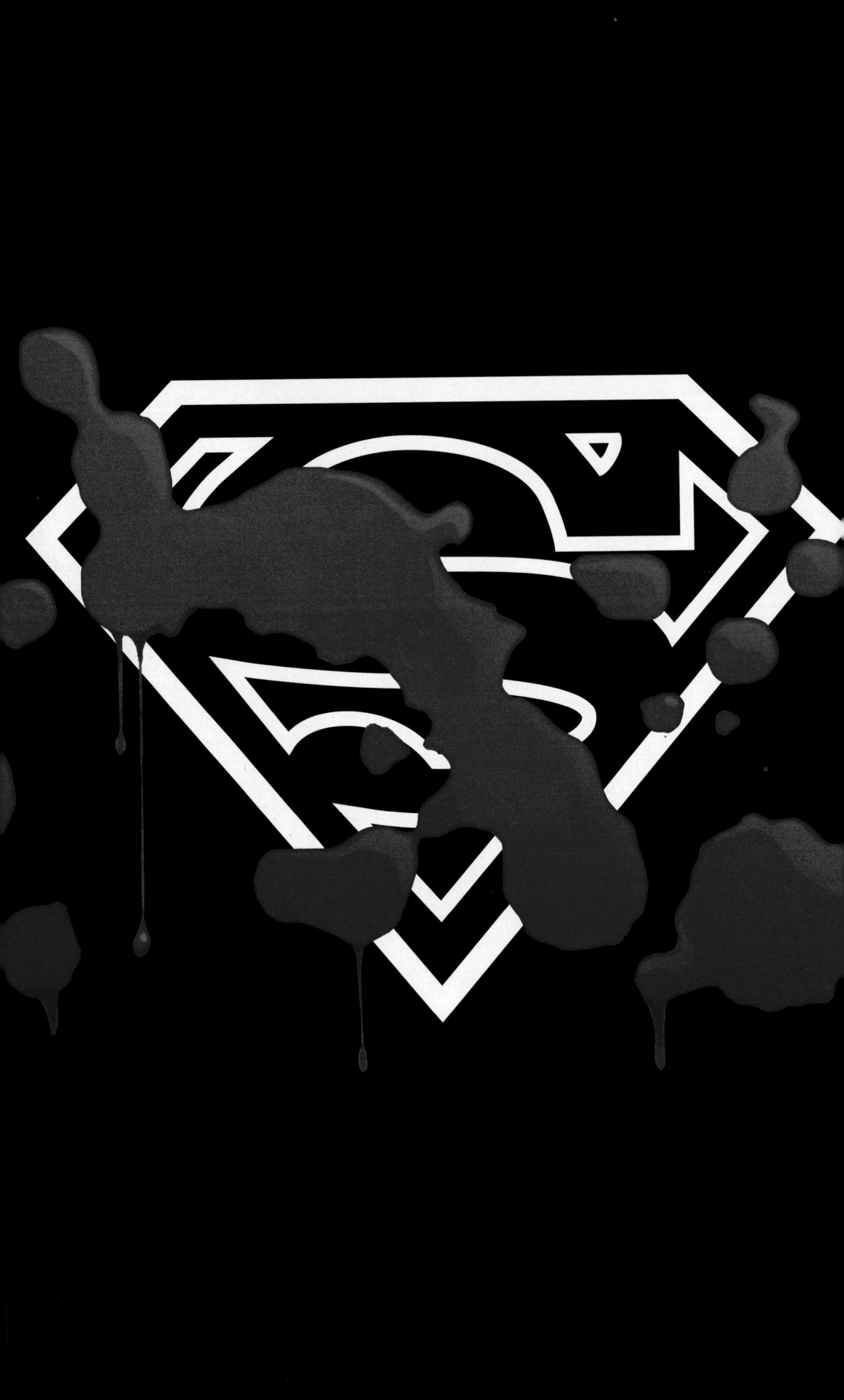

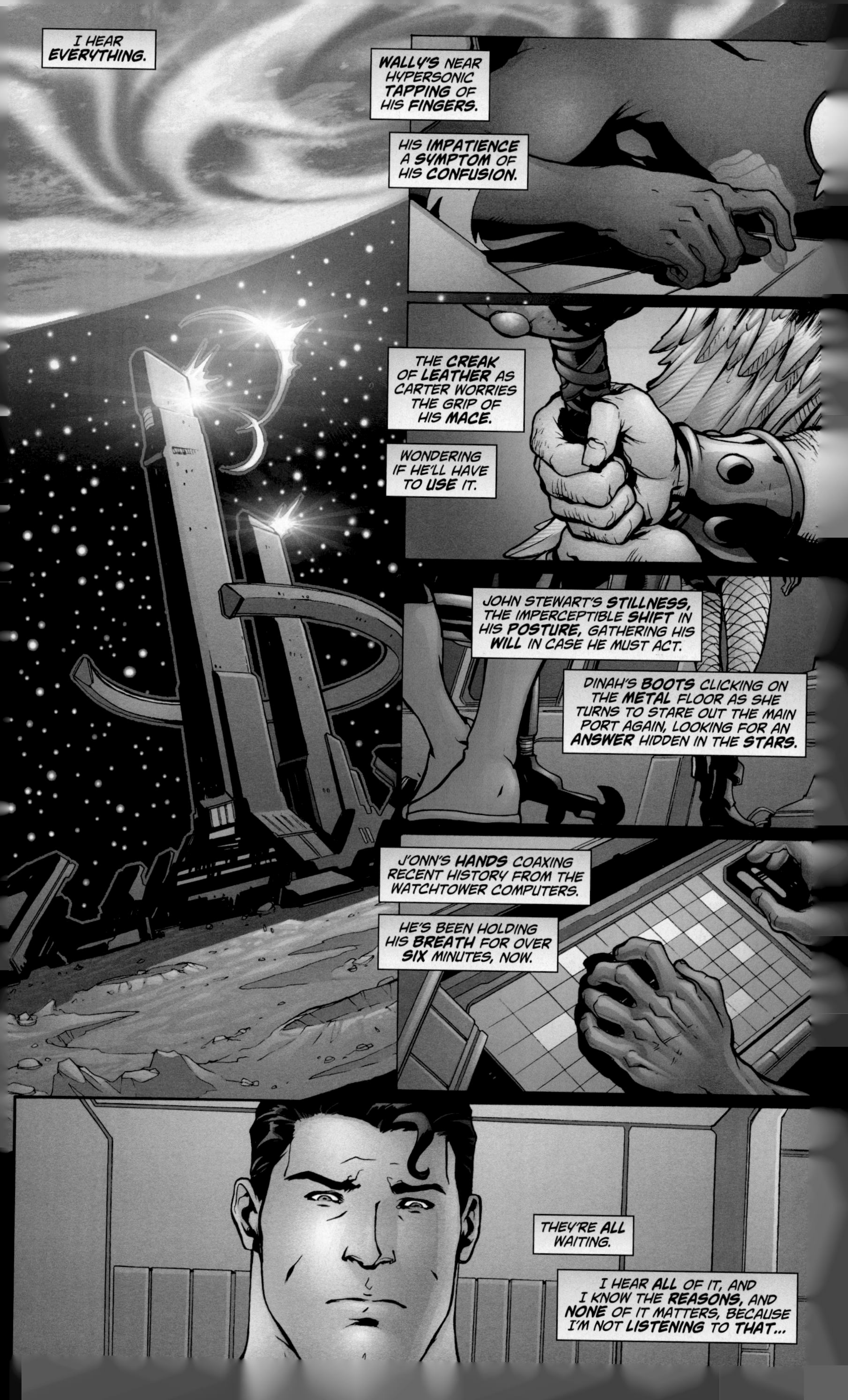

I HEAR EVERYTHING.
WALLY'S NEAR HYPERSONIC TAPPING OF HIS FINGERS.
HIS IMPATIENCE A SYMPTOM OF HIS CONFUSION.
THE CREAK OF LEATHER AS CARTER WORRIES THE GRIP OF HIS MACE.
WONDERING IF HE'LL HAVE TO USE IT.
JOHN STEWART'S STILLNESS, THE IMPERCEPTIBLE SHIFT IN HIS POSTURE, GATHERING HIS WILL IN CASE HE MUST ACT.
DINAH'S BOOTS CLICKING ON THE METAL FLOOR AS SHE TURNS TO STARE OUT THE MAIN PORT AGAIN, LOOKING FOR AN ANSWER HIDDEN IN THE STARS.
J'ONN'S HANDS COAXING RECENT HISTORY FROM THE WATCHTOWER COMPUTERS.
HE'S BEEN HOLDING HIS BREATH FOR OVER SIX MINUTES, NOW.
THEY'RE ALL WAITING.
I HEAR ALL OF IT, AND I KNOW THE REASONS, AND NONE OF IT MATTERS, BECAUSE I'M NOT LISTENING TO THAT...

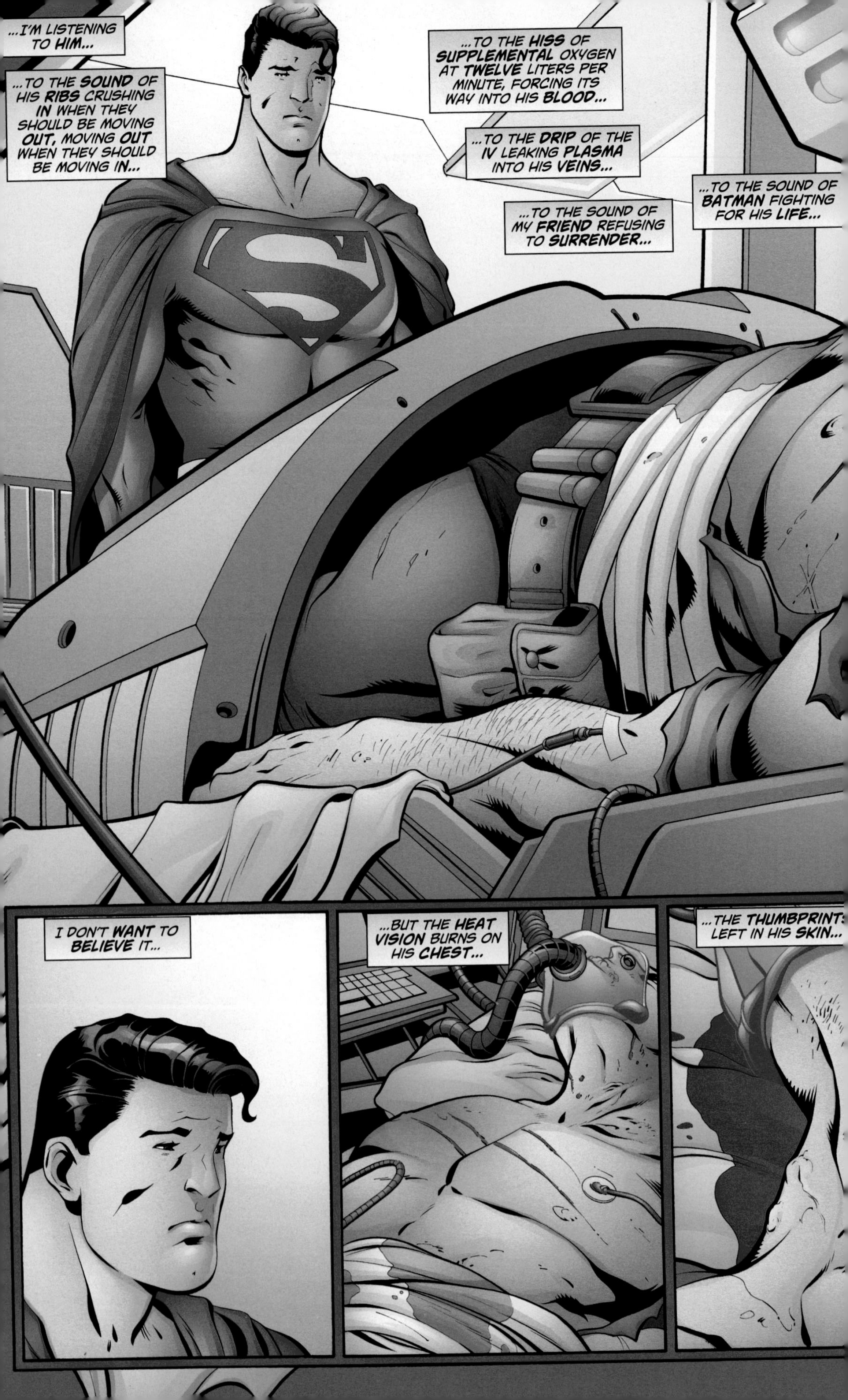
...I'M LISTENING TO HIM...
...TO THE SOUND OF HIS RIBS CRUSHING IN WHEN THEY SHOULD BE MOVING OUT, MOVING OUT WHEN THEY SHOULD BE MOVING IN...
...TO THE HISS OF SUPPLEMENTAL OXYGEN AT TWELVE LITERS PER MINUTE, FORCING ITS WAY INTO HIS BLOOD...
...TO THE DRIP OF THE IV LEAKING PLASMA INTO HIS VEINS...
...TO THE SOUND OF MY FRIEND REFUSING TO SURRENDER...
...TO THE SOUND OF BATMAN FIGHTING FOR HIS LIFE...
I DON'T WANT TO BELIEVE IT...
...BUT THE HEAT VISION BURNS ON HIS CHEST...
...THE THUMBPRINTS LEFT IN HIS SKIN...

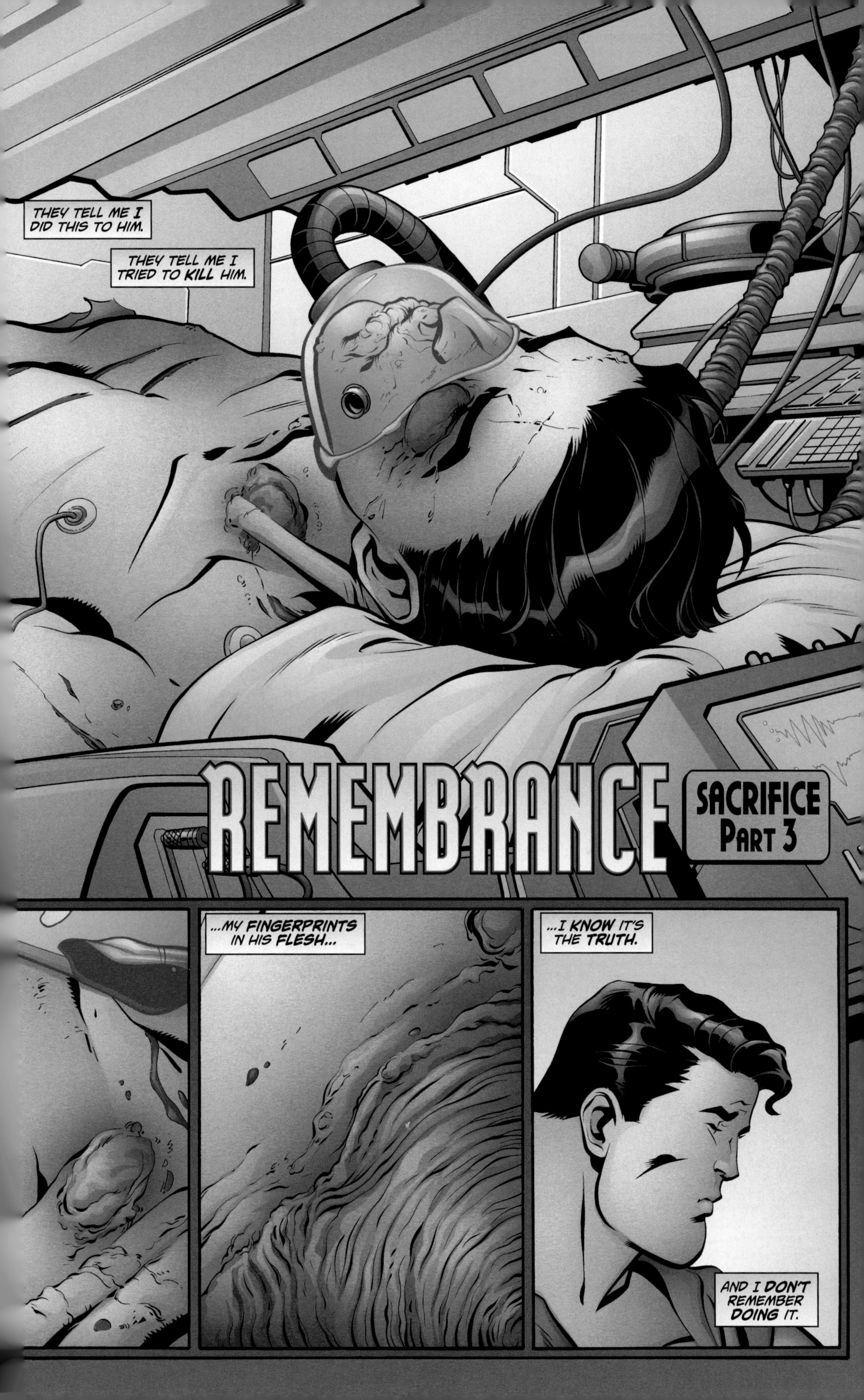

THEY TELL ME I DID THIS TO HIM.
THEY TELL ME I TRIED TO KILL HIM.
REMEMBRANCE
SACRIFICE PART 3
...MY FINGERPRINTS IN HIS FLESH...
...I KNOW IT'S THE TRUTH.
AND I DON'T REMEMBER DOING IT.

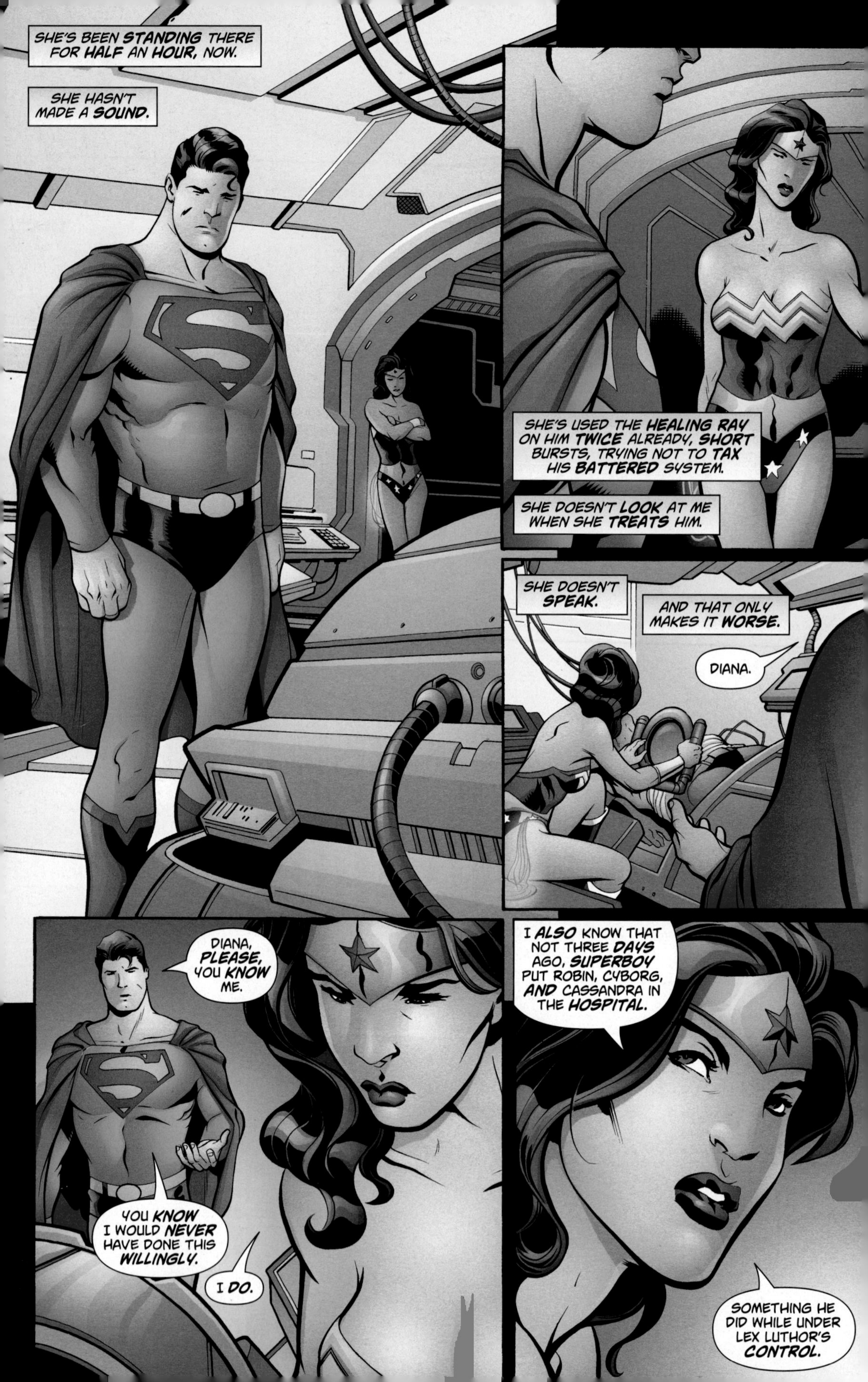
SHE'S BEEN STANDING THERE FOR HALF AN HOUR, NOW.
SHE HASN'T MADE A SOUND.
SHE'S USED THE HEALING RAY ON HIM TWICE ALREADY, SHORT BURSTS, TRYING NOT TO TAX HIS BATTERED SYSTEM.
SHE DOESN'T LOOK AT ME WHEN SHE TREATS HIM.
SHE DOESN'T SPEAK.
AND THAT ONLY MAKES IT WORSE.
DIANA.
DIANA, PLEASE, YOU KNOW ME.
YOU KNOW I WOULD NEVER HAVE DONE THIS WILLINGLY.
I DO.
I ALSO KNOW THAT NOT THREE DAYS AGO, SUPERBOY PUT ROBIN, CYBORG, AND CASSANDRA IN THE HOSPITAL.
SOMETHING HE DID WHILE UNDER LEX LUTHOR'S CONTROL.

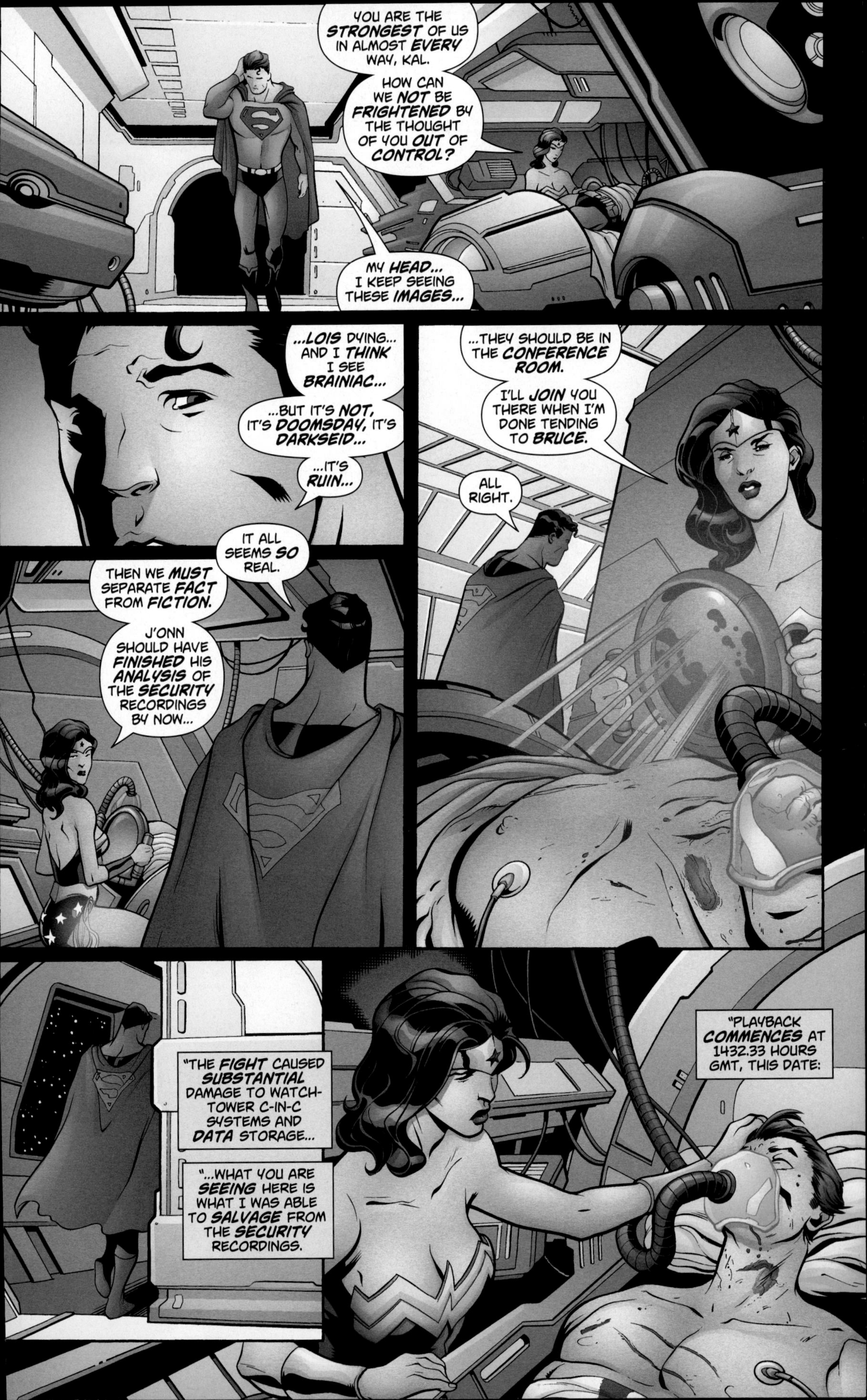
YOU ARE THE STRONGEST OF US IN ALMOST EVERY WAY, KAL.
HOW CAN WE NOT BE FRIGHTENED BY THE THOUGHT OF YOU OUT OF CONTROL?
MY HEAD... I KEEP SEEING THESE IMAGES...
...LOIS DYING... AND I THINK I SEE BRAINIAC...
...BUT IT'S NOT, IT'S DOOMSDAY, IT'S DARKSEID...
...IT'S RUIN...
IT ALL SEEMS SO REAL.
THEN WE MUST SEPARATE FACT FROM FICTION.
J'ONN SHOULD HAVE FINISHED HIS ANALYSIS OF THE SECURITY RECORDINGS BY NOW...
...THEY SHOULD BE IN THE CONFERENCE ROOM.
I'LL JOIN YOU THERE WHEN I'M DONE TENDING TO BRUCE.
ALL RIGHT.
"THE FIGHT CAUSED SUBSTANTIAL DAMAGE TO WATCH-TOWER C-IN-C SYSTEMS AND DATA STORAGE...
"...WHAT YOU ARE SEEING HERE IS WHAT I WAS ABLE TO SALVAGE FROM THE SECURITY RECORDINGS.
"PLAYBACK COMMENCES AT 1432.33 HOURS GMT, THIS DATE:

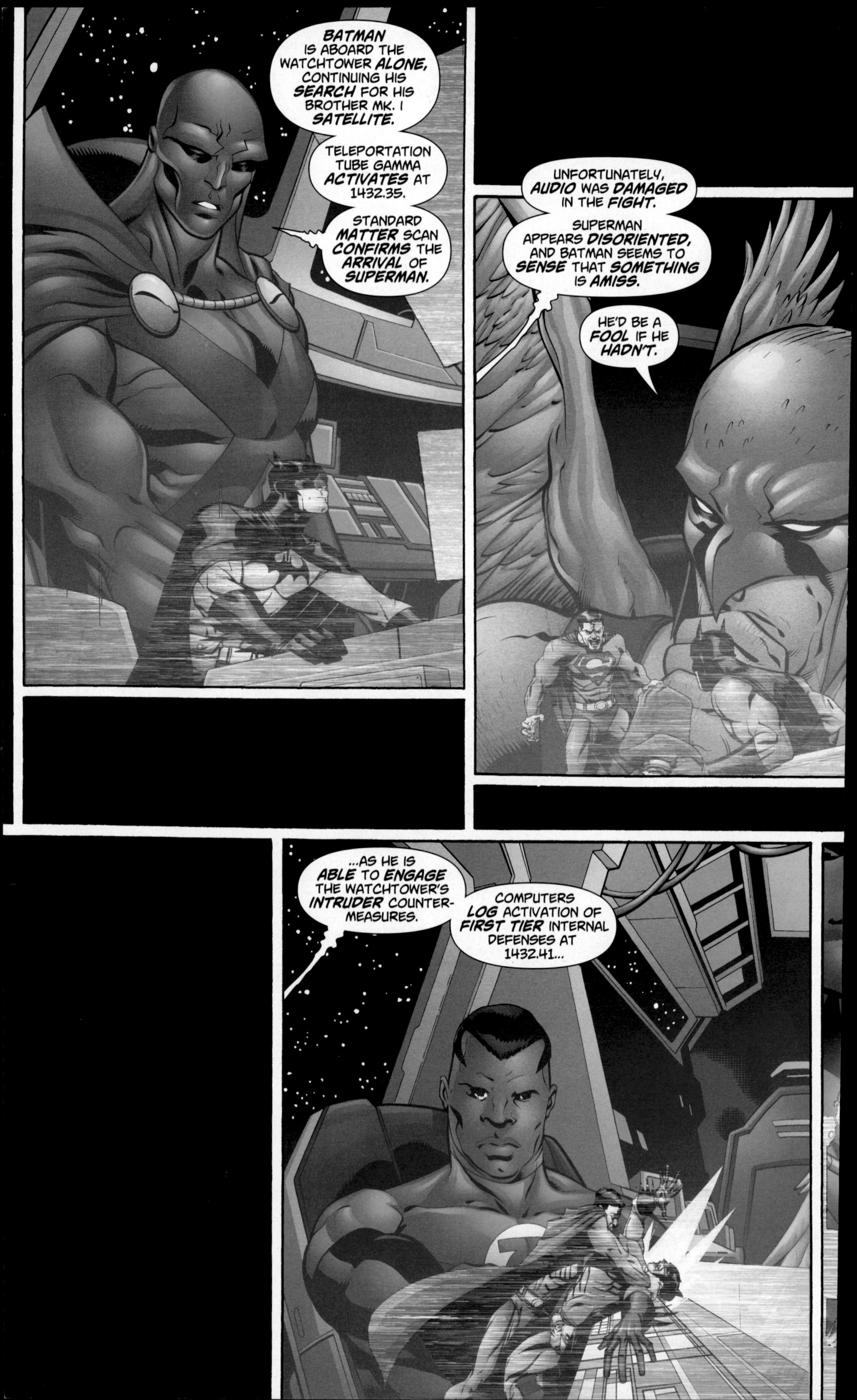
BATMAN IS ABOARD THE WATCHTOWER ALONE, CONTINUING HIS SEARCH FOR HIS BROTHER MK. I SATELLITE.
TELEPORTATION TUBE GAMMA ACTIVATES AT 1432.35.
STANDARD MATTER SCAN CONFIRMS THE ARRIVAL OF SUPERMAN.
UNFORTUNATELY, AUDIO WAS DAMAGED IN THE FIGHT.
SUPERMAN APPEARS DISORIENTED, AND BATMAN SEEMS TO SENSE THAT SOMETHING IS AMISS.
HE'D BE A FOOL IF HE HADN'T.
...AS HE IS ABLE TO ENGAGE THE WATCHTOWER'S INTRUDER COUNTER-MEASURES.
COMPUTERS LOG ACTIVATION OF FIRST TIER INTERNAL DEFENSES AT 1432.41...

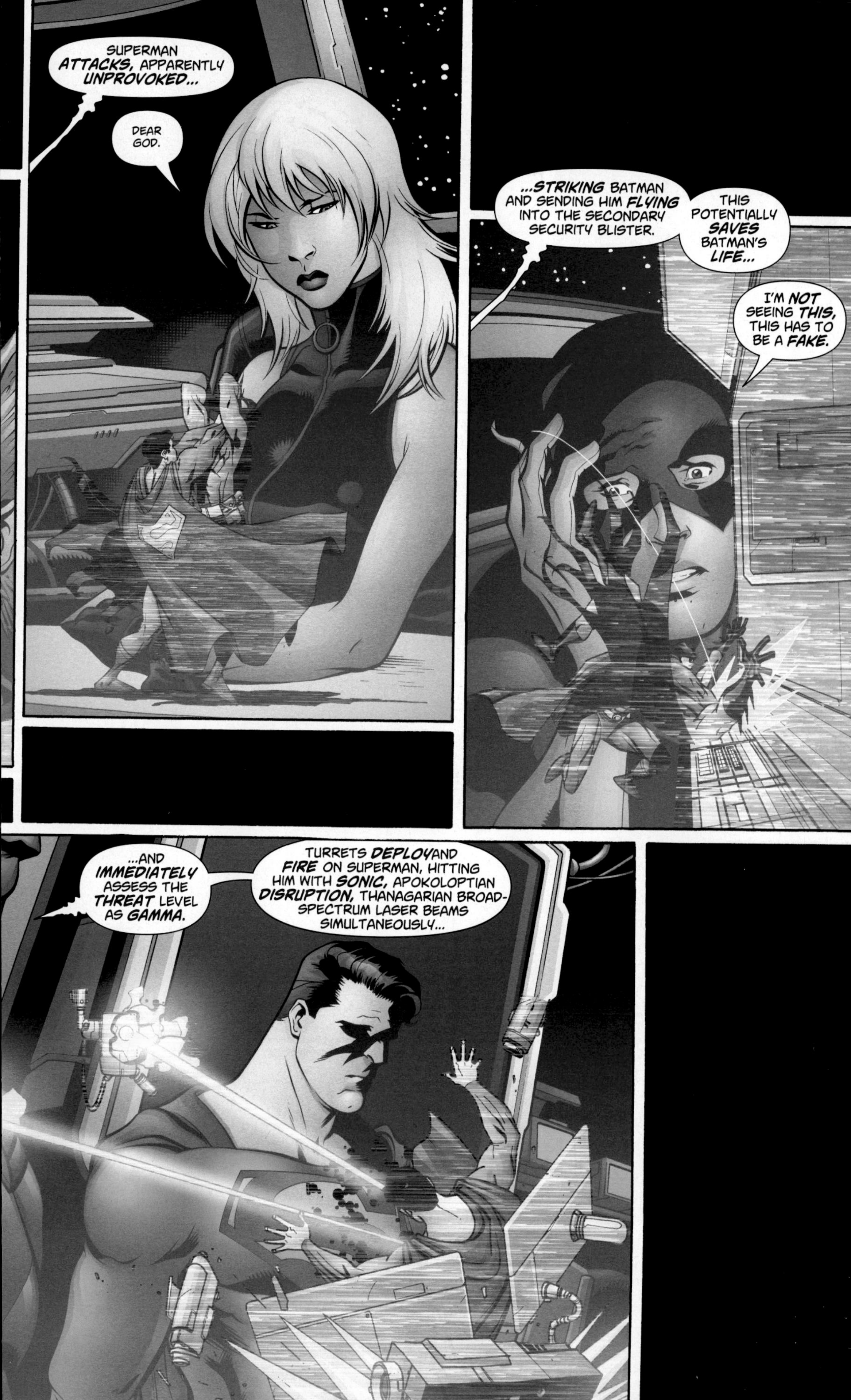

SUPERMAN ATTACKS, APPARENTLY UNPROVOKED...
DEAR GOD.
...STRIKING BATMAN AND SENDING HIM FLYING INTO THE SECONDARY SECURITY BLISTER.
THIS POTENTIALLY SAVES BATMAN'S LIFE...
I'M NOT SEEING THIS, THIS HAS TO BE A FAKE.
...AND IMMEDIATELY ASSESS THE THREAT LEVEL AS GAMMA.
TURRETS DEPLOY AND FIRE ON SUPERMAN, HITTING HIM WITH SONIC, APOKOLOPTIAN DISRUPTION, THANAGARIAN BROAD-SPECTRUM LASER BEAMS SIMULTANEOUSLY...

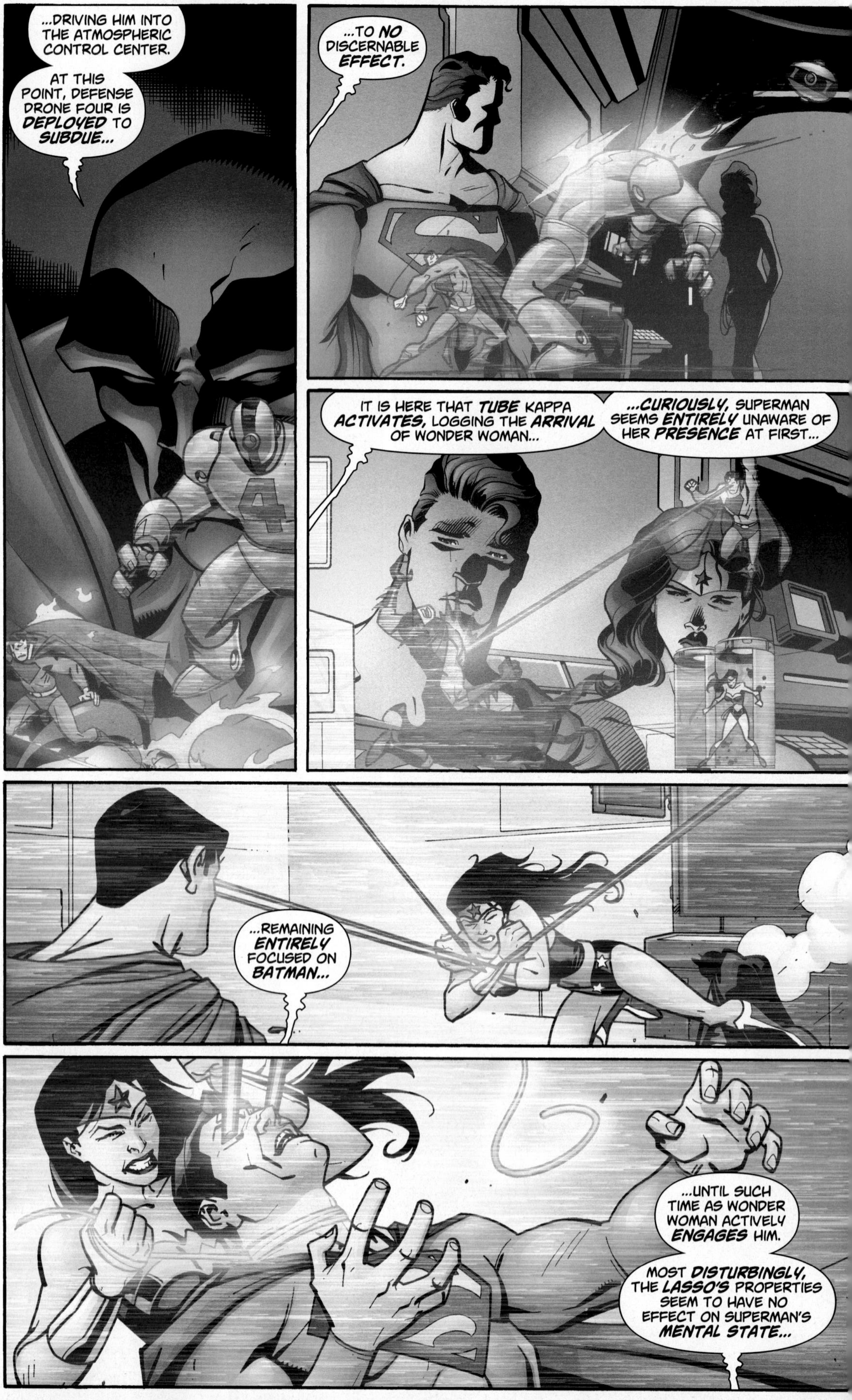

...DRIVING HIM INTO THE ATMOSPHERIC CONTROL CENTER.
AT THIS POINT, DEFENSE DRONE FOUR IS DEPLOYED TO SUBDUE...
...TO NO DISCERNABLE EFFECT.
IT IS HERE THAT TUBE KAPPA ACTIVATES, LOGGING THE ARRIVAL OF WONDER WOMAN...
...CURIOUSLY, SUPERMAN SEEMS ENTIRELY UNAWARE OF HER PRESENCE AT FIRST...
...REMAINING ENTIRELY FOCUSED ON BATMAN...
...UNTIL SUCH TIME AS WONDER WOMAN ACTIVELY ENGAGES HIM.
MOST DISTURBINGLY, THE LASSO'S PROPERTIES SEEM TO HAVE NO EFFECT ON SUPERMAN'S MENTAL STATE...

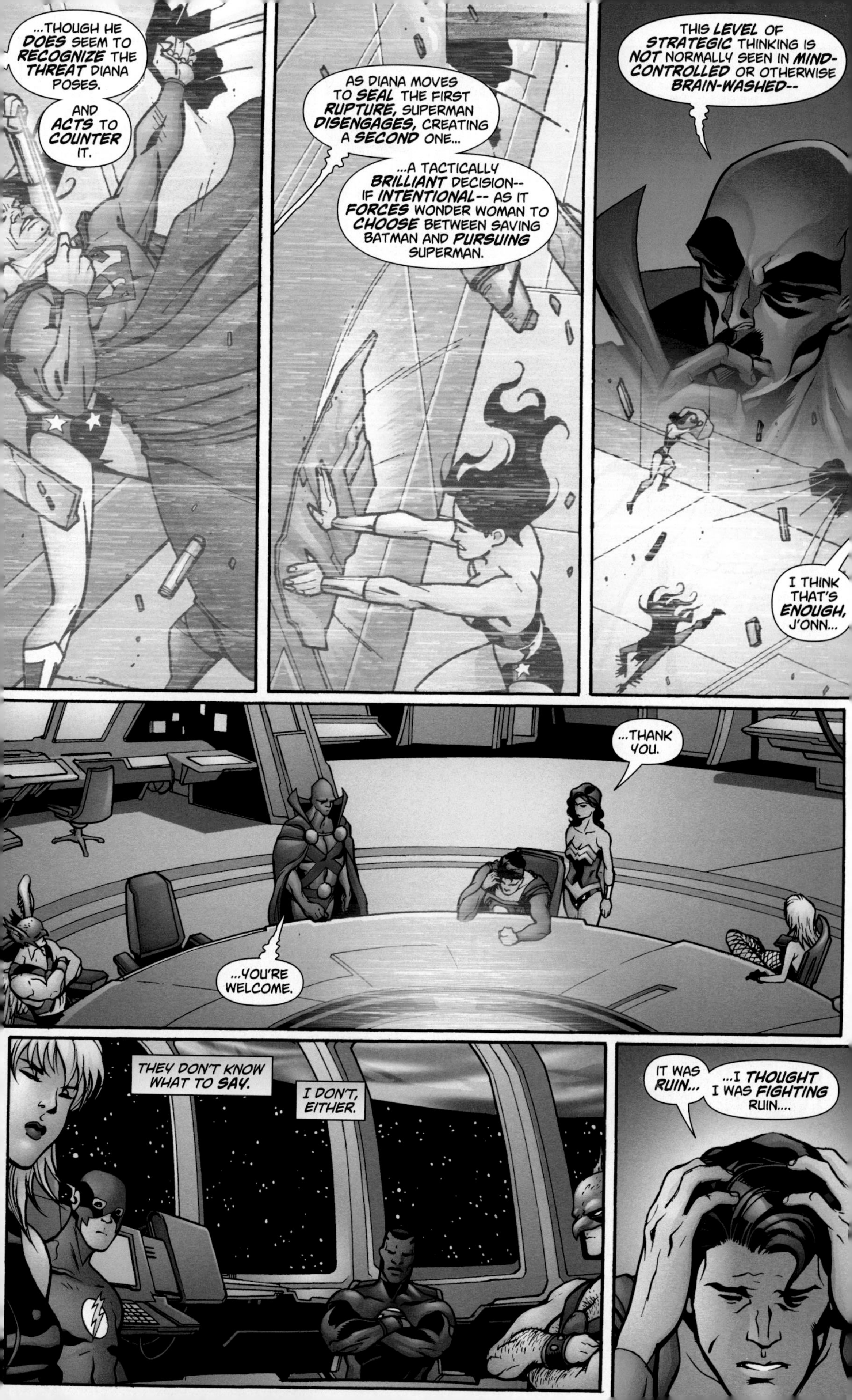
...THOUGH HE DOES SEEM TO RECOGNIZE THE THREAT DIANA POSES.
AND ACTS TO COUNTER IT.
AS DIANA MOVES TO SEAL THE FIRST RUPTURE, SUPERMAN DISENGAGES, CREATING A SECOND ONE...
...A TACTICALLY BRILLIANT DECISION-- IF INTENTIONAL-- AS IT FORCES WONDER WOMAN TO CHOOSE BETWEEN SAVING BATMAN AND PURSUING SUPERMAN.
THIS LEVEL OF STRATEGIC THINKING IS NOT NORMALLY SEEN IN MIND-CONTROLLED OR OTHERWISE BRAIN-WASHED--
I THINK THAT'S ENOUGH, J'ONN...
...THANK YOU.
...YOU'RE WELCOME.
THEY DON'T KNOW WHAT TO SAY.
I DON'T, EITHER.
IT WAS RUIN...
...I THOUGHT I WAS FIGHTING RUIN....

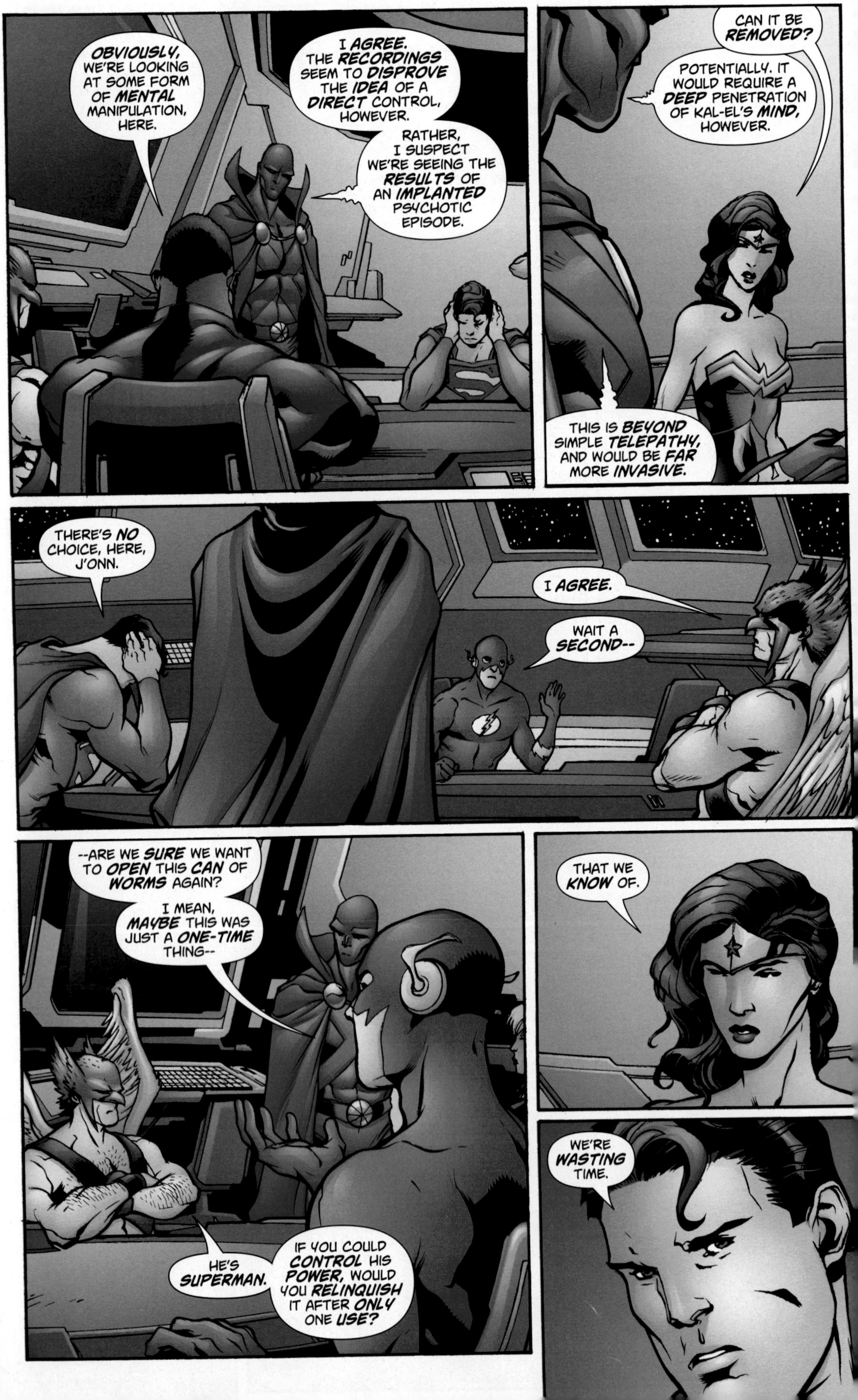

OBVIOUSLY, WE'RE LOOKING AT SOME FORM OF MENTAL MANIPULATION, HERE.
I AGREE. THE RECORDINGS SEEM TO DISPROVE THE IDEA OF A DIRECT CONTROL, HOWEVER.
RATHER, I SUSPECT WE'RE SEEING THE RESULTS OF AN IMPLANTED PSYCHOTIC EPISODE.
CAN IT BE REMOVED?
POTENTIALLY. IT WOULD REQUIRE A DEEP PENETRATION OF KAL-EL'S MIND, HOWEVER.
THIS IS BEYOND SIMPLE TELEPATHY, AND WOULD BE FAR MORE INVASIVE.
THERE'S NO CHOICE, HERE, J'ONN.
I AGREE.
WAIT A SECOND--
--ARE WE SURE WE WANT TO OPEN THIS CAN OF WORMS AGAIN?
I MEAN, MAYBE THIS WAS JUST A ONE-TIME THING--
HE'S SUPERMAN.
IF YOU COULD CONTROL HIS POWER, WOULD YOU RELINQUISH IT AFTER ONLY ONE USE?
THAT WE KNOW OF.
WE'RE WASTING TIME.

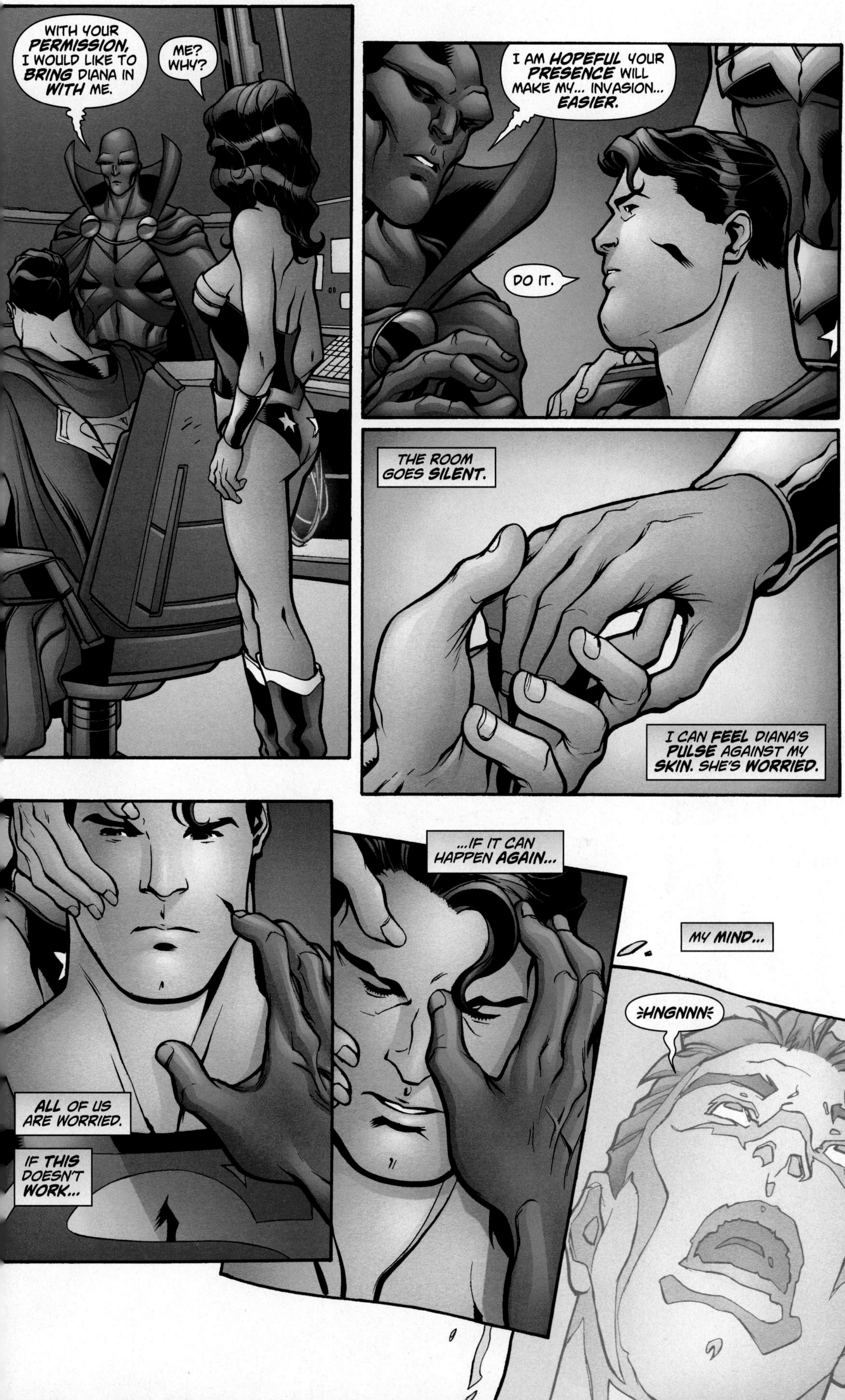

WITH YOUR PERMISSION, I WOULD LIKE TO BRING DIANA IN WITH ME.
ME? WHY?
I AM HOPEFUL YOUR PRESENCE WILL MAKE MY... INVASION... EASIER.
DO IT.
THE ROOM GOES SILENT.
I CAN FEEL DIANA'S PULSE AGAINST MY SKIN. SHE'S WORRIED.
ALL OF US ARE WORRIED.
IF THIS DOESN'T WORK...
...IF IT CAN HAPPEN AGAIN...
MY MIND...
HNGNNN

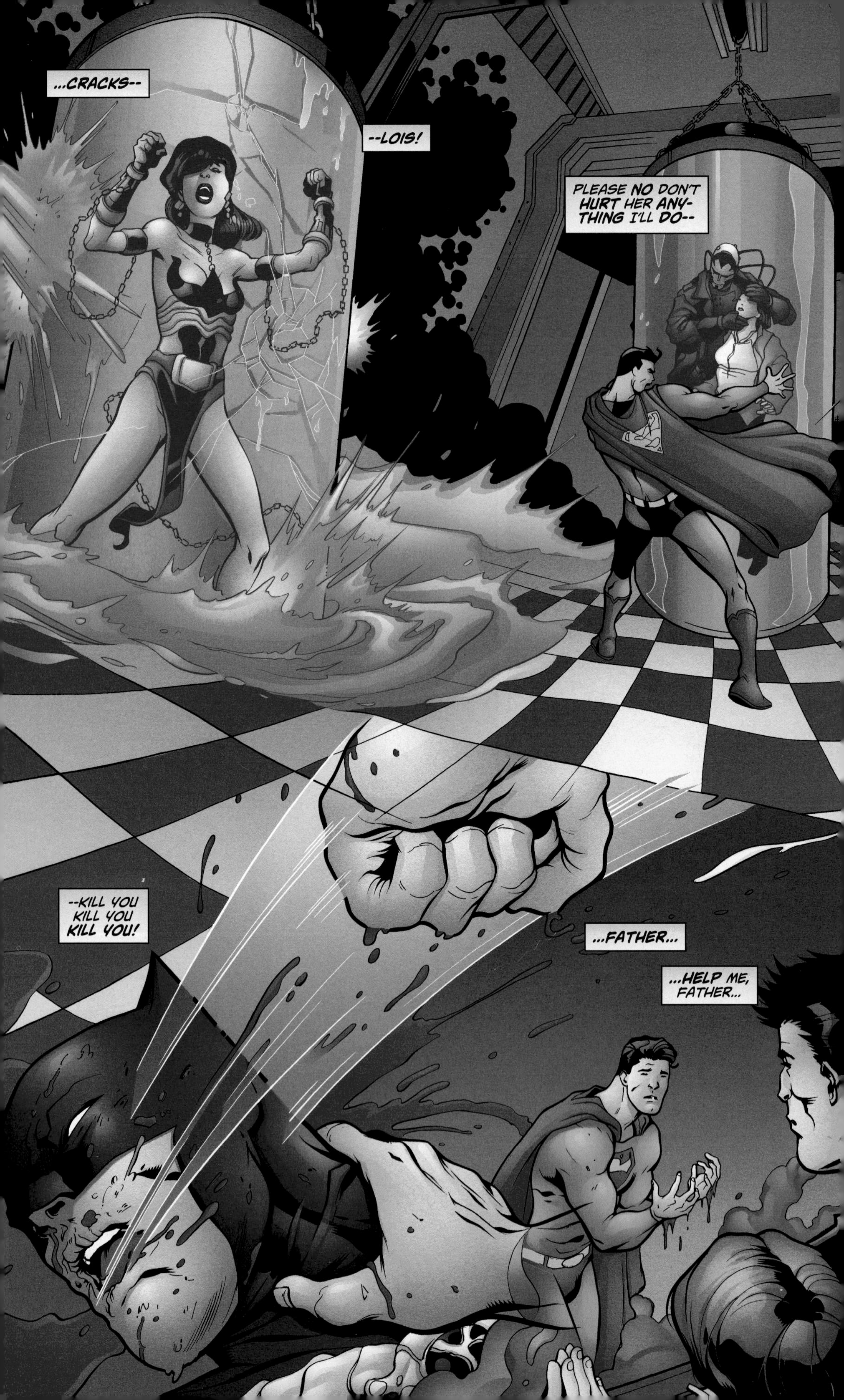
...CRACKS--
--LOIS!
PLEASE NO DON'T HURT HER ANYTHING I'LL DO--
--KILL YOU KILL YOU KILL YOU!
...FATHER...
...HELP ME, FATHER...

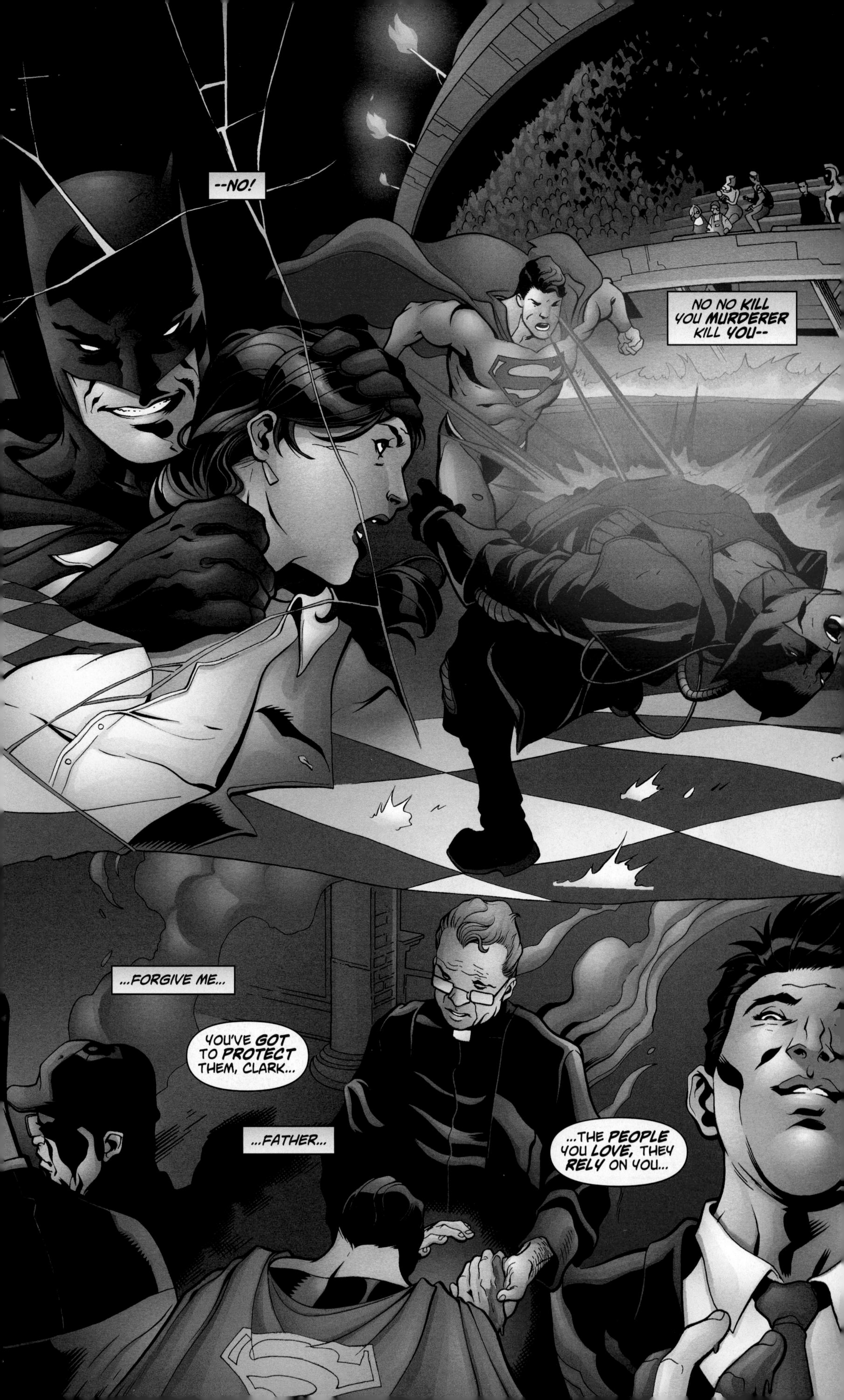
--NO!
NO NO KILL YOU MURDERER KILL YOU--
...FORGIVE ME...
YOU'VE GOT TO PROTECT THEM, CLARK...
...FATHER...
...THE PEOPLE YOU LOVE, THEY RELY ON YOU...

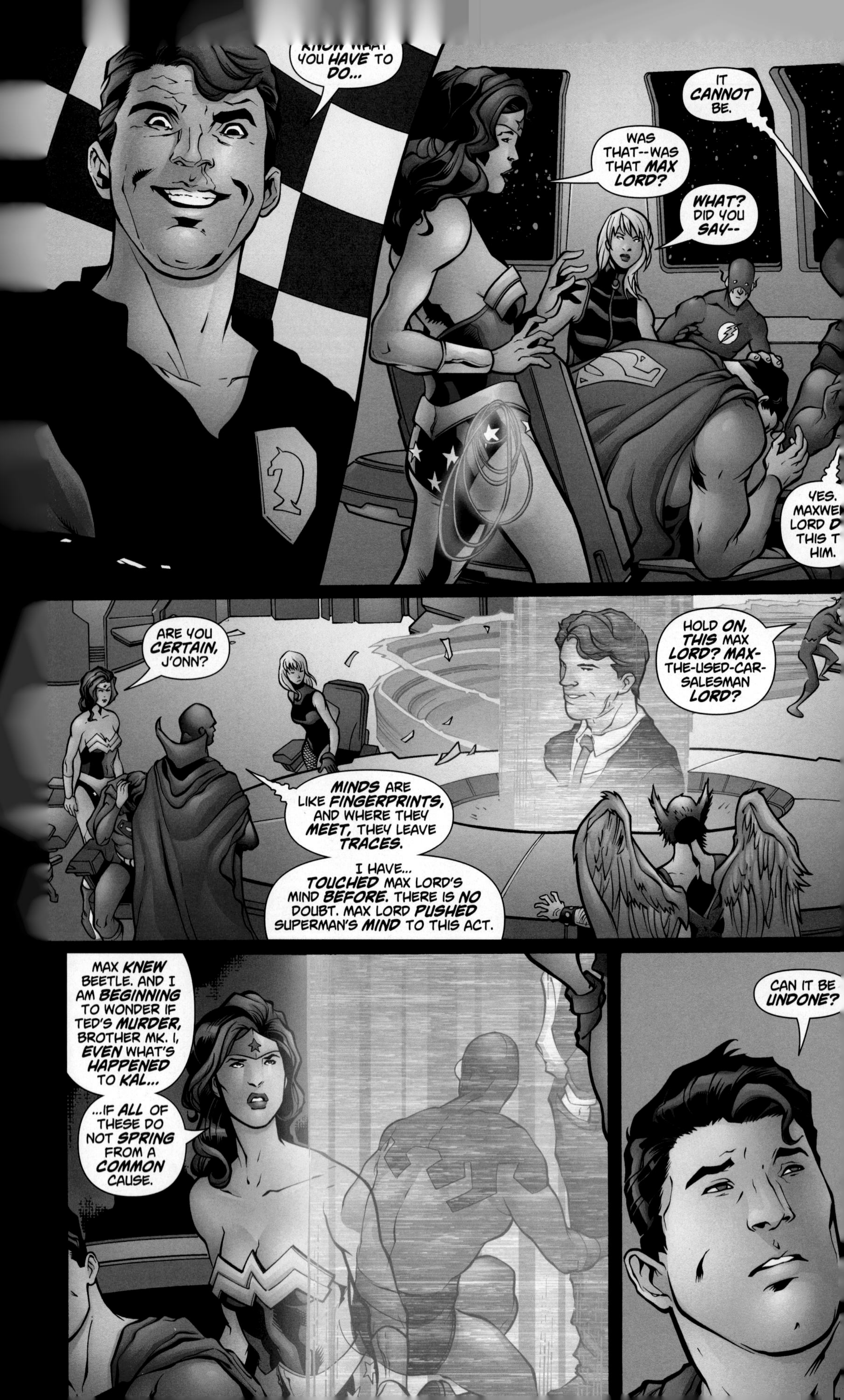

YOU HAVE TO DO...
WAS THAT--WAS THAT MAX LORD?
IT CANNOT BE.
WHAT? DID YOU SAY--
YES. MAXWE LORD D THIS T HIM.
ARE YOU CERTAIN, J'ONN?
HOLD ON, THIS MAX LORD? MAX-THE-USED-CAR-SALESMAN LORD?
MINDS ARE LIKE FINGERPRINTS, AND WHERE THEY MEET, THEY LEAVE TRACES.
I HAVE... TOUCHED MAX LORD'S MIND BEFORE. THERE IS NO DOUBT. MAX LORD PUSHED SUPERMAN'S MIND TO THIS ACT.
MAX KNEW BEETLE. AND I AM BEGINNING TO WONDER IF TED'S MURDER, BROTHER MK. I, EVEN WHAT'S HAPPENED TO KAL...
...IF ALL OF THESE DO NOT SPRING FROM A COMMON CAUSE.
CAN IT BE UNDONE?

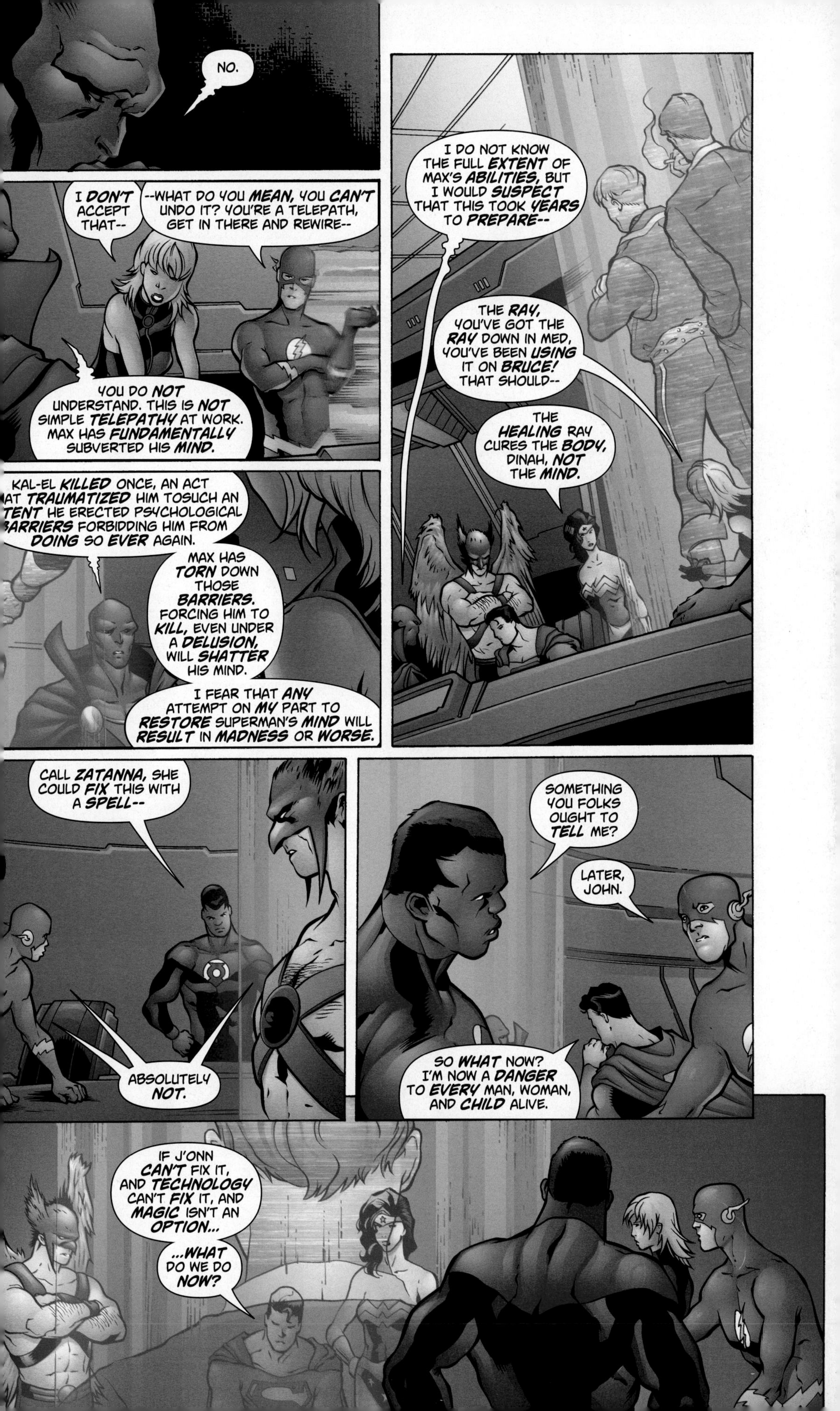

NO.
I DON'T ACCEPT THAT--
--WHAT DO YOU MEAN, YOU CAN'T UNDO IT? YOU'RE A TELEPATH, GET IN THERE AND REWIRE--
YOU DO NOT UNDERSTAND. THIS IS NOT SIMPLE TELEPATHY AT WORK. MAX HAS FUNDAMENTALLY SUBVERTED HIS MIND.
KAL-EL KILLED ONCE, AN ACT AT TRAUMATIZED HIM TOSUCH AN TENT HE ERECTED PSYCHOLOGICAL ARRIERS FORBIDDING HIM FROM DOING SO EVER AGAIN.
MAX HAS TORN DOWN THOSE BARRIERS. FORCING HIM TO KILL, EVEN UNDER A DELUSION, WILL SHATTER HIS MIND.
I FEAR THAT ANY ATTEMPT ON MY PART TO RESTORE SUPERMAN'S MIND WILL RESULT IN MADNESS OR WORSE.
I DO NOT KNOW THE FULL EXTENT OF MAX'S ABILITIES, BUT I WOULD SUSPECT THAT THIS TOOK YEARS TO PREPARE--
THE RAY, YOU'VE GOT THE RAY DOWN IN MED, YOU'VE BEEN USING IT ON BRUCE! THAT SHOULD--
THE HEALING RAY CURES THE BODY, DINAH, NOT THE MIND.
CALL ZATANNA, SHE COULD FIX THIS WITH A SPELL--
ABSOLUTELY NOT.
SOMETHING YOU FOLKS OUGHT TO TELL ME?
LATER, JOHN.
SO WHAT NOW? I'M NOW A DANGER TO EVERY MAN, WOMAN, AND CHILD ALIVE.
IF J'ONN CAN'T FIX IT, AND TECHNOLOGY CAN'T FIX IT, AND MAGIC ISN'T AN OPTION...
...WHAT DO WE DO NOW?

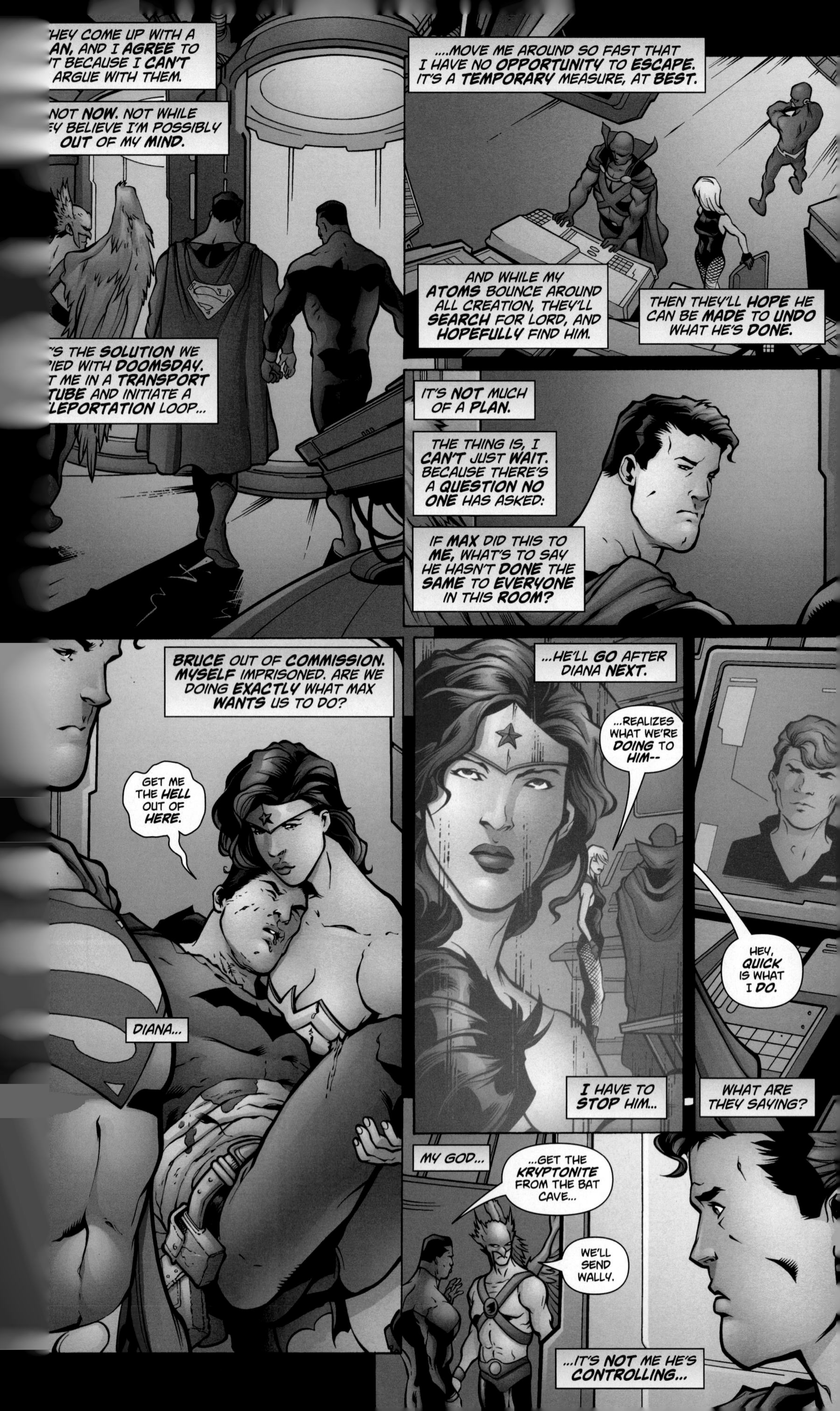

HEY COME UP WITH A
AN, AND I AGREE TO
T BECAUSE I CAN'T
ARGUE WITH THEM.
NOT NOW. NOT WHILE
Y BELIEVE I'M POSSIBLY
OUT OF MY MIND.
'S THE SOLUTION WE
PIED WITH DOOMSDAY.
T ME IN A TRANSPORT
TUBE AND INITIATE A
LEPORTATION LOOP...
....MOVE ME AROUND SO FAST THAT I HAVE NO OPPORTUNITY TO ESCAPE. IT'S A TEMPORARY MEASURE, AT BEST.
AND WHILE MY ATOMS BOUNCE AROUND ALL CREATION, THEY'LL SEARCH FOR LORD, AND HOPEFULLY FIND HIM.
THEN THEY'LL HOPE HE CAN BE MADE TO UNDO WHAT HE'S DONE.
IT'S NOT MUCH OF A PLAN.
THE THING IS, I CAN'T JUST WAIT. BECAUSE THERE'S A QUESTION NO ONE HAS ASKED:
IF MAX DID THIS TO ME, WHAT'S TO SAY HE HASN'T DONE THE SAME TO EVERYONE IN THIS ROOM?
BRUCE OUT OF COMMISSION. MYSELF IMPRISONED. ARE WE DOING EXACTLY WHAT MAX WANTS US TO DO?
GET ME THE HELL OUT OF HERE.
DIANA...
...HE'LL GO AFTER DIANA NEXT.
...REALIZES WHAT WE'RE DOING TO HIM--
I HAVE TO STOP HIM...
HEY, QUICK IS WHAT I DO.
WHAT ARE THEY SAYING?
MY GOD...
...GET THE KRYPTONITE FROM THE BAT CAVE...
WE'LL SEND WALLY.
...IT'S NOT ME HE'S CONTROLLING...

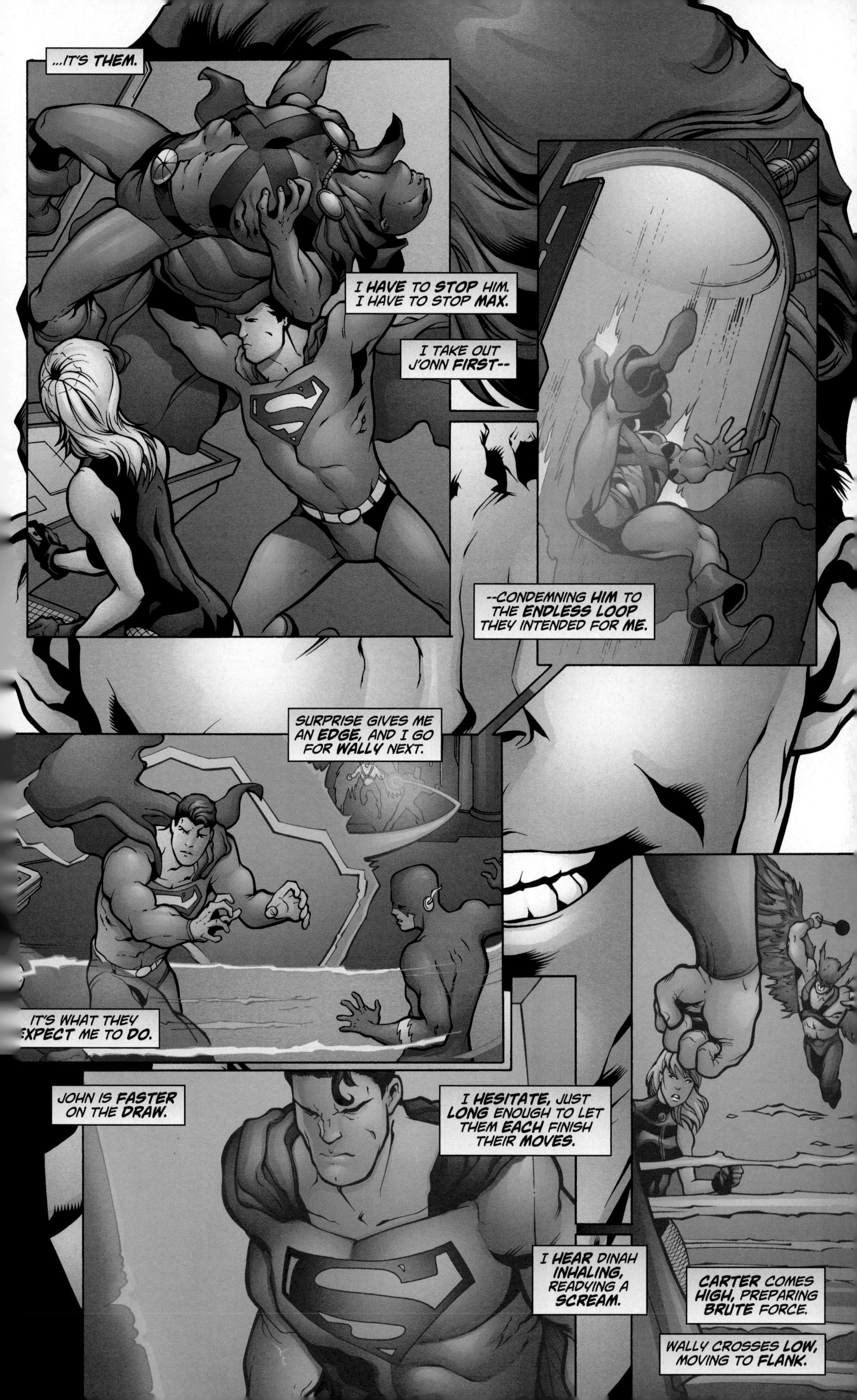
...IT'S THEM.
I HAVE TO STOP HIM. I HAVE TO STOP MAX.
I TAKE OUT J'ONN FIRST--
--CONDEMNING HIM TO THE ENDLESS LOOP THEY INTENDED FOR ME.
SURPRISE GIVES ME AN EDGE, AND I GO FOR WALLY NEXT.
IT'S WHAT THEY EXPECT ME TO DO.
JOHN IS FASTER ON THE DRAW.
I HESITATE, JUST LONG ENOUGH TO LET THEM EACH FINISH THEIR MOVES.
I HEAR DINAH INHALING, READYING A SCREAM.
CARTER COMES HIGH, PREPARING BRUTE FORCE.
WALLY CROSSES LOW, MOVING TO FLANK.

WHEN THEY'RE **WHERE** I **WANT** THEM, I **MOVE**.

WALLY IS **FAST** ENOUGH TO **SEE** IT COMING--

--BUT **NOT** FAST ENOUGH TO DO ANYTHING **ABOUT** IT.

I HIT THE **CONSTRUCT** WITH **EVERYTHING** I HAVE, THE FORCE OF MY PUNCH VERSUS THE **FORCE** OF JOHN'S **WILL**.

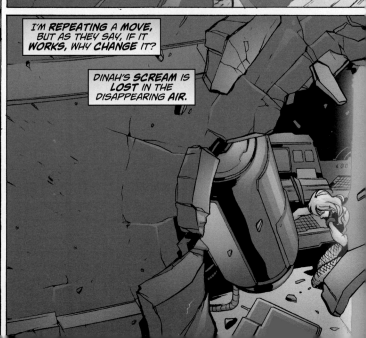

I'M REPEATING A MOVE, BUT AS THEY SAY, IF IT **WORKS,** WHY **CHANGE** IT?

DINAH'S **SCREAM** IS **LOST** IN THE DISAPPEARING **AIR**.

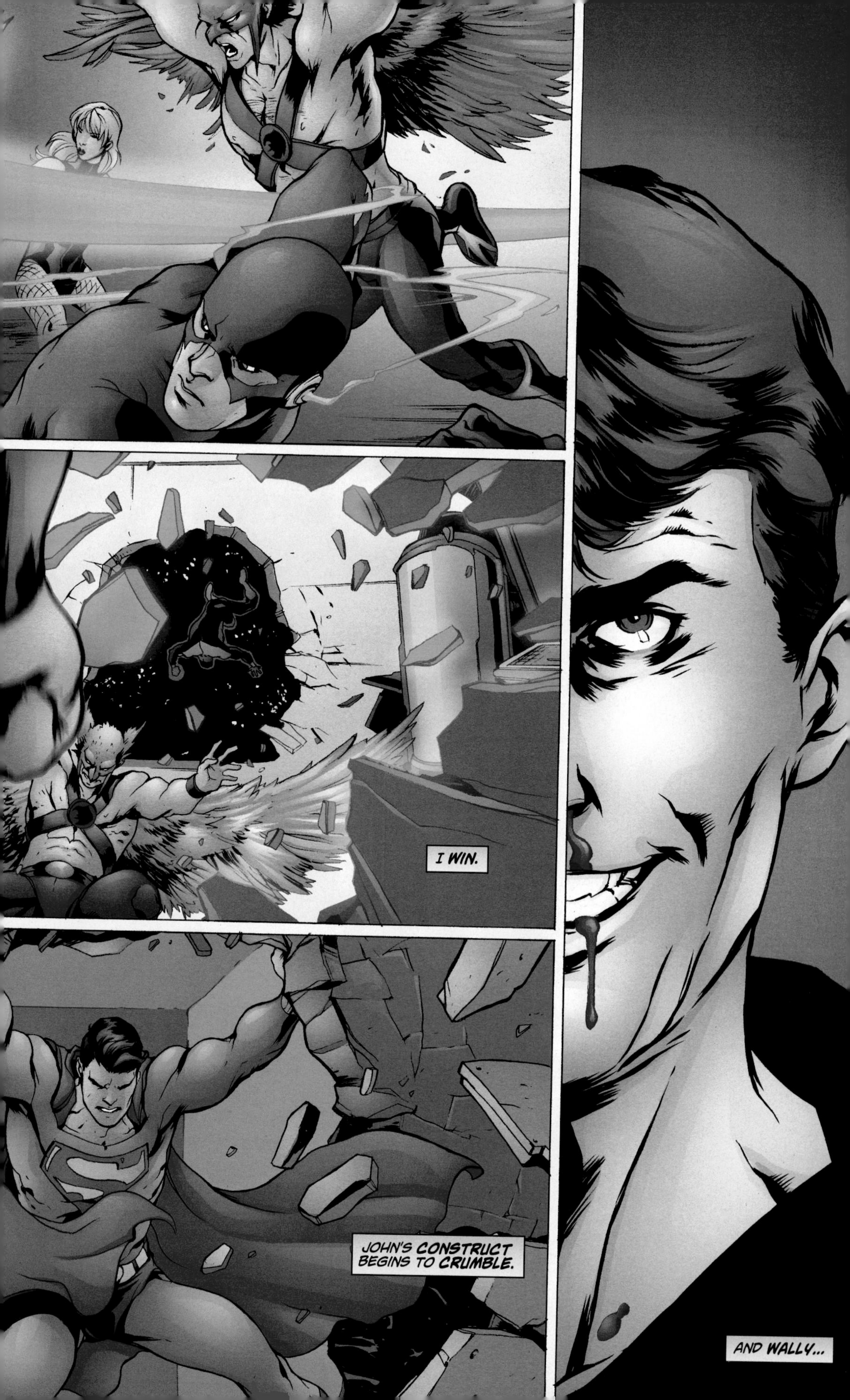
I WIN.
JOHN'S CONSTRUCT BEGINS TO CRUMBLE.
AND WALLY...

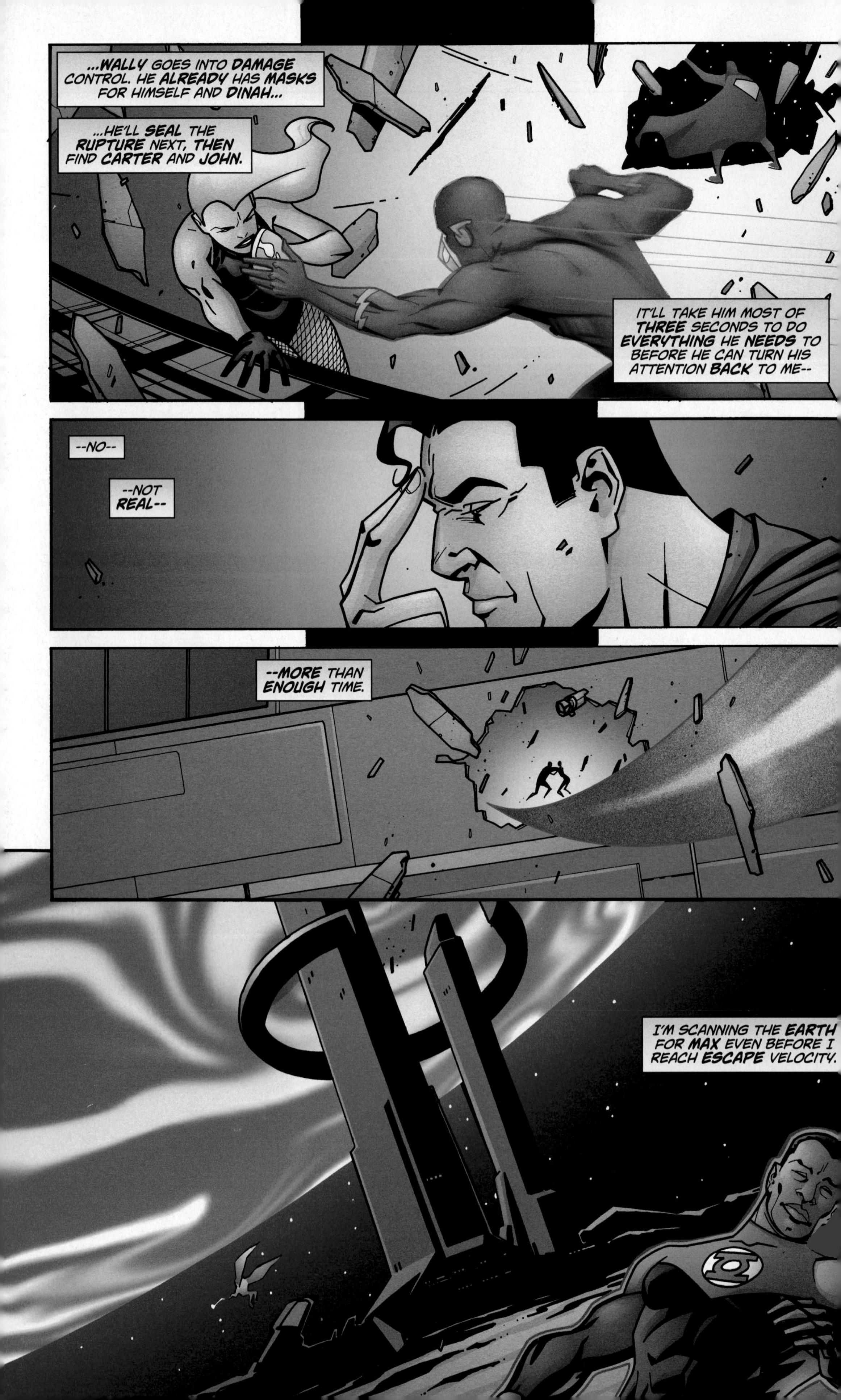
...WALLY GOES INTO DAMAGE CONTROL. HE ALREADY HAS MASKS FOR HIMSELF AND DINAH...
...HE'LL SEAL THE RUPTURE NEXT, THEN FIND CARTER AND JOHN.
IT'LL TAKE HIM MOST OF THREE SECONDS TO DO EVERYTHING HE NEEDS TO BEFORE HE CAN TURN HIS ATTENTION BACK TO ME--
--NO--
--NOT REAL--
--MORE THAN ENOUGH TIME.
I'M SCANNING THE EARTH FOR MAX EVEN BEFORE I REACH ESCAPE VELOCITY.

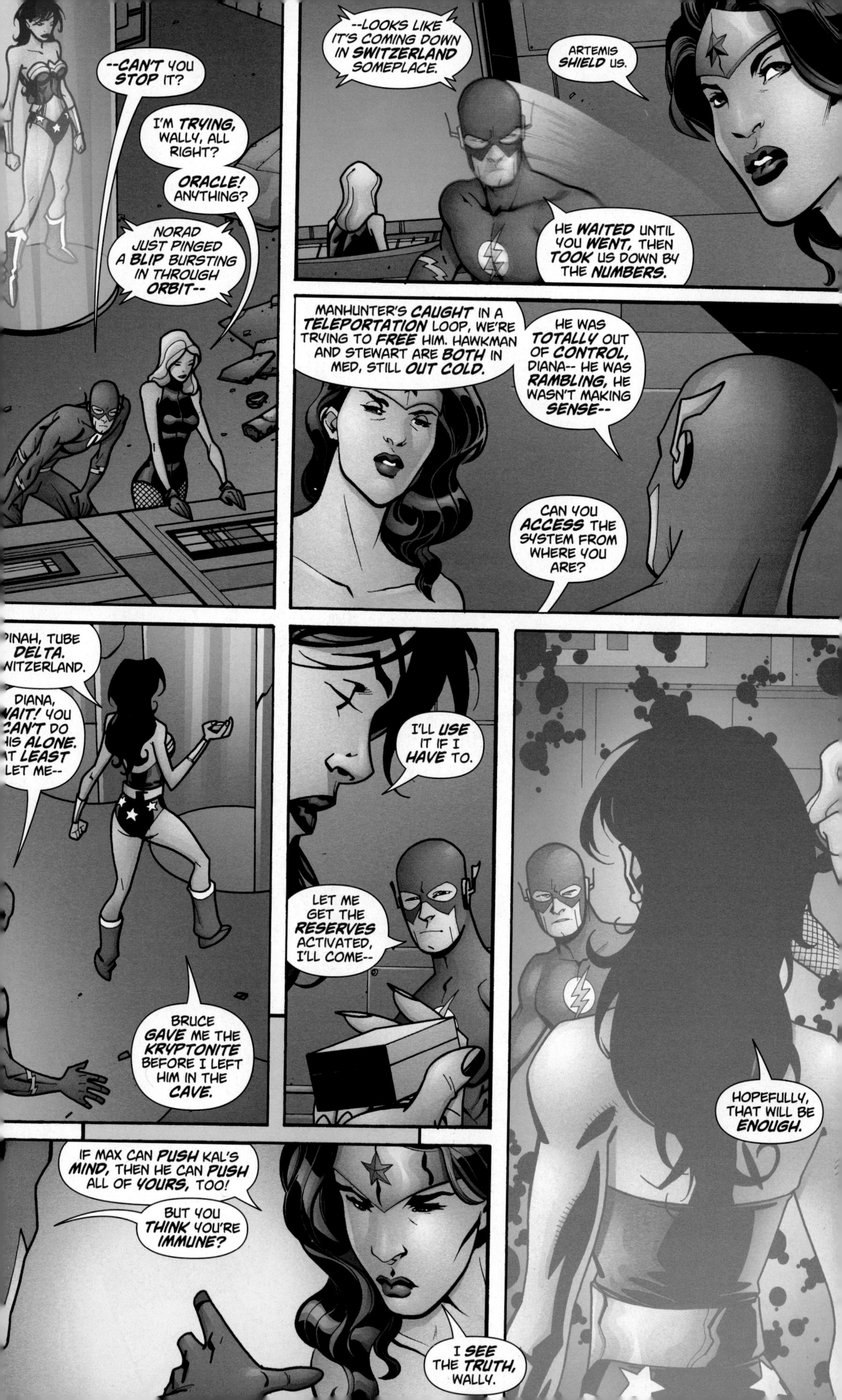
--CAN'T YOU STOP IT?
I'M TRYING, WALLY, ALL RIGHT?
ORACLE! ANYTHING?
NORAD JUST PINGED A BLIP BURSTING IN THROUGH ORBIT--
--LOOKS LIKE IT'S COMING DOWN IN SWITZERLAND SOMEPLACE.
ARTEMIS SHIELD US.
HE WAITED UNTIL YOU WENT, THEN TOOK US DOWN BY THE NUMBERS.
MANHUNTER'S CAUGHT IN A TELEPORTATION LOOP, WE'RE TRYING TO FREE HIM. HAWKMAN AND STEWART ARE BOTH IN MED, STILL OUT COLD.
HE WAS TOTALLY OUT OF CONTROL, DIANA-- HE WAS RAMBLING, HE WASN'T MAKING SENSE--
CAN YOU ACCESS THE SYSTEM FROM WHERE YOU ARE?
INAH, TUBE DELTA. WITZERLAND.
DIANA, WAIT! YOU CAN'T DO HIS ALONE. T LEAST LET ME--
BRUCE GAVE ME THE KRYPTONITE BEFORE I LEFT HIM IN THE CAVE.
I'LL USE IT IF I HAVE TO.
LET ME GET THE RESERVES ACTIVATED, I'LL COME--
HOPEFULLY, THAT WILL BE ENOUGH.
IF MAX CAN PUSH KAL'S MIND, THEN HE CAN PUSH ALL OF YOURS, TOO!
BUT YOU THINK YOU'RE IMMUNE?
I SEE THE TRUTH, WALLY.

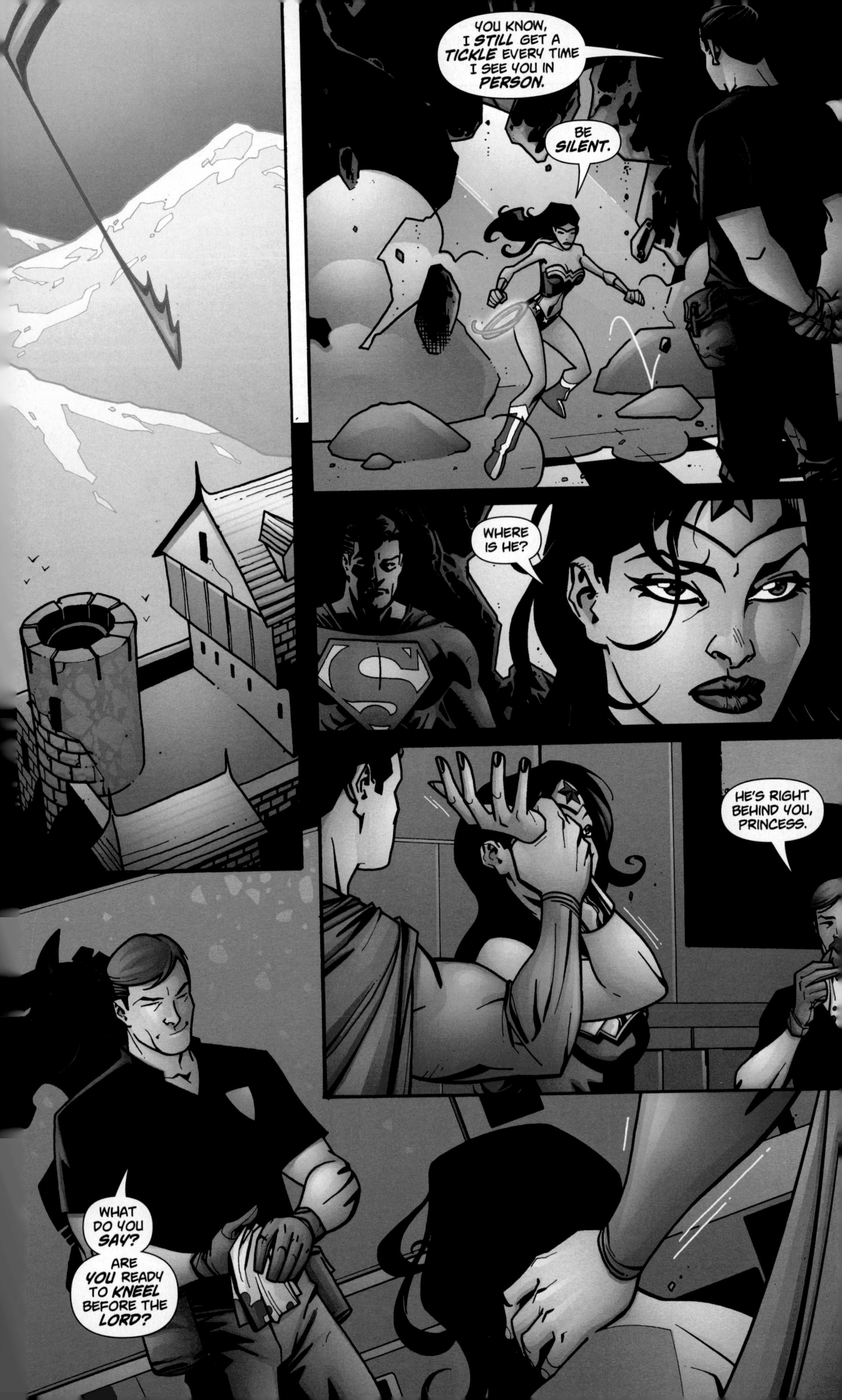
YOU KNOW, I STILL GET A TICKLE EVERY TIME I SEE YOU IN PERSON.
BE SILENT.
WHERE IS HE?
HE'S RIGHT BEHIND YOU, PRINCESS.
WHAT DO YOU SAY?
ARE YOU READY TO KNEEL BEFORE THE LORD?

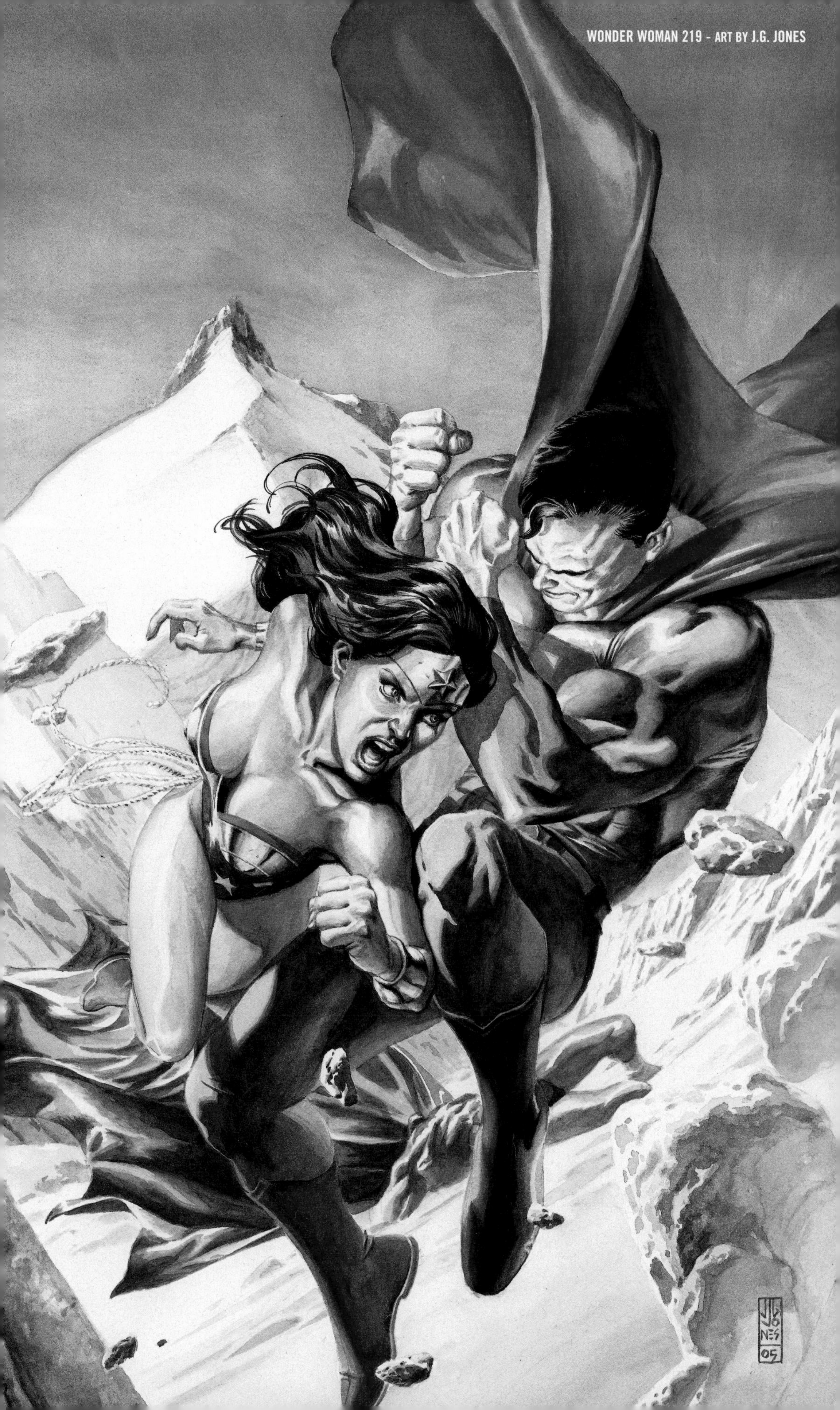

WONDER WOMAN 219 - ART BY J.G. JONES

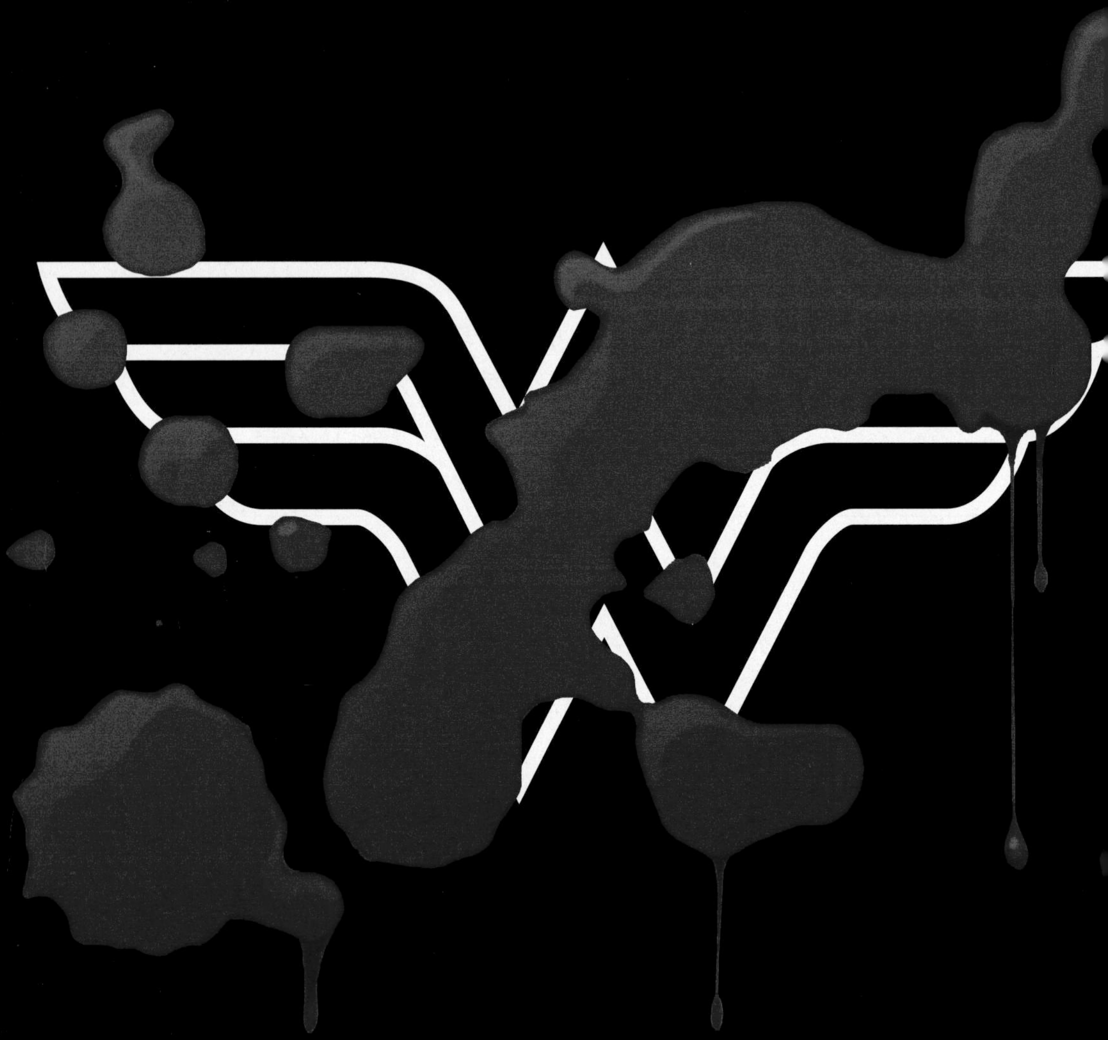

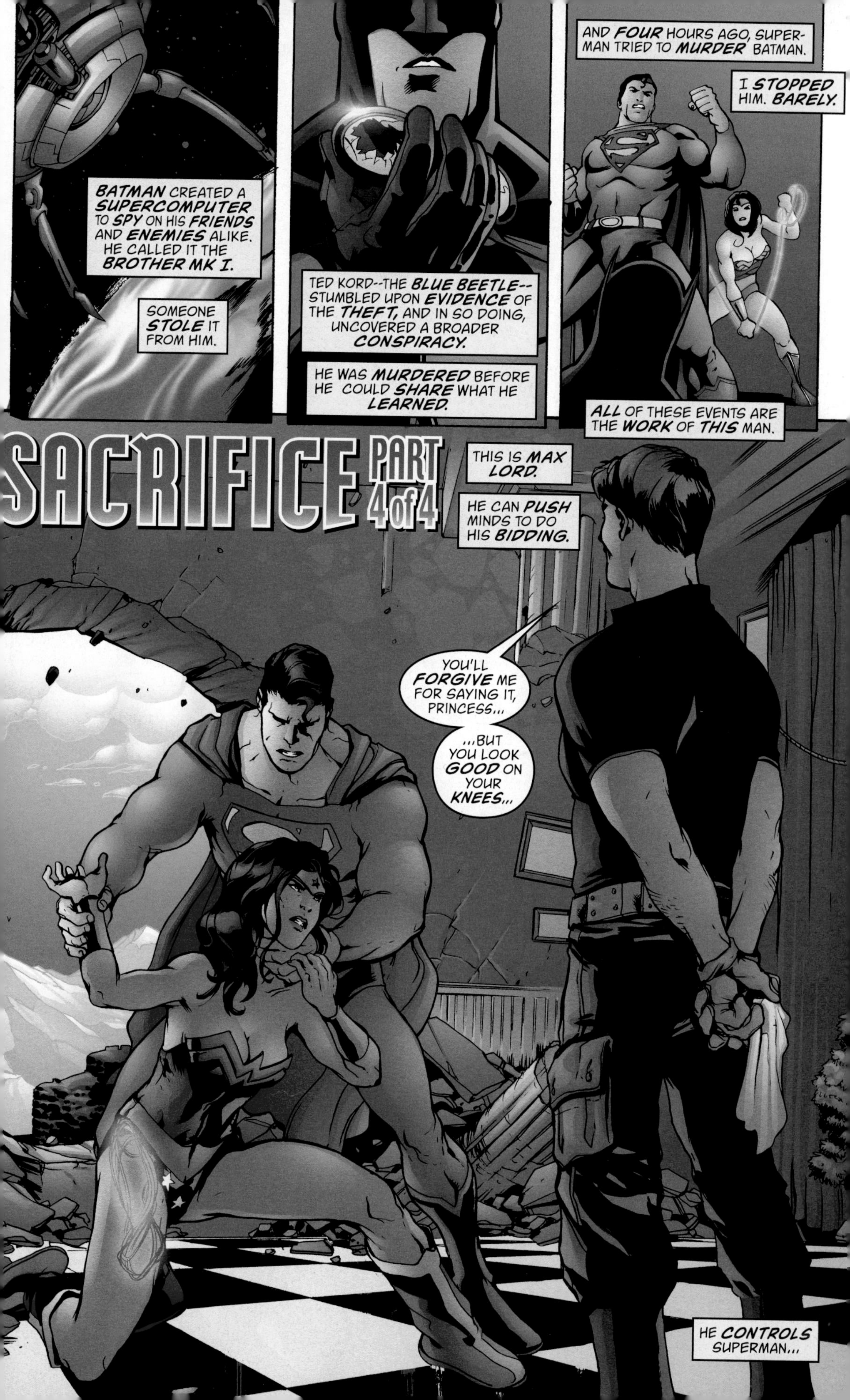
BATMAN CREATED A SUPERCOMPUTER TO SPY ON HIS FRIENDS AND ENEMIES ALIKE. HE CALLED IT THE BROTHER MK I.
SOMEONE STOLE IT FROM HIM.
TED KORD--THE BLUE BEETLE--STUMBLED UPON EVIDENCE OF THE THEFT, AND IN SO DOING, UNCOVERED A BROADER CONSPIRACY.
HE WAS MURDERED BEFORE HE COULD SHARE WHAT HE LEARNED.
AND FOUR HOURS AGO, SUPER-MAN TRIED TO MURDER BATMAN.
I STOPPED HIM. BARELY.
ALL OF THESE EVENTS ARE THE WORK OF THIS MAN.
SACRIFICE PART 4 of 4
THIS IS MAX LORD.
HE CAN PUSH MINDS TO DO HIS BIDDING.
YOU'LL FORGIVE ME FOR SAYING IT, PRINCESS...
...BUT YOU LOOK GOOD ON YOUR KNEES...
HE CONTROLS SUPERMAN...

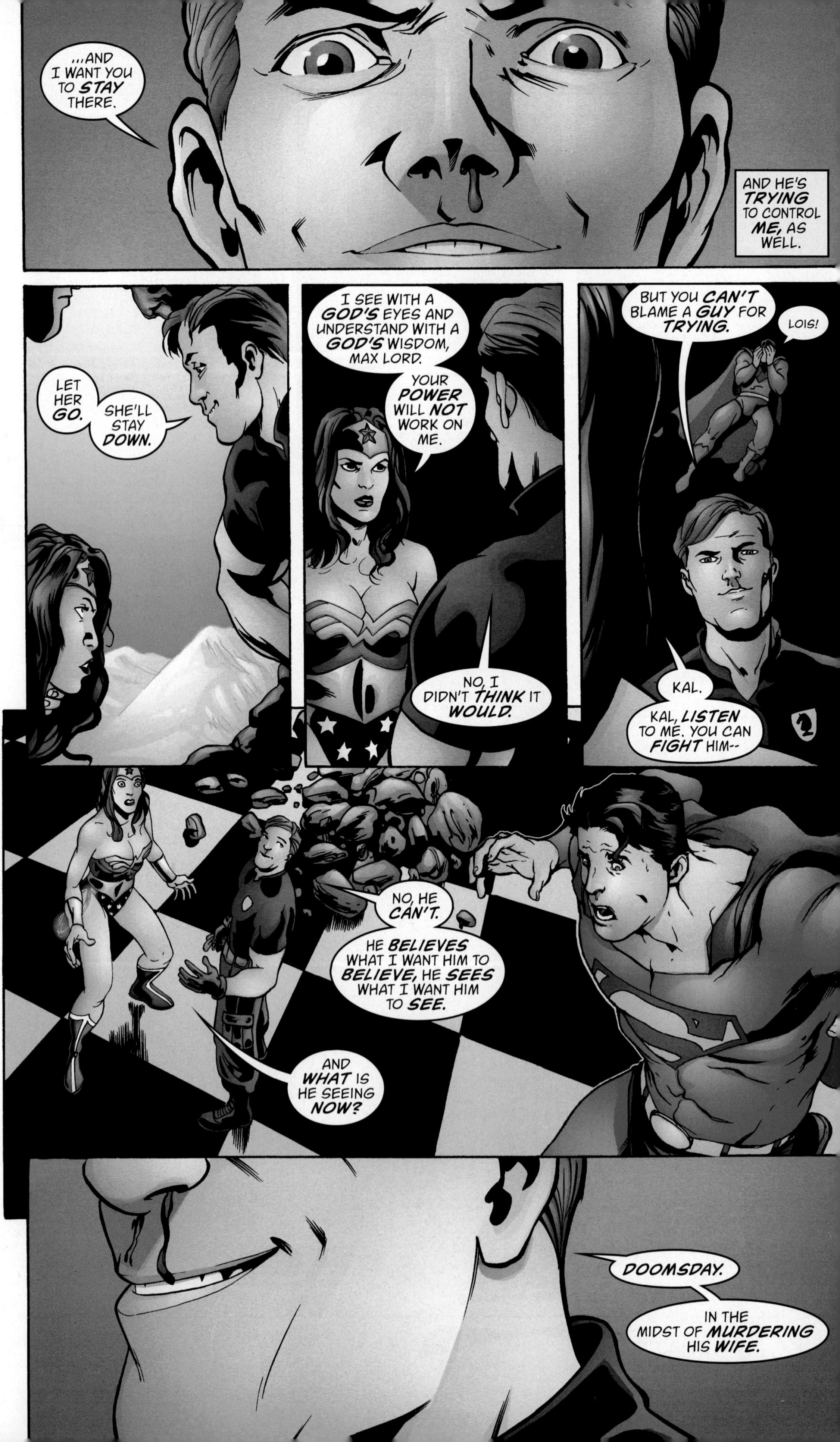
...AND I WANT YOU TO STAY THERE.
AND HE'S TRYING TO CONTROL ME, AS WELL.
LET HER GO.
SHE'LL STAY DOWN.
I SEE WITH A GOD'S EYES AND UNDERSTAND WITH A GOD'S WISDOM, MAX LORD.
YOUR POWER WILL NOT WORK ON ME.
NO, I DIDN'T THINK IT WOULD.
BUT YOU CAN'T BLAME A GUY FOR TRYING.
LOIS!
KAL.
KAL, LISTEN TO ME. YOU CAN FIGHT HIM--
NO, HE CAN'T.
HE BELIEVES WHAT I WANT HIM TO BELIEVE, HE SEES WHAT I WANT HIM TO SEE.
AND WHAT IS HE SEEING NOW?
DOOMSDAY.
IN THE MIDST OF MURDERING HIS WIFE.

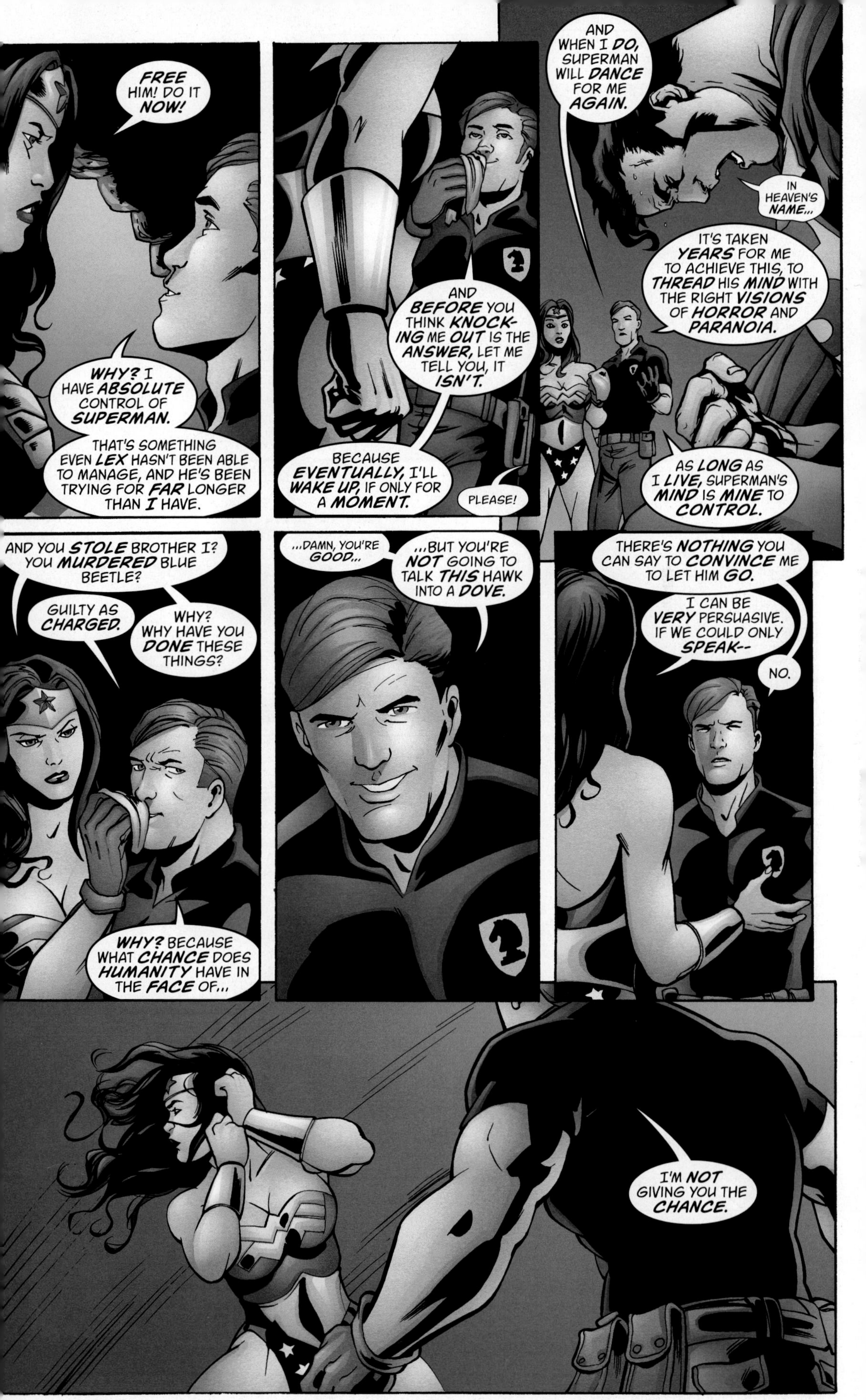
FREE HIM! DO IT NOW!
WHY? I HAVE ABSOLUTE CONTROL OF SUPERMAN.
THAT'S SOMETHING EVEN LEX HASN'T BEEN ABLE TO MANAGE, AND HE'S BEEN TRYING FOR FAR LONGER THAN I HAVE.
AND BEFORE YOU THINK KNOCKING ME OUT IS THE ANSWER, LET ME TELL YOU, IT ISN'T.
BECAUSE EVENTUALLY, I'LL WAKE UP, IF ONLY FOR A MOMENT.
PLEASE!
AND WHEN I DO, SUPERMAN WILL DANCE FOR ME AGAIN.
IN HEAVEN'S NAME...
IT'S TAKEN YEARS FOR ME TO ACHIEVE THIS, TO THREAD HIS MIND WITH THE RIGHT VISIONS OF HORROR AND PARANOIA.
AS LONG AS I LIVE, SUPERMAN'S MIND IS MINE TO CONTROL.
AND YOU STOLE BROTHER I? YOU MURDERED BLUE BEETLE?
GUILTY AS CHARGED.
WHY? WHY HAVE YOU DONE THESE THINGS?
WHY? BECAUSE WHAT CHANCE DOES HUMANITY HAVE IN THE FACE OF...
...DAMN, YOU'RE GOOD...
...BUT YOU'RE NOT GOING TO TALK THIS HAWK INTO A DOVE.
THERE'S NOTHING YOU CAN SAY TO CONVINCE ME TO LET HIM GO.
I CAN BE VERY PERSUASIVE. IF WE COULD ONLY SPEAK--
NO.
I'M NOT GIVING YOU THE CHANCE.

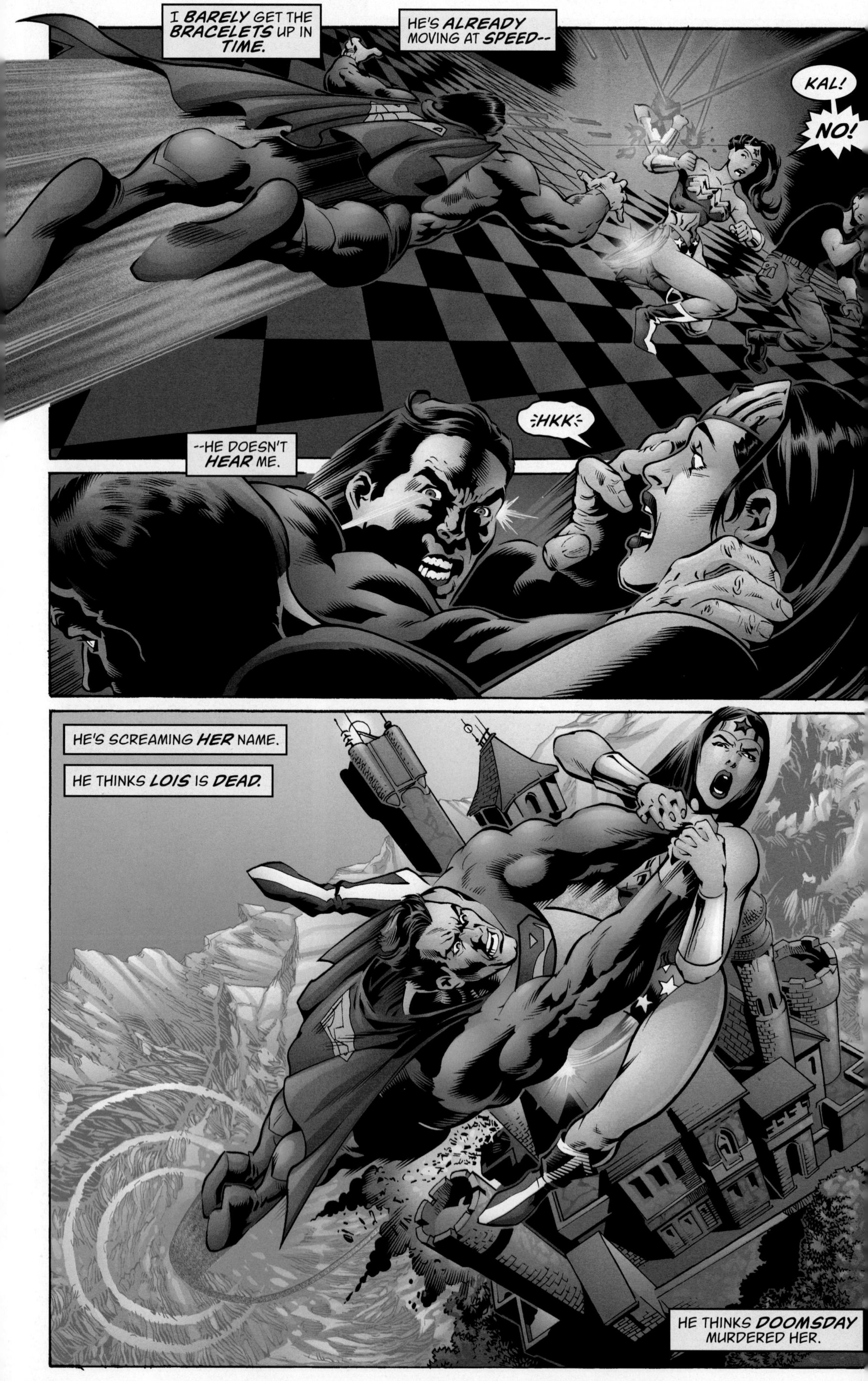
I BARELY GET THE BRACELETS UP IN TIME.
HE'S ALREADY MOVING AT SPEED--
KAL!
NO!
--HE DOESN'T HEAR ME.
HKK
HE'S SCREAMING HER NAME.
HE THINKS LOIS IS DEAD.
HE THINKS DOOMSDAY MURDERED HER.

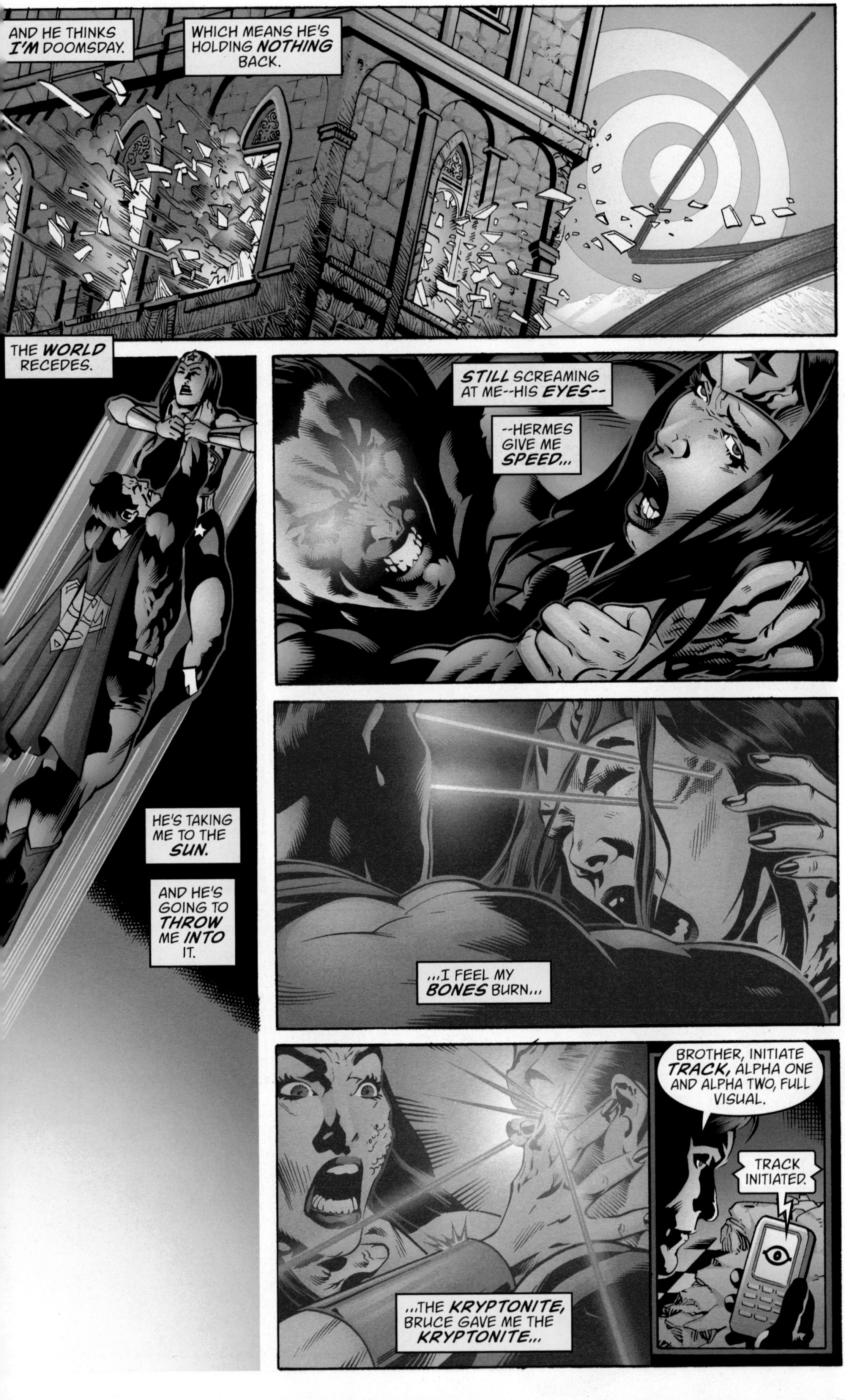

AND HE THINKS I'M DOOMSDAY.
WHICH MEANS HE'S HOLDING NOTHING BACK.
THE WORLD RECEDES.
STILL SCREAMING AT ME--HIS EYES--
--HERMES GIVE ME SPEED...
HE'S TAKING ME TO THE SUN.
AND HE'S GOING TO THROW ME INTO IT.
...I FEEL MY BONES BURN...
...THE KRYPTONITE, BRUCE GAVE ME THE KRYPTONITE...
BROTHER, INITIATE TRACK, ALPHA ONE AND ALPHA TWO, FULL VISUAL.
TRACK INITIATED.

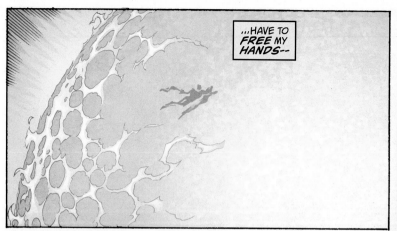

...HAVE TO *FREE* MY *HANDS*--

--*BREAK* HIS *GRIP*--

--QUICK--

--HAVE TO BE--

--QUICK--

VISUAL ACQUIRED.

BEGIN *RECORD-ING.*

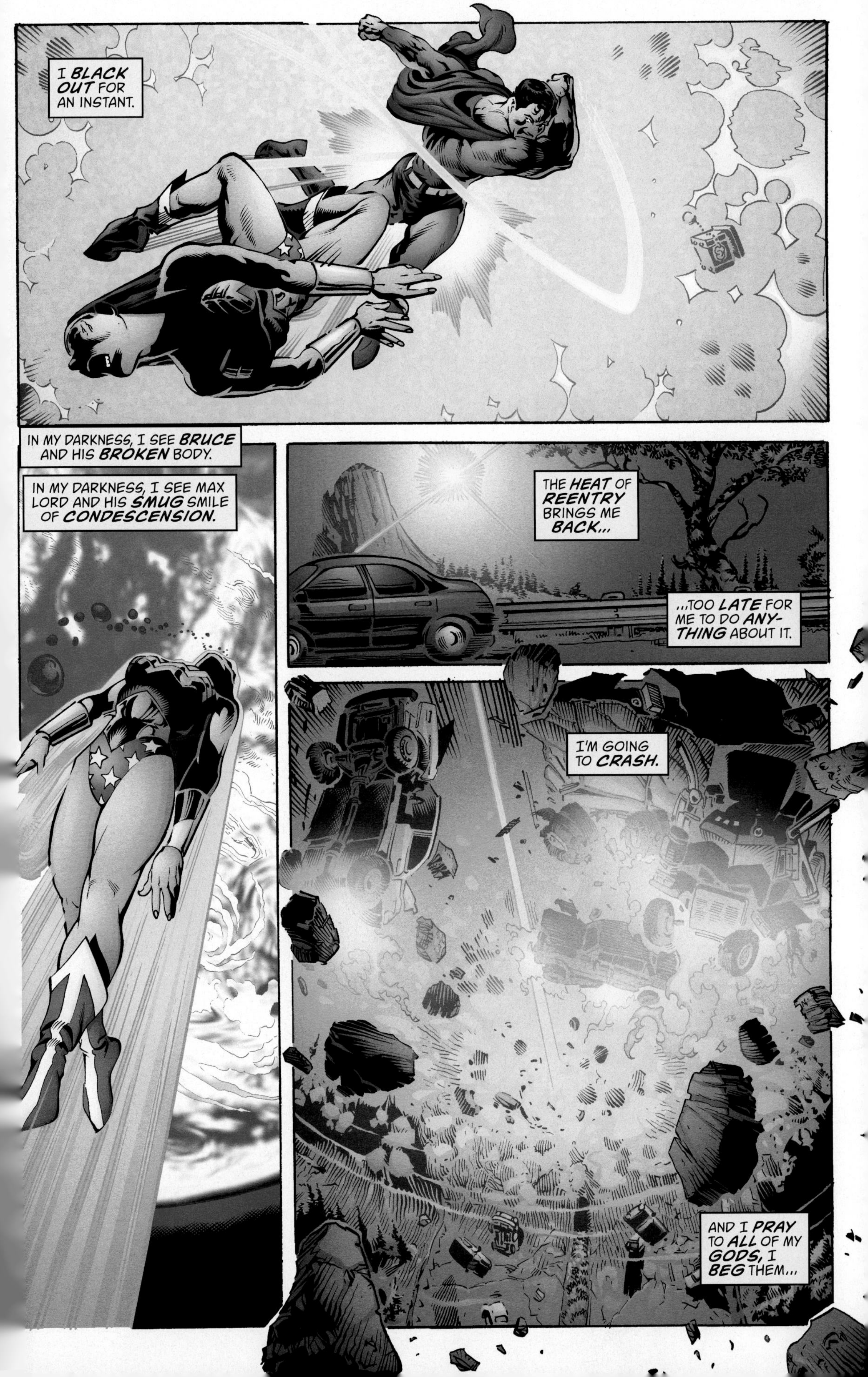
I BLACK OUT FOR AN INSTANT.
IN MY DARKNESS, I SEE BRUCE AND HIS BROKEN BODY.
IN MY DARKNESS, I SEE MAX LORD AND HIS SMUG SMILE OF CONDESCENSION.
THE HEAT OF REENTRY BRINGS ME BACK...
...TOO LATE FOR ME TO DO ANYTHING ABOUT IT.
I'M GOING TO CRASH.
AND I PRAY TO ALL OF MY GODS, I BEG THEM...

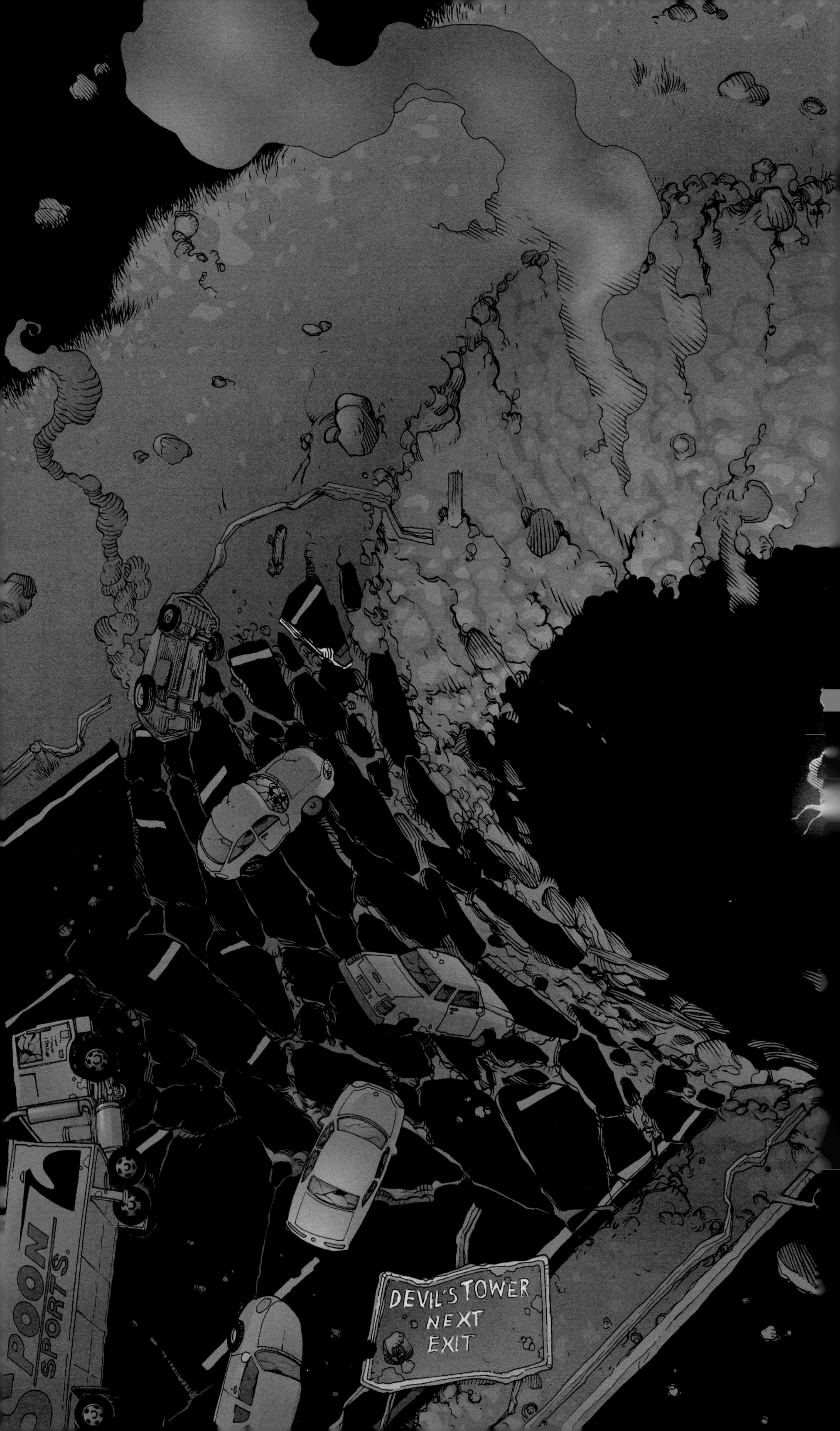
DEVIL'S TOWER
NEXT
EXIT
SPOON
SPORTS.

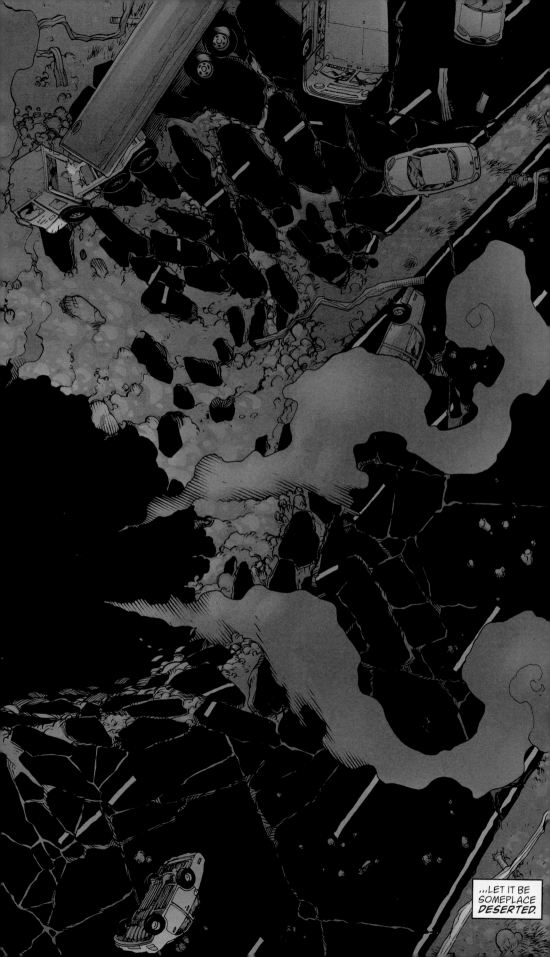

...LET IT BE SOMEPLACE DESERTED.

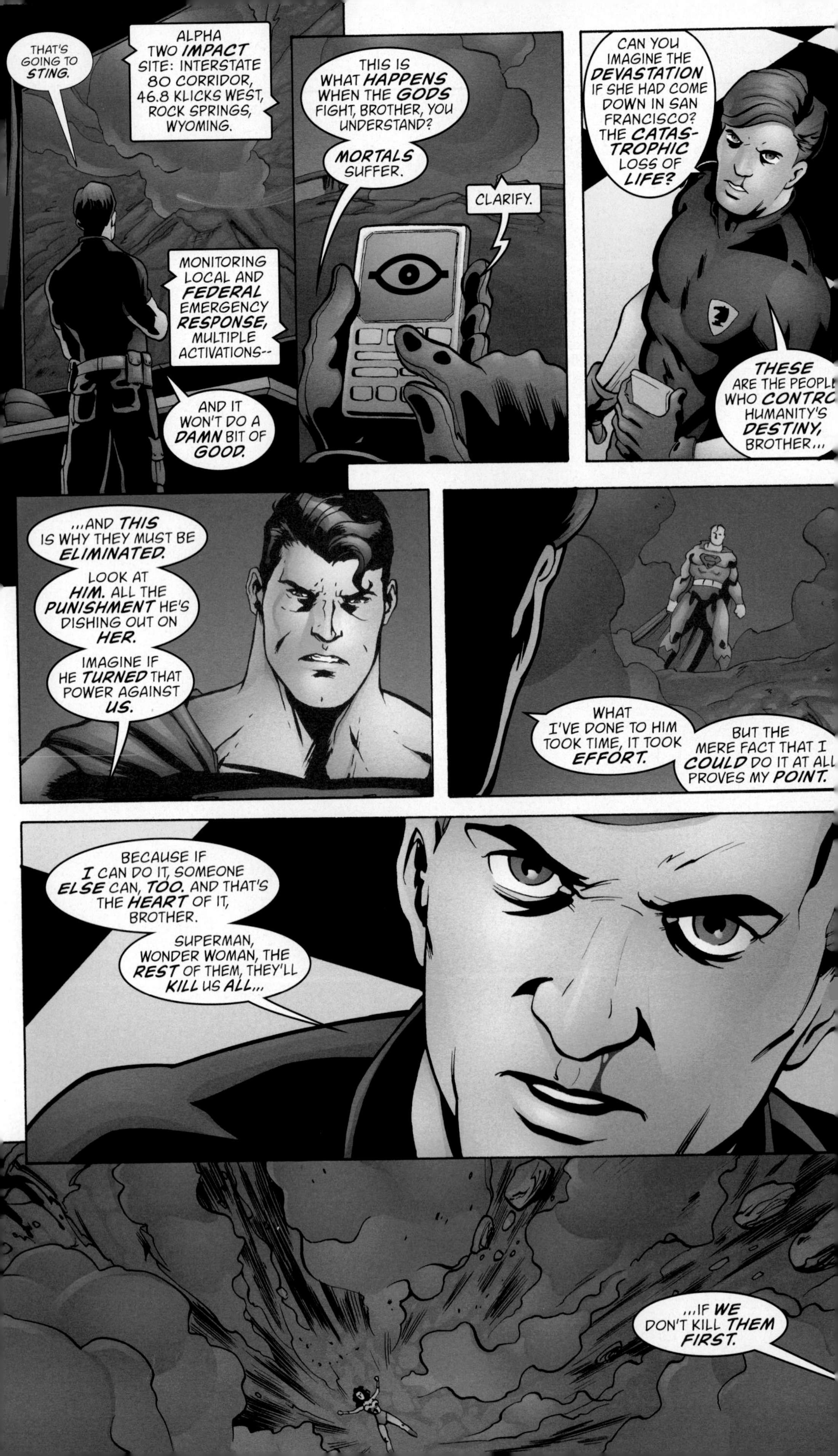
THAT'S GOING TO STING.
ALPHA TWO IMPACT SITE: INTERSTATE 80 CORRIDOR, 46.8 KLICKS WEST, ROCK SPRINGS, WYOMING.
MONITORING LOCAL AND FEDERAL EMERGENCY RESPONSE, MULTIPLE ACTIVATIONS--
AND IT WON'T DO A DAMN BIT OF GOOD.
THIS IS WHAT HAPPENS WHEN THE GODS FIGHT, BROTHER, YOU UNDERSTAND?
MORTALS SUFFER.
CLARIFY.
CAN YOU IMAGINE THE DEVASTATION IF SHE HAD COME DOWN IN SAN FRANCISCO? THE CATAS-TROPHIC LOSS OF LIFE?
THESE ARE THE PEOPL WHO CONTRO HUMANITY'S DESTINY, BROTHER...
...AND THIS IS WHY THEY MUST BE ELIMINATED.
LOOK AT HIM. ALL THE PUNISHMENT HE'S DISHING OUT ON HER.
IMAGINE IF HE TURNED THAT POWER AGAINST US.
WHAT I'VE DONE TO HIM TOOK TIME, IT TOOK EFFORT.
BUT THE MERE FACT THAT I COULD DO IT AT ALL PROVES MY POINT.
BECAUSE IF I CAN DO IT, SOMEONE ELSE CAN, TOO. AND THAT'S THE HEART OF IT, BROTHER.
SUPERMAN, WONDER WOMAN, THE REST OF THEM, THEY'LL KILL US ALL...
...IF WE DON'T KILL THEM FIRST.

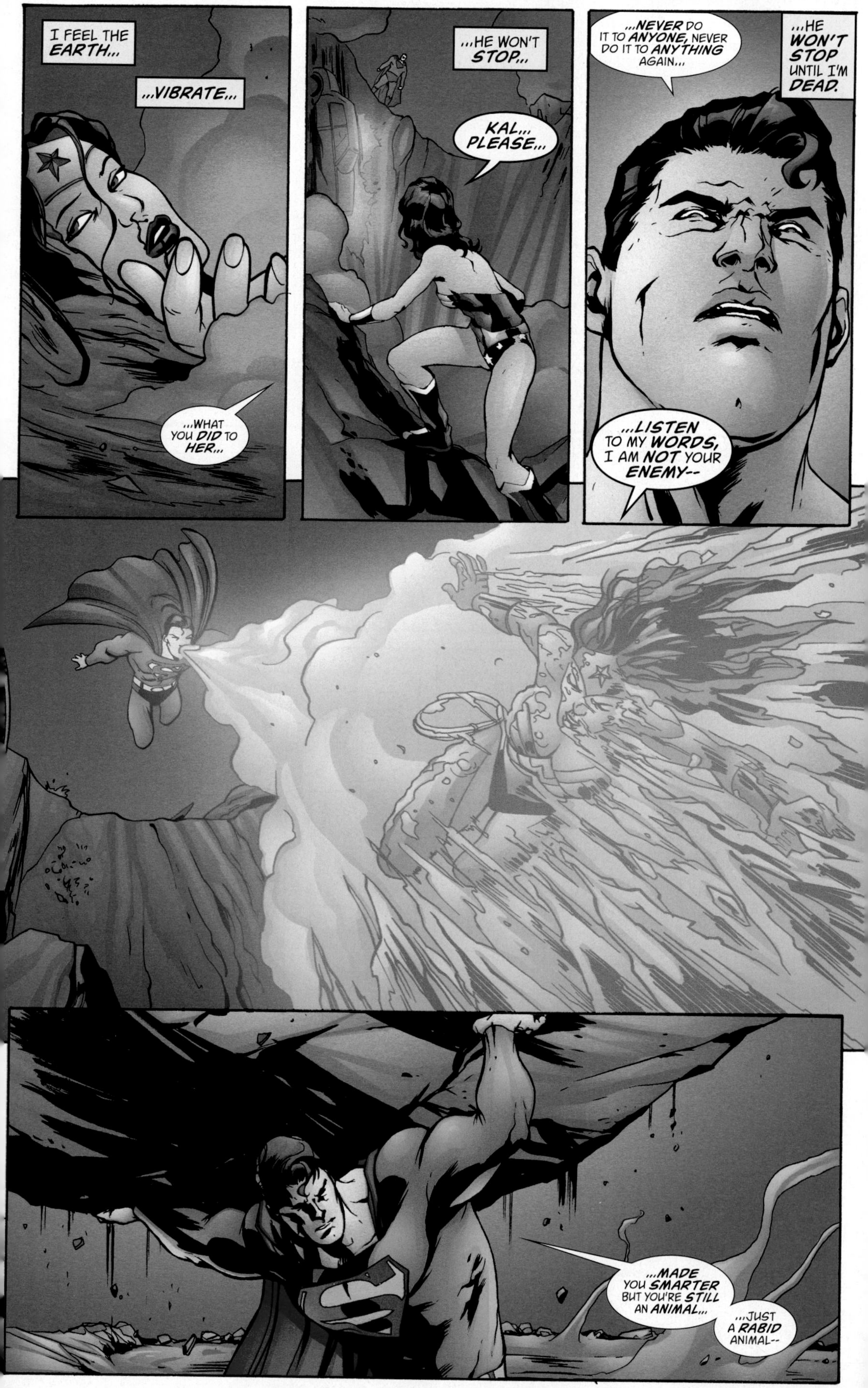
I FEEL THE EARTH...
...VIBRATE...
...WHAT YOU DID TO HER...
...HE WON'T STOP...
KAL... PLEASE...
...NEVER DO IT TO ANYONE, NEVER DO IT TO ANYTHING AGAIN...
...HE WON'T STOP UNTIL I'M DEAD.
...LISTEN TO MY WORDS, I AM NOT YOUR ENEMY--
...MADE YOU SMARTER BUT YOU'RE STILL AN ANIMAL...
...JUST A RABID ANIMAL--

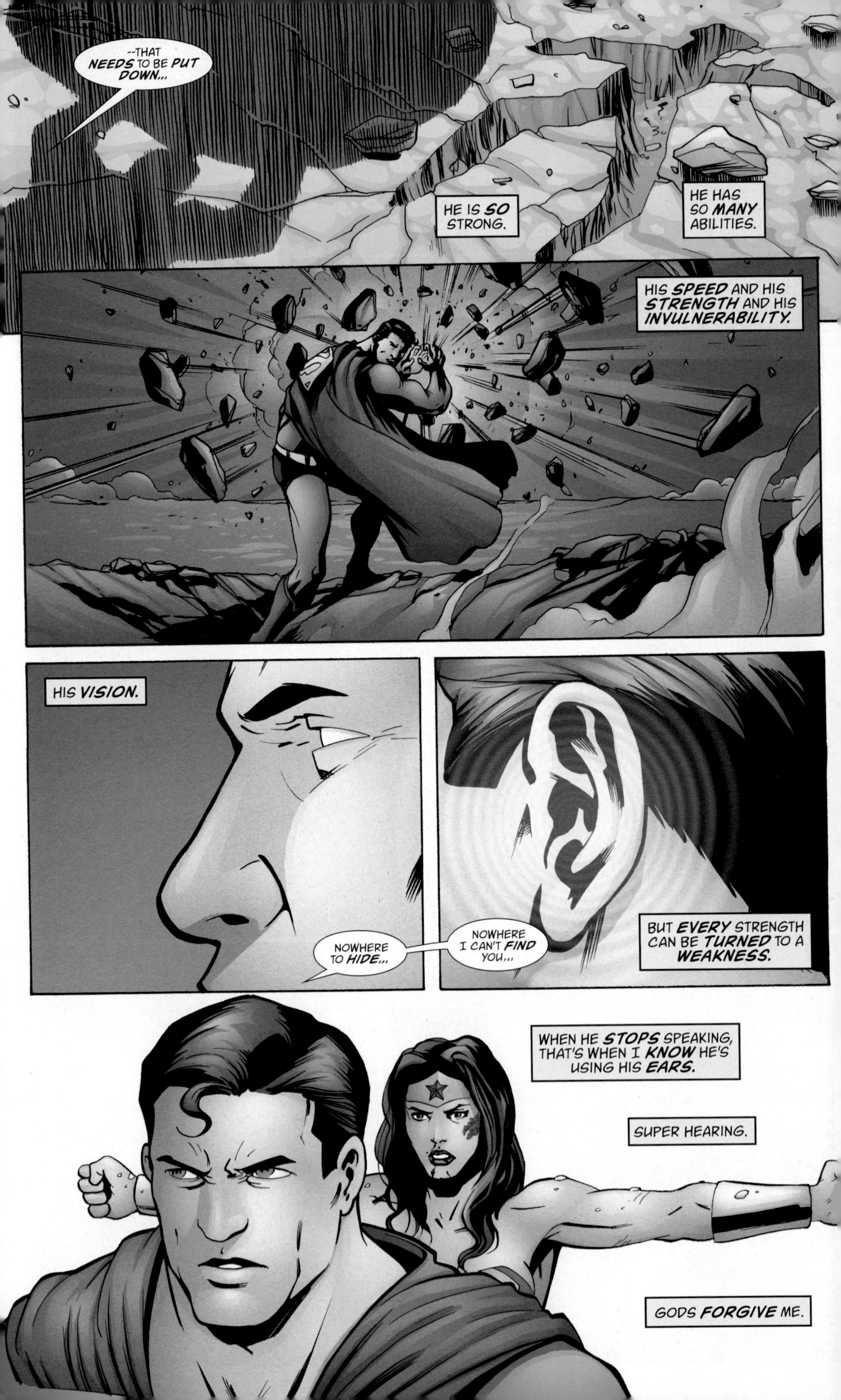
--THAT NEEDS TO BE PUT DOWN...
HE IS SO STRONG.
HE HAS SO MANY ABILITIES.
HIS SPEED AND HIS STRENGTH AND HIS INVULNERABILITY.
HIS VISION.
NOWHERE TO HIDE...
NOWHERE I CAN'T FIND YOU...
BUT EVERY STRENGTH CAN BE TURNED TO A WEAKNESS.
WHEN HE STOPS SPEAKING, THAT'S WHEN I KNOW HE'S USING HIS EARS.
SUPER HEARING.
GODS FORGIVE ME.

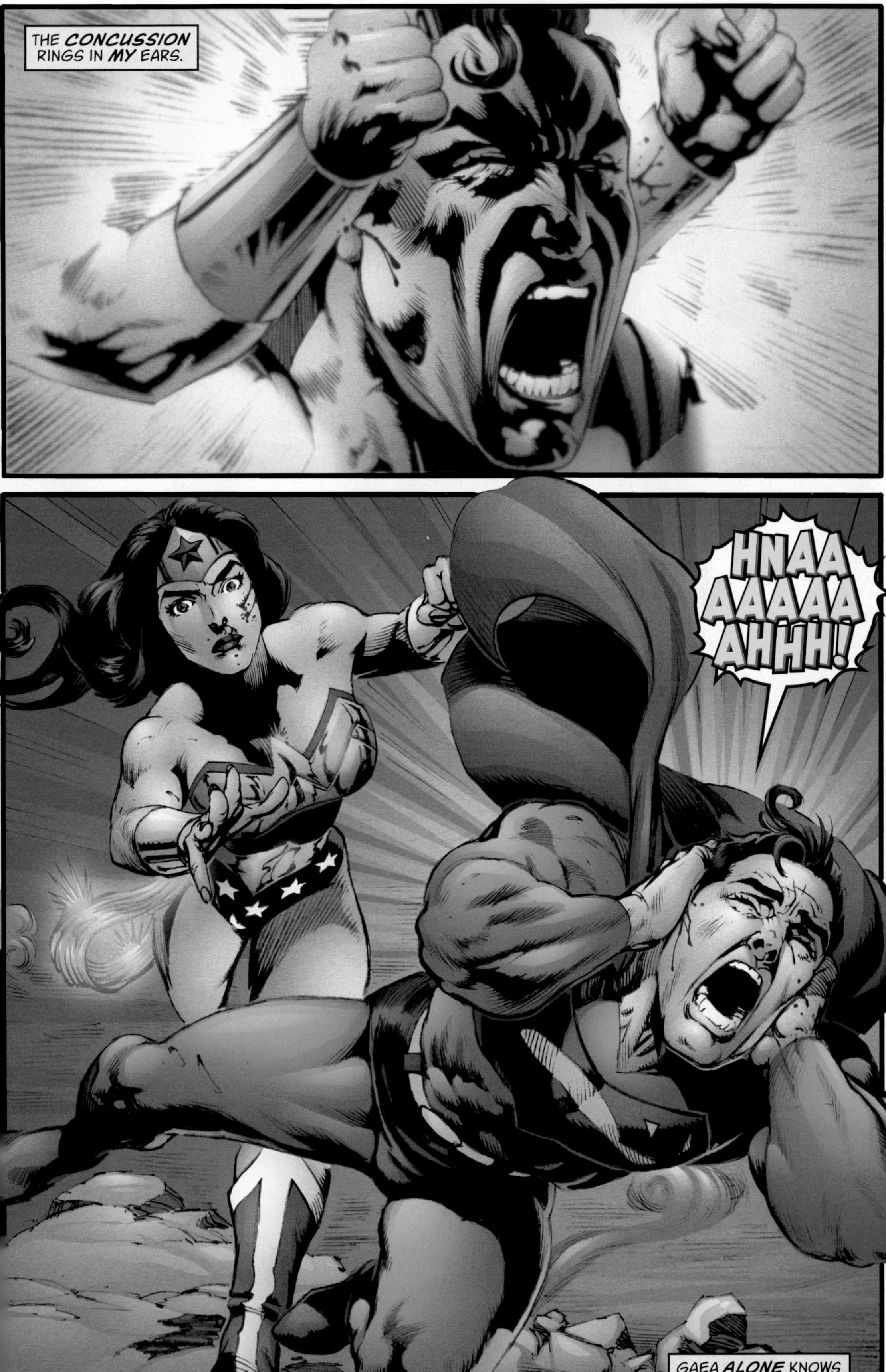
THE CONCUSSION RINGS IN MY EARS.
HNAA AAAAA AHHH!
GAEA ALONE KNOWS WHAT IT DOES TO HIS.

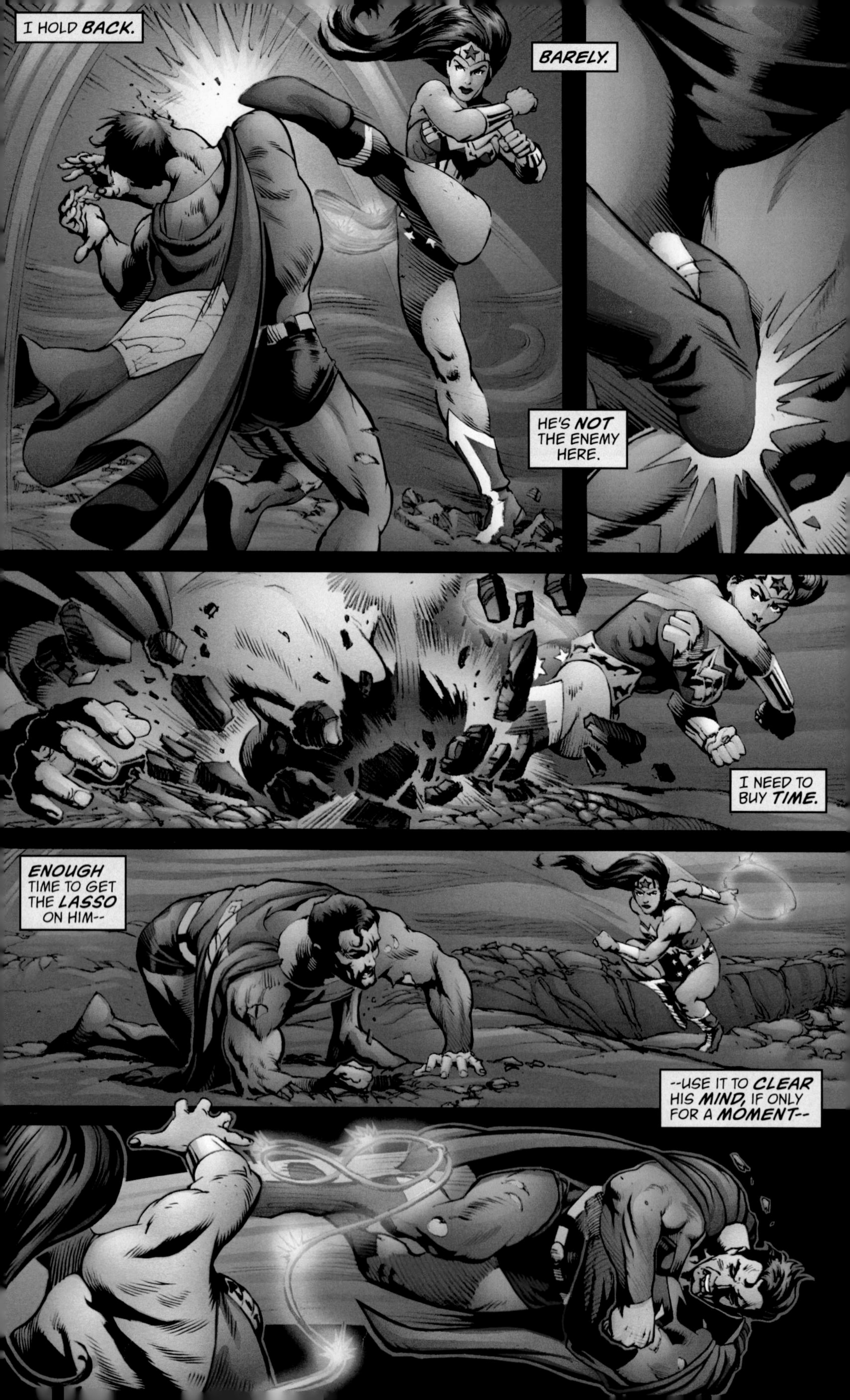
I HOLD BACK.
BARELY.
HE'S NOT THE ENEMY HERE.
I NEED TO BUY TIME.
ENOUGH TIME TO GET THE LASSO ON HIM--
--USE IT TO CLEAR HIS MIND, IF ONLY FOR A MOMENT--

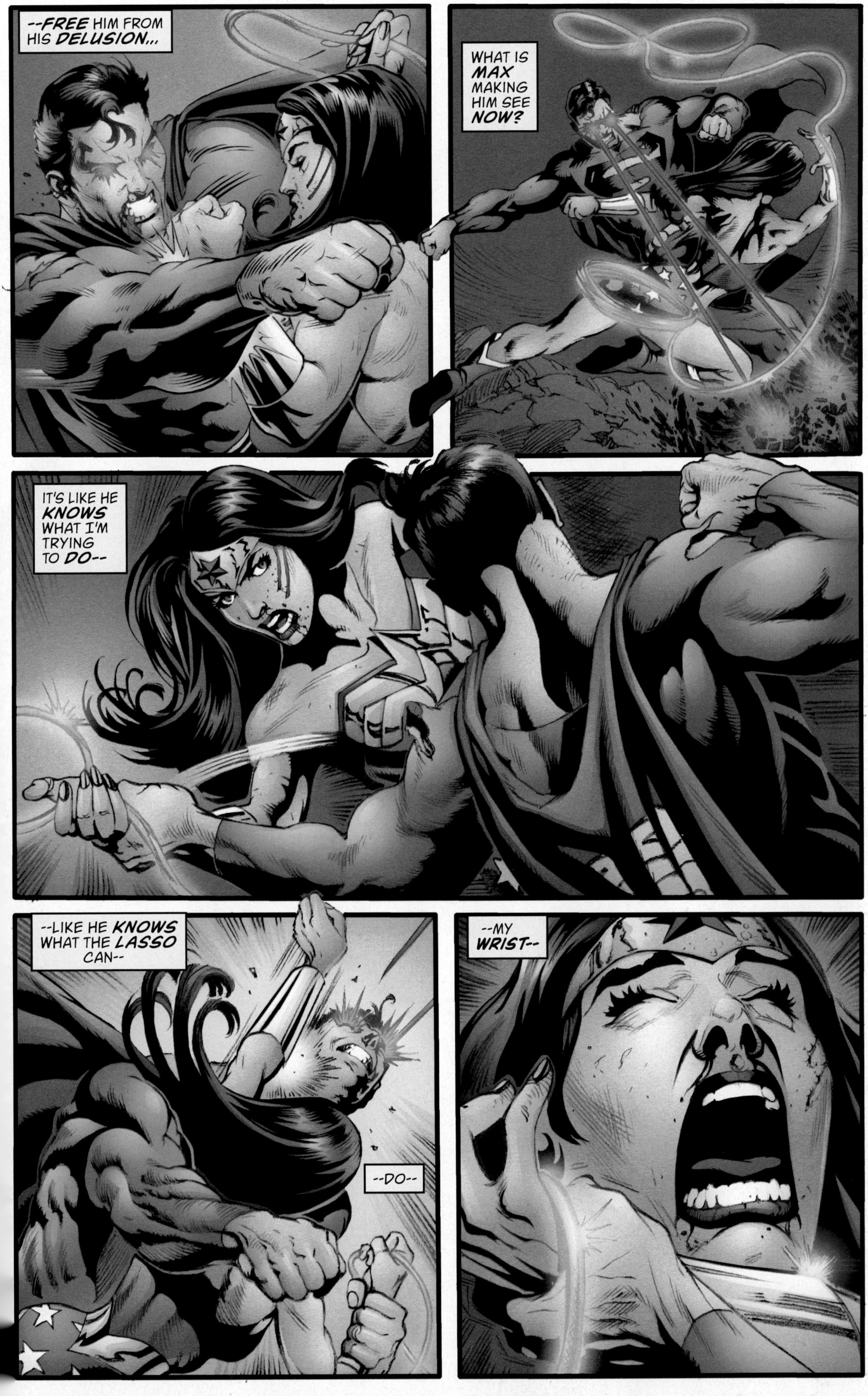
--FREE HIM FROM HIS DELUSION...
WHAT IS MAX MAKING HIM SEE NOW?
IT'S LIKE HE KNOWS WHAT I'M TRYING TO DO--
--LIKE HE KNOWS WHAT THE LASSO CAN--
--DO--
--MY WRIST--

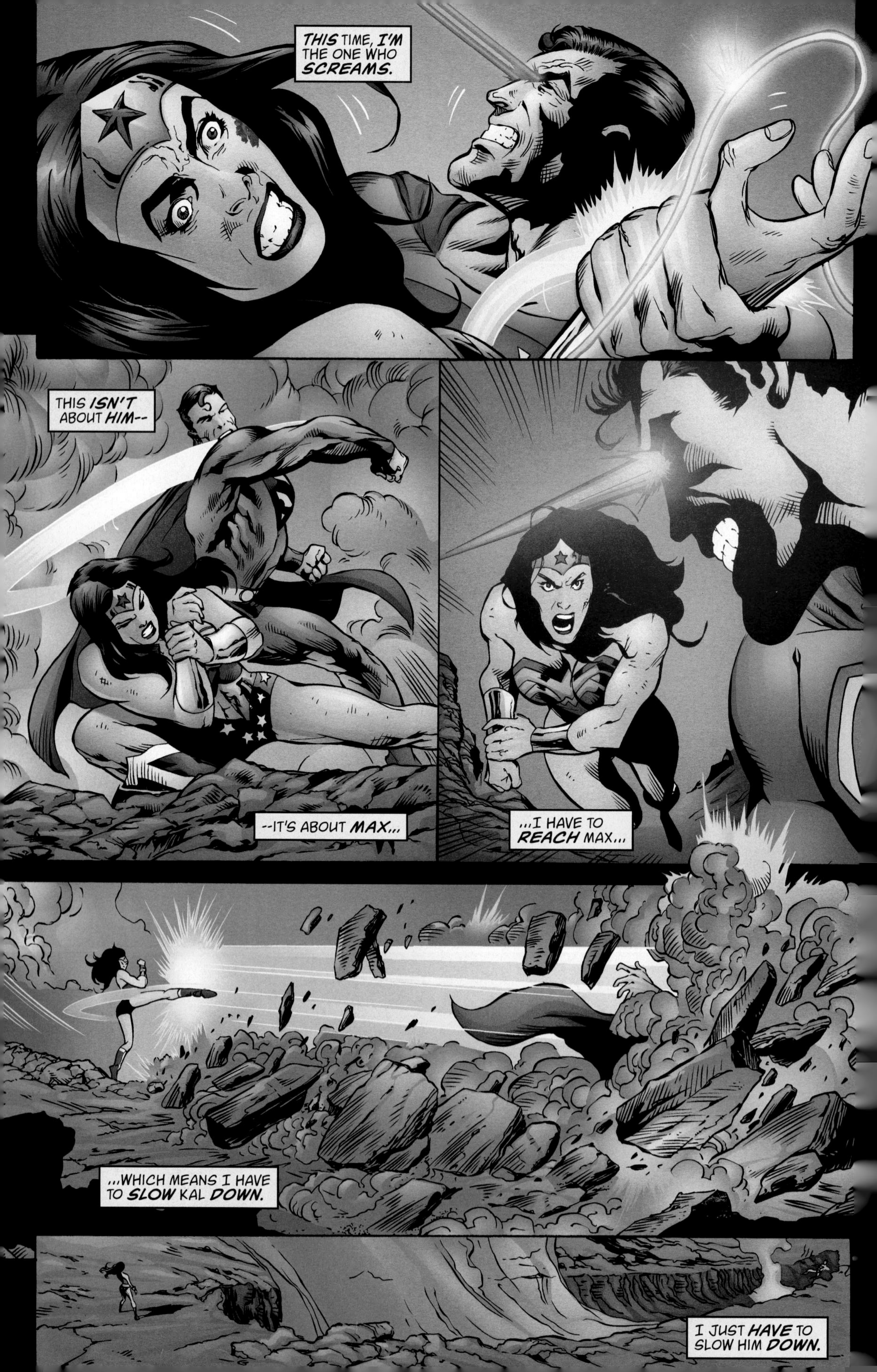
THIS TIME, I'M THE ONE WHO SCREAMS.
THIS ISN'T ABOUT HIM--
--IT'S ABOUT MAX...
...I HAVE TO REACH MAX...
...WHICH MEANS I HAVE TO SLOW KAL DOWN.
I JUST HAVE TO SLOW HIM DOWN.

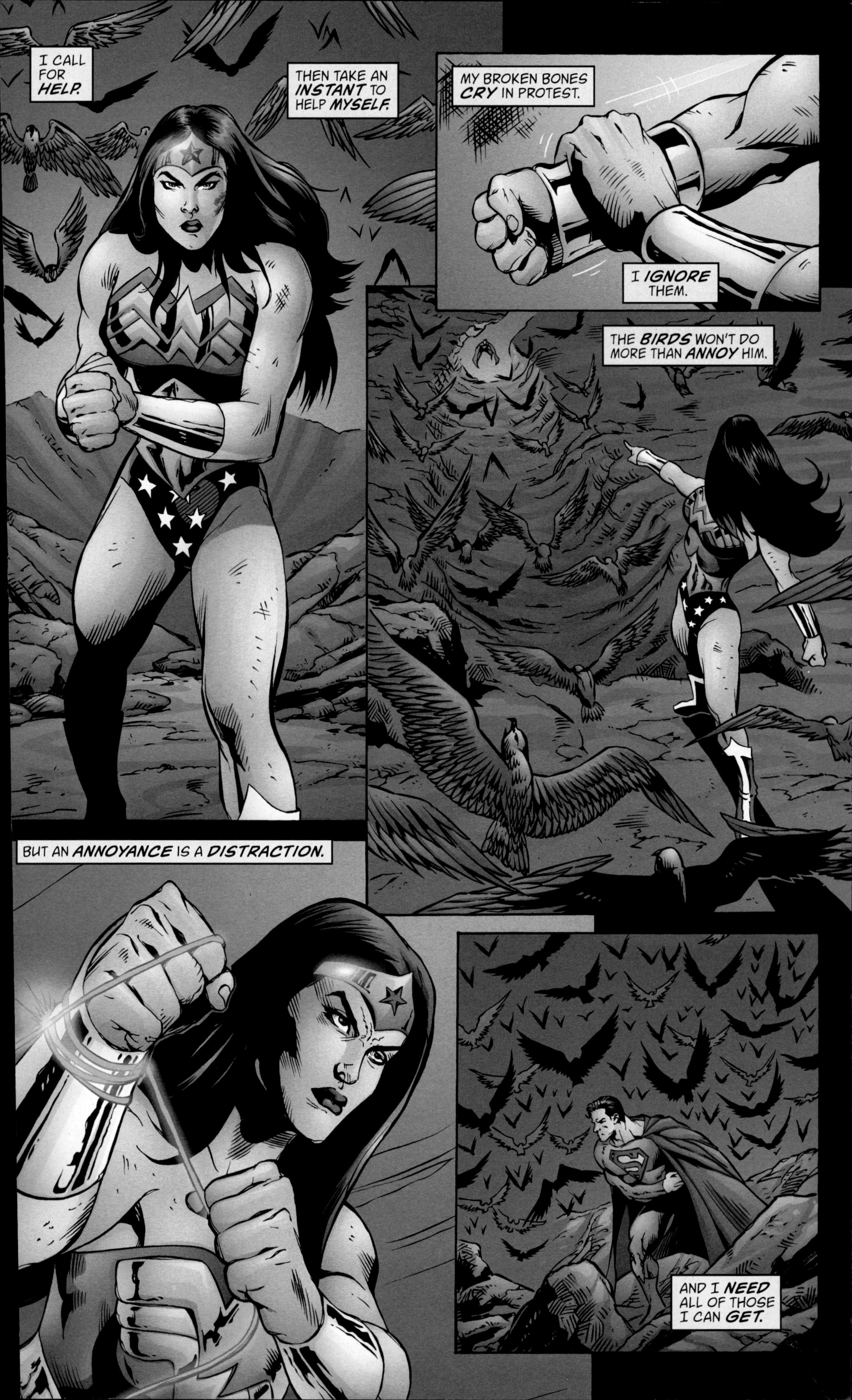
I CALL FOR HELP.
THEN TAKE AN INSTANT TO HELP MYSELF.
MY BROKEN BONES CRY IN PROTEST.
I IGNORE THEM.
THE BIRDS WON'T DO MORE THAN ANNOY HIM.
BUT AN ANNOYANCE IS A DISTRACTION.
AND I NEED ALL OF THOSE I CAN GET.

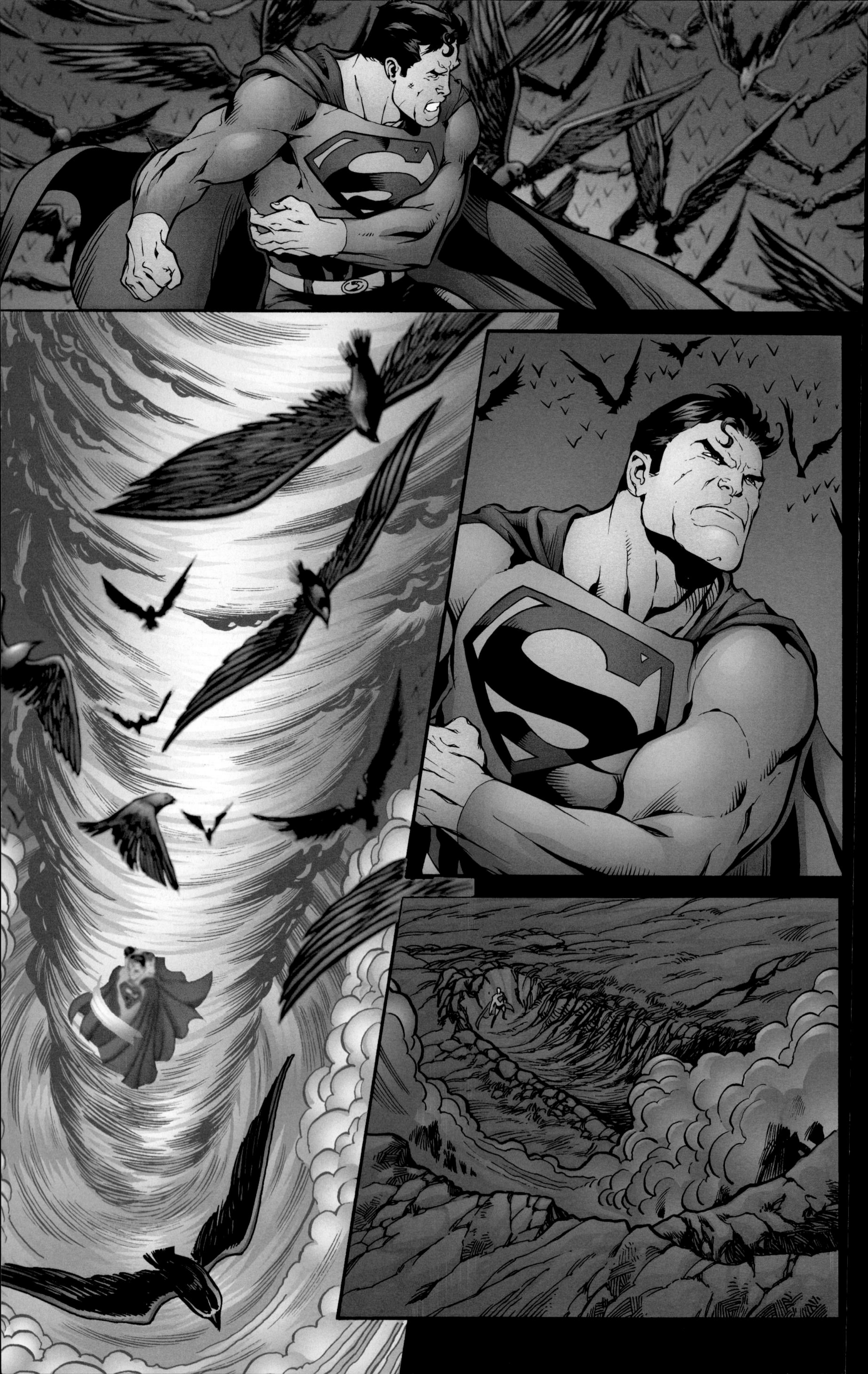

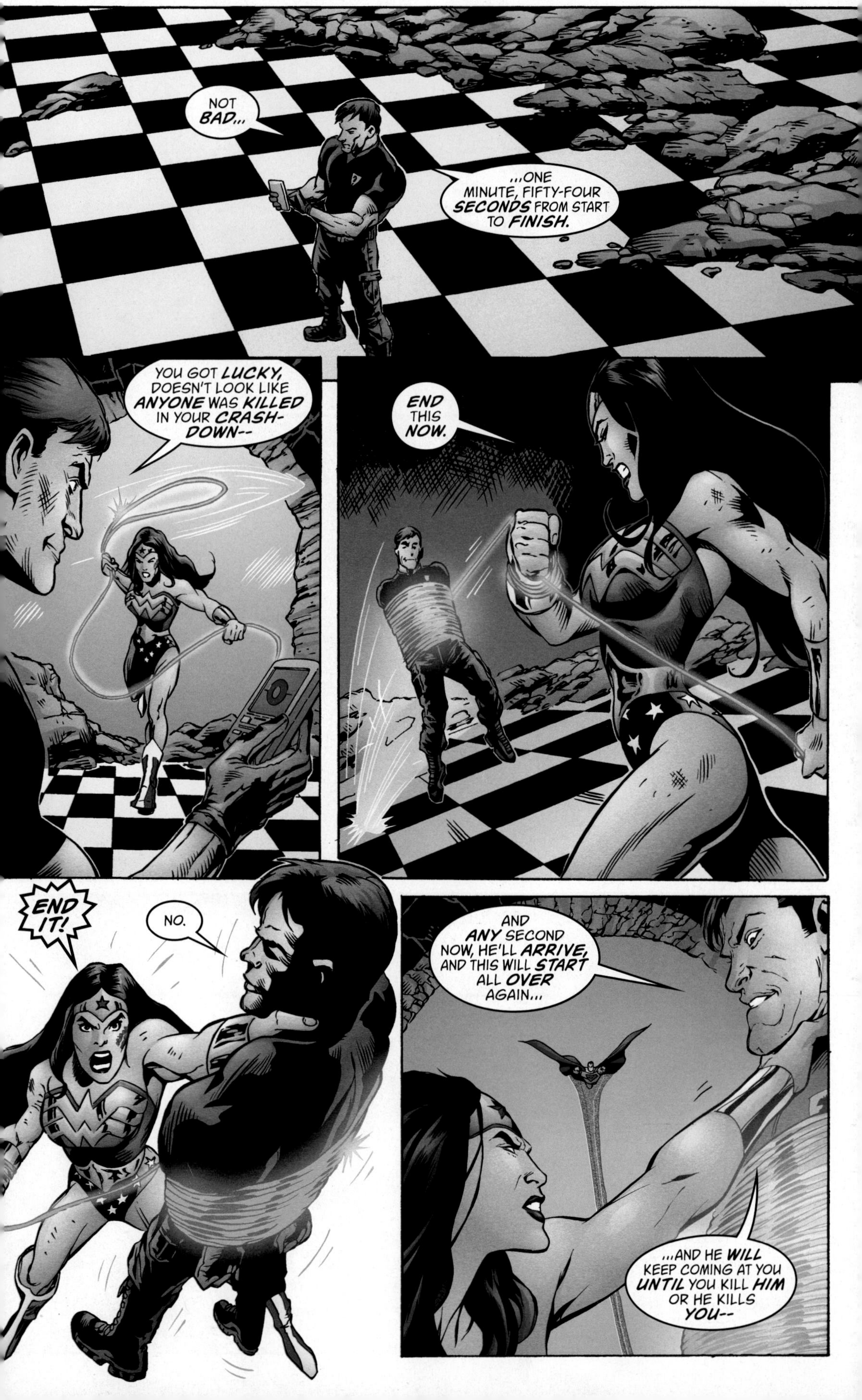
NOT BAD...
...ONE MINUTE, FIFTY-FOUR SECONDS FROM START TO FINISH.
YOU GOT LUCKY, DOESN'T LOOK LIKE ANYONE WAS KILLED IN YOUR CRASH-DOWN--
END THIS NOW.
END IT!
NO.
AND ANY SECOND NOW, HE'LL ARRIVE, AND THIS WILL START ALL OVER AGAIN...
...AND HE WILL KEEP COMING AT YOU UNTIL YOU KILL HIM OR HE KILLS YOU--

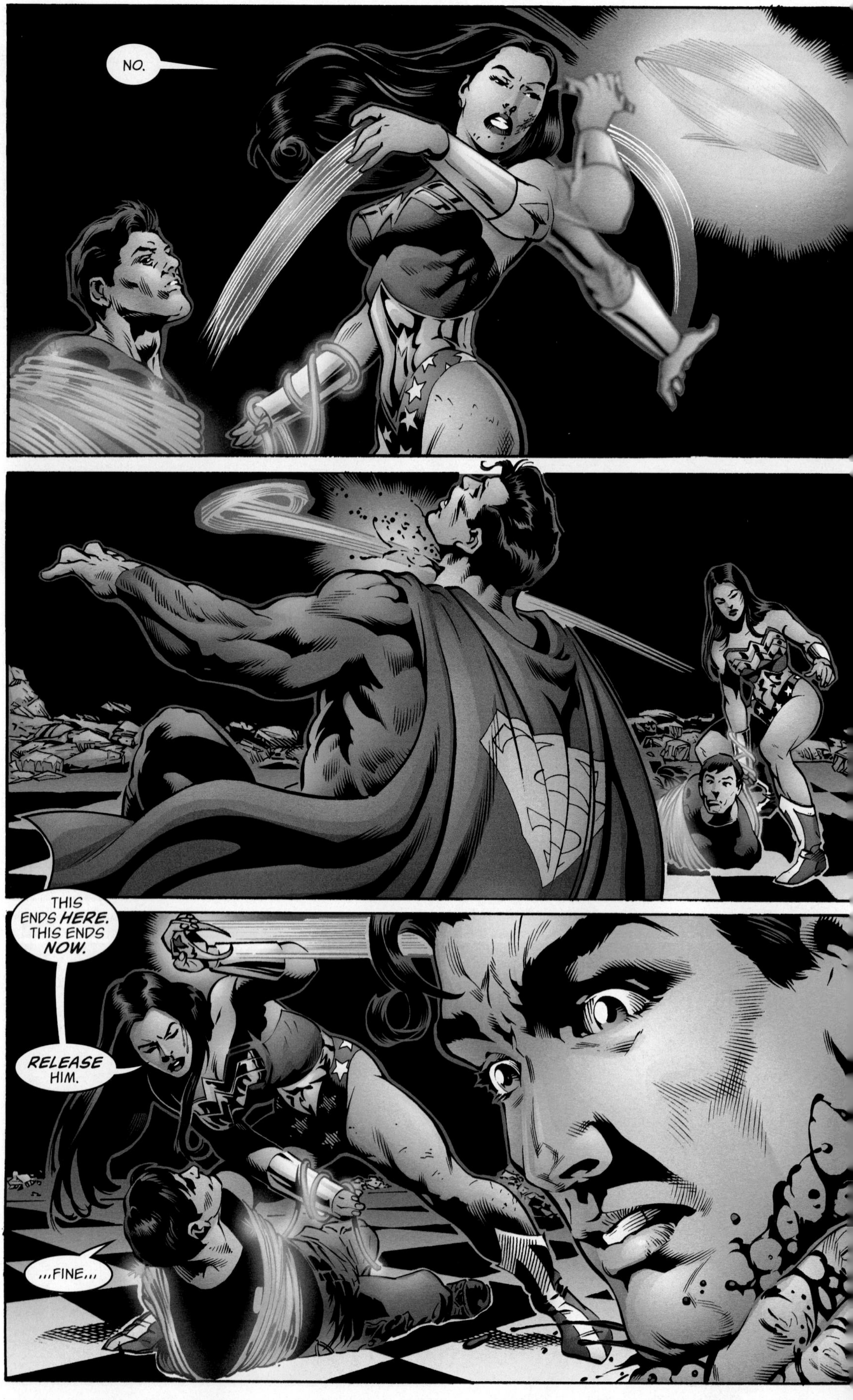
NO.
THIS ENDS *HERE*. THIS ENDS *NOW*.
RELEASE HIM.
...FINE...

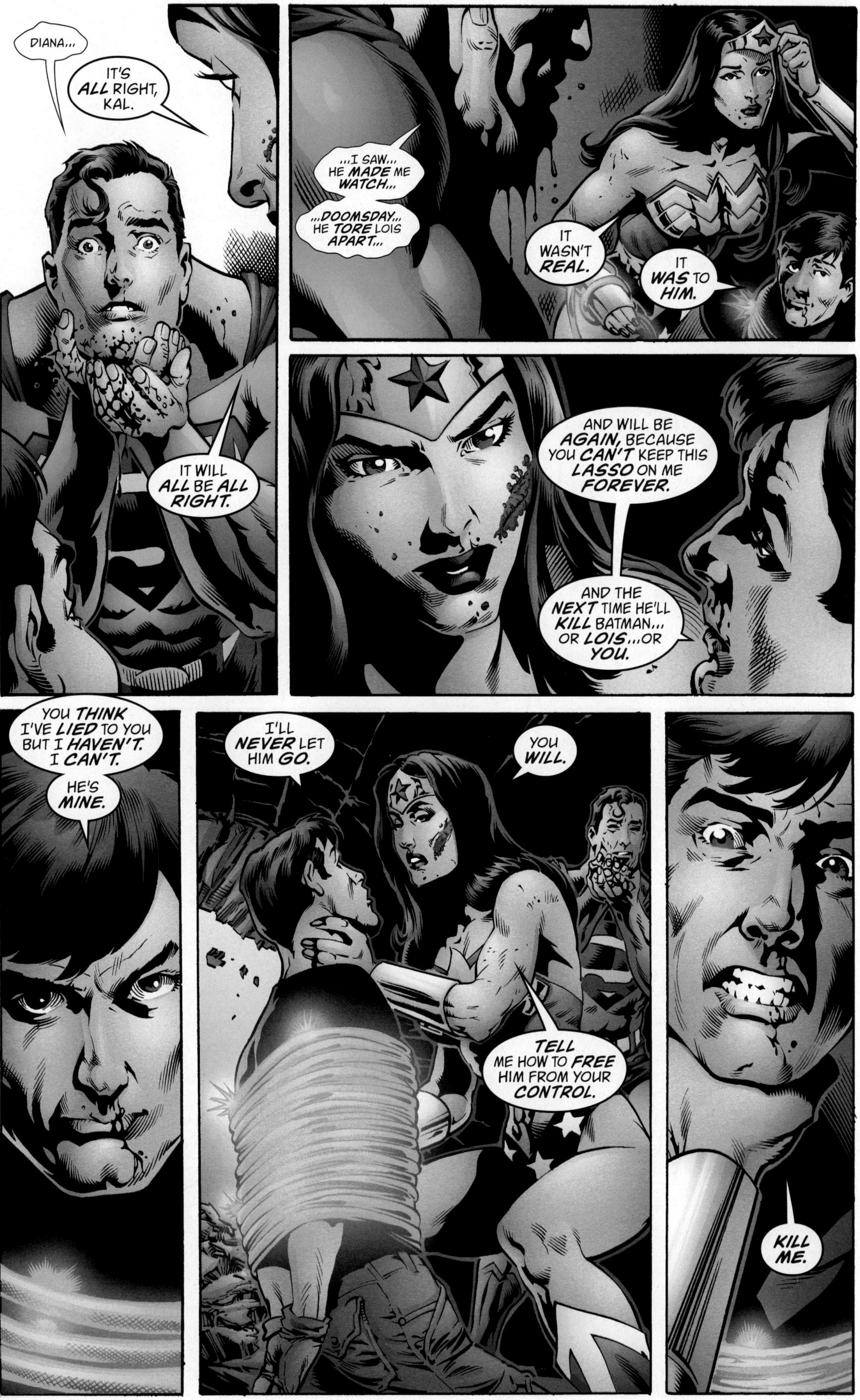
DIANA...
IT'S ALL RIGHT, KAL.
...I SAW... HE MADE ME WATCH...
...DOOMSDAY... HE TORE LOIS APART...
IT WASN'T REAL.
IT WAS TO HIM.
IT WILL ALL BE ALL RIGHT.
AND WILL BE AGAIN, BECAUSE YOU CAN'T KEEP THIS LASSO ON ME FOREVER.
AND THE NEXT TIME HE'LL KILL BATMAN... OR LOIS... OR YOU.
YOU THINK I'VE LIED TO YOU BUT I HAVEN'T. I CAN'T.
HE'S MINE.
I'LL NEVER LET HIM GO.
YOU WILL.
TELL ME HOW TO FREE HIM FROM YOUR CONTROL.
KILL ME.

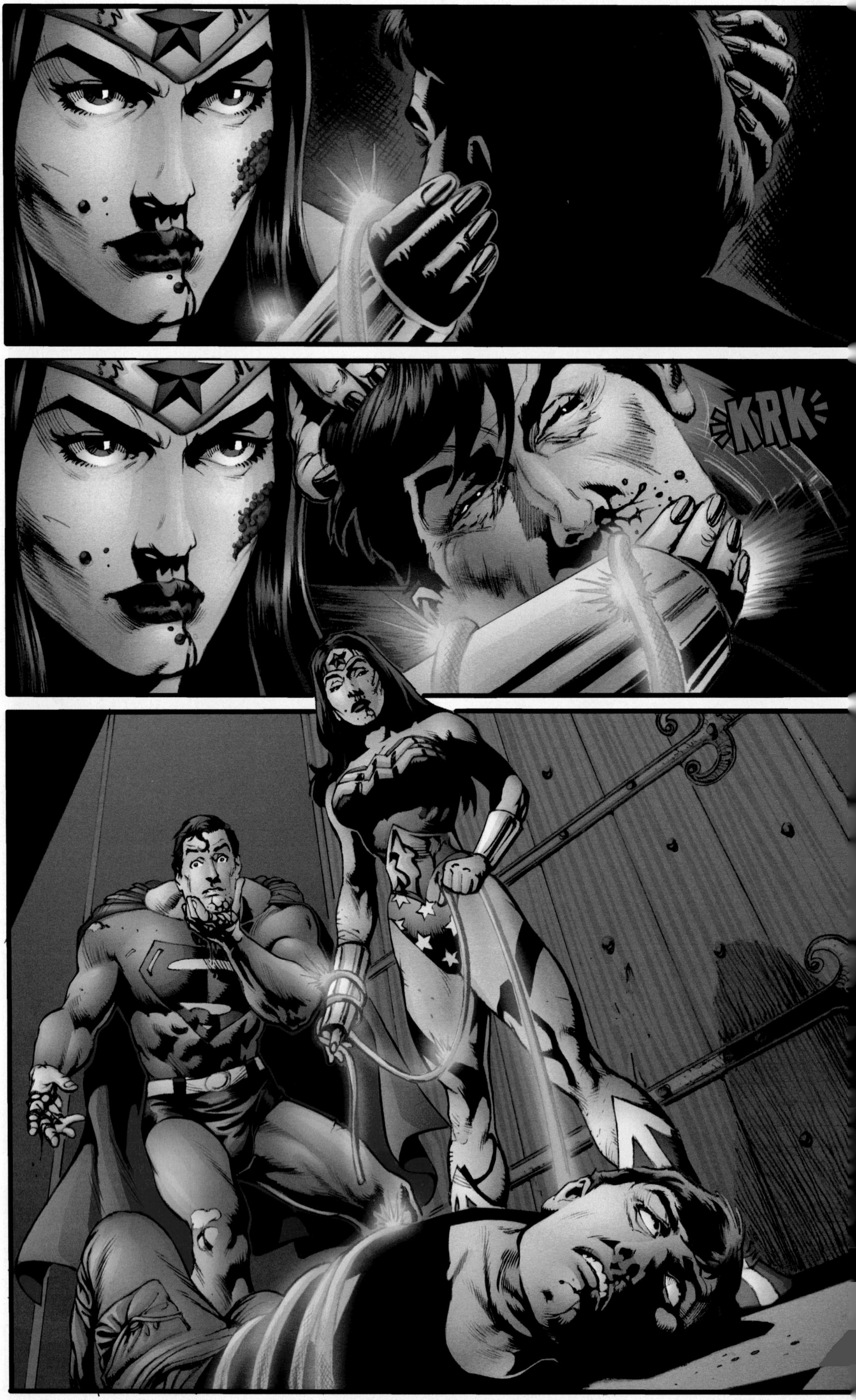
KRK

WONDER WOMAN 220 - ART BY J.G. JONES

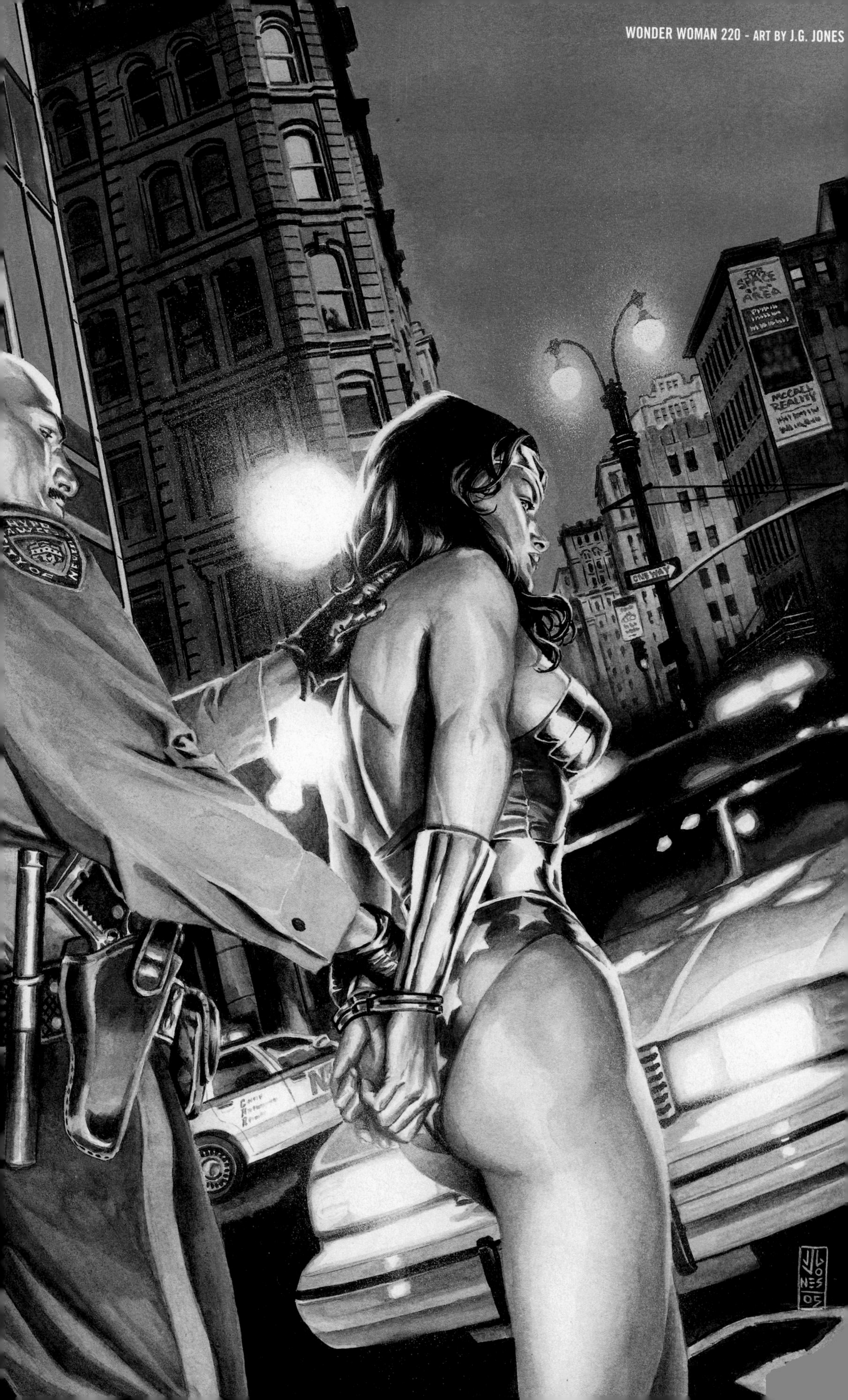
MCCALL REALTY
ONE WAY

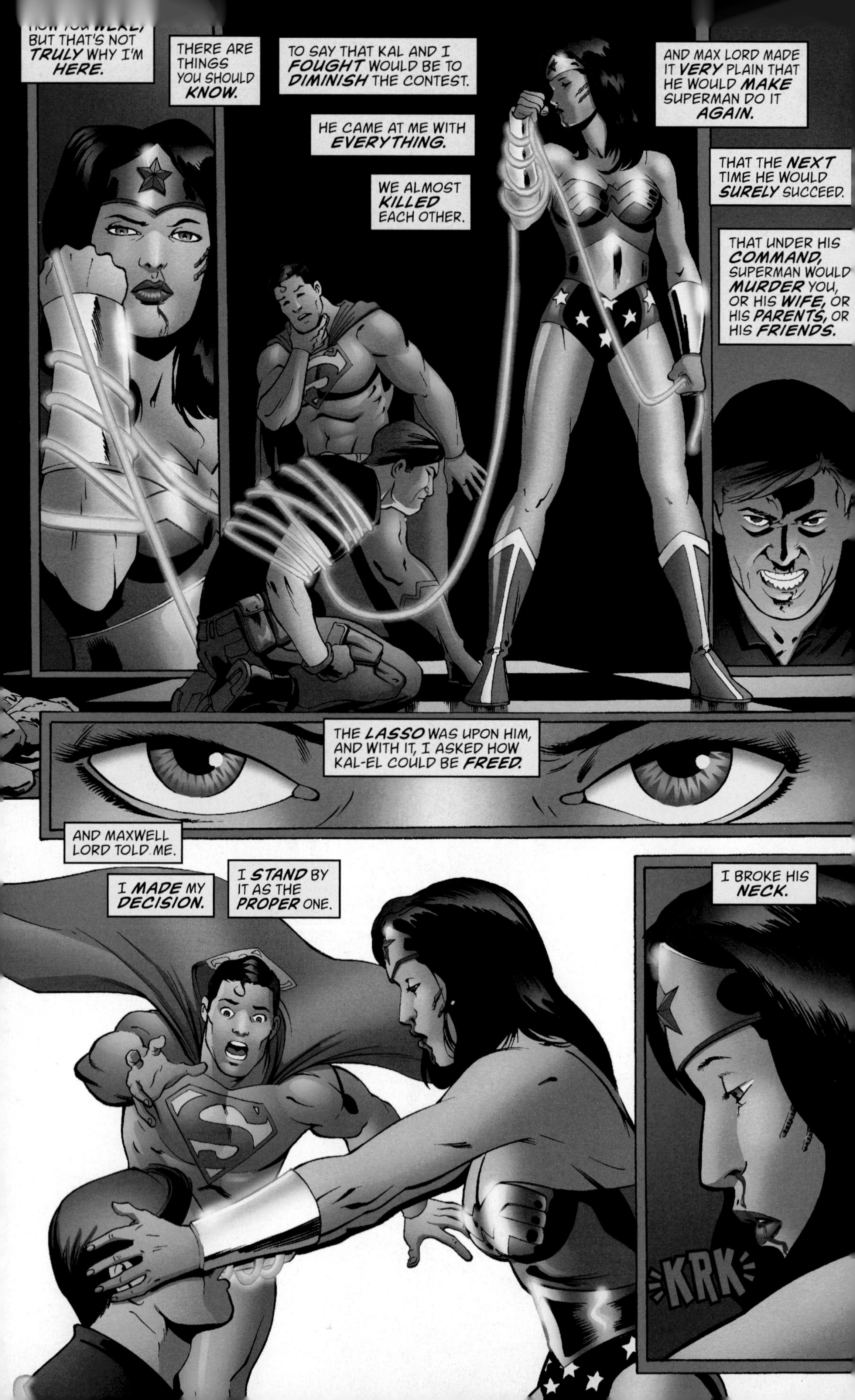
BUT THAT'S NOT TRULY WHY I'M HERE.
THERE ARE THINGS YOU SHOULD KNOW.
TO SAY THAT KAL AND I FOUGHT WOULD BE TO DIMINISH THE CONTEST.
HE CAME AT ME WITH EVERYTHING.
WE ALMOST KILLED EACH OTHER.
AND MAX LORD MADE IT VERY PLAIN THAT HE WOULD MAKE SUPERMAN DO IT AGAIN.
THAT THE NEXT TIME HE WOULD SURELY SUCCEED.
THAT UNDER HIS COMMAND, SUPERMAN WOULD MURDER YOU, OR HIS WIFE, OR HIS PARENTS, OR HIS FRIENDS.
THE LASSO WAS UPON HIM, AND WITH IT, I ASKED HOW KAL-EL COULD BE FREED.
AND MAXWELL LORD TOLD ME.
I MADE MY DECISION.
I STAND BY IT AS THE PROPER ONE.
I BROKE HIS NECK.
KRK

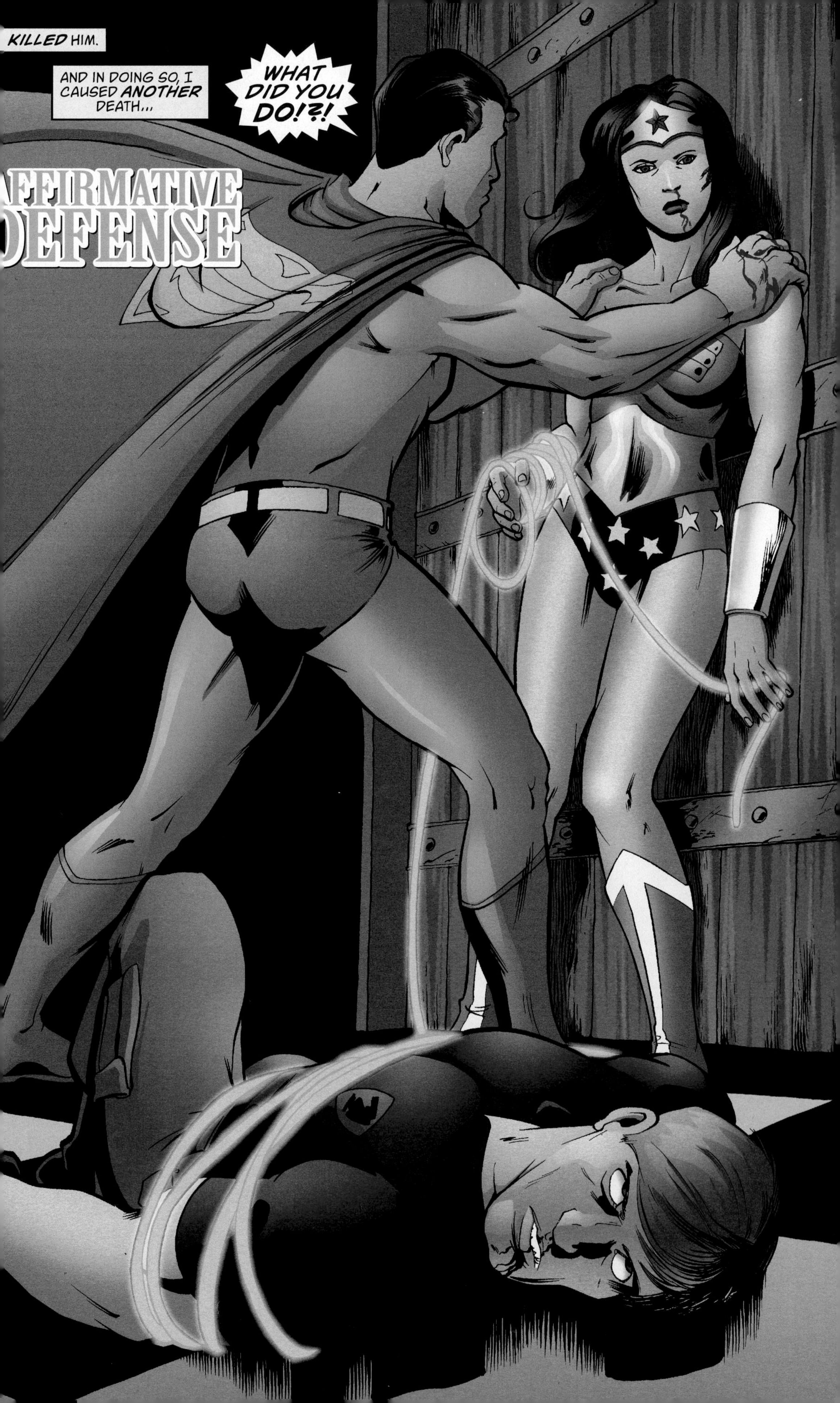

KILLED HIM.
AND IN DOING SO, I CAUSED ANOTHER DEATH...
WHAT DID YOU DO!?!
AFFIRMATIVE DEFENSE

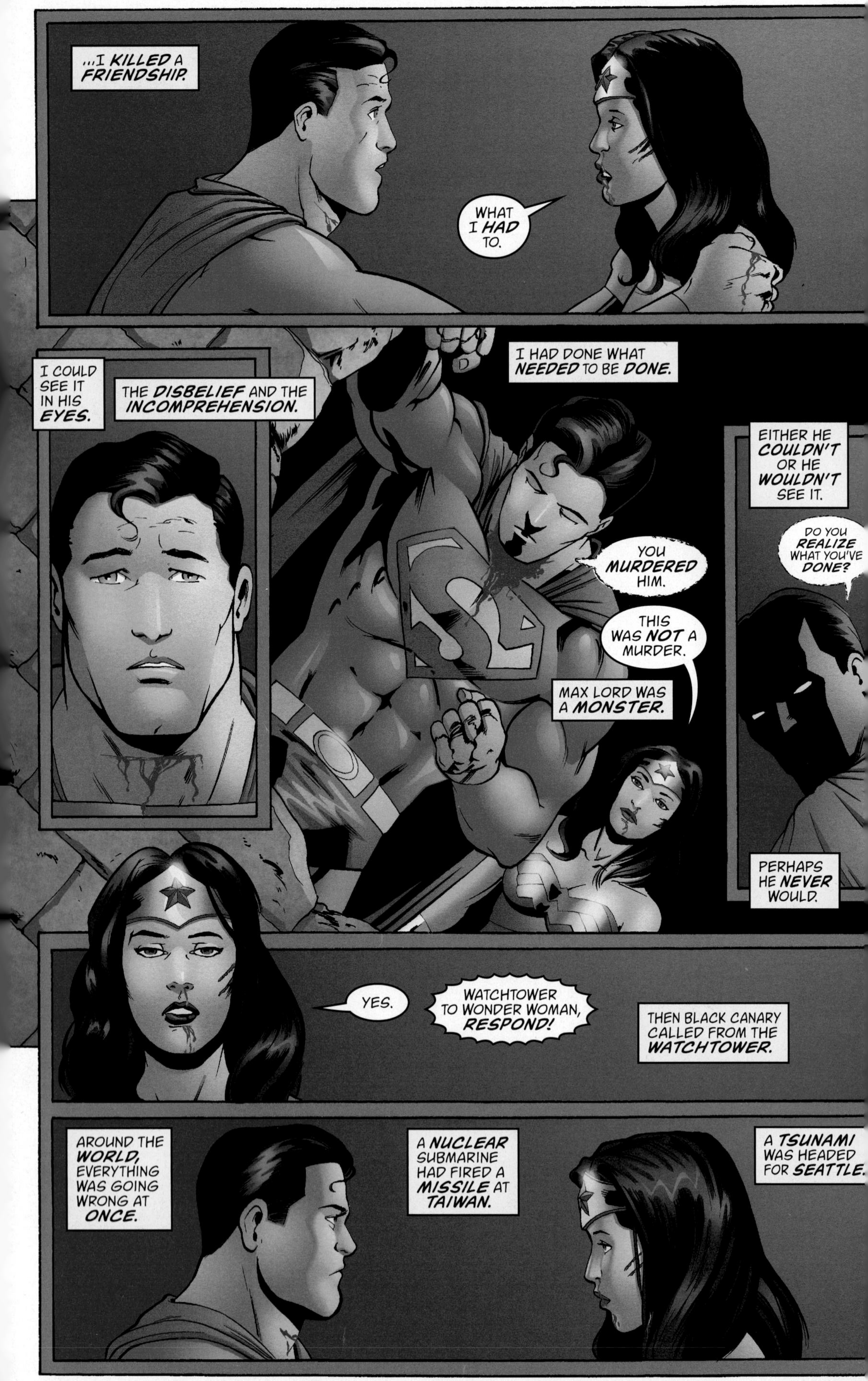

...I KILLED A FRIENDSHIP.
WHAT I HAD TO.
I COULD SEE IT IN HIS EYES.
THE DISBELIEF AND THE INCOMPREHENSION.
I HAD DONE WHAT NEEDED TO BE DONE.
YOU MURDERED HIM.
THIS WAS NOT A MURDER.
MAX LORD WAS A MONSTER.
EITHER HE COULDN'T OR HE WOULDN'T SEE IT.
DO YOU REALIZE WHAT YOU'VE DONE?
PERHAPS HE NEVER WOULD.
YES.
WATCHTOWER TO WONDER WOMAN, RESPOND!
THEN BLACK CANARY CALLED FROM THE WATCHTOWER.
AROUND THE WORLD, EVERYTHING WAS GOING WRONG AT ONCE.
A NUCLEAR SUBMARINE HAD FIRED A MISSILE AT TAIWAN.
A TSUNAMI WAS HEADED FOR SEATTLE.

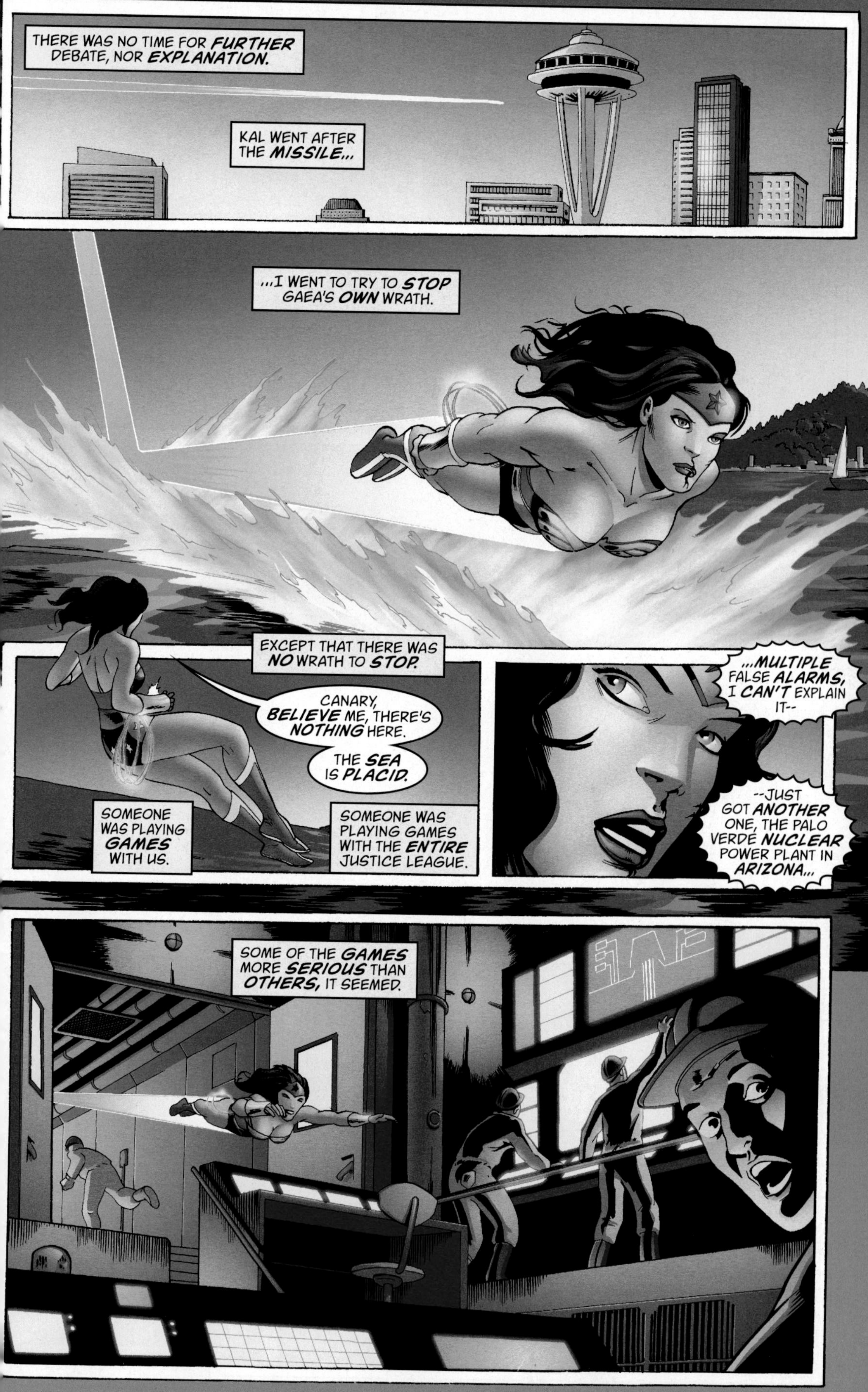
THERE WAS NO TIME FOR FURTHER DEBATE, NOR EXPLANATION.
KAL WENT AFTER THE MISSILE...
...I WENT TO TRY TO STOP GAEA'S OWN WRATH.
EXCEPT THAT THERE WAS NO WRATH TO STOP.
CANARY, BELIEVE ME, THERE'S NOTHING HERE.
THE SEA IS PLACID.
SOMEONE WAS PLAYING GAMES WITH US.
SOMEONE WAS PLAYING GAMES WITH THE ENTIRE JUSTICE LEAGUE.
...MULTIPLE FALSE ALARMS, I CAN'T EXPLAIN IT--
--JUST GOT ANOTHER ONE, THE PALO VERDE NUCLEAR POWER PLANT IN ARIZONA...
SOME OF THE GAMES MORE SERIOUS THAN OTHERS, IT SEEMED.

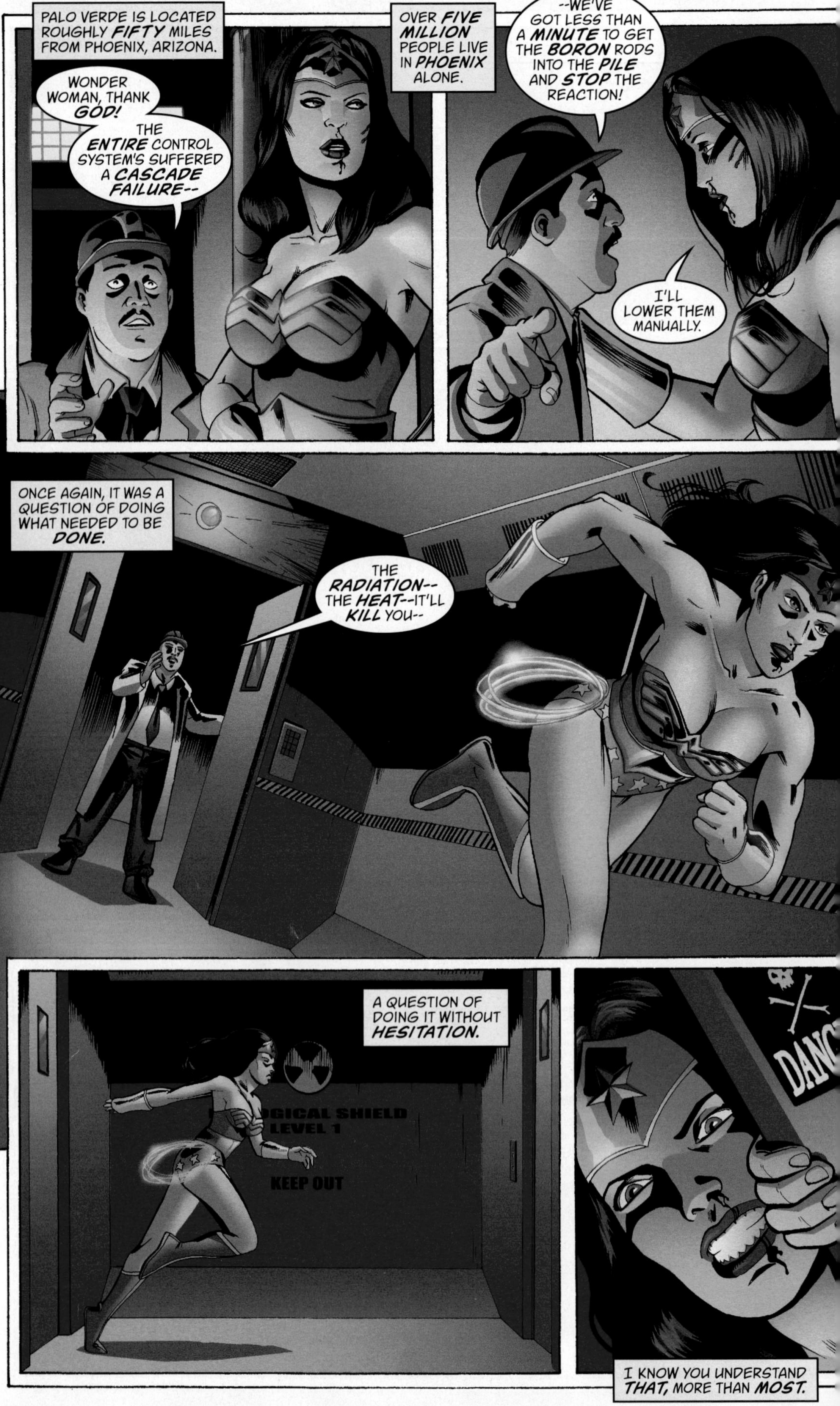

PALO VERDE IS LOCATED ROUGHLY FIFTY MILES FROM PHOENIX, ARIZONA.
WONDER WOMAN, THANK GOD!
THE ENTIRE CONTROL SYSTEM'S SUFFERED A CASCADE FAILURE--
OVER FIVE MILLION PEOPLE LIVE IN PHOENIX ALONE.
--WE'VE GOT LESS THAN A MINUTE TO GET THE BORON RODS INTO THE PILE AND STOP THE REACTION!
I'LL LOWER THEM MANUALLY.
ONCE AGAIN, IT WAS A QUESTION OF DOING WHAT NEEDED TO BE DONE.
THE RADIATION-- THE HEAT--IT'LL KILL YOU--
A QUESTION OF DOING IT WITHOUT HESITATION.
LEVEL 1
KEEP OUT
I KNOW YOU UNDERSTAND THAT, MORE THAN MOST.

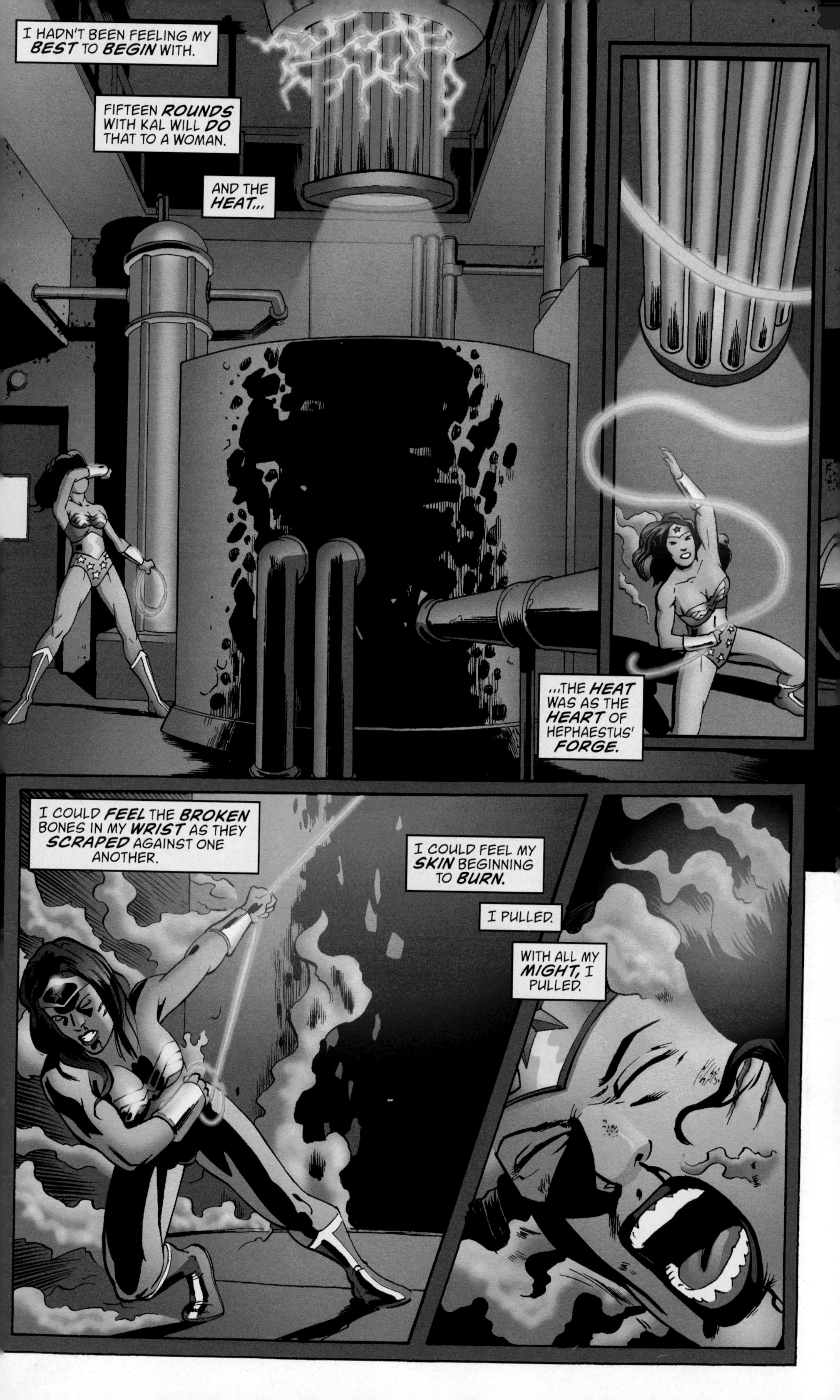
I HADN'T BEEN FEELING MY BEST TO BEGIN WITH.
FIFTEEN ROUNDS WITH KAL WILL DO THAT TO A WOMAN.
AND THE HEAT...
...THE HEAT WAS AS THE HEART OF HEPHAESTUS' FORGE.
I COULD FEEL THE BROKEN BONES IN MY WRIST AS THEY SCRAPED AGAINST ONE ANOTHER.
I COULD FEEL MY SKIN BEGINNING TO BURN.
I PULLED.
WITH ALL MY MIGHT, I PULLED.

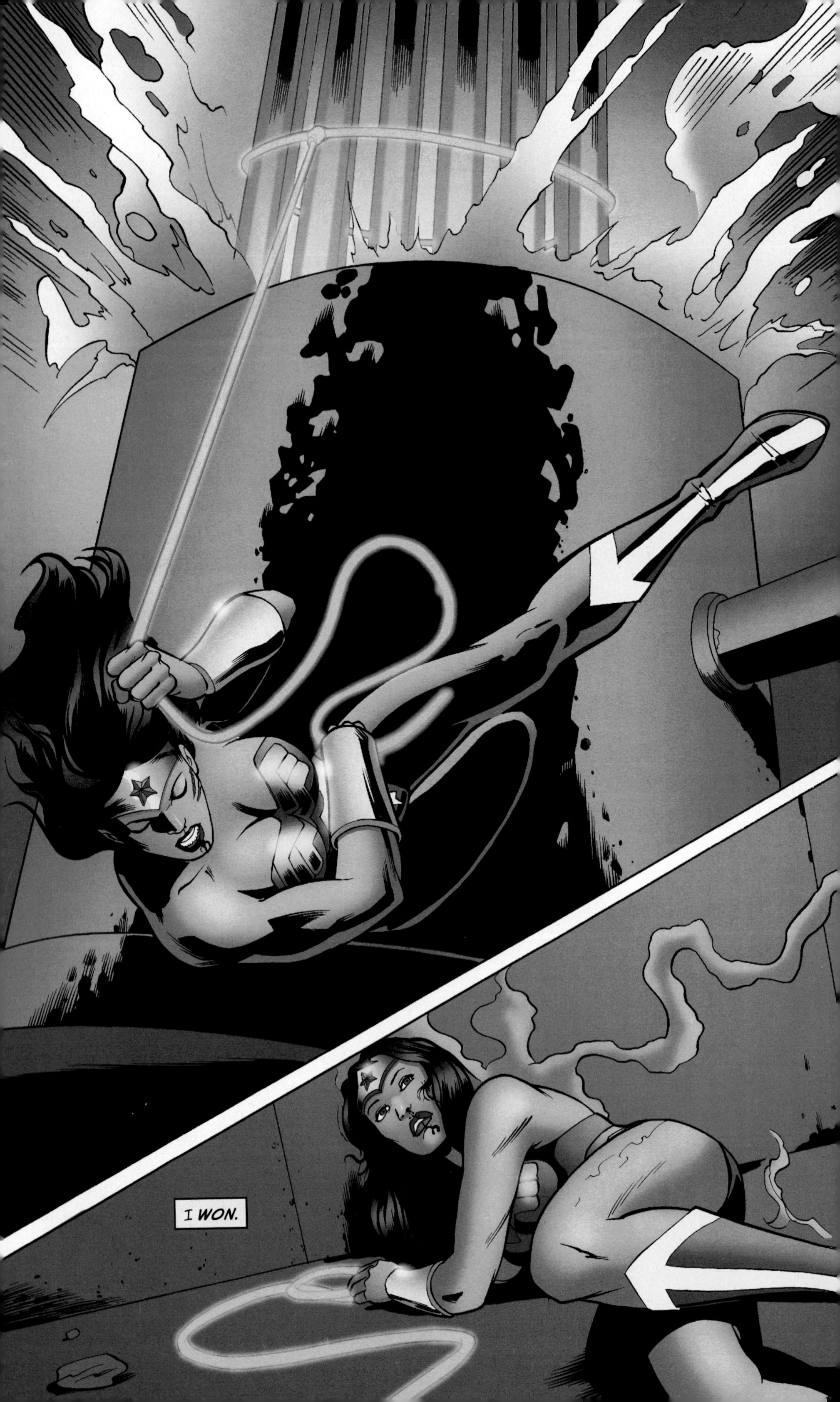
I WON.

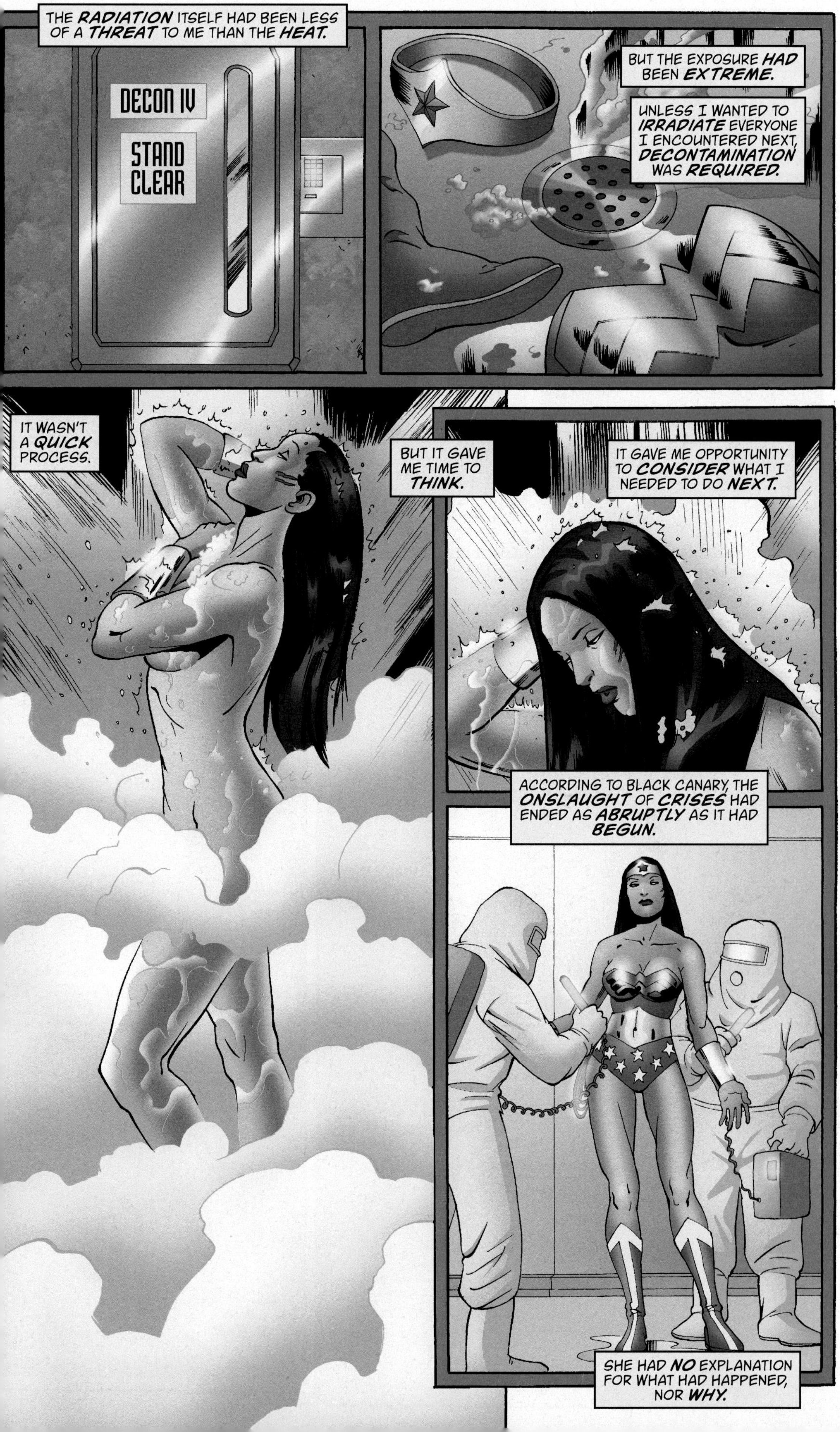
THE RADIATION ITSELF HAD BEEN LESS OF A THREAT TO ME THAN THE HEAT.
DECON IV
STAND CLEAR
BUT THE EXPOSURE HAD BEEN EXTREME.
UNLESS I WANTED TO IRRADIATE EVERYONE I ENCOUNTERED NEXT, DECONTAMINATION WAS REQUIRED.
IT WASN'T A QUICK PROCESS.
BUT IT GAVE ME TIME TO THINK.
IT GAVE ME OPPORTUNITY TO CONSIDER WHAT I NEEDED TO DO NEXT.
ACCORDING TO BLACK CANARY, THE ONSLAUGHT OF CRISES HAD ENDED AS ABRUPTLY AS IT HAD BEGUN.
SHE HAD NO EXPLANATION FOR WHAT HAD HAPPENED, NOR WHY.

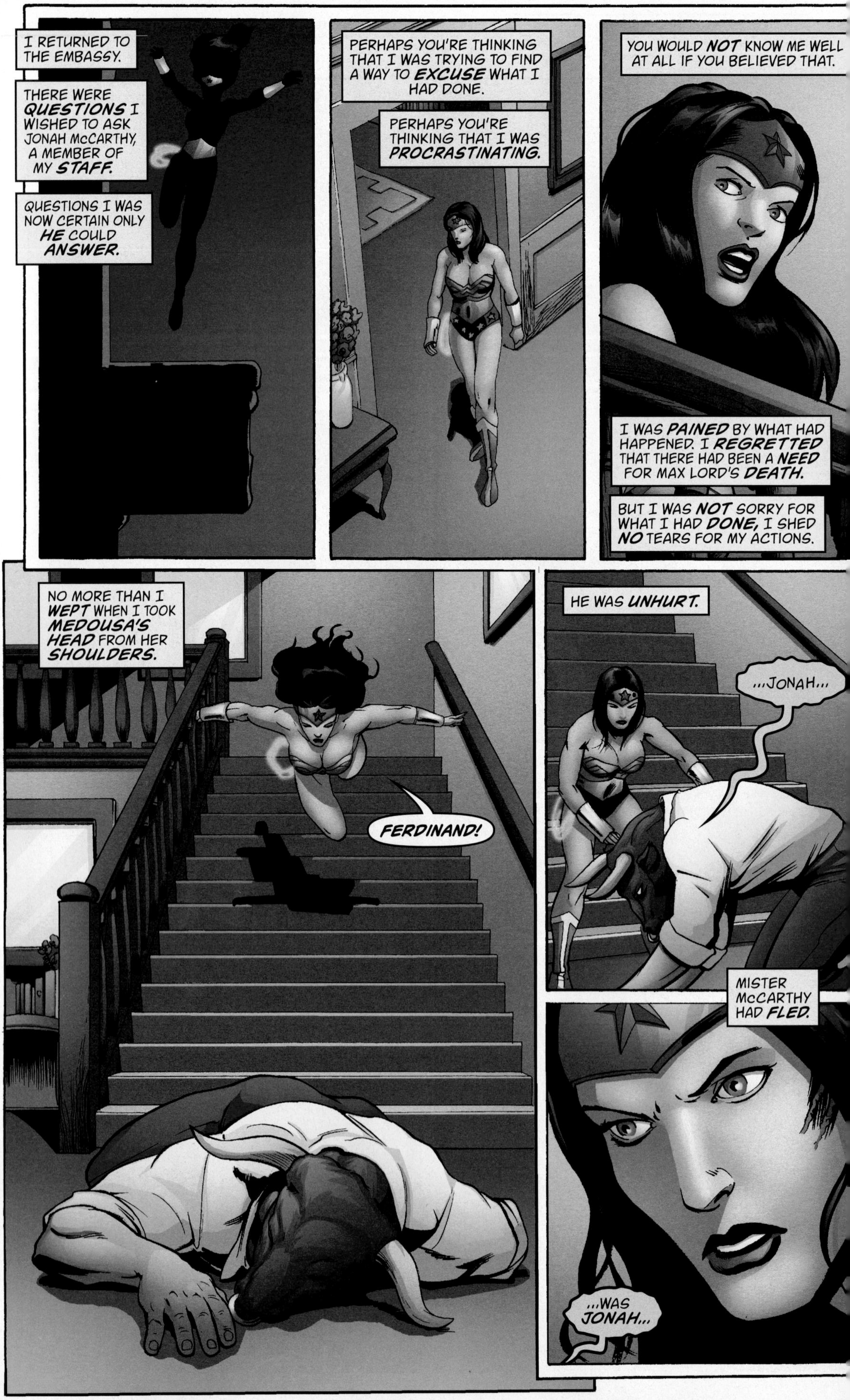

I RETURNED TO THE EMBASSY.
THERE WERE QUESTIONS I WISHED TO ASK JONAH McCARTHY, A MEMBER OF MY STAFF.
QUESTIONS I WAS NOW CERTAIN ONLY HE COULD ANSWER.
PERHAPS YOU'RE THINKING THAT I WAS TRYING TO FIND A WAY TO EXCUSE WHAT I HAD DONE.
PERHAPS YOU'RE THINKING THAT I WAS PROCRASTINATING.
YOU WOULD NOT KNOW ME WELL AT ALL IF YOU BELIEVED THAT.
I WAS PAINED BY WHAT HAD HAPPENED. I REGRETTED THAT THERE HAD BEEN A NEED FOR MAX LORD'S DEATH.
BUT I WAS NOT SORRY FOR WHAT I HAD DONE, I SHED NO TEARS FOR MY ACTIONS.
NO MORE THAN I WEPT WHEN I TOOK MEDOUSA'S HEAD FROM HER SHOULDERS.
FERDINAND!
HE WAS UNHURT.
...JONAH...
MISTER McCARTHY HAD FLED.
...WAS JONAH...

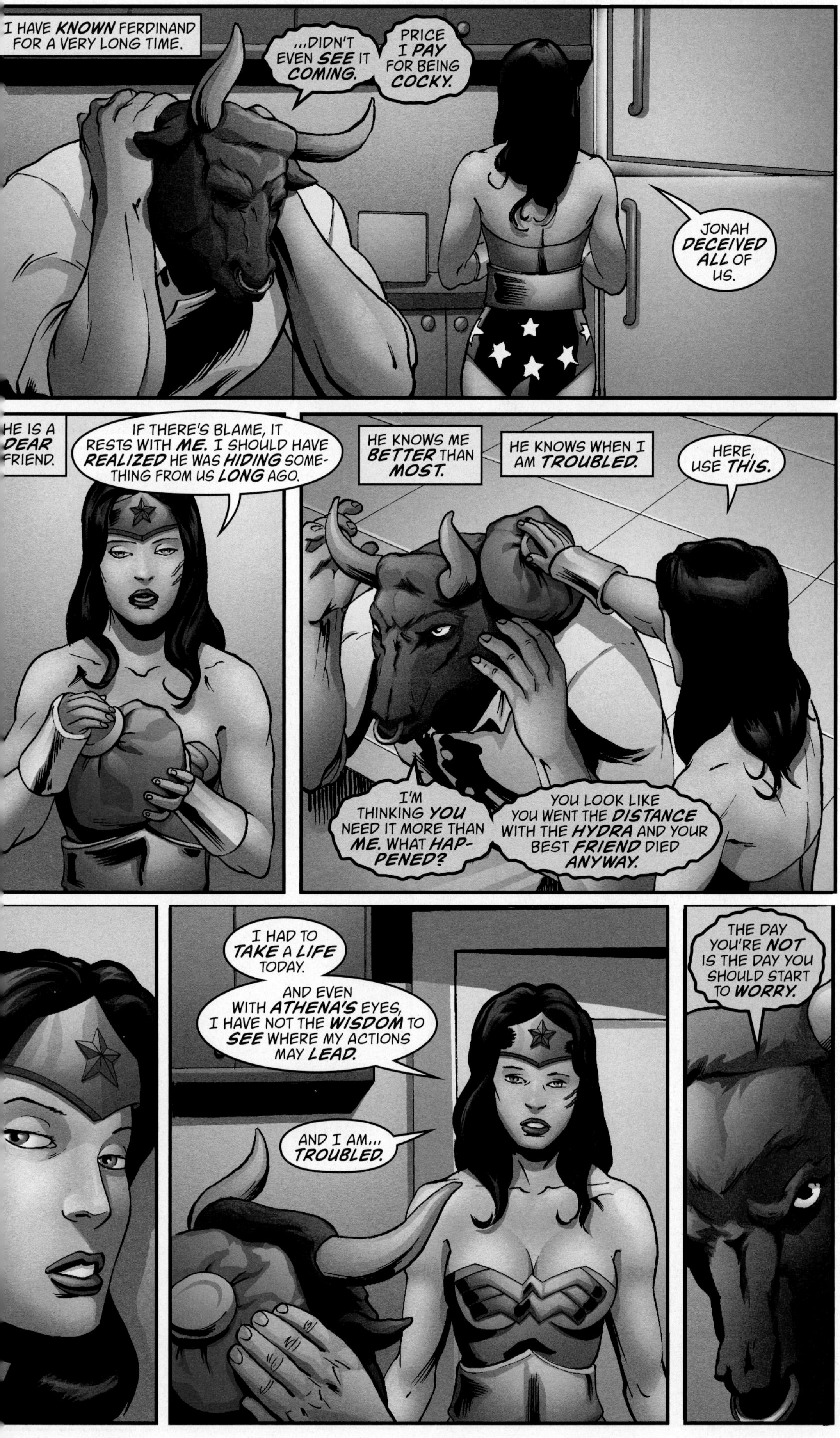

I HAVE KNOWN FERDINAND FOR A VERY LONG TIME.
...DIDN'T EVEN SEE IT COMING.
PRICE I PAY FOR BEING COCKY.
JONAH DECEIVED ALL OF US.
HE IS A DEAR FRIEND.
IF THERE'S BLAME, IT RESTS WITH ME. I SHOULD HAVE REALIZED HE WAS HIDING SOME-THING FROM US LONG AGO.
HE KNOWS ME BETTER THAN MOST.
HE KNOWS WHEN I AM TROUBLED.
HERE, USE THIS.
I'M THINKING YOU NEED IT MORE THAN ME. WHAT HAP-PENED?
YOU LOOK LIKE YOU WENT THE DISTANCE WITH THE HYDRA AND YOUR BEST FRIEND DIED ANYWAY.
I HAD TO TAKE A LIFE TODAY.
AND EVEN WITH ATHENA'S EYES, I HAVE NOT THE WISDOM TO SEE WHERE MY ACTIONS MAY LEAD.
AND I AM... TROUBLED.
THE DAY YOU'RE NOT IS THE DAY YOU SHOULD START TO WORRY.

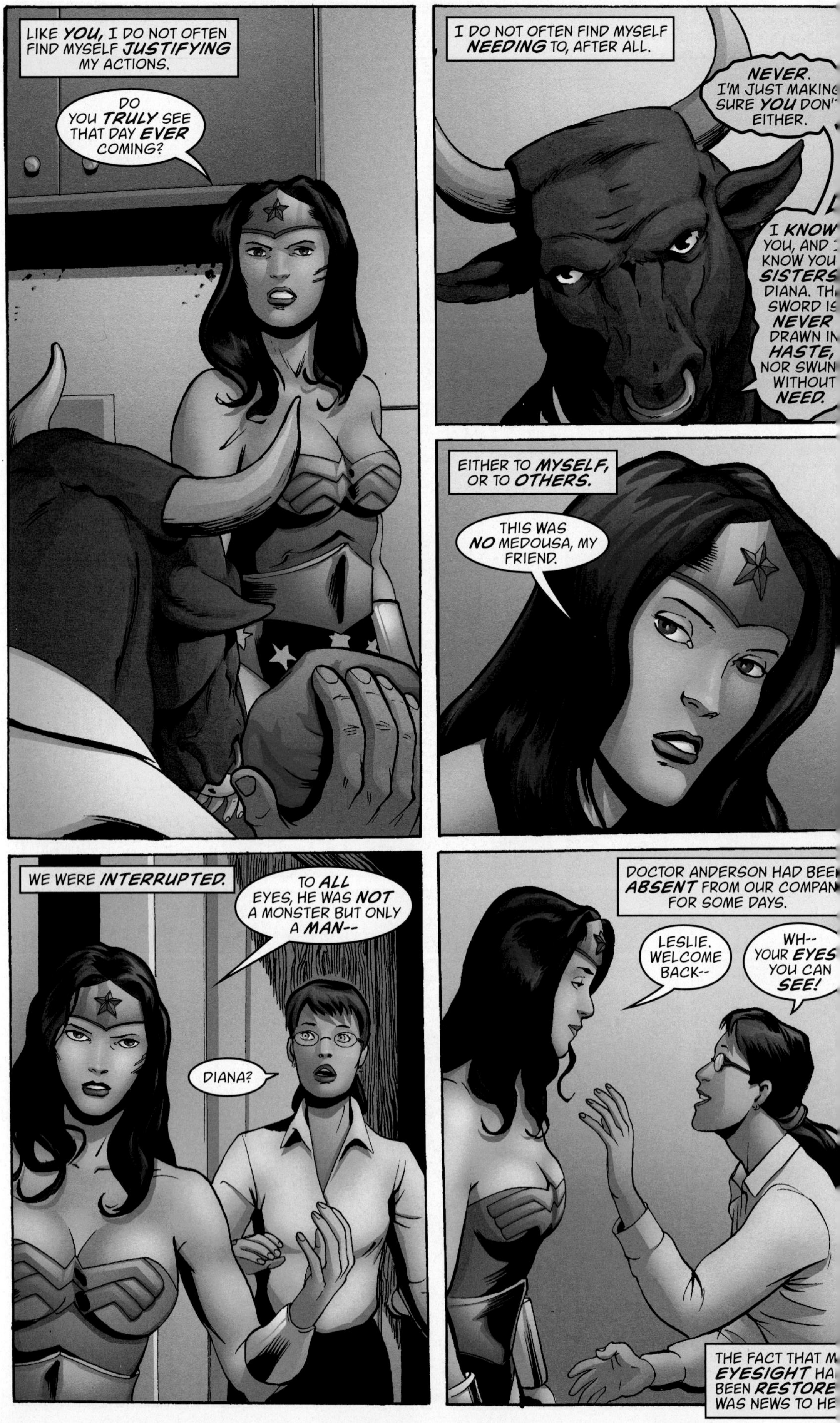
LIKE YOU, I DO NOT OFTEN FIND MYSELF JUSTIFYING MY ACTIONS.
DO YOU TRULY SEE THAT DAY EVER COMING?
I DO NOT OFTEN FIND MYSELF NEEDING TO, AFTER ALL.
NEVER. I'M JUST MAKIN SURE YOU DON EITHER.
I KNOW YOU, AND KNOW YOU SISTERS DIANA. TH SWORD IS NEVER DRAWN IN HASTE, NOR SWUN WITHOUT NEED.
EITHER TO MYSELF, OR TO OTHERS.
THIS WAS NO MEDOUSA, MY FRIEND.
WE WERE INTERRUPTED.
TO ALL EYES, HE WAS NOT A MONSTER BUT ONLY A MAN--
DIANA?
DOCTOR ANDERSON HAD BEE ABSENT FROM OUR COMPAN FOR SOME DAYS.
LESLIE. WELCOME BACK--
WH-- YOUR EYES YOU CAN SEE!
THE FACT THAT M EYESIGHT HA BEEN RESTORE WAS NEWS TO HE

FERDINAND HAD **BE-IEVED** HER ABSENCE **IS** DOING, THAT HE **HAD DRIVEN** LESLIE AWAY.

HELLO, LESLIE.

EVEN **WITHOUT** ATHENA'S **VISION**, THE FACT THAT SHE **DOES** IS PLAIN FOR **ALL** TO SEE.

THAT SHE COULD NOT **POSSIBLY** FEEL FOR HIM WHAT HE FEELS FOR **HER.**

FERDINAND.

PLAIN TO ALL SAVE THE TWO OF THEM.

I'M...I'M **GLAD** YOU CAME **BACK.** I'D **THOUGHT...**

NO, IT'S...IT **WASN'T** ABOUT **YOU...**

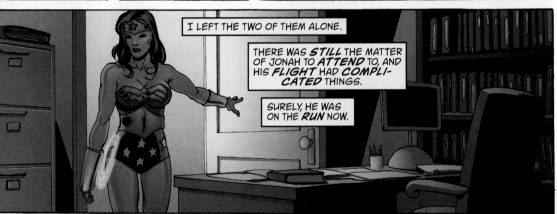

I LEFT THE TWO OF THEM ALONE.

THERE WAS **STILL** THE MATTER OF JONAH TO **ATTEND** TO, AND HIS **FLIGHT** HAD **COMPLI-CATED** THINGS.

SURELY, HE WAS ON THE **RUN** NOW.

WHERE HE **WAS,** AND **WHERE** HE WAS **GOING,** I DID NOT KNOW.

BUT A **SEARCH** OF HIS **OFFICE** SEEMED IN ORDER.

THERE WAS **NOT** MUCH TO **FIND.**

BUT WHAT I **FOUND** WAS **ENOUGH.**

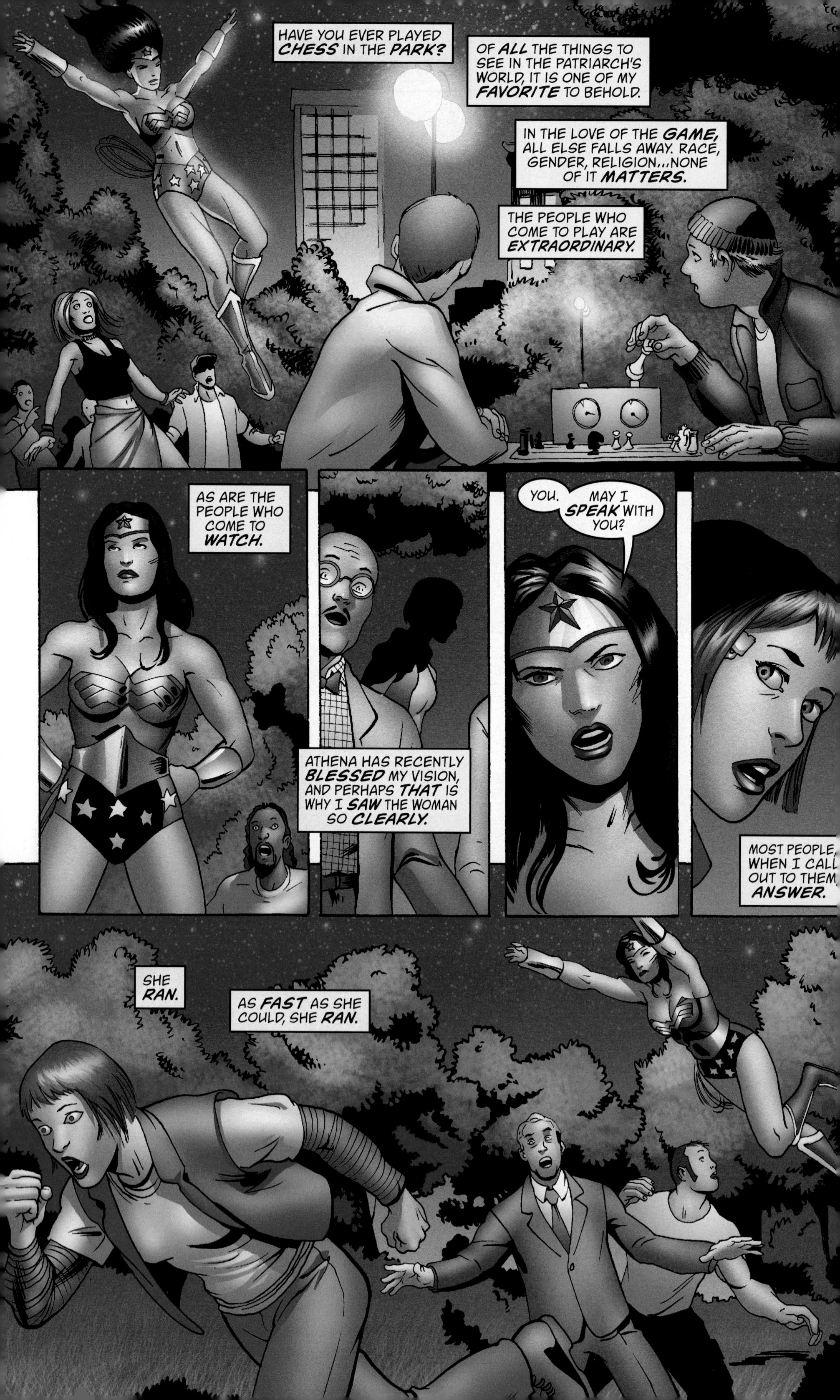
HAVE YOU EVER PLAYED CHESS IN THE PARK?
OF ALL THE THINGS TO SEE IN THE PATRIARCH'S WORLD, IT IS ONE OF MY FAVORITE TO BEHOLD.
IN THE LOVE OF THE GAME, ALL ELSE FALLS AWAY. RACE, GENDER, RELIGION...NONE OF IT MATTERS.
THE PEOPLE WHO COME TO PLAY ARE EXTRAORDINARY.
AS ARE THE PEOPLE WHO COME TO WATCH.
ATHENA HAS RECENTLY BLESSED MY VISION, AND PERHAPS THAT IS WHY I SAW THE WOMAN SO CLEARLY.
YOU.
MAY I SPEAK WITH YOU?
MOST PEOPLE, WHEN I CALL OUT TO THEM ANSWER.
SHE RAN.
AS FAST AS SHE COULD, SHE RAN.

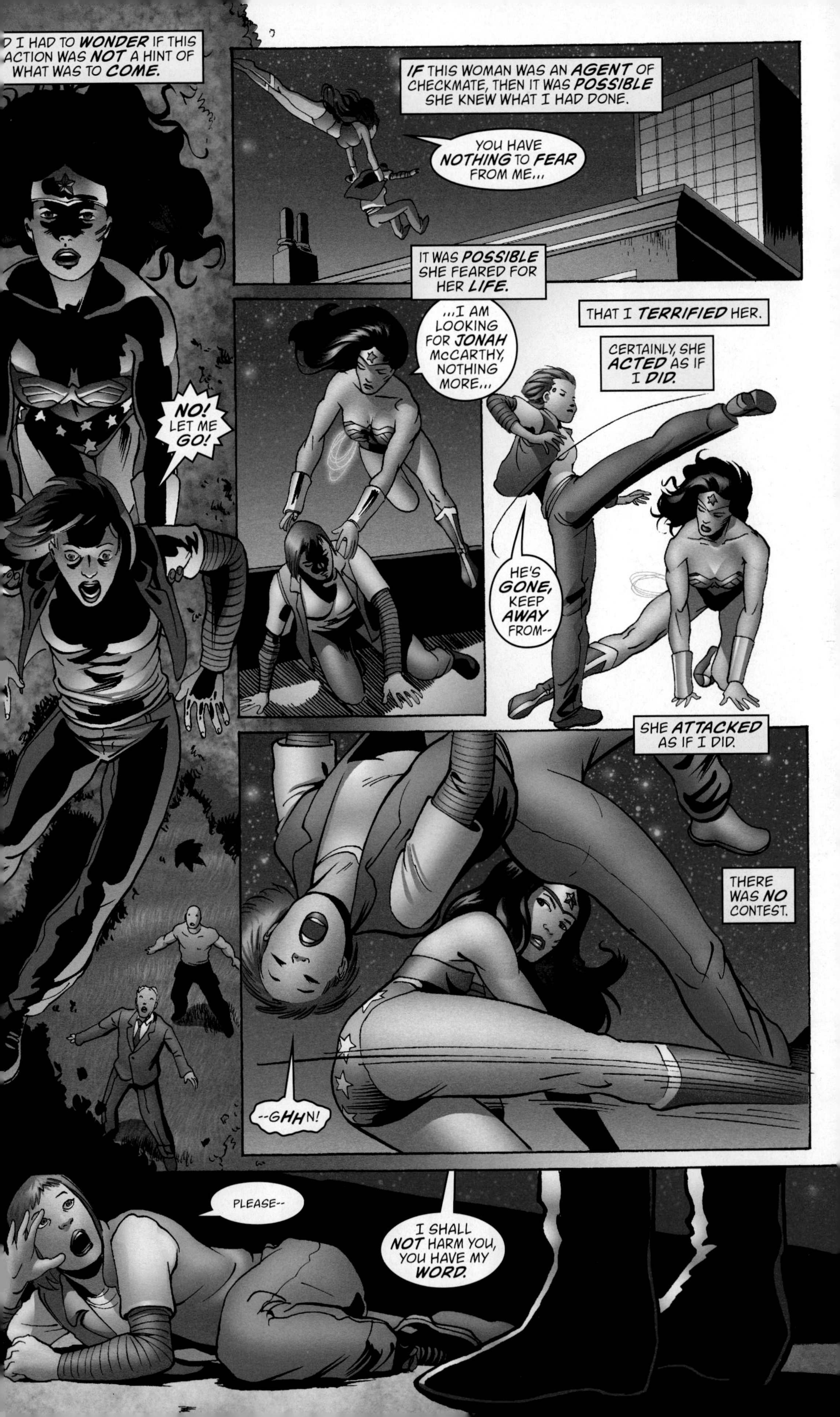

D I HAD TO WONDER IF THIS ACTION WAS NOT A HINT OF WHAT WAS TO COME.
IF THIS WOMAN WAS AN AGENT OF CHECKMATE, THEN IT WAS POSSIBLE SHE KNEW WHAT I HAD DONE.
YOU HAVE NOTHING TO FEAR FROM ME...
NO! LET ME GO!
IT WAS POSSIBLE SHE FEARED FOR HER LIFE.
...I AM LOOKING FOR JONAH McCARTHY, NOTHING MORE...
THAT I TERRIFIED HER.
CERTAINLY, SHE ACTED AS IF I DID.
HE'S GONE, KEEP AWAY FROM--
SHE ATTACKED AS IF I DID.
THERE WAS NO CONTEST.
--GHHN!
PLEASE--
I SHALL NOT HARM YOU, YOU HAVE MY WORD.

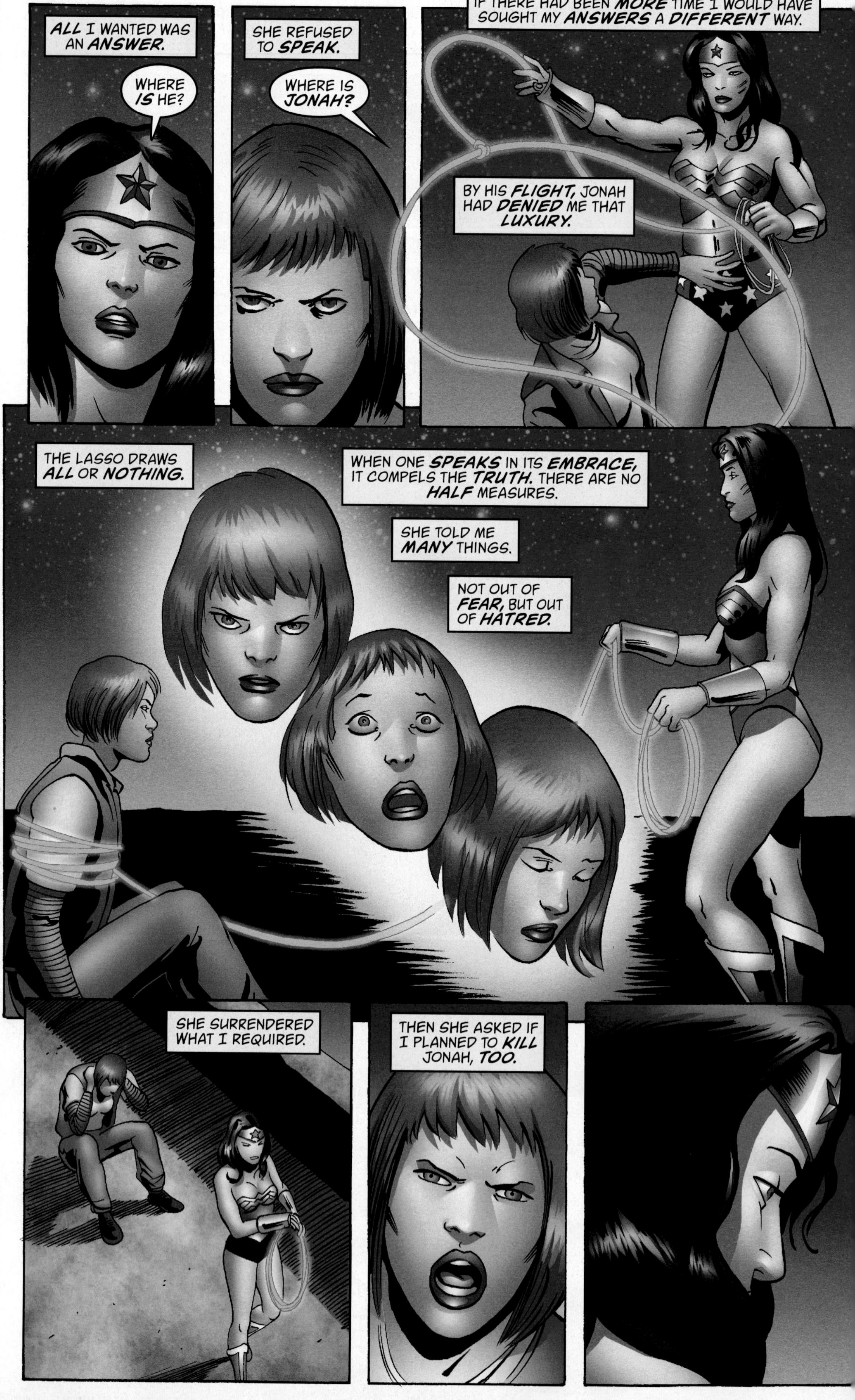
ALL I WANTED WAS AN ANSWER.
WHERE IS HE?
SHE REFUSED TO SPEAK.
WHERE IS JONAH?
IF THERE HAD BEEN MORE TIME I WOULD HAVE SOUGHT MY ANSWERS A DIFFERENT WAY.
BY HIS FLIGHT, JONAH HAD DENIED ME THAT LUXURY.
THE LASSO DRAWS ALL OR NOTHING.
WHEN ONE SPEAKS IN ITS EMBRACE, IT COMPELS THE TRUTH. THERE ARE NO HALF MEASURES.
SHE TOLD ME MANY THINGS.
NOT OUT OF FEAR, BUT OUT OF HATRED.
SHE SURRENDERED WHAT I REQUIRED.
THEN SHE ASKED IF I PLANNED TO KILL JONAH, TOO.

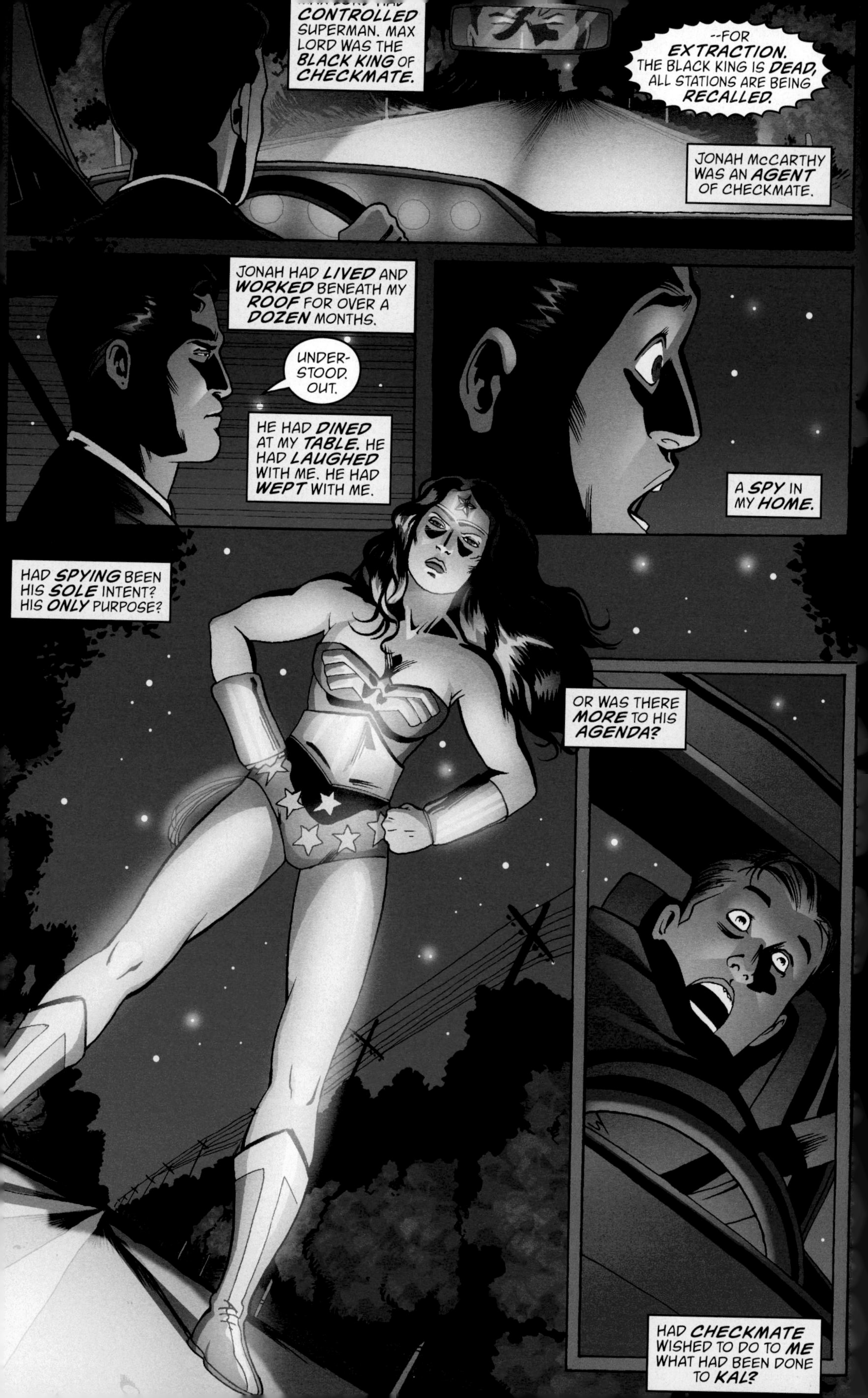
CONTROLLED SUPERMAN. MAX LORD WAS THE BLACK KING OF CHECKMATE.
--FOR EXTRACTION. THE BLACK KING IS DEAD, ALL STATIONS ARE BEING RECALLED.
JONAH McCARTHY WAS AN AGENT OF CHECKMATE.
JONAH HAD LIVED AND WORKED BENEATH MY ROOF FOR OVER A DOZEN MONTHS.
UNDER-STOOD. OUT.
HE HAD DINED AT MY TABLE. HE HAD LAUGHED WITH ME. HE HAD WEPT WITH ME.
A SPY IN MY HOME.
HAD SPYING BEEN HIS SOLE INTENT? HIS ONLY PURPOSE?
OR WAS THERE MORE TO HIS AGENDA?
HAD CHECKMATE WISHED TO DO TO ME WHAT HAD BEEN DONE TO KAL?

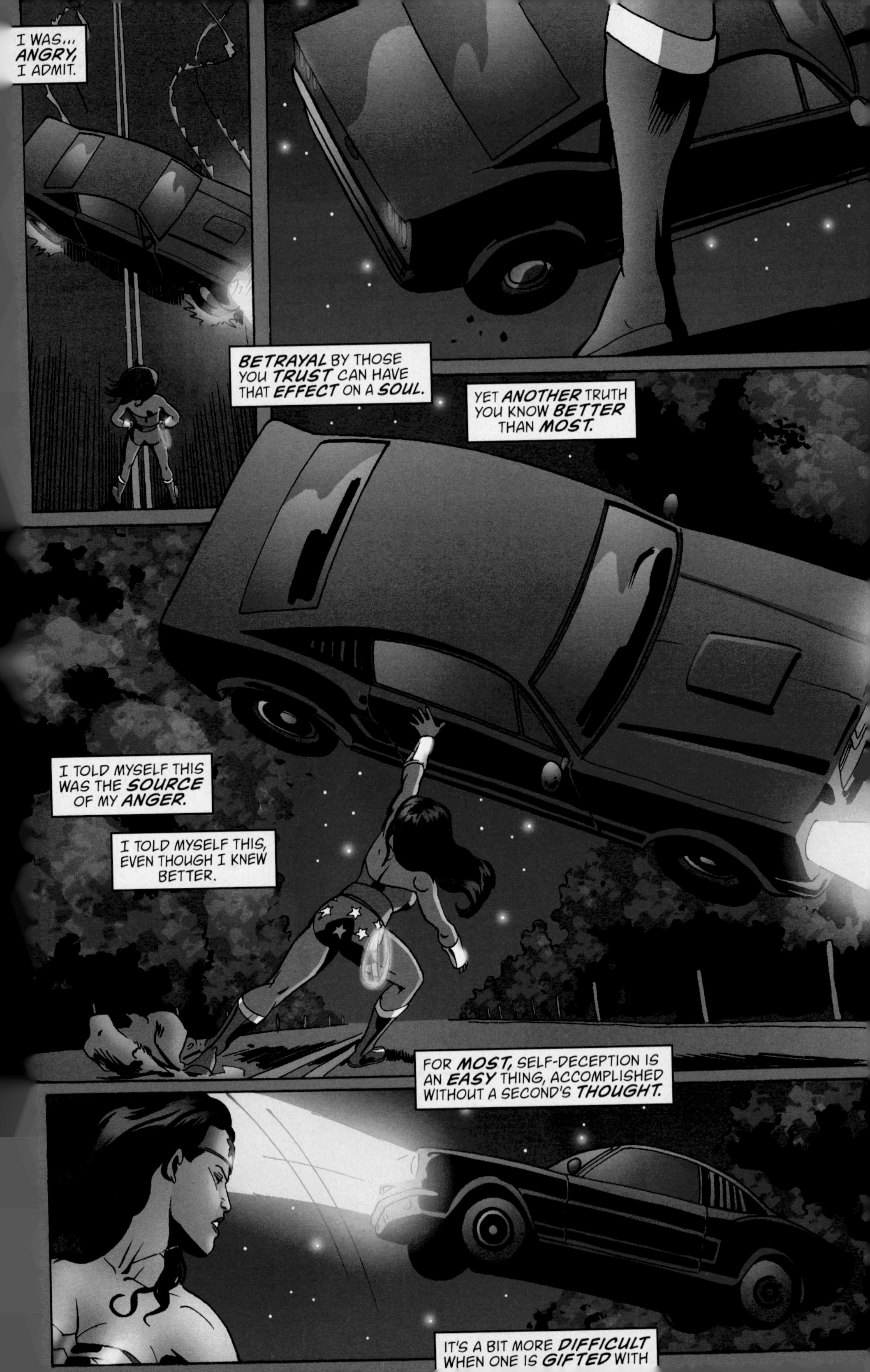
I WAS... ANGRY, I ADMIT.
BETRAYAL BY THOSE YOU TRUST CAN HAVE THAT EFFECT ON A SOUL.
YET ANOTHER TRUTH YOU KNOW BETTER THAN MOST.
I TOLD MYSELF THIS WAS THE SOURCE OF MY ANGER.
I TOLD MYSELF THIS, EVEN THOUGH I KNEW BETTER.
FOR MOST, SELF-DECEPTION IS AN EASY THING, ACCOMPLISHED WITHOUT A SECOND'S THOUGHT.
IT'S A BIT MORE DIFFICULT WHEN ONE IS GIFTED WITH

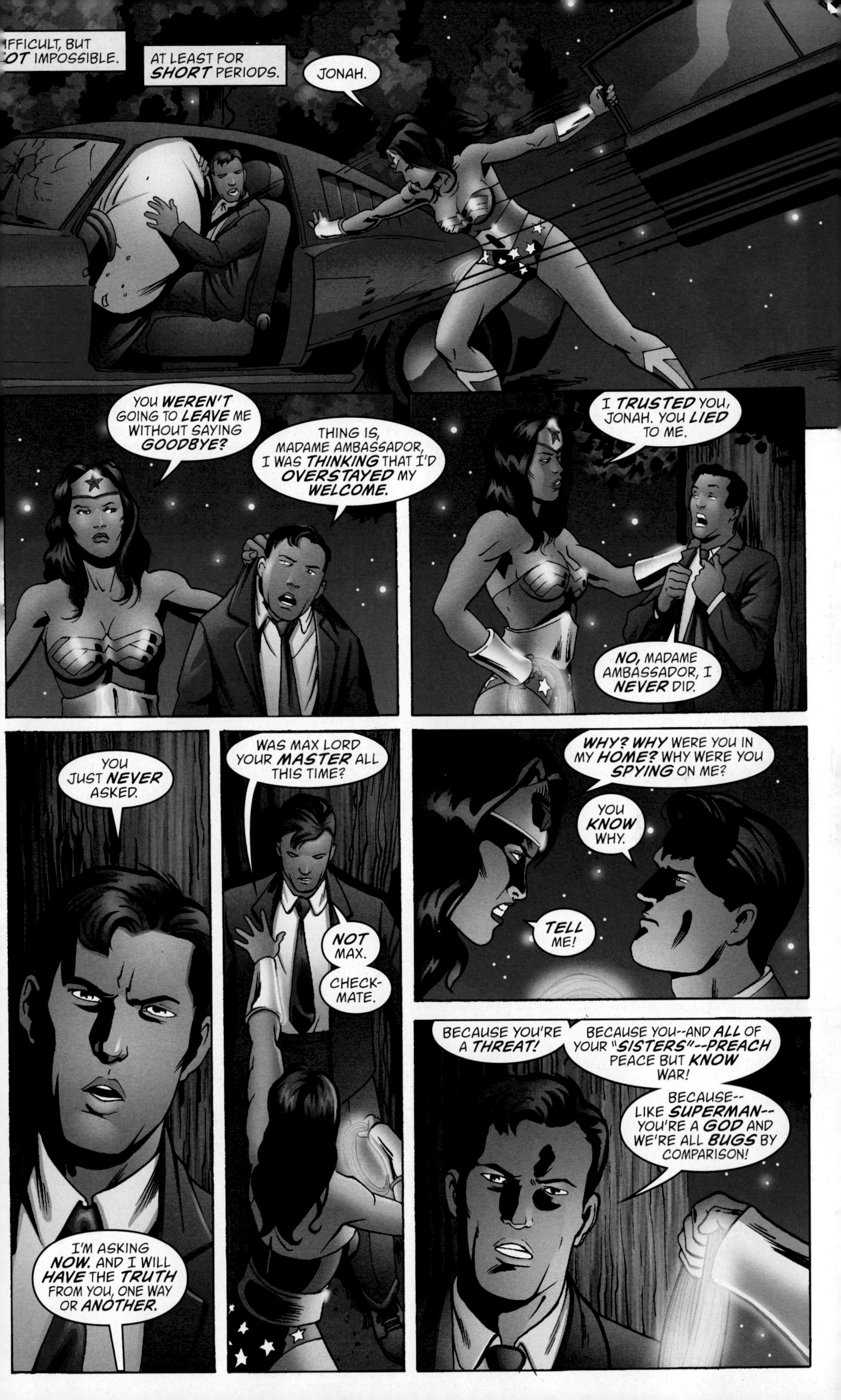

IFFICULT, BUT
OT IMPOSSIBLE.
AT LEAST FOR SHORT PERIODS.
JONAH.
YOU WEREN'T GOING TO LEAVE ME WITHOUT SAYING GOODBYE?
THING IS, MADAME AMBASSADOR, I WAS THINKING THAT I'D OVERSTAYED MY WELCOME.
I TRUSTED YOU, JONAH. YOU LIED TO ME.
NO, MADAME AMBASSADOR, I NEVER DID.
YOU JUST NEVER ASKED.
I'M ASKING NOW. AND I WILL HAVE THE TRUTH FROM YOU, ONE WAY OR ANOTHER.
WAS MAX LORD YOUR MASTER ALL THIS TIME?
NOT MAX.
CHECK-MATE.
WHY? WHY WERE YOU IN MY HOME? WHY WERE YOU SPYING ON ME?
YOU KNOW WHY.
TELL ME!
BECAUSE YOU'RE A THREAT!
BECAUSE YOU--AND ALL OF YOUR "SISTERS"--PREACH PEACE BUT KNOW WAR!
BECAUSE--LIKE SUPERMAN--YOU'RE A GOD AND WE'RE ALL BUGS BY COMPARISON!

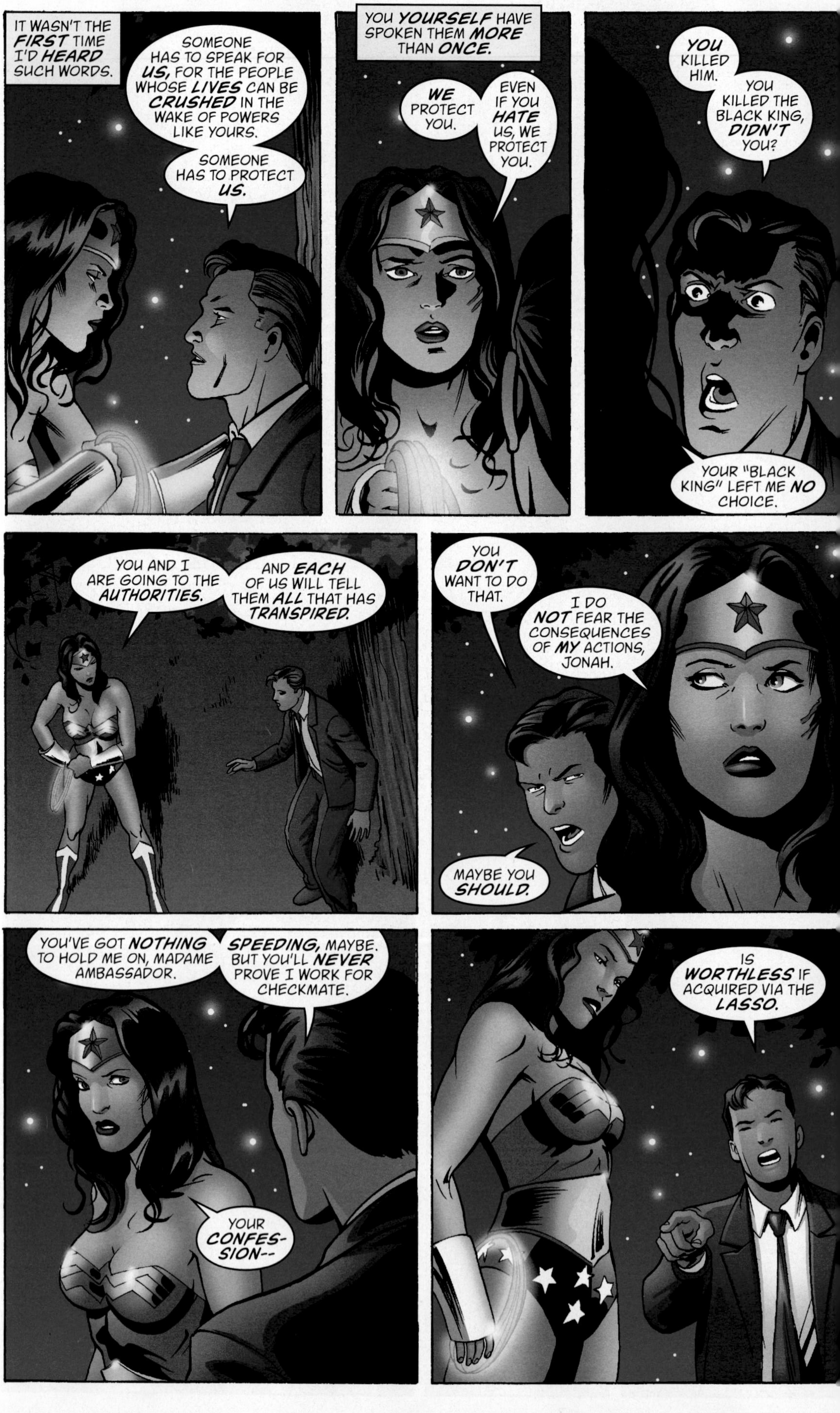
IT WASN'T THE FIRST TIME I'D HEARD SUCH WORDS.
SOMEONE HAS TO SPEAK FOR US, FOR THE PEOPLE WHOSE LIVES CAN BE CRUSHED IN THE WAKE OF POWERS LIKE YOURS.
SOMEONE HAS TO PROTECT US.
YOU YOURSELF HAVE SPOKEN THEM MORE THAN ONCE.
WE PROTECT YOU.
EVEN IF YOU HATE US, WE PROTECT YOU.
YOU KILLED HIM.
YOU KILLED THE BLACK KING, DIDN'T YOU?
YOUR "BLACK KING" LEFT ME NO CHOICE.
YOU AND I ARE GOING TO THE AUTHORITIES.
AND EACH OF US WILL TELL THEM ALL THAT HAS TRANSPIRED.
YOU DON'T WANT TO DO THAT.
I DO NOT FEAR THE CONSEQUENCES OF MY ACTIONS, JONAH.
MAYBE YOU SHOULD.
YOU'VE GOT NOTHING TO HOLD ME ON, MADAME AMBASSADOR.
SPEEDING, MAYBE. BUT YOU'LL NEVER PROVE I WORK FOR CHECKMATE.
YOUR CONFES-SION--
IS WORTHLESS IF ACQUIRED VIA THE LASSO.

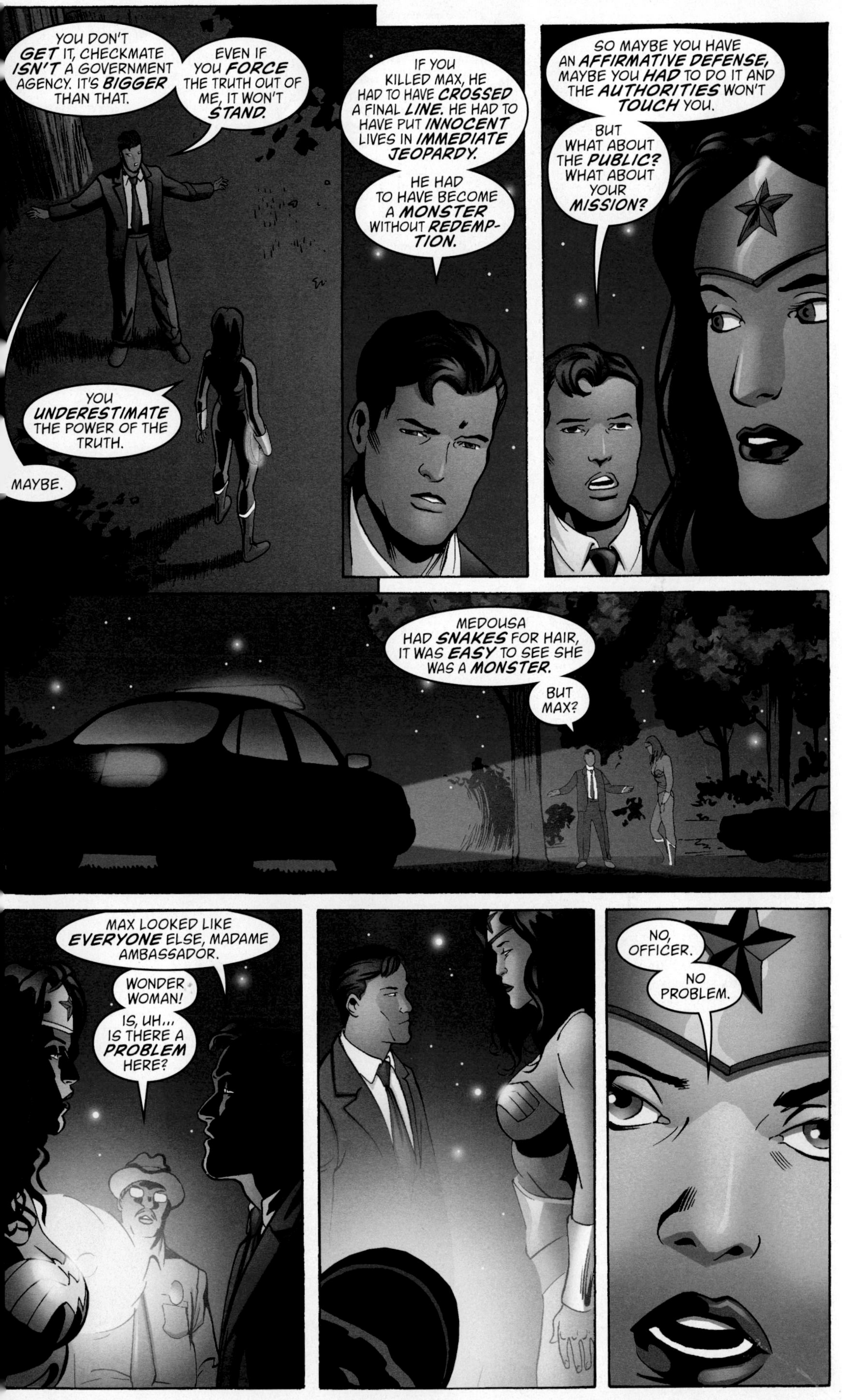
YOU DON'T GET IT, CHECKMATE ISN'T A GOVERNMENT AGENCY. IT'S BIGGER THAN THAT.
EVEN IF YOU FORCE THE TRUTH OUT OF ME, IT WON'T STAND.
YOU UNDERESTIMATE THE POWER OF THE TRUTH.
MAYBE.
IF YOU KILLED MAX, HE HAD TO HAVE CROSSED A FINAL LINE. HE HAD TO HAVE PUT INNOCENT LIVES IN IMMEDIATE JEOPARDY.
HE HAD TO HAVE BECOME A MONSTER WITHOUT REDEMP-TION.
SO MAYBE YOU HAVE AN AFFIRMATIVE DEFENSE, MAYBE YOU HAD TO DO IT AND THE AUTHORITIES WON'T TOUCH YOU.
BUT WHAT ABOUT THE PUBLIC? WHAT ABOUT YOUR MISSION?
MEDOUSA HAD SNAKES FOR HAIR, IT WAS EASY TO SEE SHE WAS A MONSTER.
BUT MAX?
MAX LOOKED LIKE EVERYONE ELSE, MADAME AMBASSADOR.
WONDER WOMAN!
IS, UH... IS THERE A PROBLEM HERE?
NO, OFFICER.
NO PROBLEM.

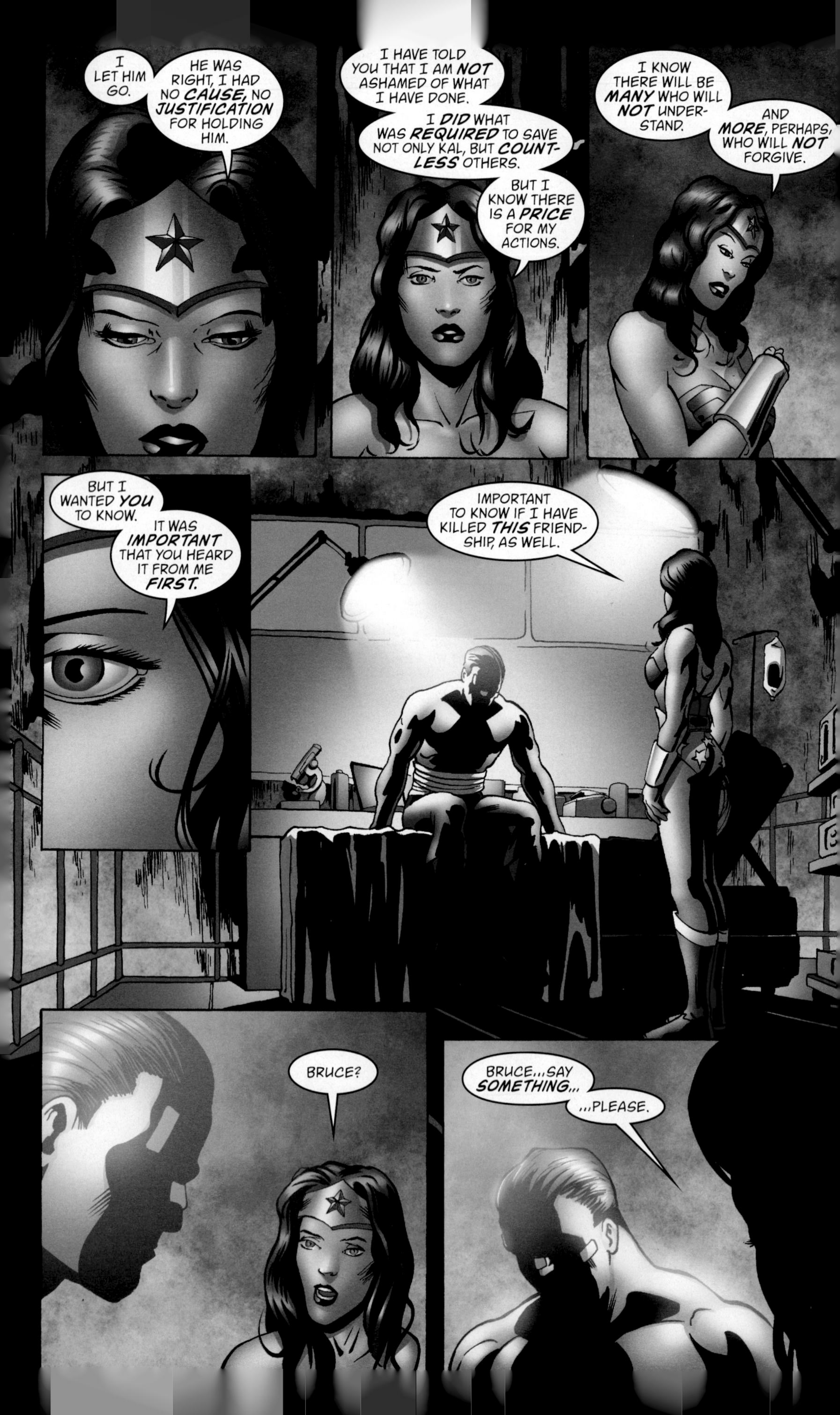
I LET HIM GO.
HE WAS RIGHT, I HAD NO CAUSE, NO JUSTIFICATION FOR HOLDING HIM.
I HAVE TOLD YOU THAT I AM NOT ASHAMED OF WHAT I HAVE DONE.
I DID WHAT WAS REQUIRED TO SAVE NOT ONLY KAL, BUT COUNT-LESS OTHERS.
BUT I KNOW THERE IS A PRICE FOR MY ACTIONS.
I KNOW THERE WILL BE MANY WHO WILL NOT UNDER-STAND.
AND MORE, PERHAPS, WHO WILL NOT FORGIVE.
BUT I WANTED YOU TO KNOW.
IT WAS IMPORTANT THAT YOU HEARD IT FROM ME FIRST.
IMPORTANT TO KNOW IF I HAVE KILLED THIS FRIEND-SHIP, AS WELL.
BRUCE?
BRUCE...SAY SOMETHING...
...PLEASE.

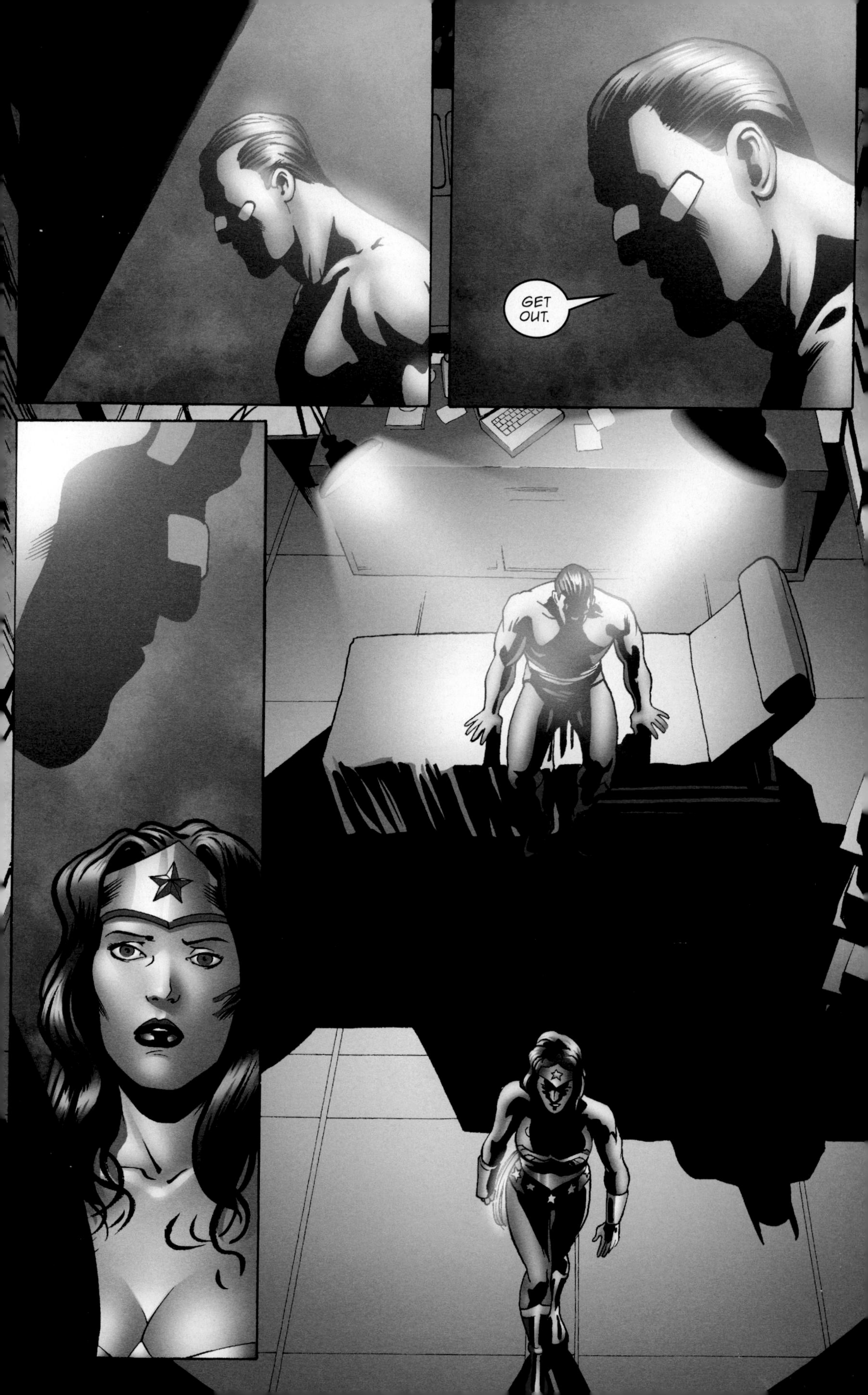
GET OUT.

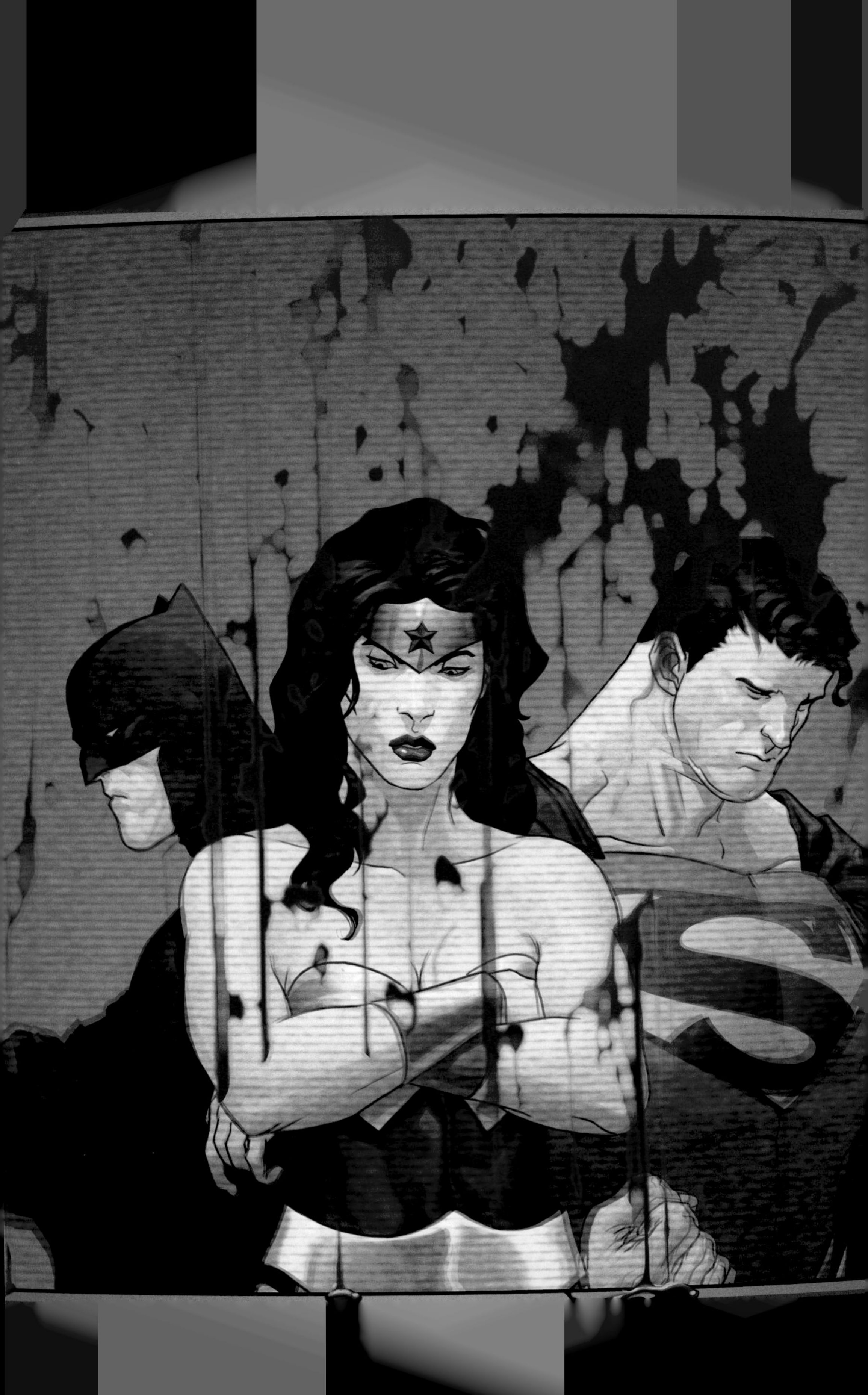

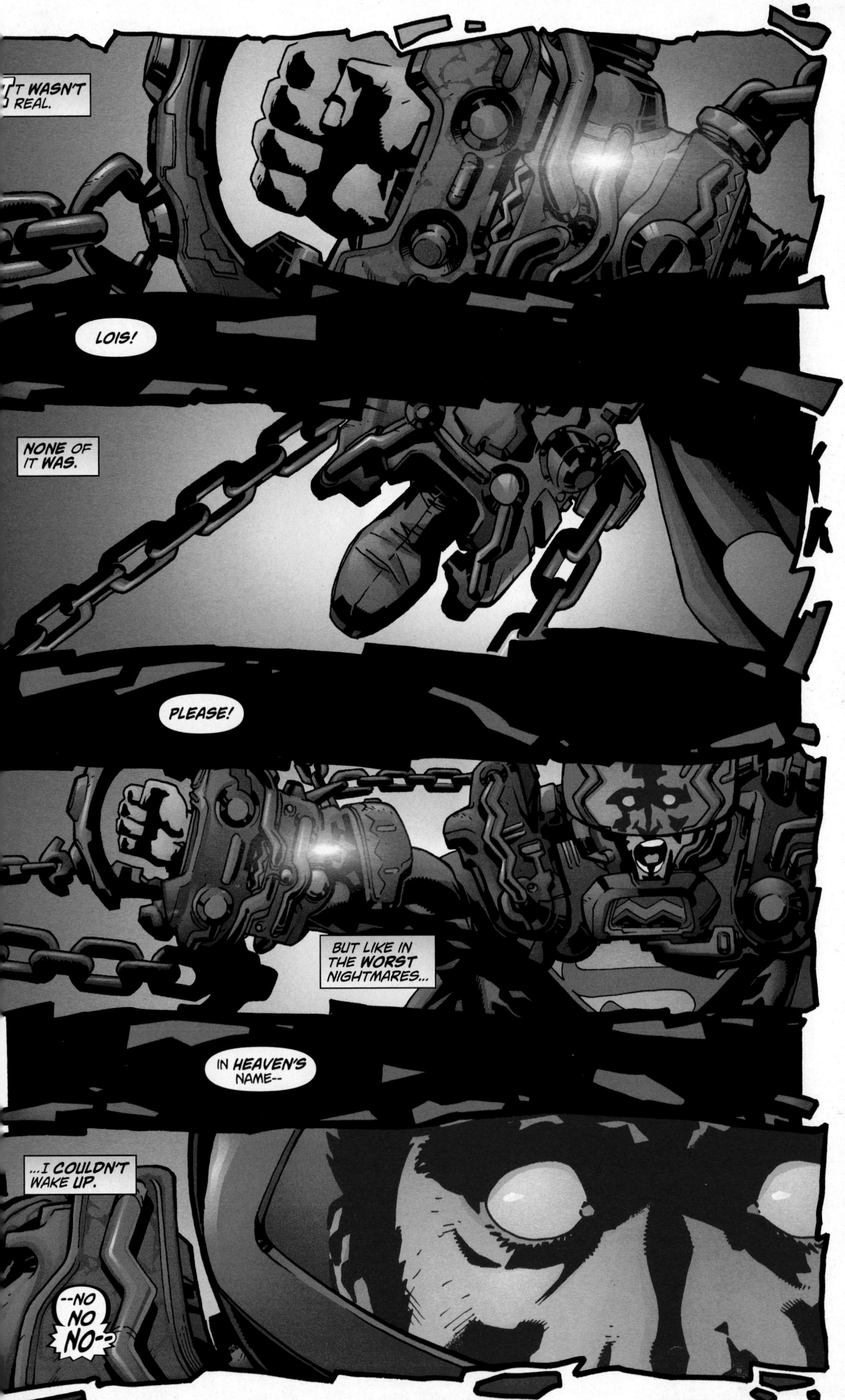
IT WASN'T REAL.
LOIS!
NONE OF IT WAS.
PLEASE!
BUT LIKE IN THE WORST NIGHTMARES...
IN HEAVEN'S NAME--
...I COULDN'T WAKE UP.
--NO NO NO--

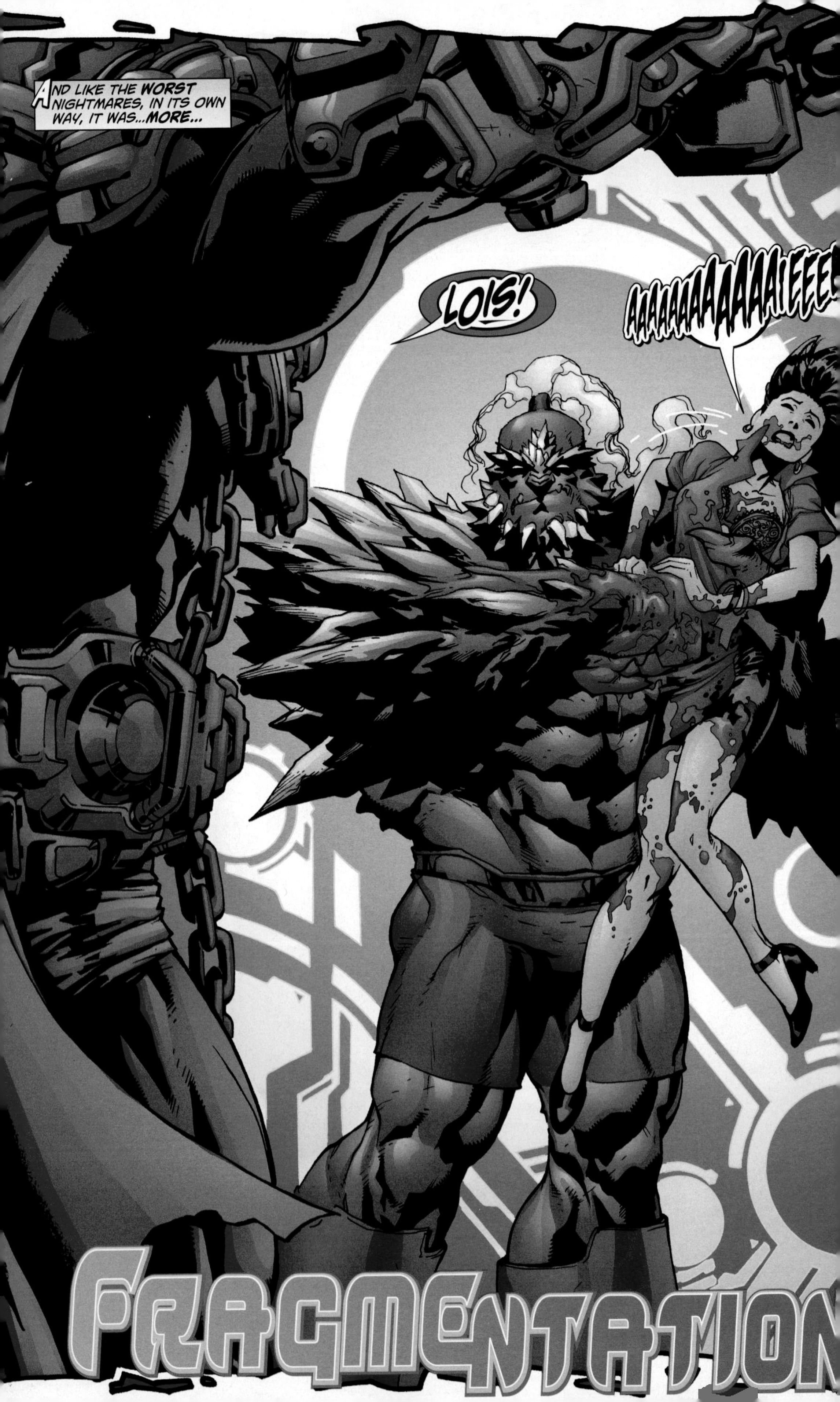
AND LIKE THE WORST NIGHTMARES, IN ITS OWN WAY, IT WAS...MORE...
LOIS!
AAAAAAAAAAAAIEEE!
FRAGMENTATION

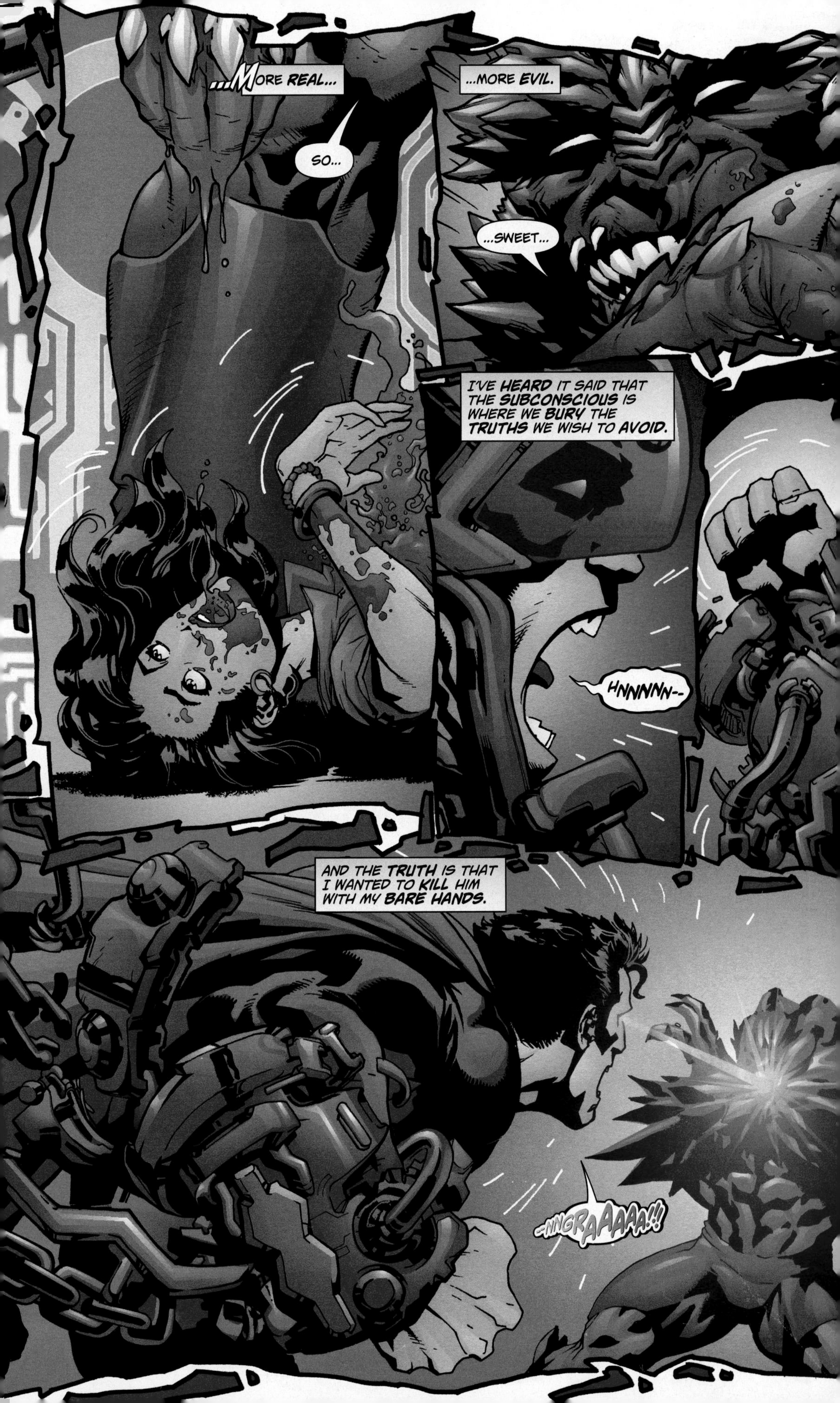
...MORE REAL...
SO...
...MORE EVIL.
...SWEET...
I'VE HEARD IT SAID THAT THE SUBCONSCIOUS IS WHERE WE BURY THE TRUTHS WE WISH TO AVOID.
HNNNNN--
AND THE TRUTH IS THAT I WANTED TO KILL HIM WITH MY BARE HANDS.
-NNGRAAAAA!!!

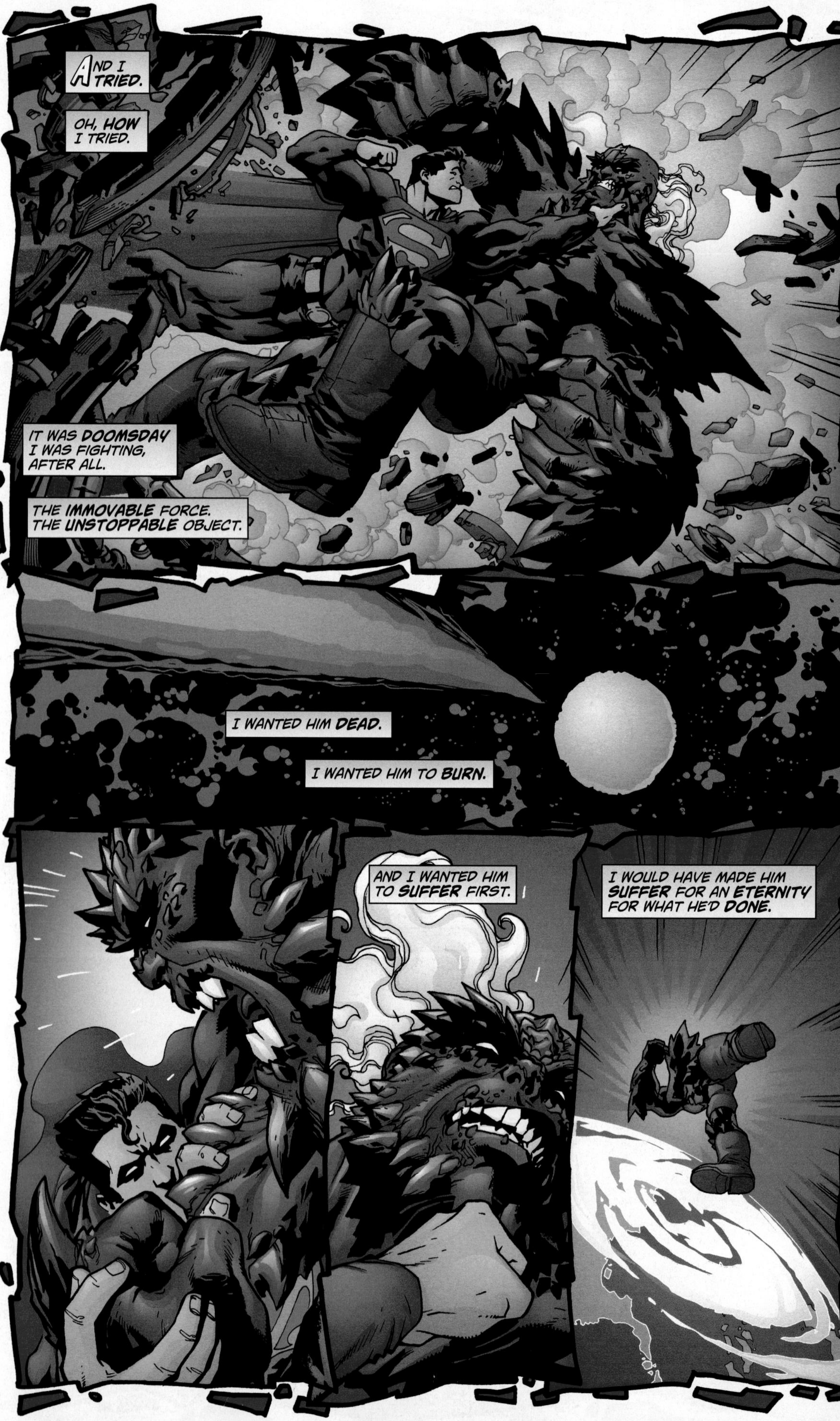

AND I TRIED.
OH, HOW I TRIED.
IT WAS DOOMSDAY I WAS FIGHTING, AFTER ALL.
THE IMMOVABLE FORCE. THE UNSTOPPABLE OBJECT.
I WANTED HIM DEAD.
I WANTED HIM TO BURN.
AND I WANTED HIM TO SUFFER FIRST.
I WOULD HAVE MADE HIM SUFFER FOR AN ETERNITY FOR WHAT HE'D DONE.

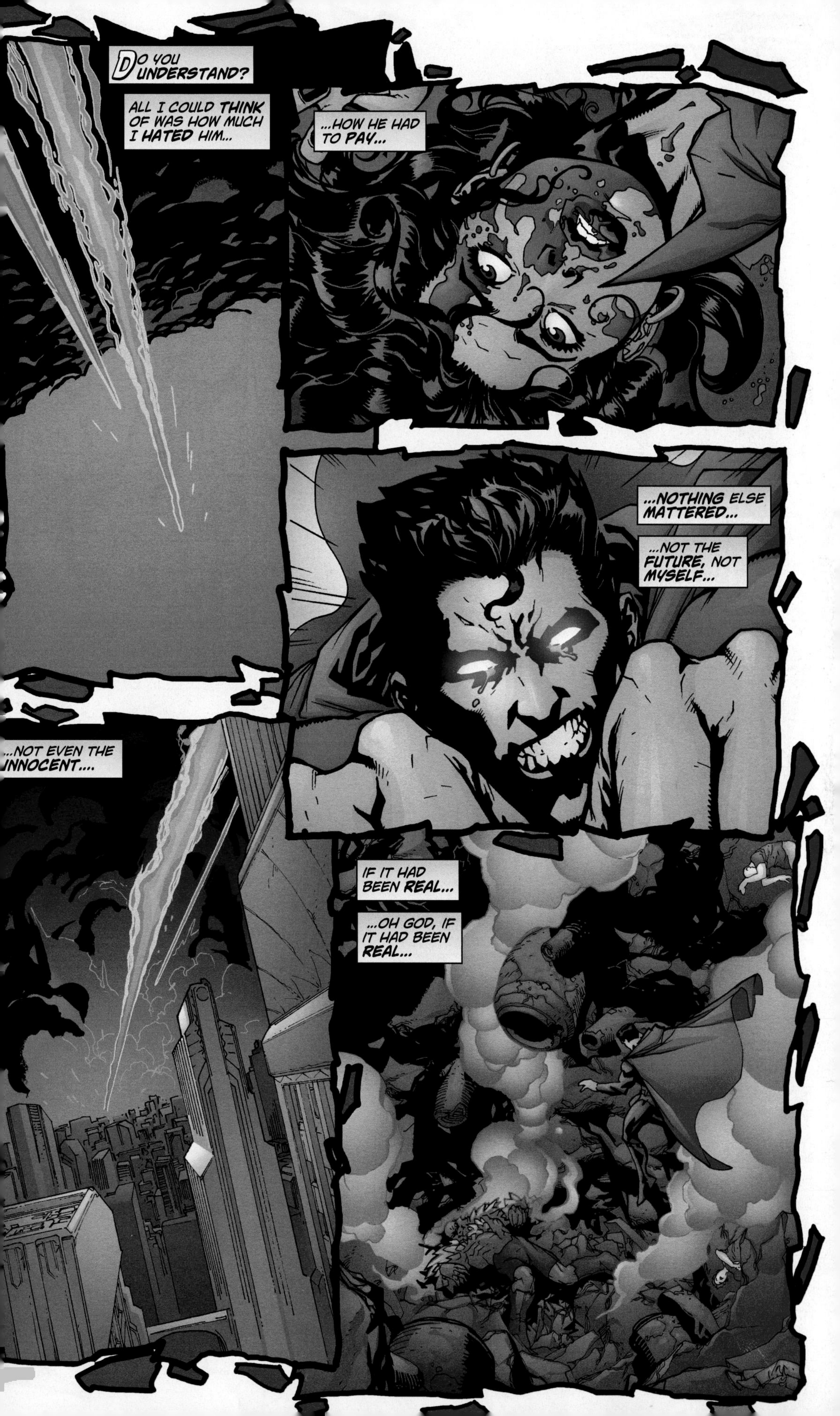
DO YOU UNDERSTAND?
ALL I COULD THINK OF WAS HOW MUCH I HATED HIM...
...HOW HE HAD TO PAY...
...NOTHING ELSE MATTERED...
...NOT THE FUTURE, NOT MYSELF...
...NOT EVEN THE INNOCENT....
IF IT HAD BEEN REAL...
...OH GOD, IF IT HAD BEEN REAL...

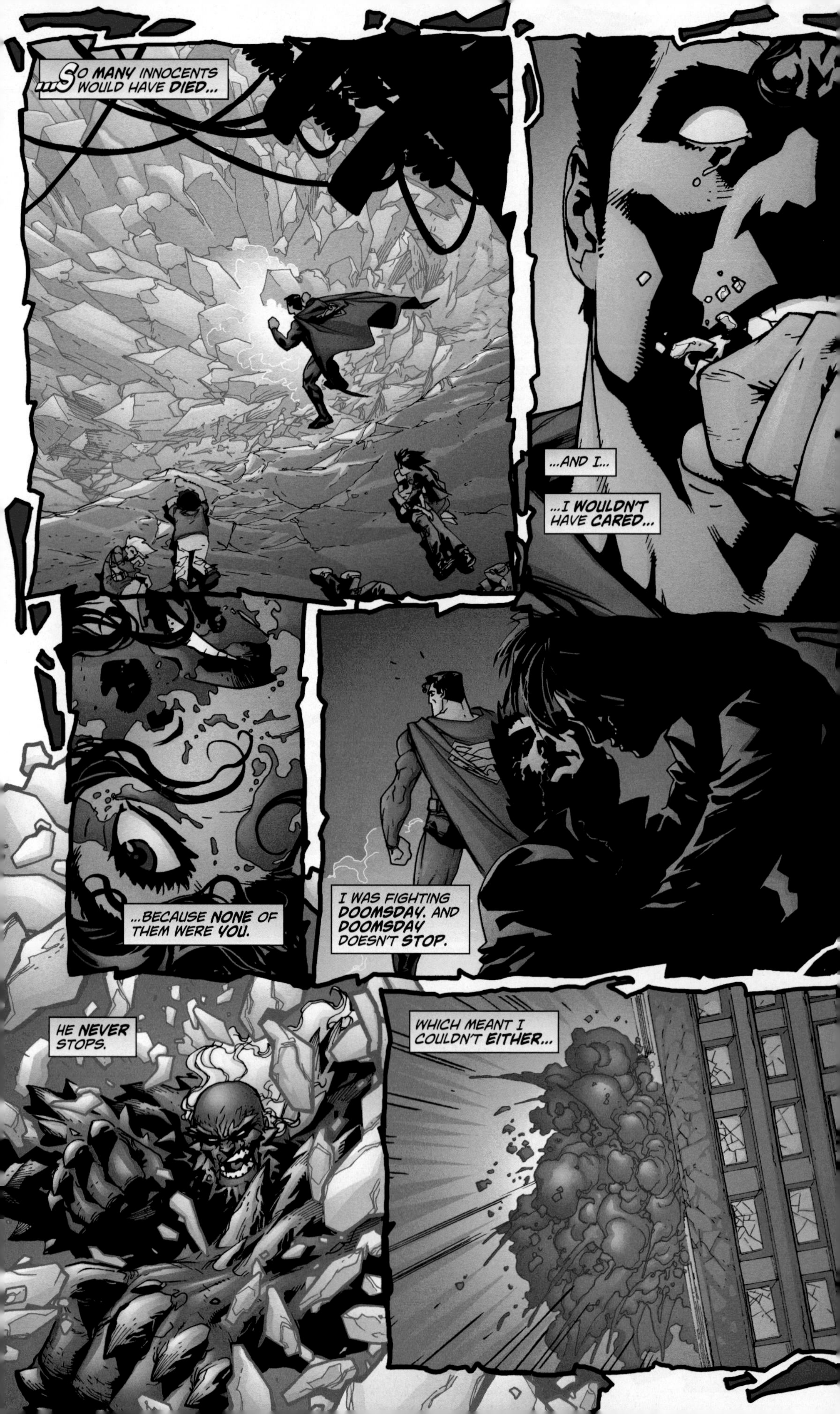
...SO MANY INNOCENTS WOULD HAVE DIED...
...AND I...
...I WOULDN'T HAVE CARED...
...BECAUSE NONE OF THEM WERE YOU.
I WAS FIGHTING DOOMSDAY. AND DOOMSDAY DOESN'T STOP.
HE NEVER STOPS.
WHICH MEANT I COULDN'T EITHER...

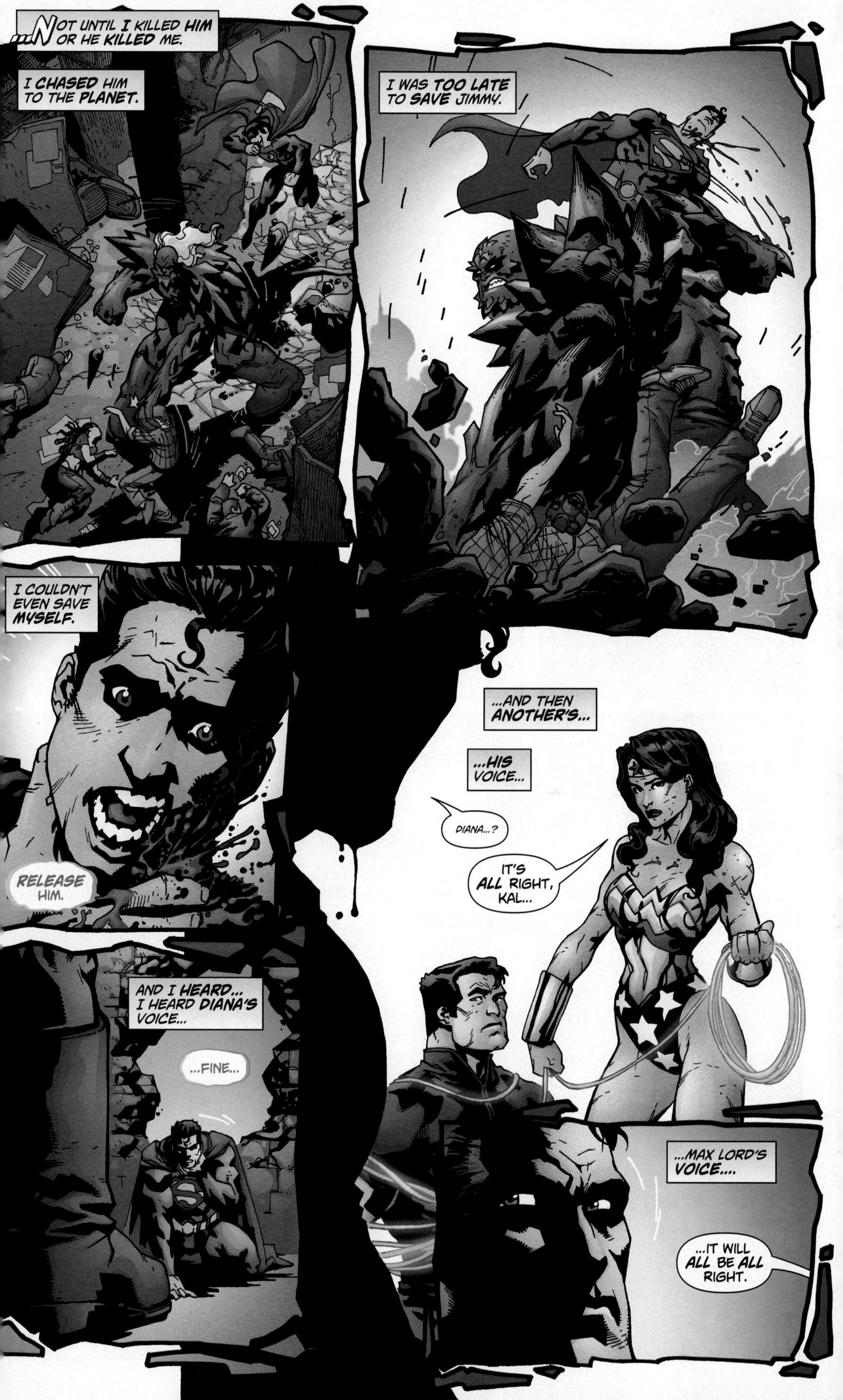
NOT UNTIL I KILLED HIM OR HE KILLED ME.
I CHASED HIM TO THE PLANET.
I WAS TOO LATE TO SAVE JIMMY.
I COULDN'T EVEN SAVE MYSELF.
RELEASE HIM.
AND I HEARD... I HEARD DIANA'S VOICE...
...FINE...
...AND THEN ANOTHER'S...
...HIS VOICE...
DIANA...?
IT'S ALL RIGHT, KAL...
...MAX LORD'S VOICE....
...IT WILL ALL BE ALL RIGHT.

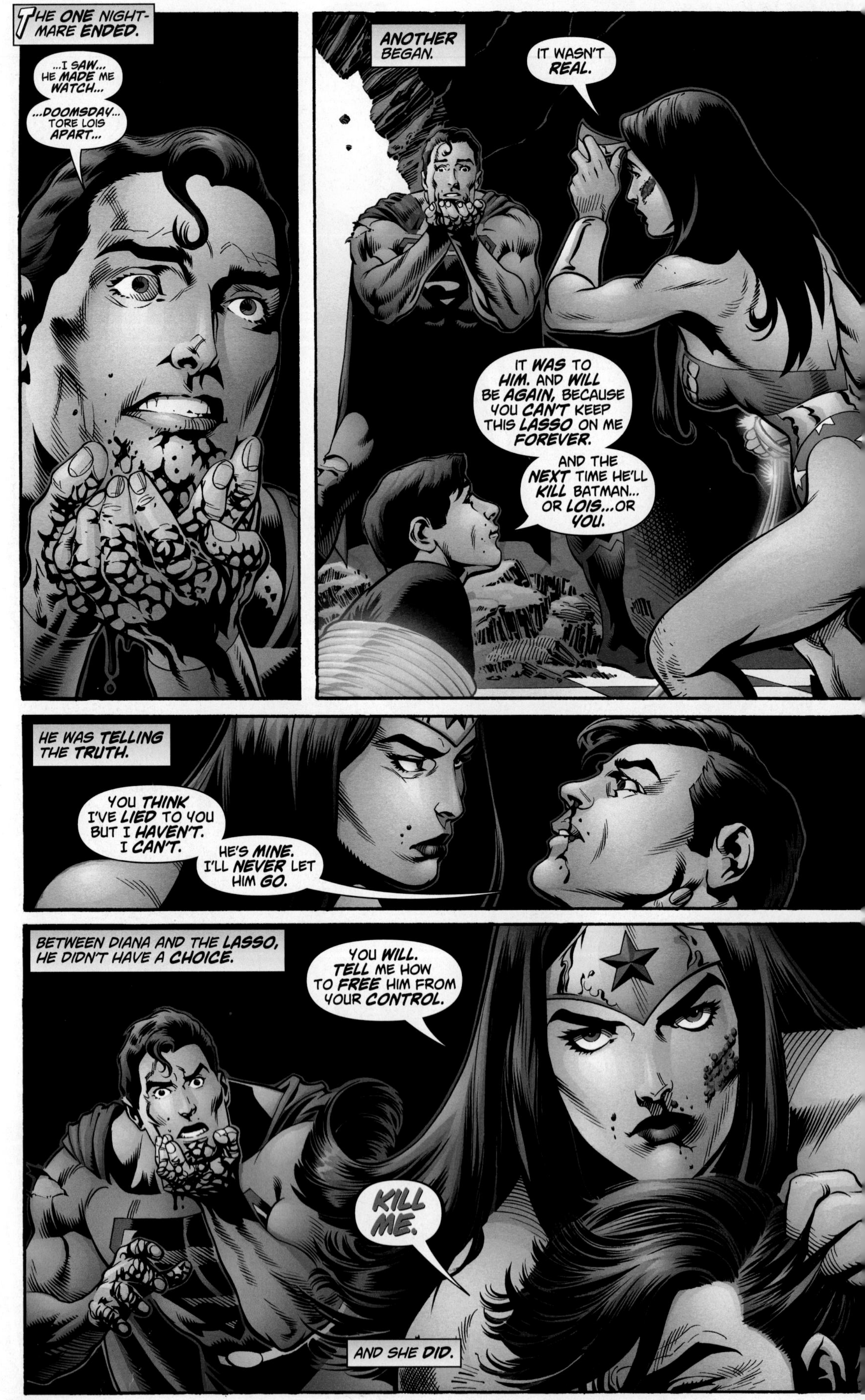
THE ONE NIGHTMARE ENDED.
...I SAW... HE MADE ME WATCH...
...DOOMSDAY... TORE LOIS APART...
ANOTHER BEGAN.
IT WASN'T REAL.
IT WAS TO HIM. AND WILL BE AGAIN, BECAUSE YOU CAN'T KEEP THIS LASSO ON ME FOREVER.
AND THE NEXT TIME HE'LL KILL BATMAN... OR LOIS...OR YOU.
HE WAS TELLING THE TRUTH.
YOU THINK I'VE LIED TO YOU BUT I HAVEN'T. I CAN'T.
HE'S MINE. I'LL NEVER LET HIM GO.
BETWEEN DIANA AND THE LASSO, HE DIDN'T HAVE A CHOICE.
YOU WILL. TELL ME HOW TO FREE HIM FROM YOUR CONTROL.
KILL ME.
AND SHE DID.

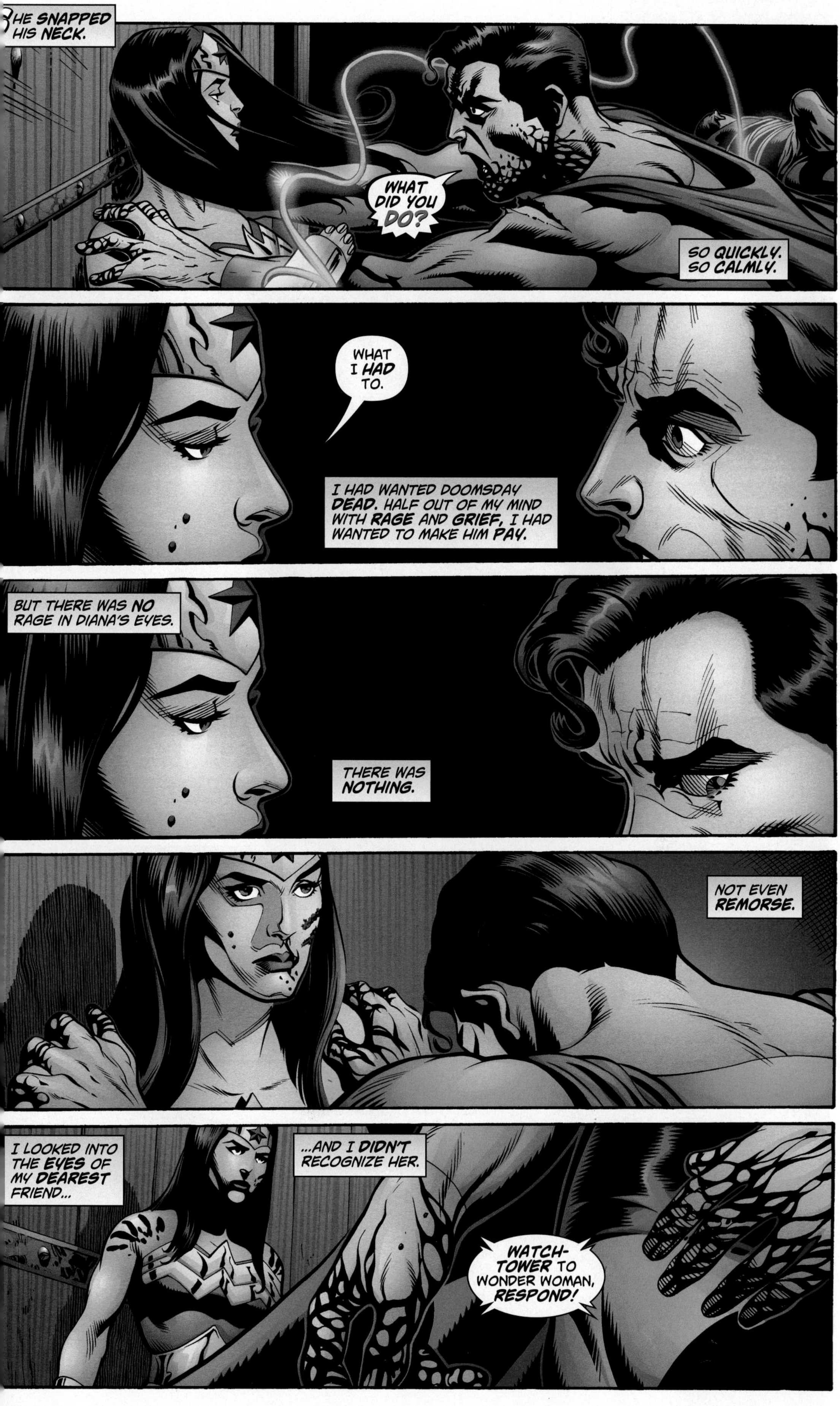

SHE SNAPPED HIS NECK.
WHAT DID YOU DO?
SO QUICKLY. SO CALMLY.
WHAT I HAD TO.
I HAD WANTED DOOMSDAY DEAD. HALF OUT OF MY MIND WITH RAGE AND GRIEF, I HAD WANTED TO MAKE HIM PAY.
BUT THERE WAS NO RAGE IN DIANA'S EYES.
THERE WAS NOTHING.
NOT EVEN REMORSE.
I LOOKED INTO THE EYES OF MY DEAREST FRIEND...
...AND I DIDN'T RECOGNIZE HER.
WATCH-TOWER TO WONDER WOMAN, RESPOND!

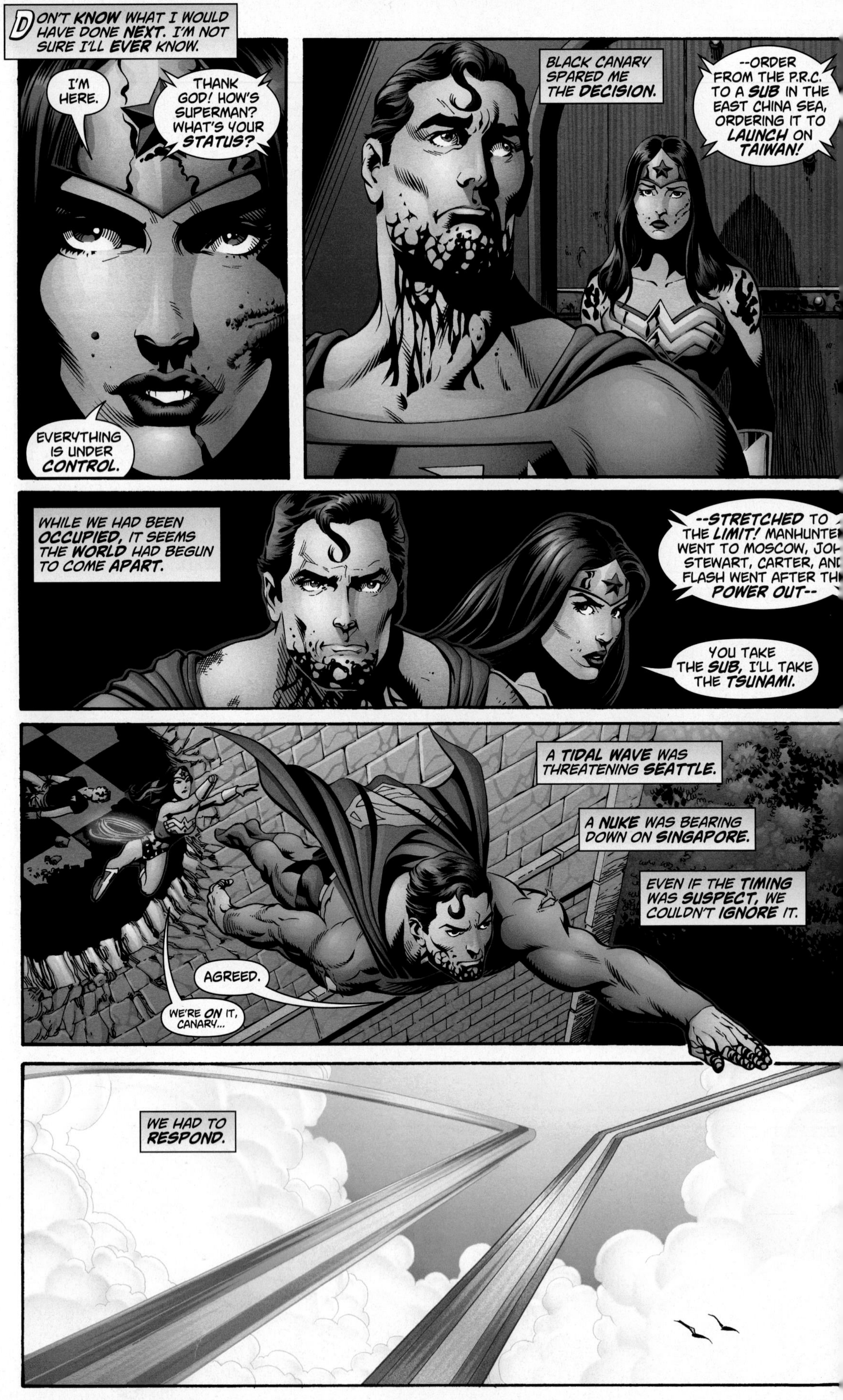
DON'T KNOW WHAT I WOULD HAVE DONE NEXT. I'M NOT SURE I'LL EVER KNOW.
I'M HERE.
THANK GOD! HOW'S SUPERMAN? WHAT'S YOUR STATUS?
EVERYTHING IS UNDER CONTROL.
BLACK CANARY SPARED ME THE DECISION.
--ORDER FROM THE P.R.C. TO A SUB IN THE EAST CHINA SEA, ORDERING IT TO LAUNCH ON TAIWAN!
WHILE WE HAD BEEN OCCUPIED, IT SEEMS THE WORLD HAD BEGUN TO COME APART.
--STRETCHED TO THE LIMIT! MANHUNTE WENT TO MOSCOW, JOH STEWART, CARTER, AND FLASH WENT AFTER TH POWER OUT--
YOU TAKE THE SUB, I'LL TAKE THE TSUNAMI.
A TIDAL WAVE WAS THREATENING SEATTLE.
A NUKE WAS BEARING DOWN ON SINGAPORE.
EVEN IF THE TIMING WAS SUSPECT, WE COULDN'T IGNORE IT.
AGREED.
WE'RE ON IT, CANARY...
WE HAD TO RESPOND.

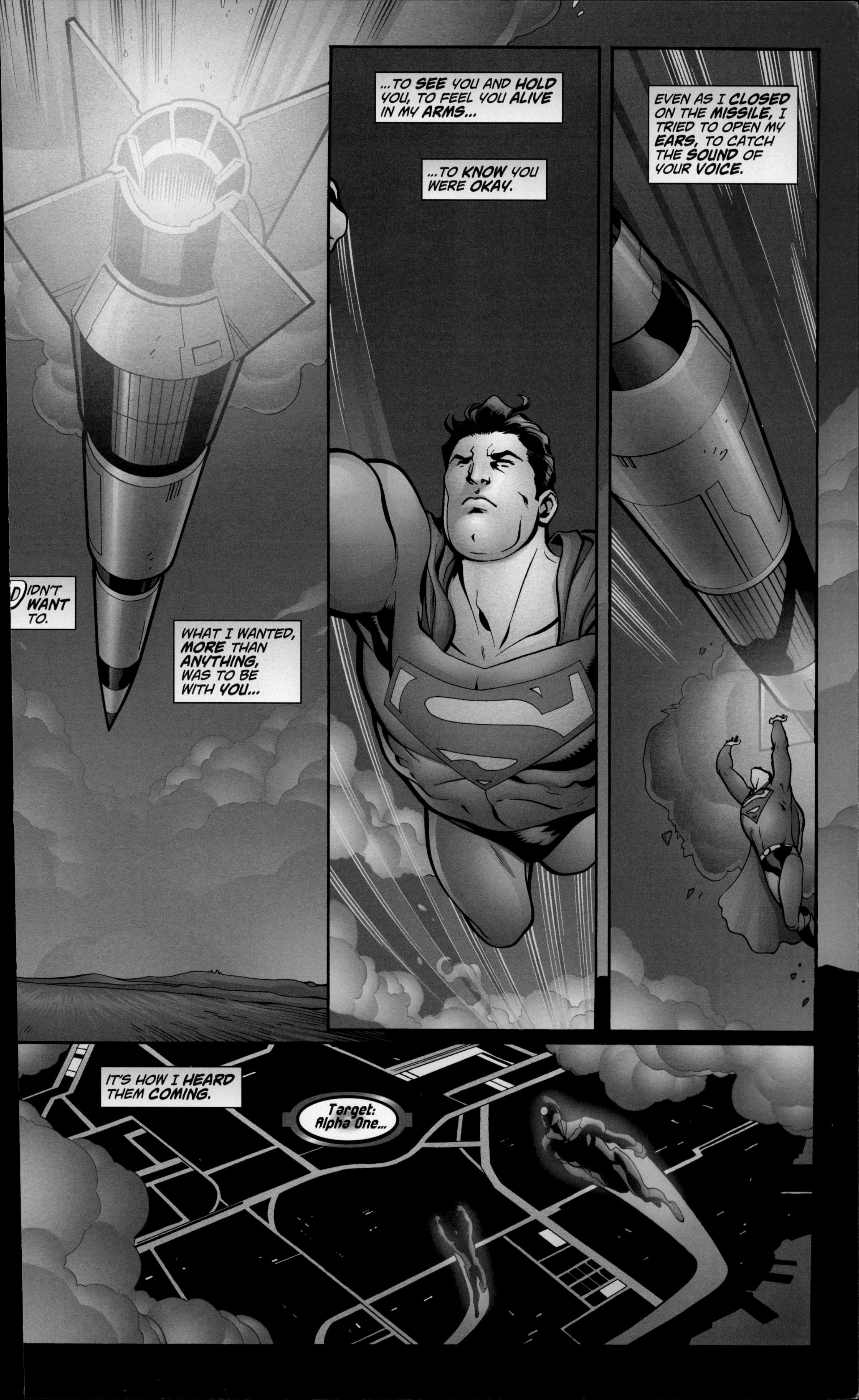

...DIDN'T WANT TO.
WHAT I WANTED, MORE THAN ANYTHING, WAS TO BE WITH YOU...
...TO SEE YOU AND HOLD YOU, TO FEEL YOU ALIVE IN MY ARMS...
...TO KNOW YOU WERE OKAY.
EVEN AS I CLOSED ON THE MISSILE, I TRIED TO OPEN MY EARS, TO CATCH THE SOUND OF YOUR VOICE.
IT'S HOW I HEARD THEM COMING.
Target: Alpha One...

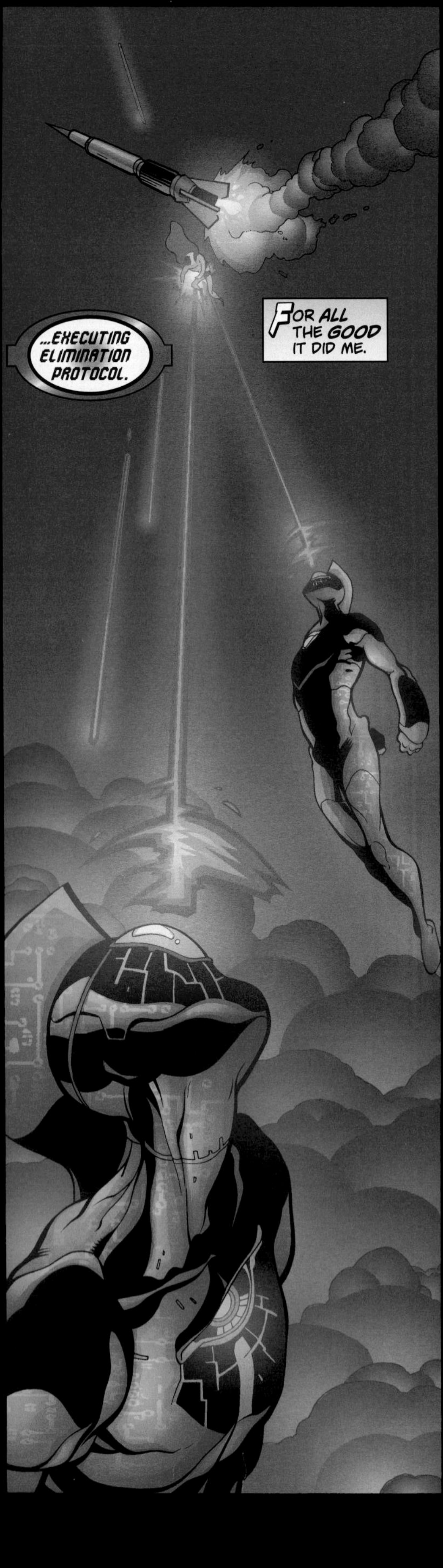
...EXECUTING ELIMINATION PROTOCOL.
FOR ALL THE GOOD IT DID ME.
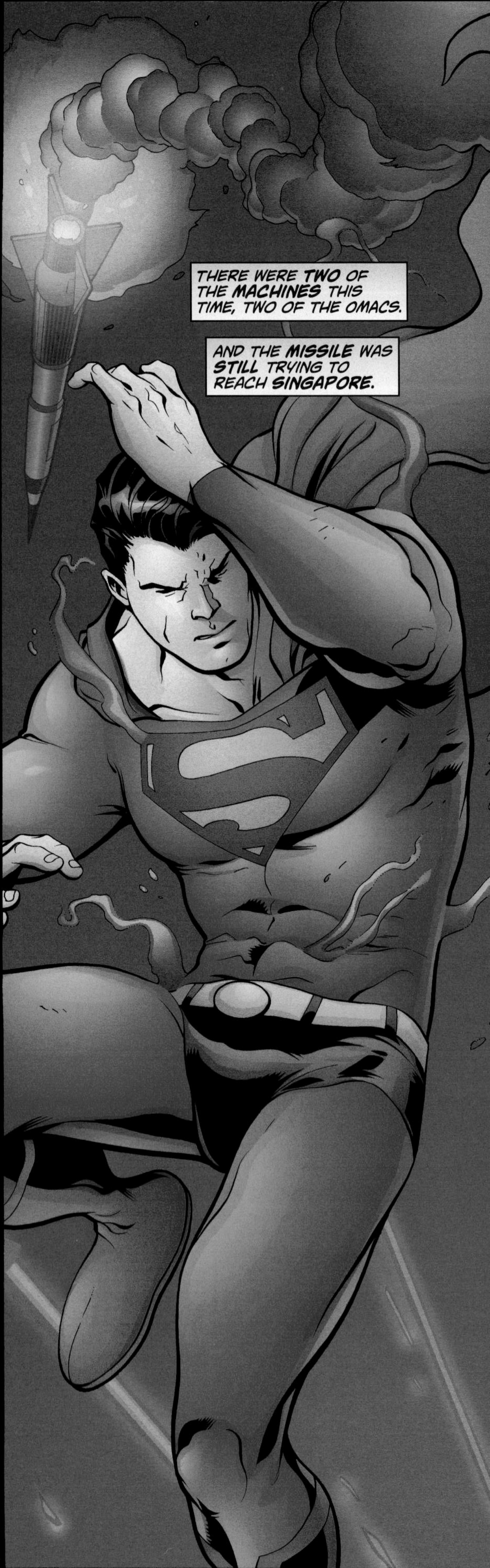
THERE WERE TWO OF THE MACHINES THIS TIME, TWO OF THE OMACS.
AND THE MISSILE WAS STILL TRYING TO REACH SINGAPORE.

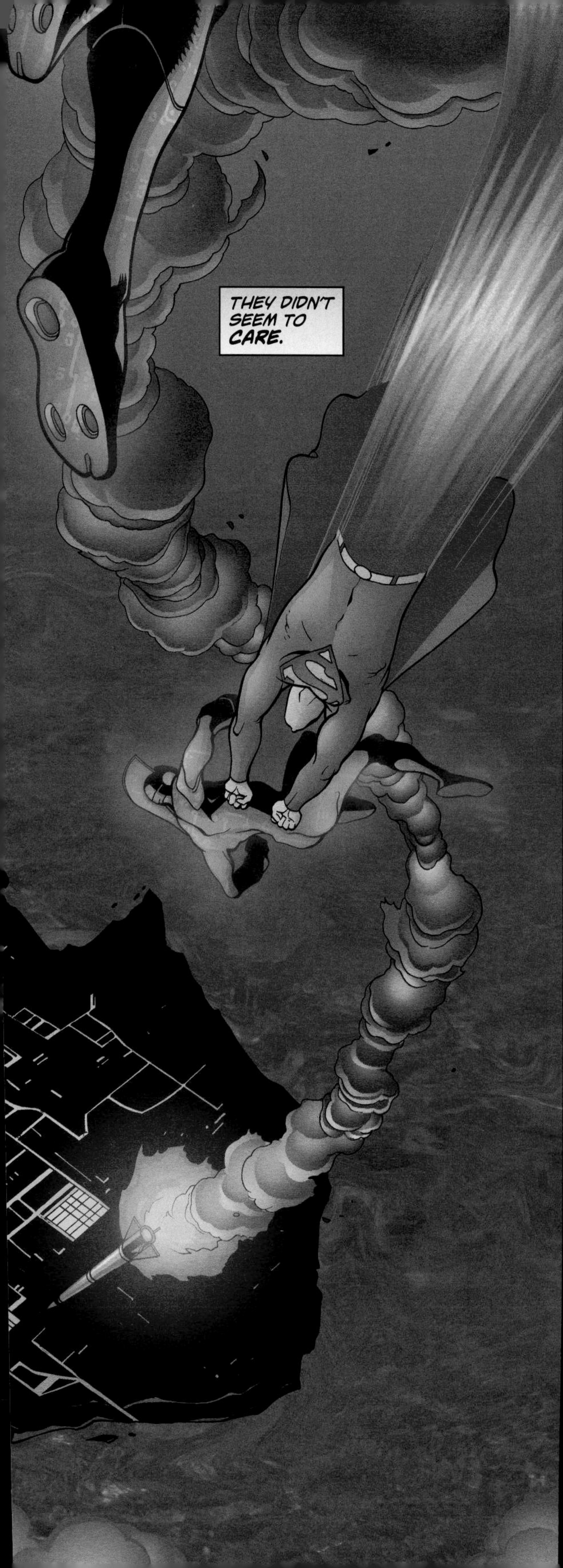
THEY DIDN'T SEEM TO CARE.

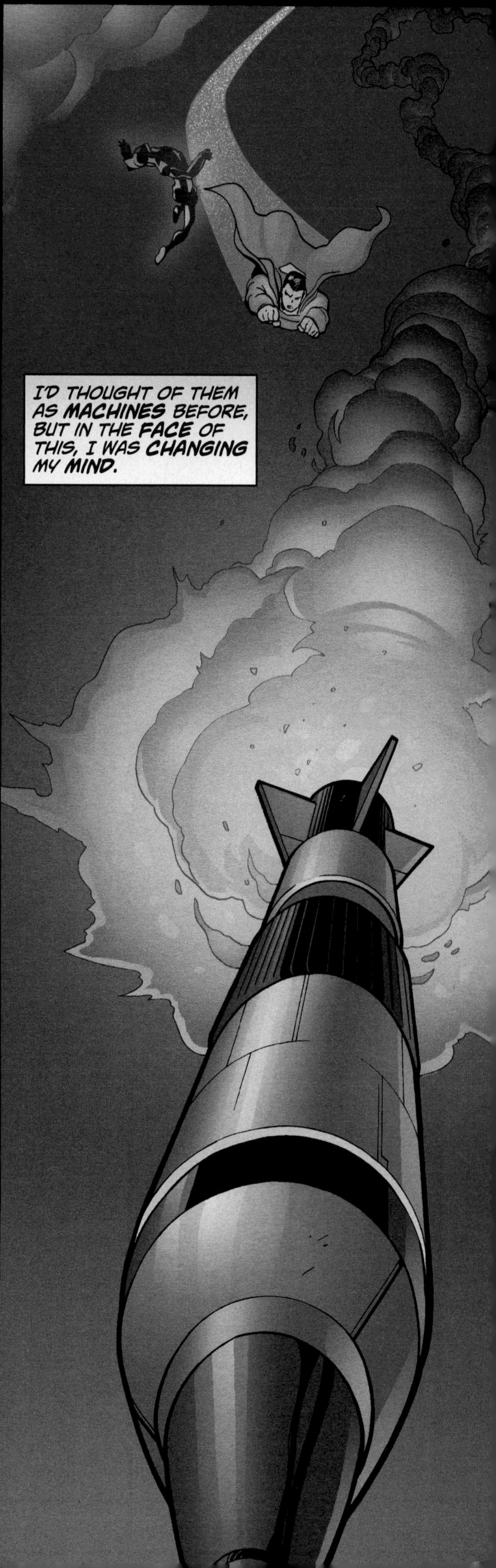
I'D THOUGHT OF THEM AS MACHINES BEFORE, BUT IN THE FACE OF THIS, I WAS CHANGING MY MIND.

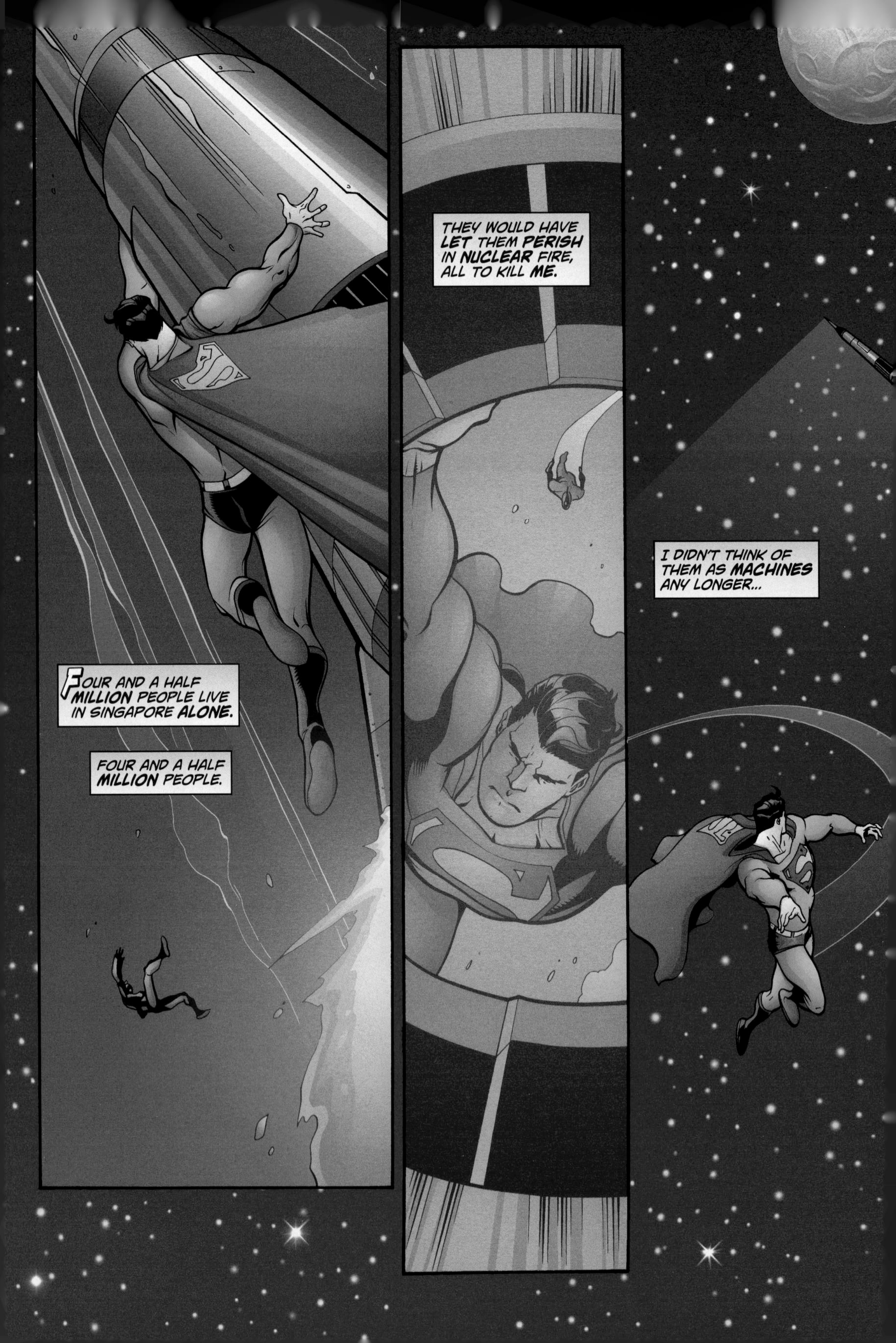
FOUR AND A HALF MILLION PEOPLE LIVE IN SINGAPORE ALONE.
FOUR AND A HALF MILLION PEOPLE.
THEY WOULD HAVE LET THEM PERISH IN NUCLEAR FIRE, ALL TO KILL ME.
I DIDN'T THINK OF THEM AS MACHINES ANY LONGER...

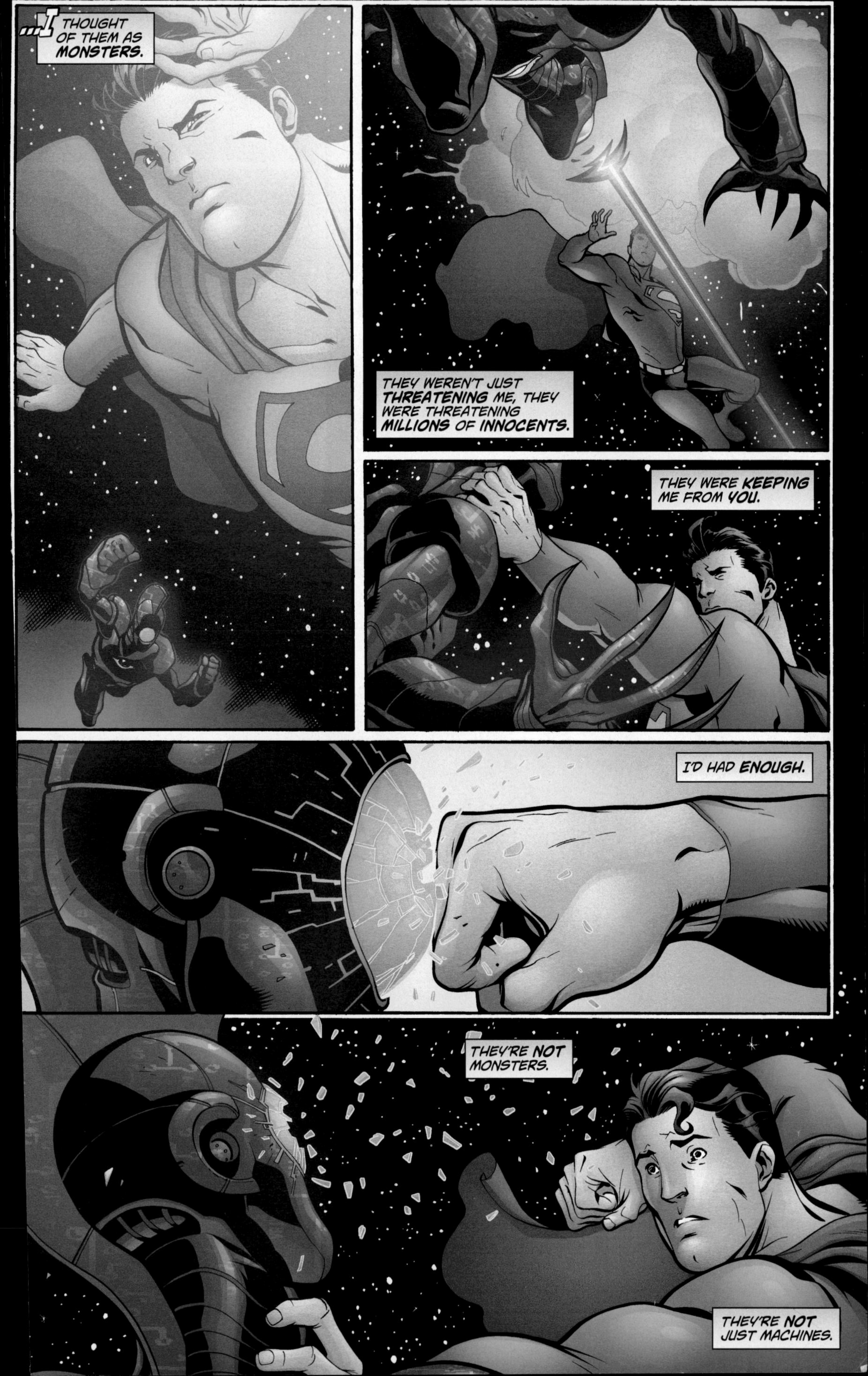
...I THOUGHT OF THEM AS MONSTERS.
THEY WEREN'T JUST THREATENING ME, THEY WERE THREATENING MILLIONS OF INNOCENTS.
THEY WERE KEEPING ME FROM YOU.
I'D HAD ENOUGH.
THEY'RE NOT MONSTERS.
THEY'RE NOT JUST MACHINES.

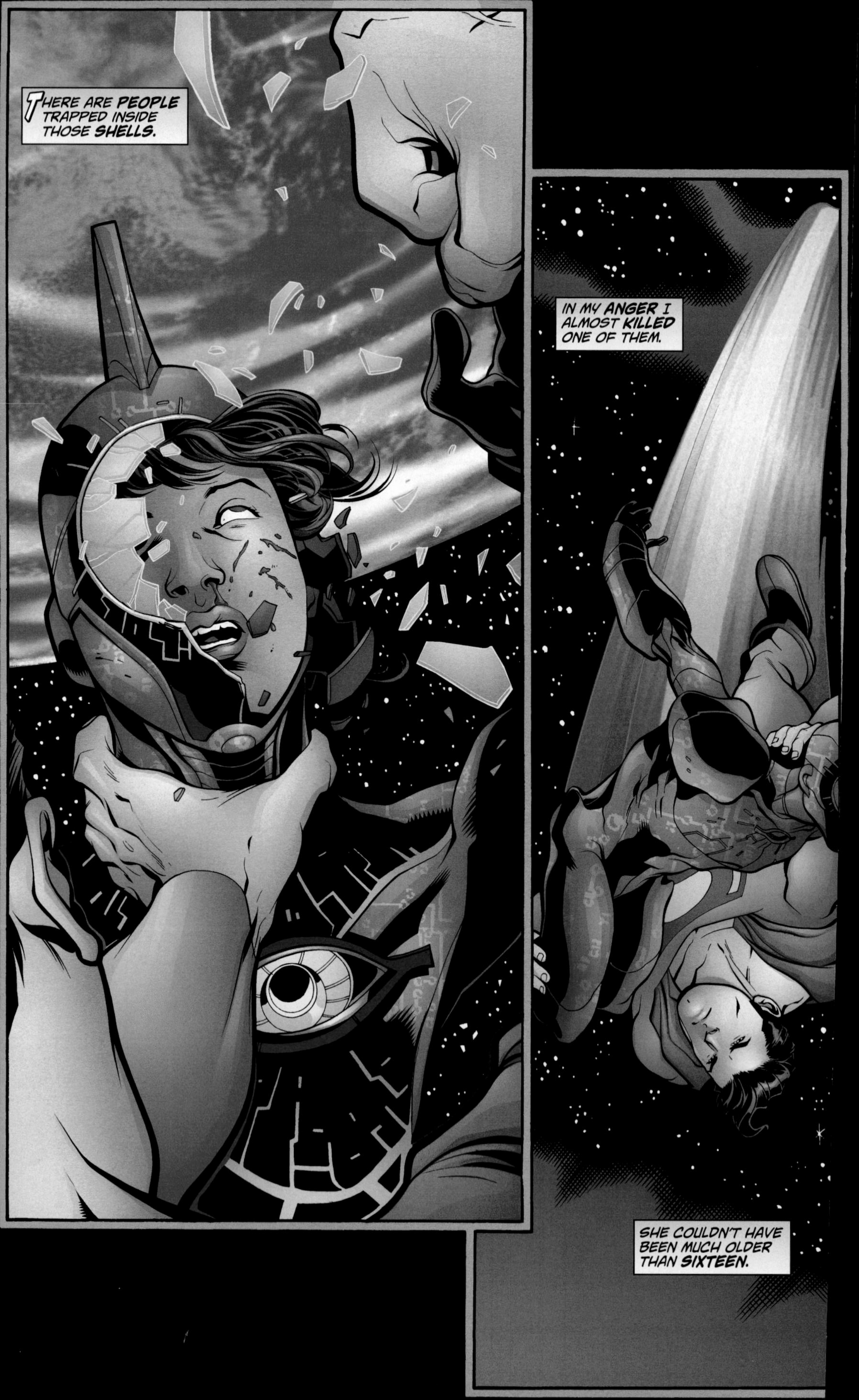
THERE ARE PEOPLE TRAPPED INSIDE THOSE SHELLS.
IN MY ANGER I ALMOST KILLED ONE OF THEM.
SHE COULDN'T HAVE BEEN MUCH OLDER THAN SIXTEEN.

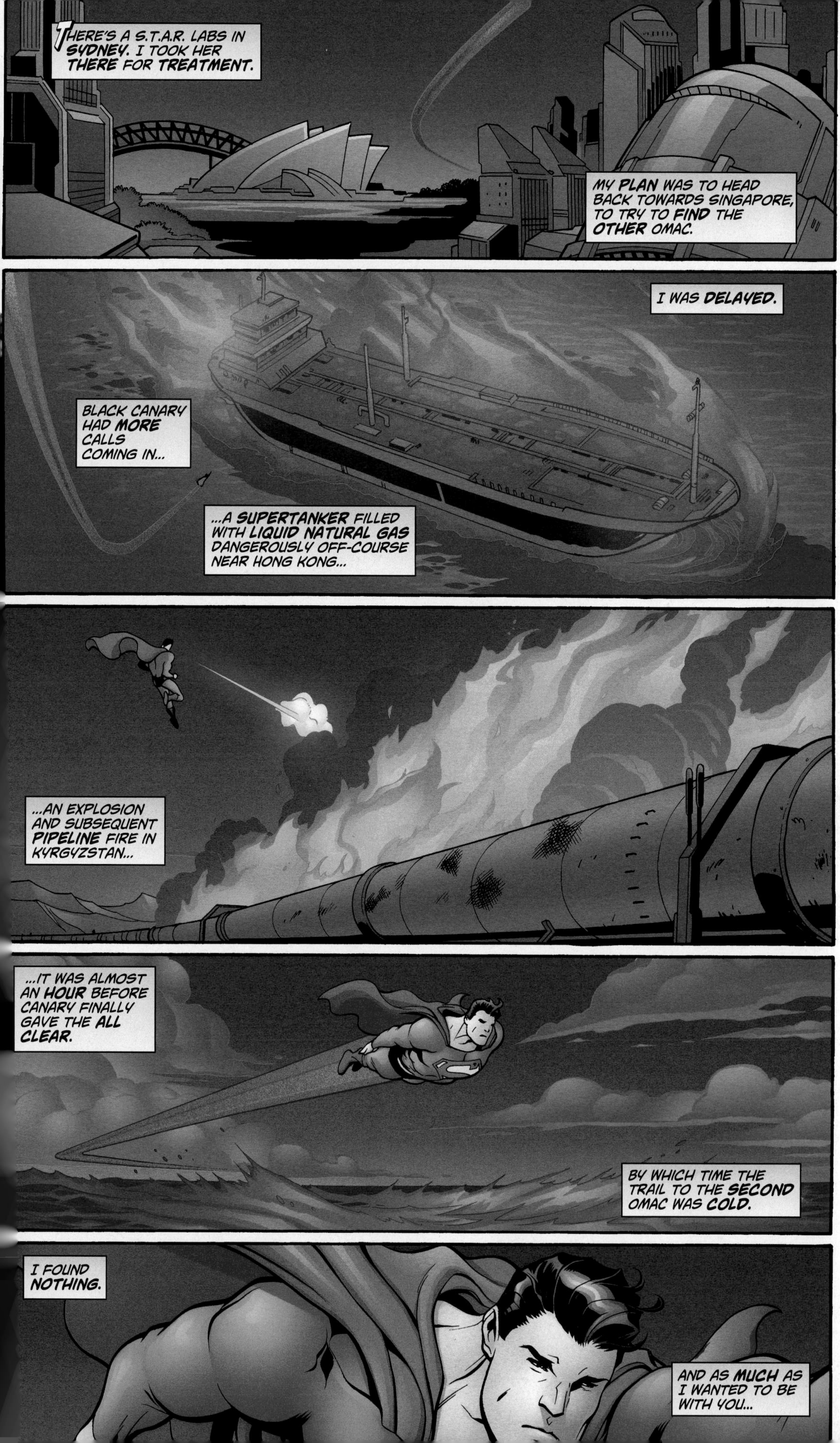
THERE'S A S.T.A.R. LABS IN SYDNEY. I TOOK HER THERE FOR TREATMENT.
MY PLAN WAS TO HEAD BACK TOWARDS SINGAPORE, TO TRY TO FIND THE OTHER OMAC.
I WAS DELAYED.
BLACK CANARY HAD MORE CALLS COMING IN...
...A SUPERTANKER FILLED WITH LIQUID NATURAL GAS DANGEROUSLY OFF-COURSE NEAR HONG KONG...
...AN EXPLOSION AND SUBSEQUENT PIPELINE FIRE IN KYRGYZSTAN...
...IT WAS ALMOST AN HOUR BEFORE CANARY FINALLY GAVE THE ALL CLEAR.
BY WHICH TIME THE TRAIL TO THE SECOND OMAC WAS COLD.
I FOUND NOTHING.
AND AS MUCH AS I WANTED TO BE WITH YOU...

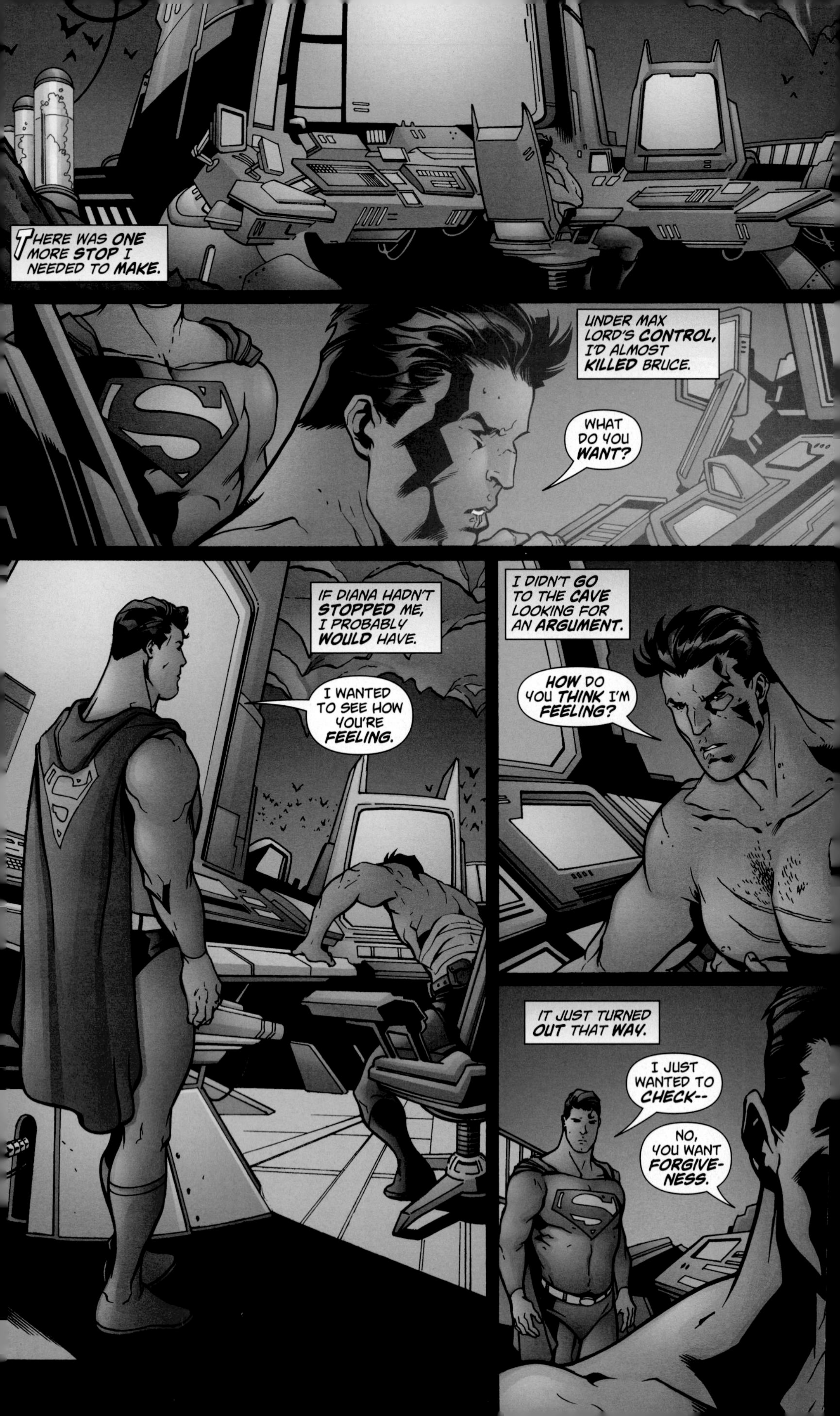
THERE WAS ONE MORE STOP I NEEDED TO MAKE.
UNDER MAX LORD'S CONTROL, I'D ALMOST KILLED BRUCE.
WHAT DO YOU WANT?
IF DIANA HADN'T STOPPED ME, I PROBABLY WOULD HAVE.
I WANTED TO SEE HOW YOU'RE FEELING.
I DIDN'T GO TO THE CAVE LOOKING FOR AN ARGUMENT.
HOW DO YOU THINK I'M FEELING?
IT JUST TURNED OUT THAT WAY.
I JUST WANTED TO CHECK--
NO, YOU WANT FORGIVE-NESS.

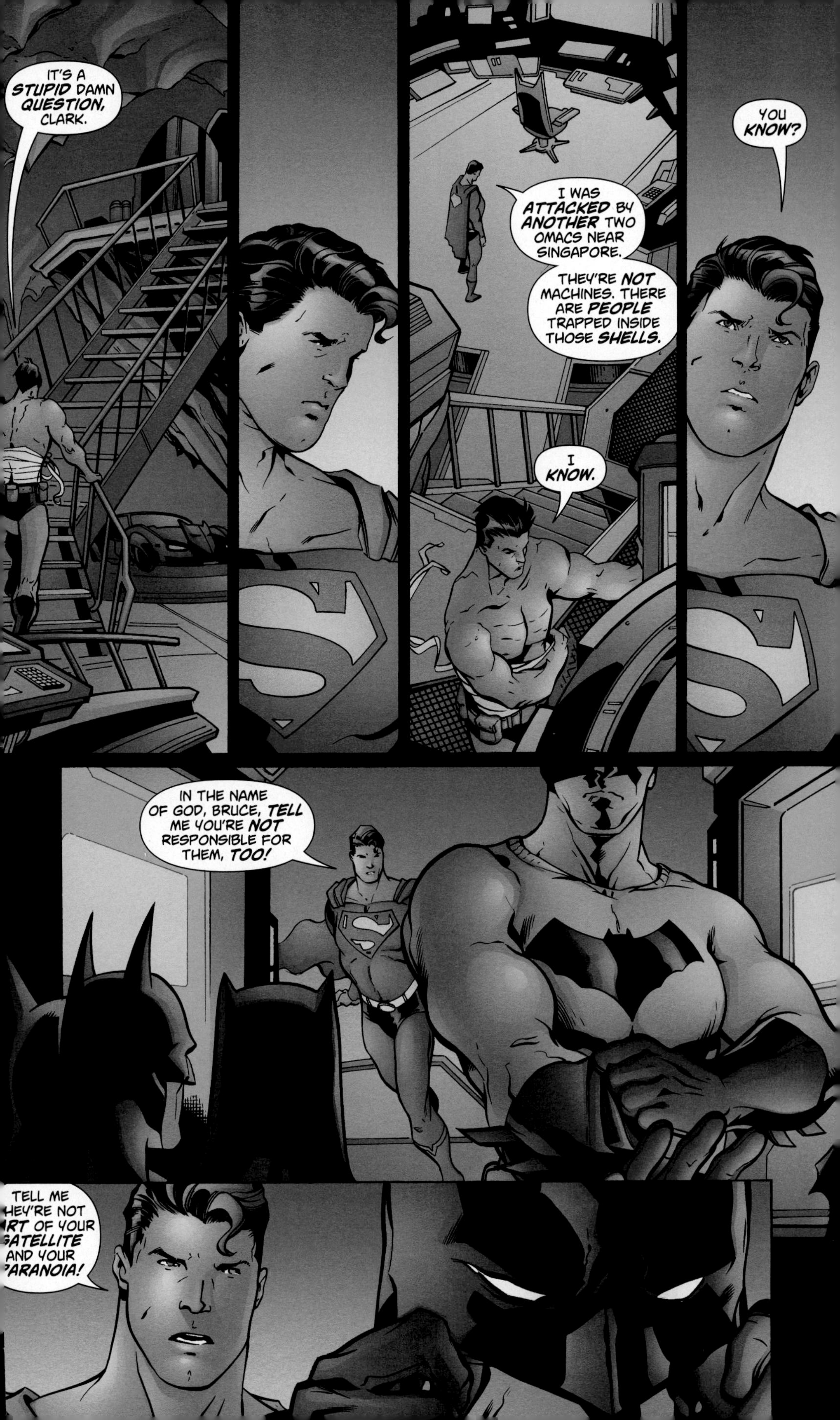
IT'S A STUPID DAMN QUESTION, CLARK.
I WAS ATTACKED BY ANOTHER TWO OMACS NEAR SINGAPORE.
THEY'RE NOT MACHINES. THERE ARE PEOPLE TRAPPED INSIDE THOSE SHELLS.
I KNOW.
YOU KNOW?
IN THE NAME OF GOD, BRUCE, TELL ME YOU'RE NOT RESPONSIBLE FOR THEM, TOO!
TELL ME
AND YOUR

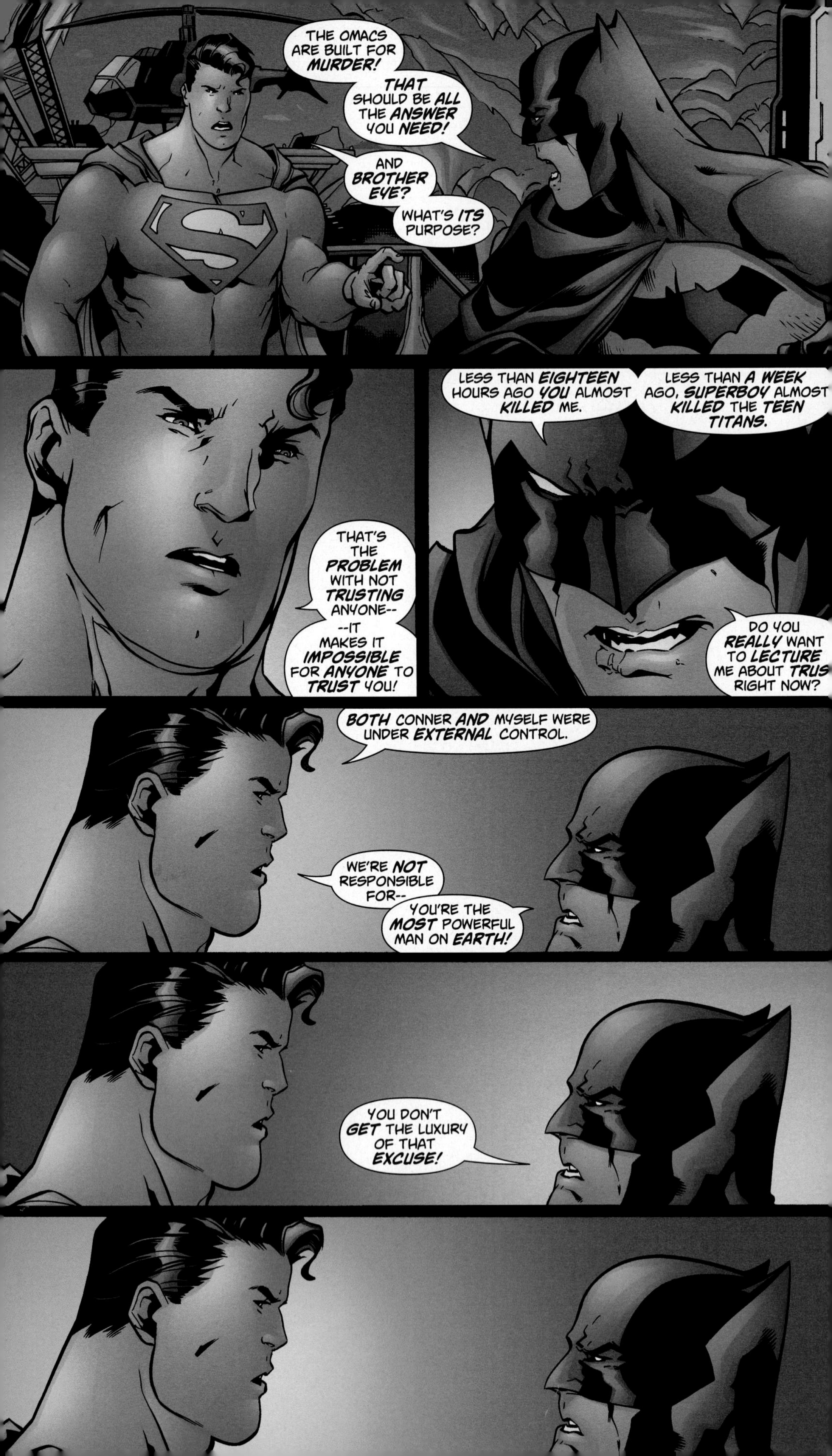
THE OMACS ARE BUILT FOR MURDER!
THAT SHOULD BE ALL THE ANSWER YOU NEED!
AND BROTHER EYE?
WHAT'S ITS PURPOSE?
LESS THAN EIGHTEEN HOURS AGO YOU ALMOST KILLED ME.
LESS THAN A WEEK AGO, SUPERBOY ALMOST KILLED THE TEEN TITANS.
THAT'S THE PROBLEM WITH NOT TRUSTING ANYONE--
--IT MAKES IT IMPOSSIBLE FOR ANYONE TO TRUST YOU!
DO YOU REALLY WANT TO LECTURE ME ABOUT TRUS RIGHT NOW?
BOTH CONNER AND MYSELF WERE UNDER EXTERNAL CONTROL.
WE'RE NOT RESPONSIBLE FOR--
YOU'RE THE MOST POWERFUL MAN ON EARTH!
YOU DON'T GET THE LUXURY OF THAT EXCUSE!

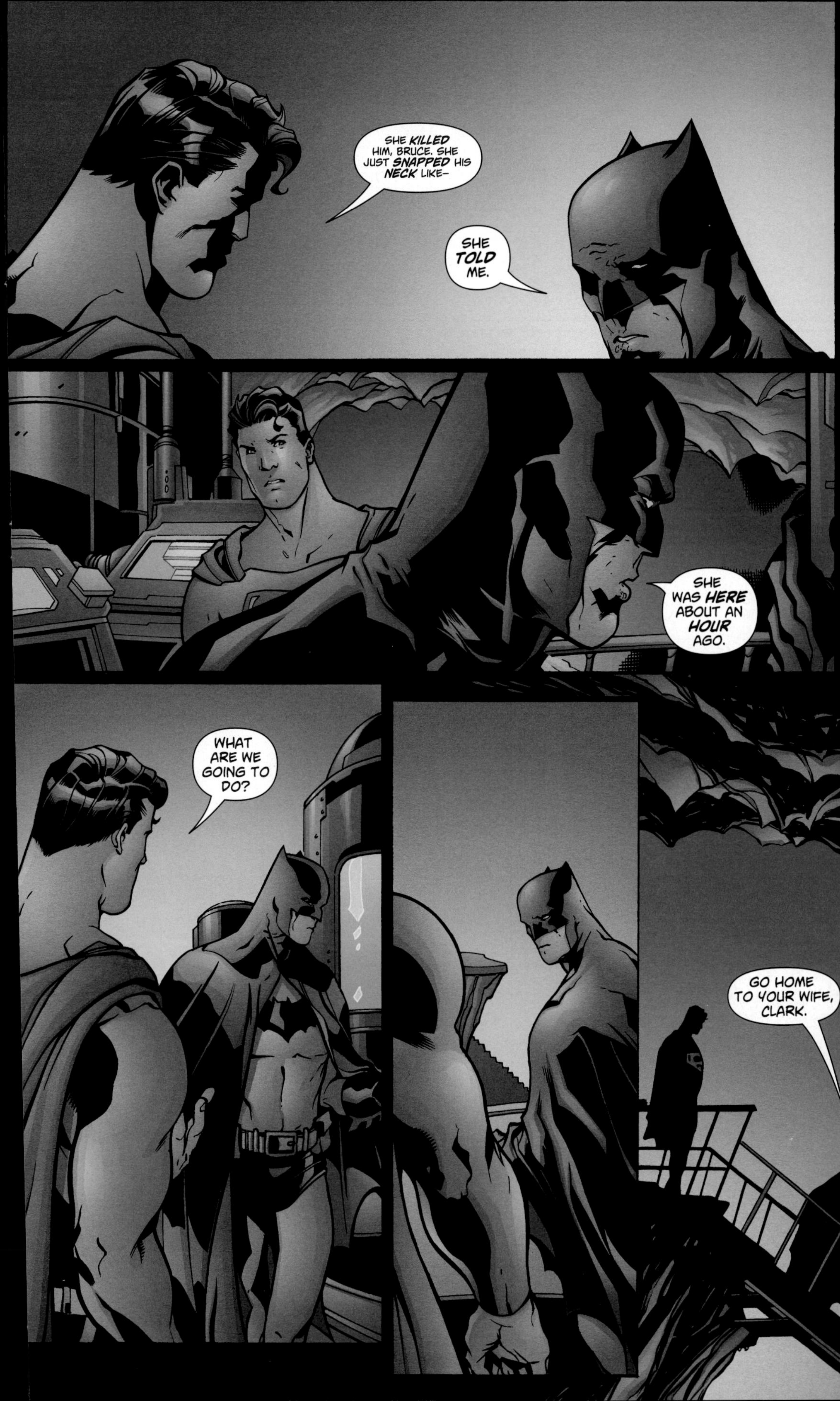
SHE KILLED HIM, BRUCE. SHE JUST SNAPPED HIS NECK LIKE–
SHE TOLD ME.
SHE WAS HERE ABOUT AN HOUR AGO.
WHAT ARE WE GOING TO DO?
GO HOME TO YOUR WIFE, CLARK.

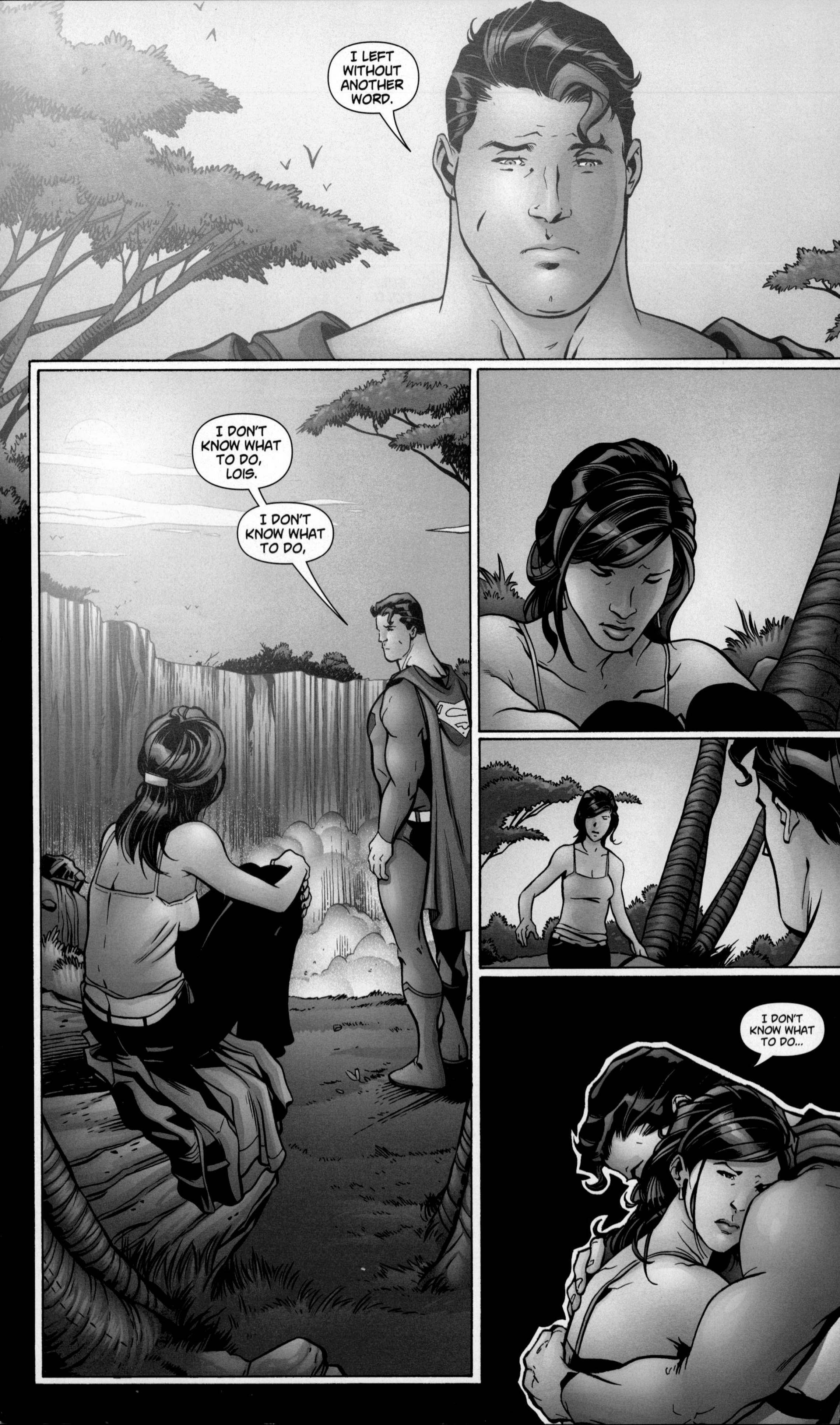
I LEFT WITHOUT ANOTHER WORD.
I DON'T KNOW WHAT TO DO, LOIS.
I DON'T KNOW WHAT TO DO,
I DON'T KNOW WHAT TO DO...

SUPERMAN 220 - ART BY ED BENES

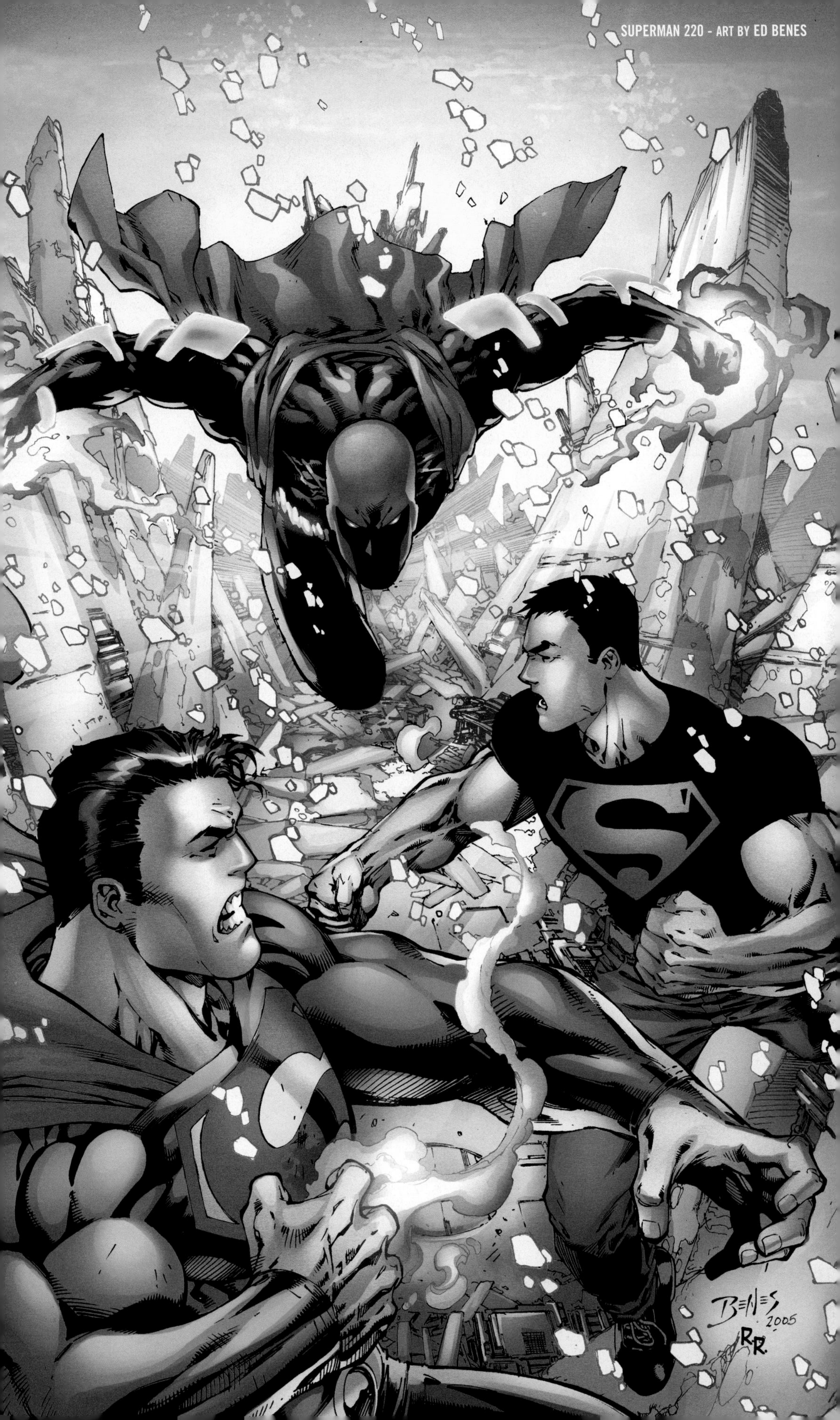

BENES 2005
R.R.

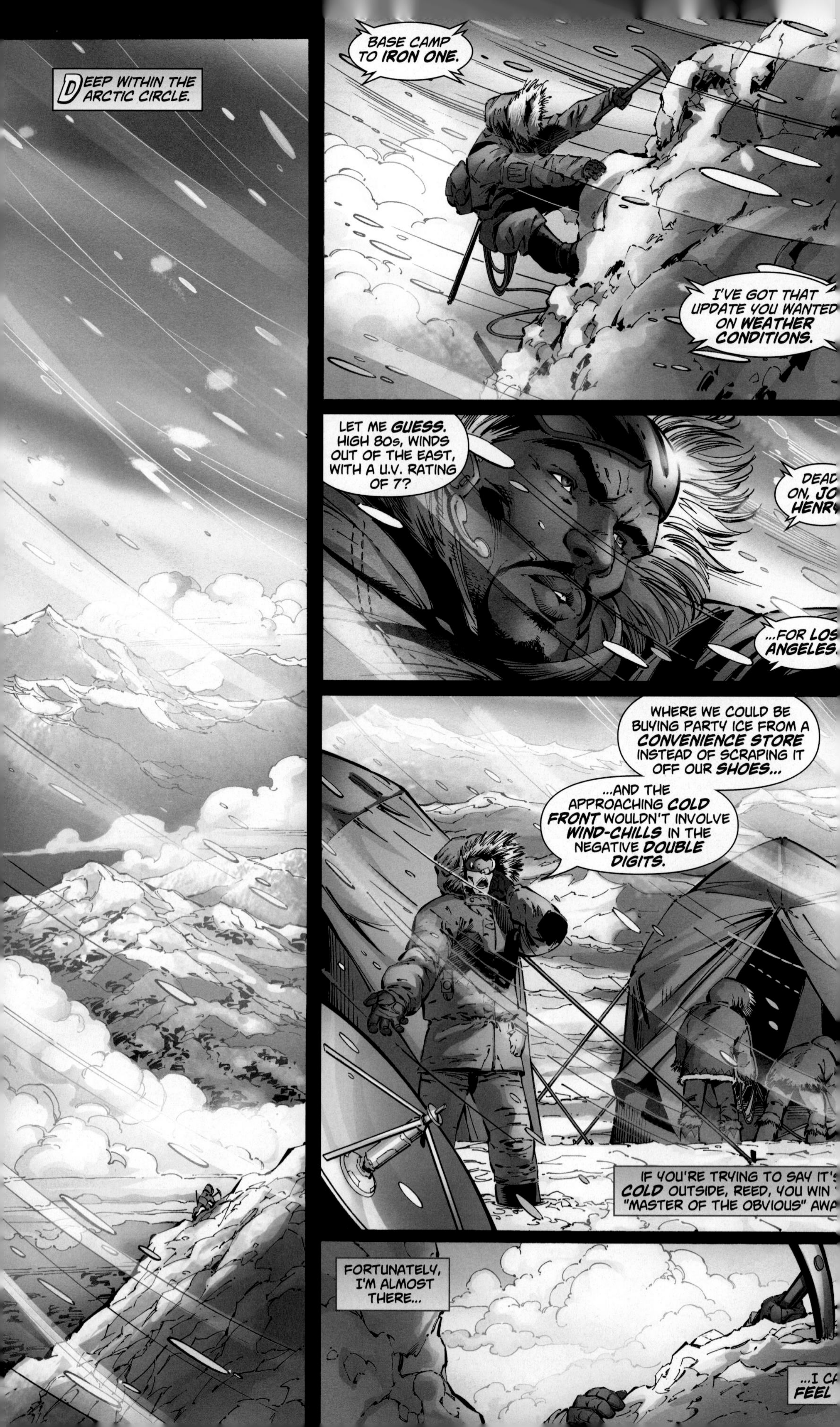
DEEP WITHIN THE ARCTIC CIRCLE.
BASE CAMP TO IRON ONE.
I'VE GOT THAT UPDATE YOU WANTED ON WEATHER CONDITIONS.
LET ME GUESS. HIGH 80s, WINDS OUT OF THE EAST, WITH A U.V. RATING OF 7?
DEAD ON, JO HENR
...FOR LOS ANGELES.
WHERE WE COULD BE BUYING PARTY ICE FROM A CONVENIENCE STORE INSTEAD OF SCRAPING IT OFF OUR SHOES...
...AND THE APPROACHING COLD FRONT WOULDN'T INVOLVE WIND-CHILLS IN THE NEGATIVE DOUBLE DIGITS.
IF YOU'RE TRYING TO SAY IT'S COLD OUTSIDE, REED, YOU WIN "MASTER OF THE OBVIOUS" AWA
FORTUNATELY, I'M ALMOST THERE...
...I CA FEEL

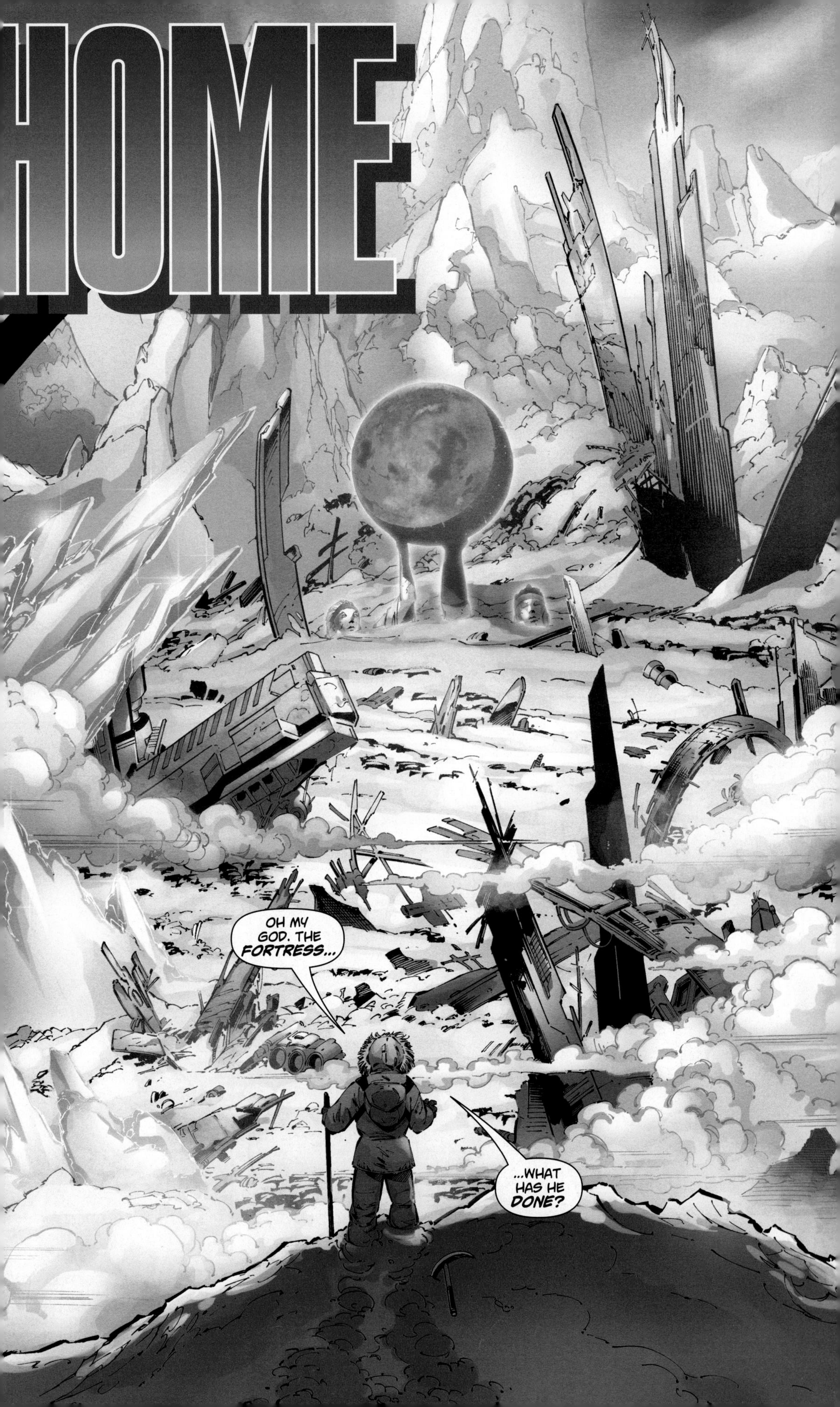
HOME
OH MY GOD. THE FORTRESS...
...WHAT HAS HE DONE?

WHATEVER.

AT LEAST YOU'RE FINALLY NOT LOOKING AT ME LIKE I'M A *TIME-BOMB* ABOUT TO GO OFF...

...ONE JOHN DEERE, COMING UP...

CONNER, WAIT!

MARTHA GAVE ME THE HEADS UP.

I THOUGHT IT WAS SUPPOSED TO BE *IMPOSSIBLE* TO GET A TRACTOR STUCK IN THE MUD.

NO, CONNER. IT'S IMPOSSIBLE FOR PEOPLE TO *FLY*.

TAKE IT FROM A KANSAS FARMER, *TRACTORS* GET STUCK ALL THE TIME.

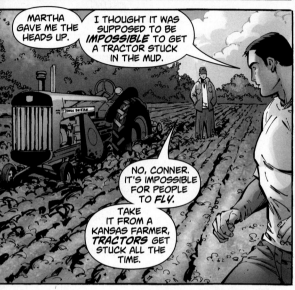

YOU NEED TO START *WATCHING* HOW YOU USE YOUR POWERS EVEN OUT HERE.

LEX LUTHOR'S BOUND TO BE *LOOKING* FOR YOU.

GREAT.

AND THAT'S ONLY AN ISSUE *NOW* BECAUSE...

BECAUSE THERE'S NO SUCH THING AS "REMOTE." LUTHOR HAS HIS FINGERS IN A MILLION HIGH-TECH PIES.

BETWEEN SATELLITE SURVEILLANCE AND HIGH ALTITUDE SPY PLANES, THE WORLD'S NOT AS *BIG* AS IT USED TO BE.

AND AFTER ALL *CLARK'S* BEEN THROUGH WITH THAT MANIAC...

...IT DOESN'T HURT TO BE *CAUTIOUS*.

RIGHT *CLARK*.

SEEING HOW WELL *YOU GUYS* ARE HANDLING MY SITUATION, I CA[N] WAIT FOR THA[T] CONVERSATION[.]

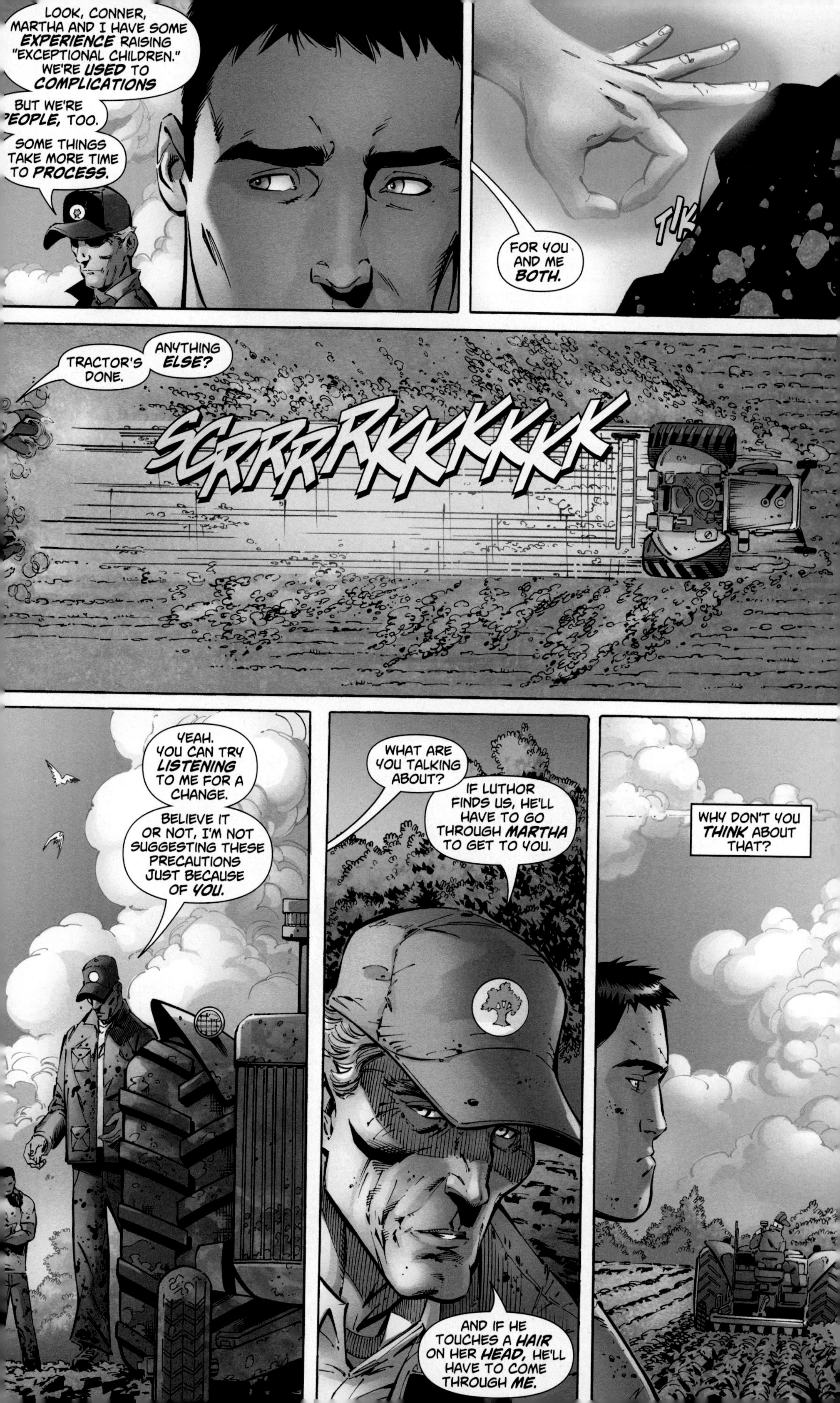
LOOK, CONNER, MARTHA AND I HAVE SOME EXPERIENCE RAISING "EXCEPTIONAL CHILDREN." WE'RE USED TO COMPLICATIONS
BUT WE'RE PEOPLE, TOO.
SOME THINGS TAKE MORE TIME TO PROCESS.
FOR YOU AND ME BOTH.
TIK
TRACTOR'S DONE.
ANYTHING ELSE?
SCRRRRKKKKKK
YEAH. YOU CAN TRY LISTENING TO ME FOR A CHANGE.
BELIEVE IT OR NOT, I'M NOT SUGGESTING THESE PRECAUTIONS JUST BECAUSE OF YOU.
WHAT ARE YOU TALKING ABOUT?
IF LUTHOR FINDS US, HE'LL HAVE TO GO THROUGH MARTHA TO GET TO YOU.
AND IF HE TOUCHES A HAIR ON HER HEAD, HE'LL HAVE TO COME THROUGH ME.
WHY DON'T YOU THINK ABOUT THAT?

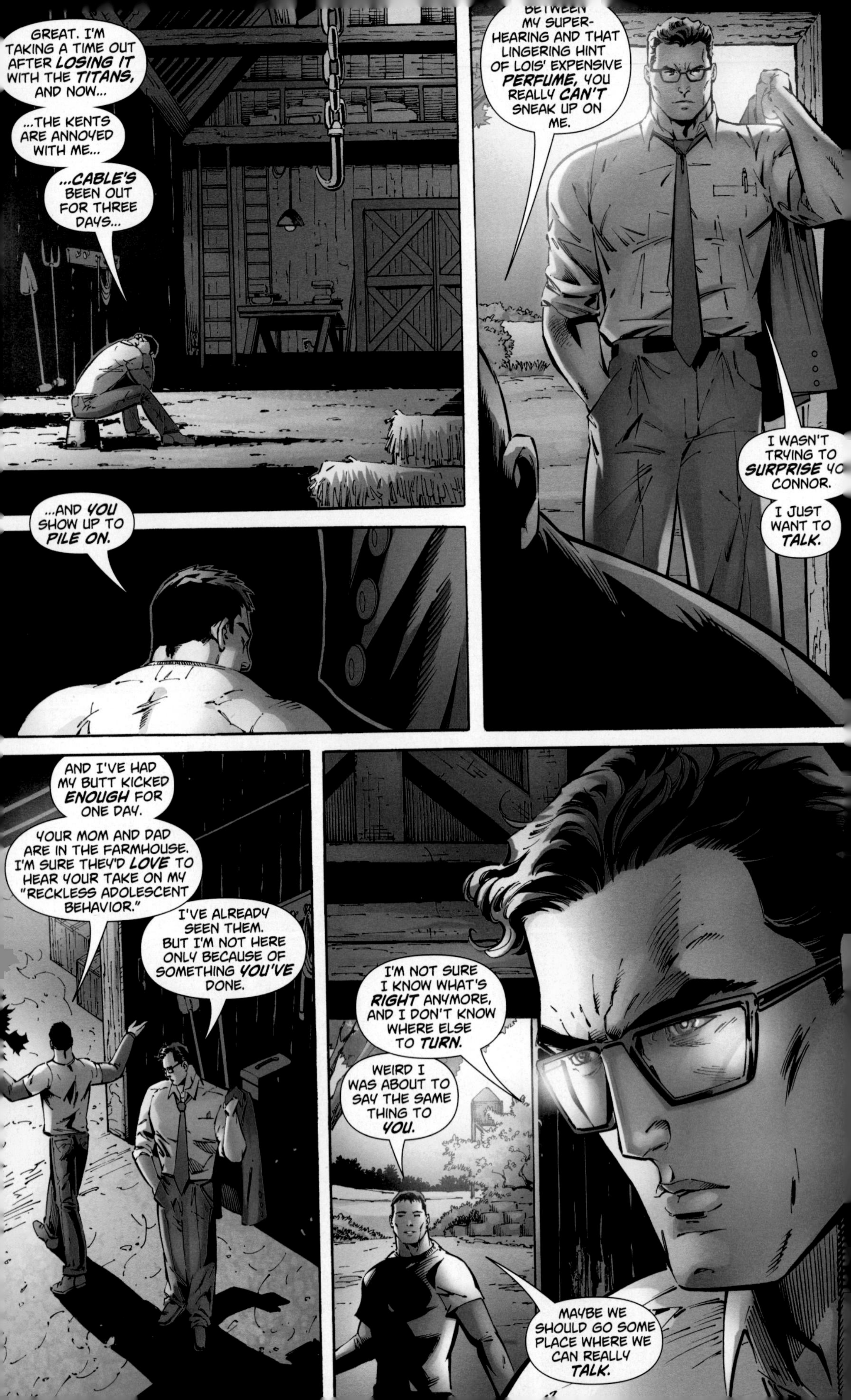
GREAT. I'M TAKING A TIME OUT AFTER LOSING IT WITH THE TITANS, AND NOW...
...THE KENTS ARE ANNOYED WITH ME...
...CABLE'S BEEN OUT FOR THREE DAYS...
...AND YOU SHOW UP TO PILE ON.
BETWEEN MY SUPER-HEARING AND THAT LINGERING HINT OF LOIS' EXPENSIVE PERFUME, YOU REALLY CAN'T SNEAK UP ON ME.
I WASN'T TRYING TO SURPRISE YO CONNOR.
I JUST WANT TO TALK.
AND I'VE HAD MY BUTT KICKED ENOUGH FOR ONE DAY.
YOUR MOM AND DAD ARE IN THE FARMHOUSE. I'M SURE THEY'D LOVE TO HEAR YOUR TAKE ON MY "RECKLESS ADOLESCENT BEHAVIOR."
I'VE ALREADY SEEN THEM. BUT I'M NOT HERE ONLY BECAUSE OF SOMETHING YOU'VE DONE.
I'M NOT SURE I KNOW WHAT'S RIGHT ANYMORE, AND I DON'T KNOW WHERE ELSE TO TURN.
WEIRD I WAS ABOUT TO SAY THE SAME THING TO YOU.
MAYBE WE SHOULD GO SOME PLACE WHERE WE CAN REALLY TALK.

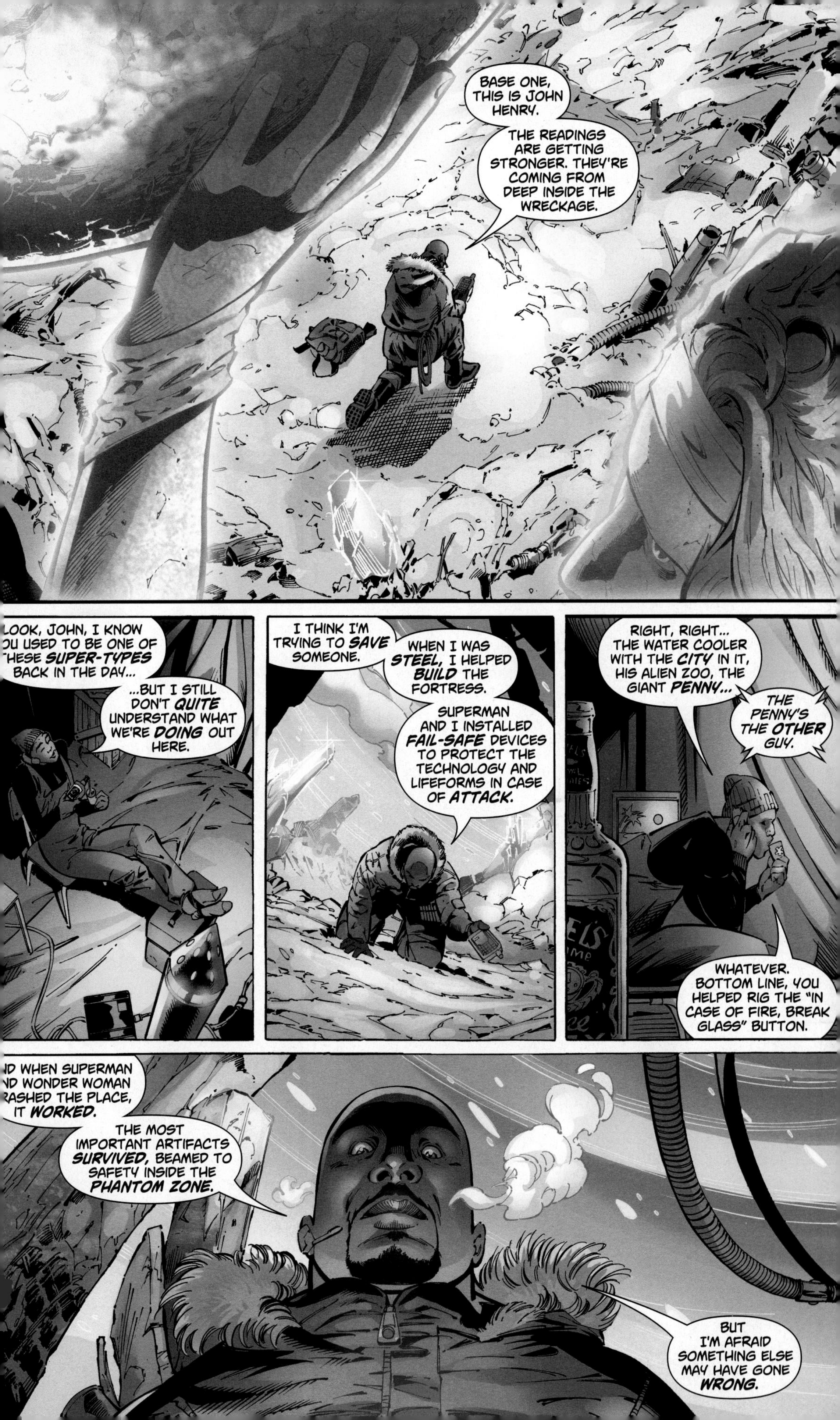

BASE ONE, THIS IS JOHN HENRY.
THE READINGS ARE GETTING STRONGER. THEY'RE COMING FROM DEEP INSIDE THE WRECKAGE.
LOOK, JOHN, I KNOW YOU USED TO BE ONE OF THESE SUPER-TYPES BACK IN THE DAY...
...BUT I STILL DON'T QUITE UNDERSTAND WHAT WE'RE DOING OUT HERE.
I THINK I'M TRYING TO SAVE SOMEONE.
WHEN I WAS STEEL, I HELPED BUILD THE FORTRESS.
SUPERMAN AND I INSTALLED FAIL-SAFE DEVICES TO PROTECT THE TECHNOLOGY AND LIFEFORMS IN CASE OF ATTACK.
RIGHT, RIGHT... THE WATER COOLER WITH THE CITY IN IT, HIS ALIEN ZOO, THE GIANT PENNY...
THE PENNY'S THE OTHER GUY.
WHATEVER. BOTTOM LINE, YOU HELPED RIG THE "IN CASE OF FIRE, BREAK GLASS" BUTTON.
AND WHEN SUPERMAN AND WONDER WOMAN TRASHED THE PLACE, IT WORKED.
THE MOST IMPORTANT ARTIFACTS SURVIVED, BEAMED TO SAFETY INSIDE THE PHANTOM ZONE.
BUT I'M AFRAID SOMETHING ELSE MAY HAVE GONE WRONG.

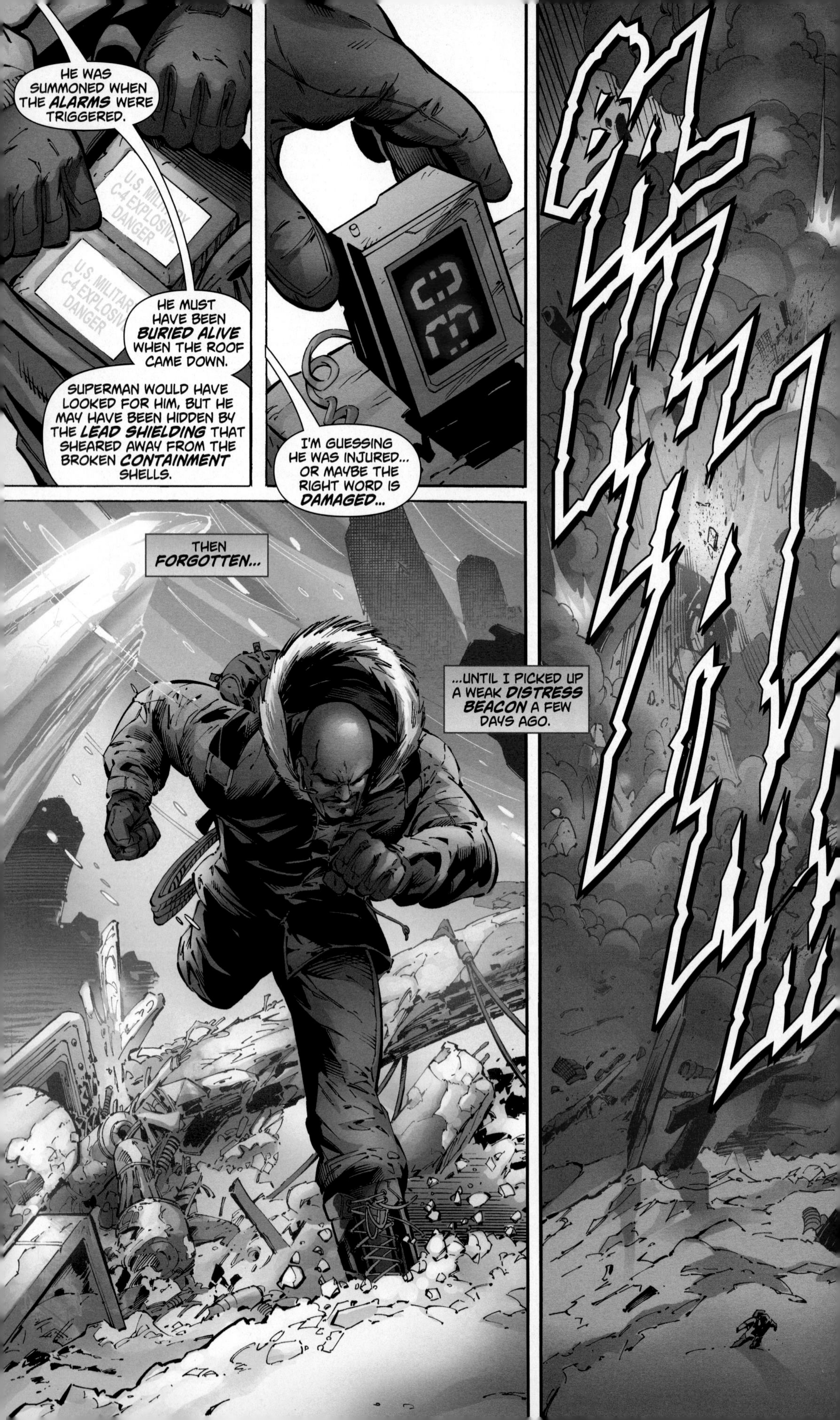
HE WAS SUMMONED WHEN THE ALARMS WERE TRIGGERED.
U.S. MILITARY C-4 EXPLOSIVE DANGER
U.S. MILITARY C-4 EXPLOSIVE DANGER
HE MUST HAVE BEEN BURIED ALIVE WHEN THE ROOF CAME DOWN.
SUPERMAN WOULD HAVE LOOKED FOR HIM, BUT HE MAY HAVE BEEN HIDDEN BY THE LEAD SHIELDING THAT SHEARED AWAY FROM THE BROKEN CONTAINMENT SHELLS.
I'M GUESSING HE WAS INJURED... OR MAYBE THE RIGHT WORD IS DAMAGED...
THEN FORGOTTEN...
...UNTIL I PICKED UP A WEAK DISTRESS BEACON A FEW DAYS AGO.

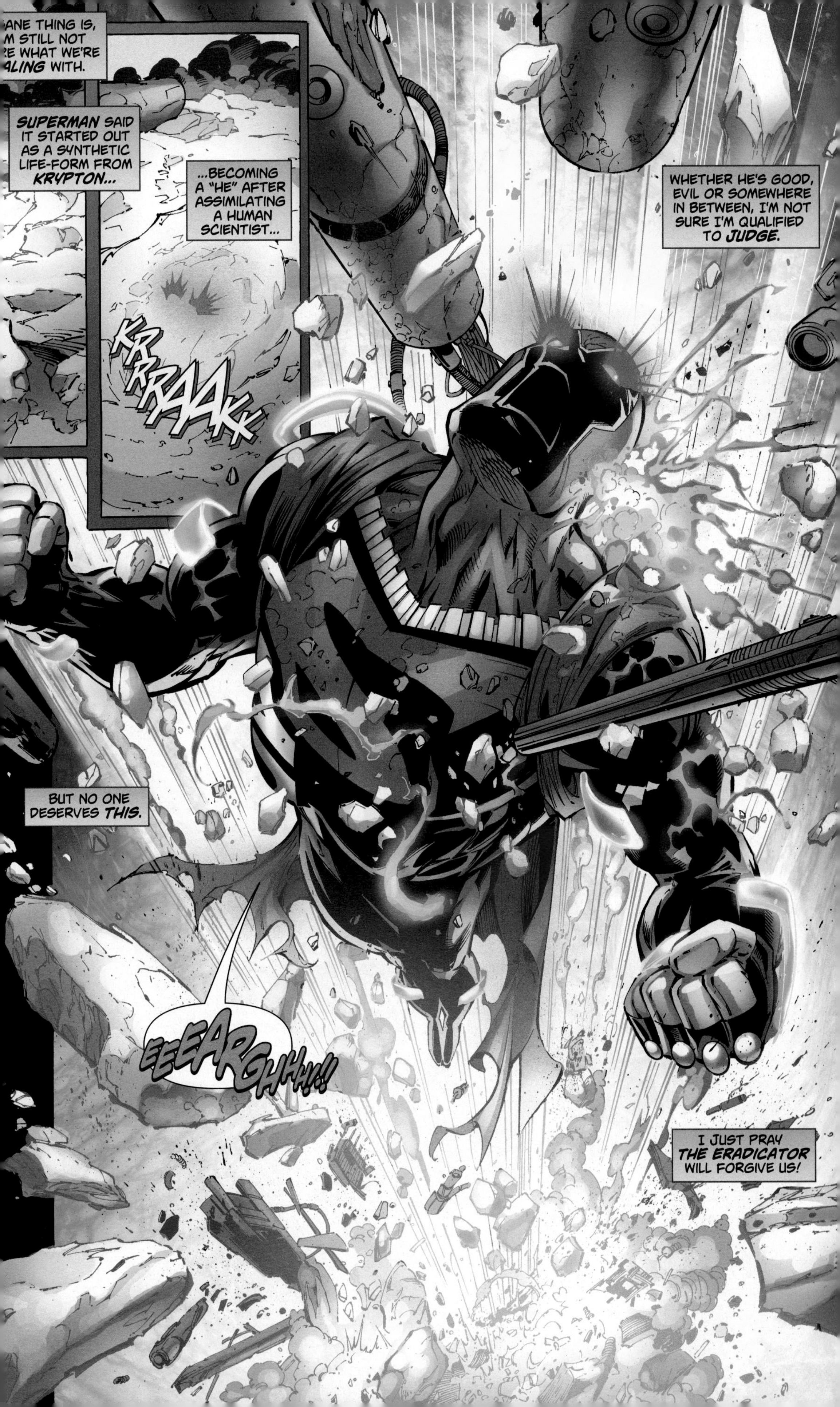
ANE THING IS, M STILL NOT E WHAT WE'RE ALING WITH.
SUPERMAN SAID IT STARTED OUT AS A SYNTHETIC LIFE-FORM FROM KRYPTON...
...BECOMING A "HE" AFTER ASSIMILATING A HUMAN SCIENTIST...
WHETHER HE'S GOOD, EVIL OR SOMEWHERE IN BETWEEN, I'M NOT SURE I'M QUALIFIED TO JUDGE.
KRRRAAKK
BUT NO ONE DESERVES THIS.
EEEEARGHHH!!!
I JUST PRAY THE ERADICATOR WILL FORGIVE US!

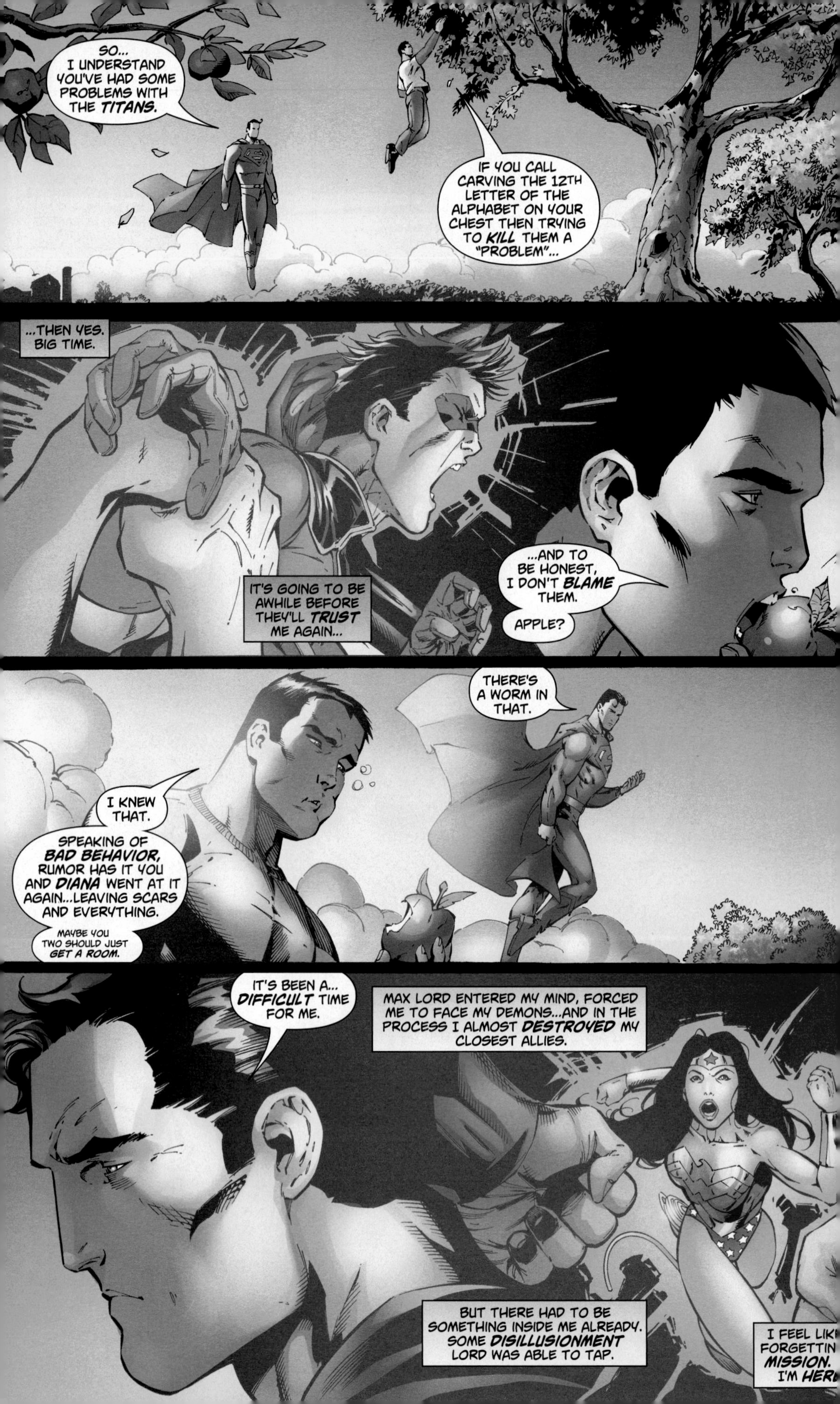
SO... I UNDERSTAND YOU'VE HAD SOME PROBLEMS WITH THE TITANS.
IF YOU CALL CARVING THE 12TH LETTER OF THE ALPHABET ON YOUR CHEST THEN TRYING TO KILL THEM A "PROBLEM"...
...THEN YES. BIG TIME.
IT'S GOING TO BE AWHILE BEFORE THEY'LL TRUST ME AGAIN...
...AND TO BE HONEST, I DON'T BLAME THEM.
APPLE?
THERE'S A WORM IN THAT.
I KNEW THAT.
SPEAKING OF BAD BEHAVIOR, RUMOR HAS IT YOU AND DIANA WENT AT IT AGAIN...LEAVING SCARS AND EVERYTHING.
MAYBE YOU TWO SHOULD JUST GET A ROOM.
IT'S BEEN A... DIFFICULT TIME FOR ME.
MAX LORD ENTERED MY MIND, FORCED ME TO FACE MY DEMONS...AND IN THE PROCESS I ALMOST DESTROYED MY CLOSEST ALLIES.
BUT THERE HAD TO BE SOMETHING INSIDE ME ALREADY. SOME DISILLUSIONMENT LORD WAS ABLE TO TAP.

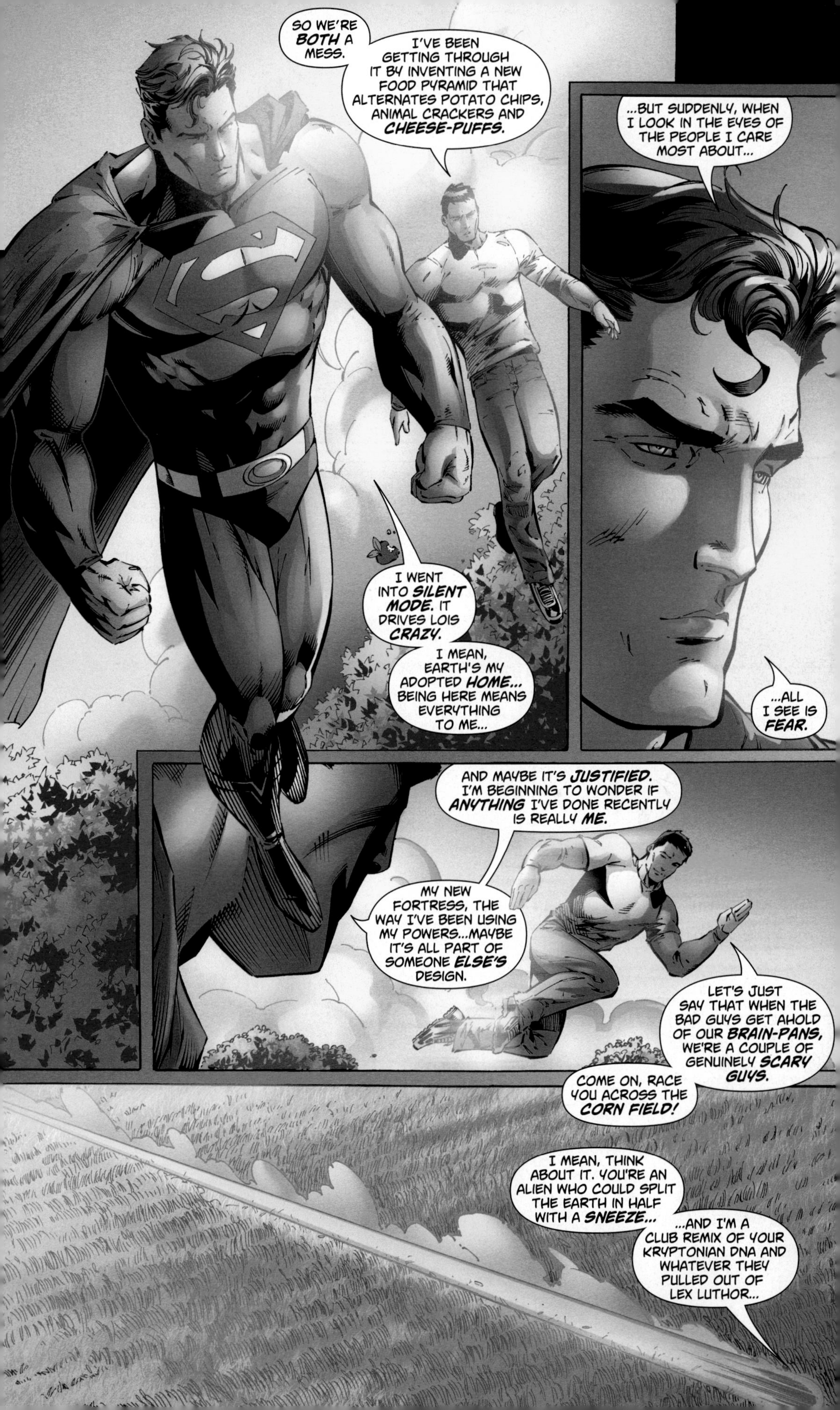

SO WE'RE BOTH A MESS.
I'VE BEEN GETTING THROUGH IT BY INVENTING A NEW FOOD PYRAMID THAT ALTERNATES POTATO CHIPS, ANIMAL CRACKERS AND CHEESE-PUFFS.
I WENT INTO SILENT MODE. IT DRIVES LOIS CRAZY.
I MEAN, EARTH'S MY ADOPTED HOME... BEING HERE MEANS EVERYTHING TO ME...
...BUT SUDDENLY, WHEN I LOOK IN THE EYES OF THE PEOPLE I CARE MOST ABOUT...
...ALL I SEE IS FEAR.
AND MAYBE IT'S JUSTIFIED. I'M BEGINNING TO WONDER IF ANYTHING I'VE DONE RECENTLY IS REALLY ME.
MY NEW FORTRESS, THE WAY I'VE BEEN USING MY POWERS...MAYBE IT'S ALL PART OF SOMEONE ELSE'S DESIGN.
LET'S JUST SAY THAT WHEN THE BAD GUYS GET AHOLD OF OUR BRAIN-PANS, WE'RE A COUPLE OF GENUINELY SCARY GUYS.
COME ON, RACE YOU ACROSS THE CORN FIELD!
I MEAN, THINK ABOUT IT. YOU'RE AN ALIEN WHO COULD SPLIT THE EARTH IN HALF WITH A SNEEZE...
...AND I'M A CLUB REMIX OF YOUR KRYPTONIAN DNA AND WHATEVER THEY PULLED OUT OF LEX LUTHOR...

WHAT?!

Uhh, YOU WIN.

SORRY. I'VE BEEN TRYING TO FIND A WAY TO GIVE YOU THE 411 ON MY LEX CONNECTION FOR AWHILE.

LIKE, BEFORE THE TERM "411" BECAME A HOKEY CLICHÉ.

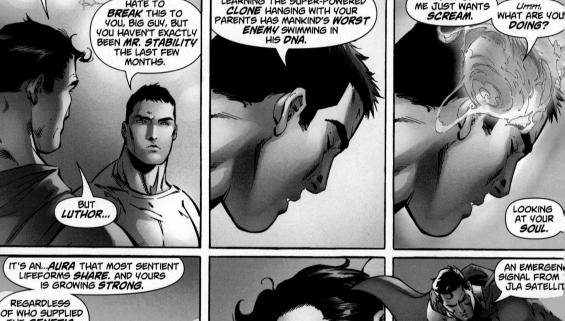

I CAN'T BELIEVE YOU NEVER TOLD ME.

I COULD HAVE HELPED. MAYBE EVEN FOUND A WAY TO PREVENT WHAT HAPPENED WITH THE TITANS.

HATE TO BREAK THIS TO YOU, BIG GUY, BUT YOU HAVEN'T EXACTLY BEEN MR. STABILITY THE LAST FEW MONTHS.

BUT LUTHOR...

TRUST ME, IT DOESN'T TAKE A PhD TO GUESS MY DUELING GENE POOLS EXPLAIN HOW I WAS MIND-CONTROLLED...

...OR YOUR REACTION TO LEARNING THE SUPER-POWERED CLONE HANGING WITH YOUR PARENTS HAS MANKIND'S WORST ENEMY SWIMMING IN HIS DNA.

PART OF ME KEEPS HOPING THERE'S SOMETHING TO THE NATURE VS NURTURE ARGUMENT...

...PART OF ME JUST WANTS SCREAM.

Umm, WHAT ARE YOU DOING?

LOOKING AT YOUR SOUL.

IT'S AN...AURA THAT MOST SENTIENT LIFEFORMS SHARE. AND YOURS IS GROWING STRONG.

REGARDLESS OF WHO SUPPLIED THE GENETIC MATERIAL, CONNER...

...YOU HAVE A BOND WITH THE HUMAN RACE.

AND YOU'RE WORRIED THAT MAYBE, BEING AN ALIEN, YOU DON'T.

FYI, CLARK, KAL, WHATEVER... FOR BETTER OR WORSE, YOU'RE PROBABLY THE MOST "HUMAN" GUY I KNOW.

WHAT IS IT?

AN EMERGEN[CY] SIGNAL FROM JLA SATELLIT[E]

SOMETHIN[G] VERY WRONG

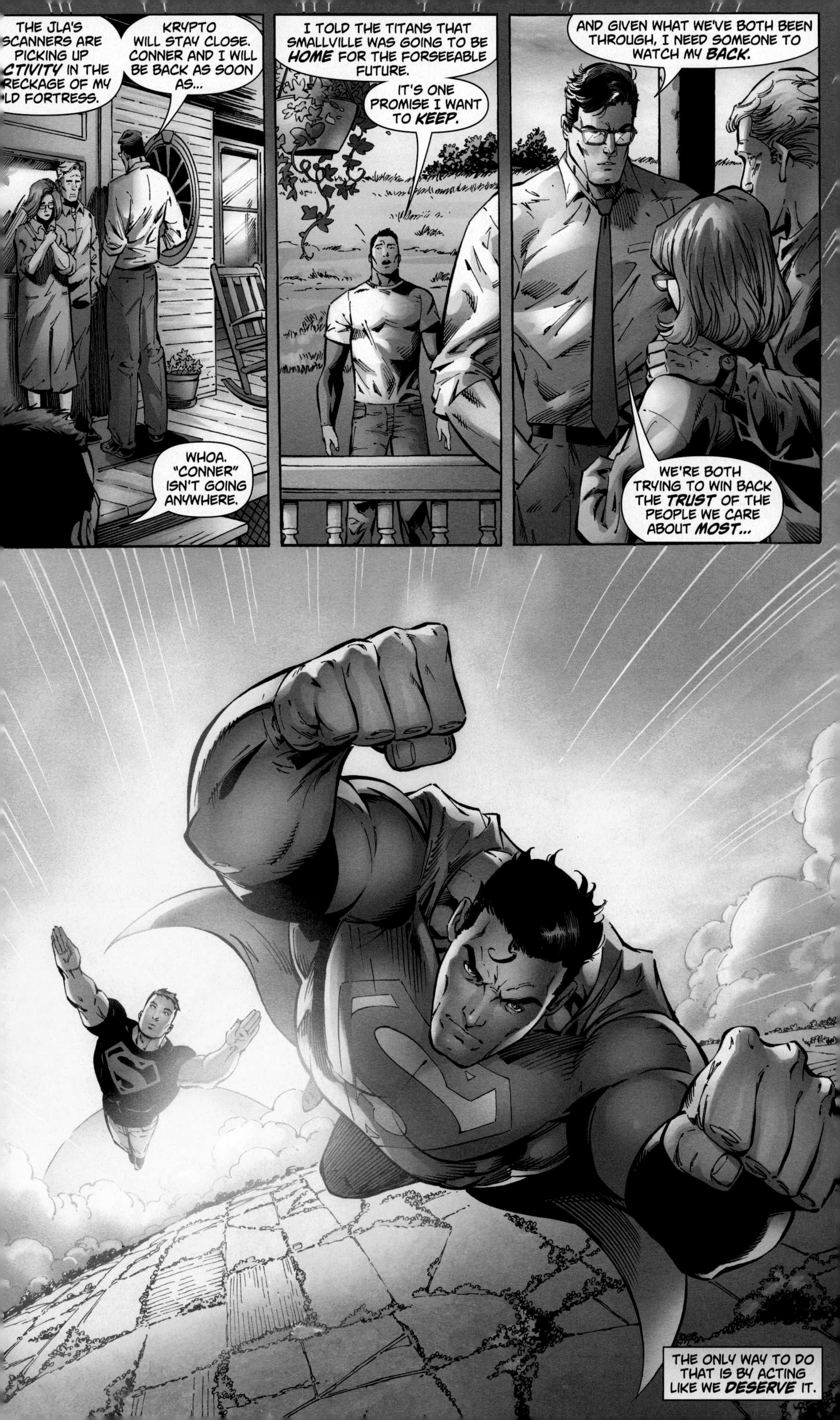
THE JLA'S SCANNERS ARE PICKING UP CTIVITY IN THE RECKAGE OF MY LD FORTRESS.
KRYPTO WILL STAY CLOSE. CONNER AND I WILL BE BACK AS SOON AS...
WHOA. "CONNER" ISN'T GOING ANYWHERE.
I TOLD THE TITANS THAT SMALLVILLE WAS GOING TO BE HOME FOR THE FORSEEABLE FUTURE.
IT'S ONE PROMISE I WANT TO KEEP.
AND GIVEN WHAT WE'VE BOTH BEEN THROUGH, I NEED SOMEONE TO WATCH MY BACK.
WE'RE BOTH TRYING TO WIN BACK THE TRUST OF THE PEOPLE WE CARE ABOUT MOST...
THE ONLY WAY TO DO THAT IS BY ACTING LIKE WE DESERVE IT.

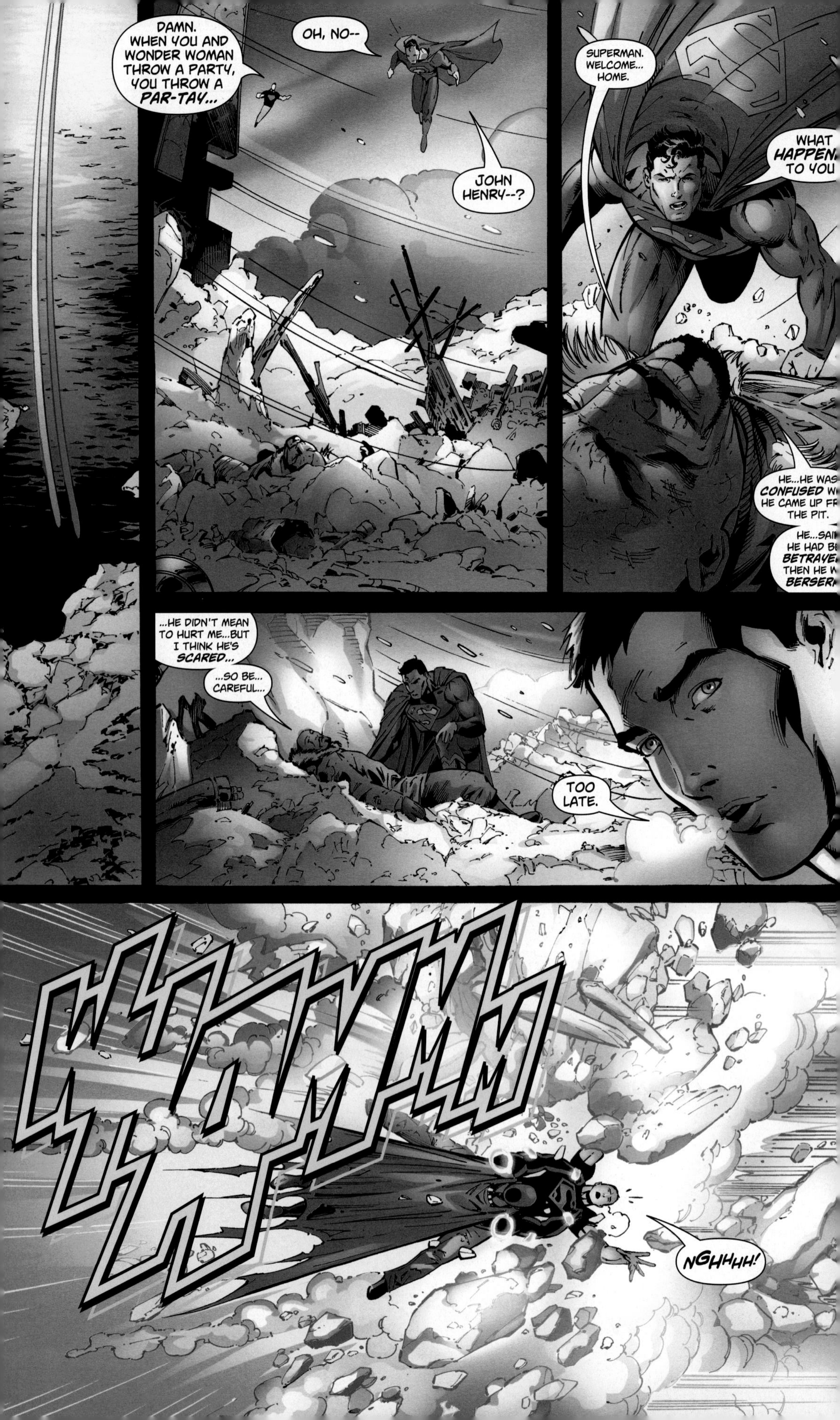
DAMN. WHEN YOU AND WONDER WOMAN THROW A PARTY, YOU THROW A PAR-TAY...
OH, NO--
JOHN HENRY--?
SUPERMAN. WELCOME... HOME.
WHAT HAPPEN TO YOU
HE...HE WAS CONFUSED W HE CAME UP FR THE PIT.
HE...SAI HE HAD B BETRAYE THEN HE W BERSER
...HE DIDN'T MEAN TO HURT ME...BUT I THINK HE'S SCARED...
...SO BE... CAREFUL...
TOO LATE.
NGHHHH!

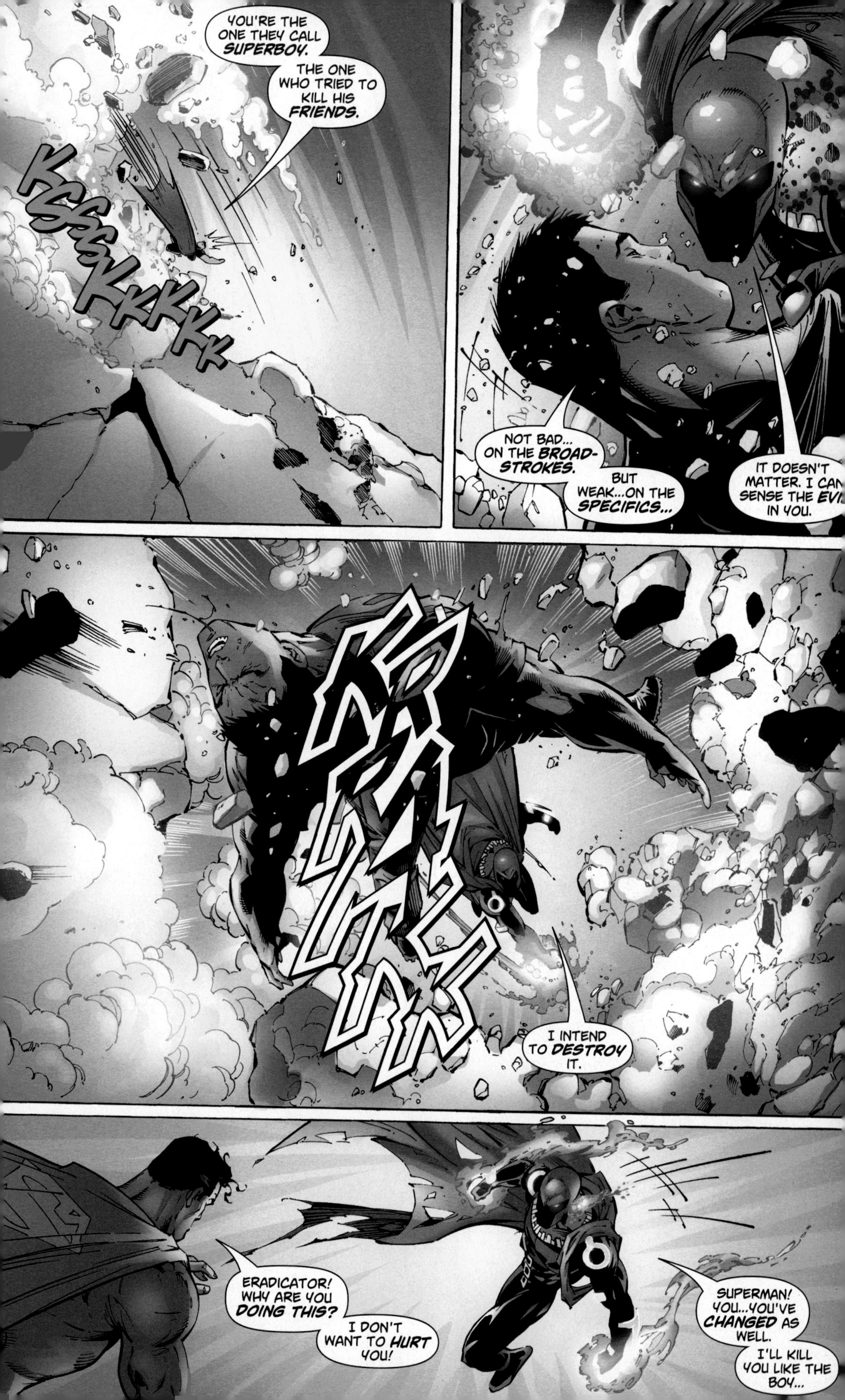

YOU'RE THE ONE THEY CALL SUPERBOY.
THE ONE WHO TRIED TO KILL HIS FRIENDS.
NOT BAD... ON THE BROAD-STROKES.
BUT WEAK...ON THE SPECIFICS...
IT DOESN'T MATTER. I CAN SENSE THE EVIL IN YOU.
I INTEND TO DESTROY IT.
ERADICATOR! WHY ARE YOU DOING THIS?
I DON'T WANT TO HURT YOU!
SUPERMAN! YOU...YOU'VE CHANGED AS WELL.
I'LL KILL YOU LIKE THE BOY...

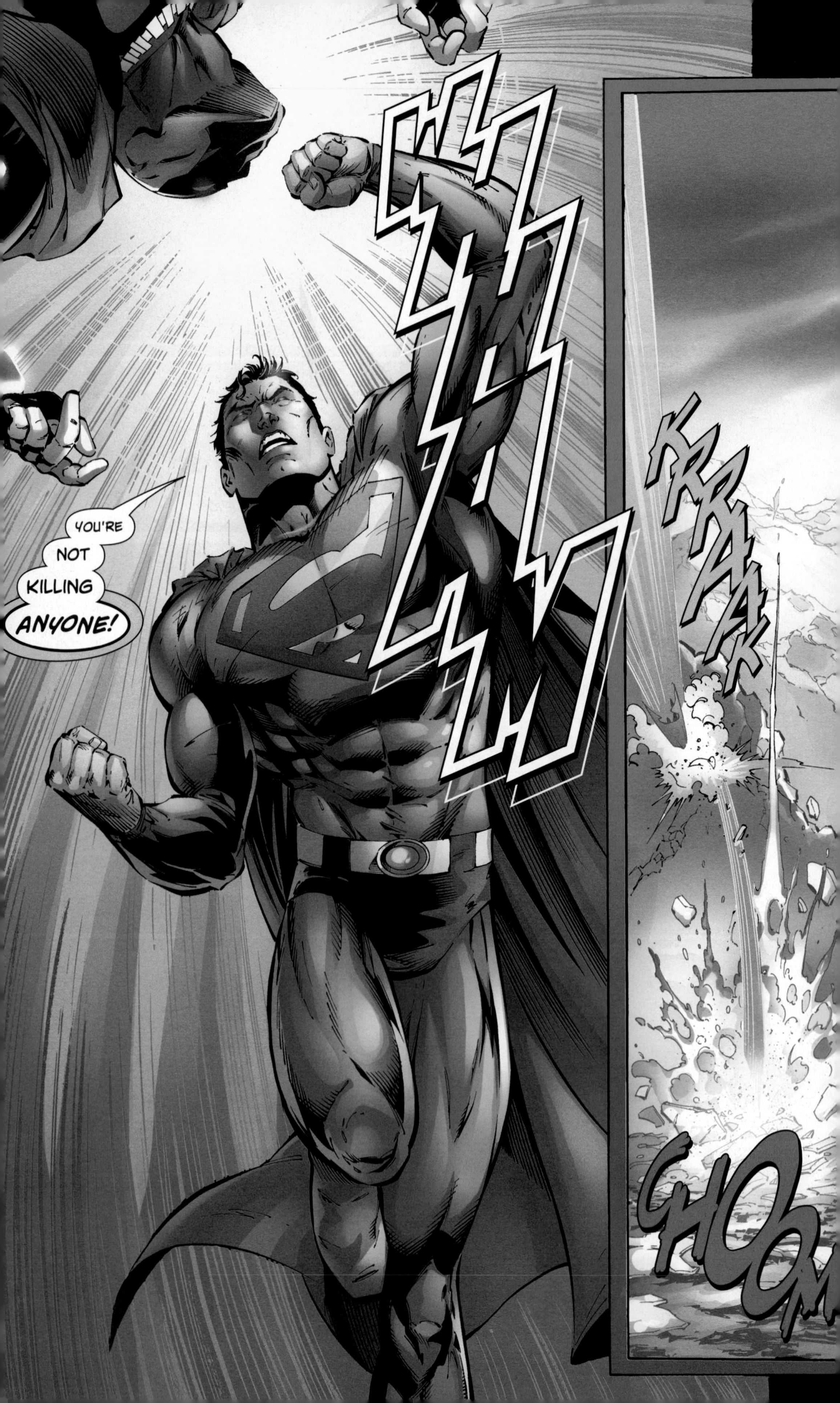

YOU'RE NOT KILLING ANYONE!
KRRAAKK

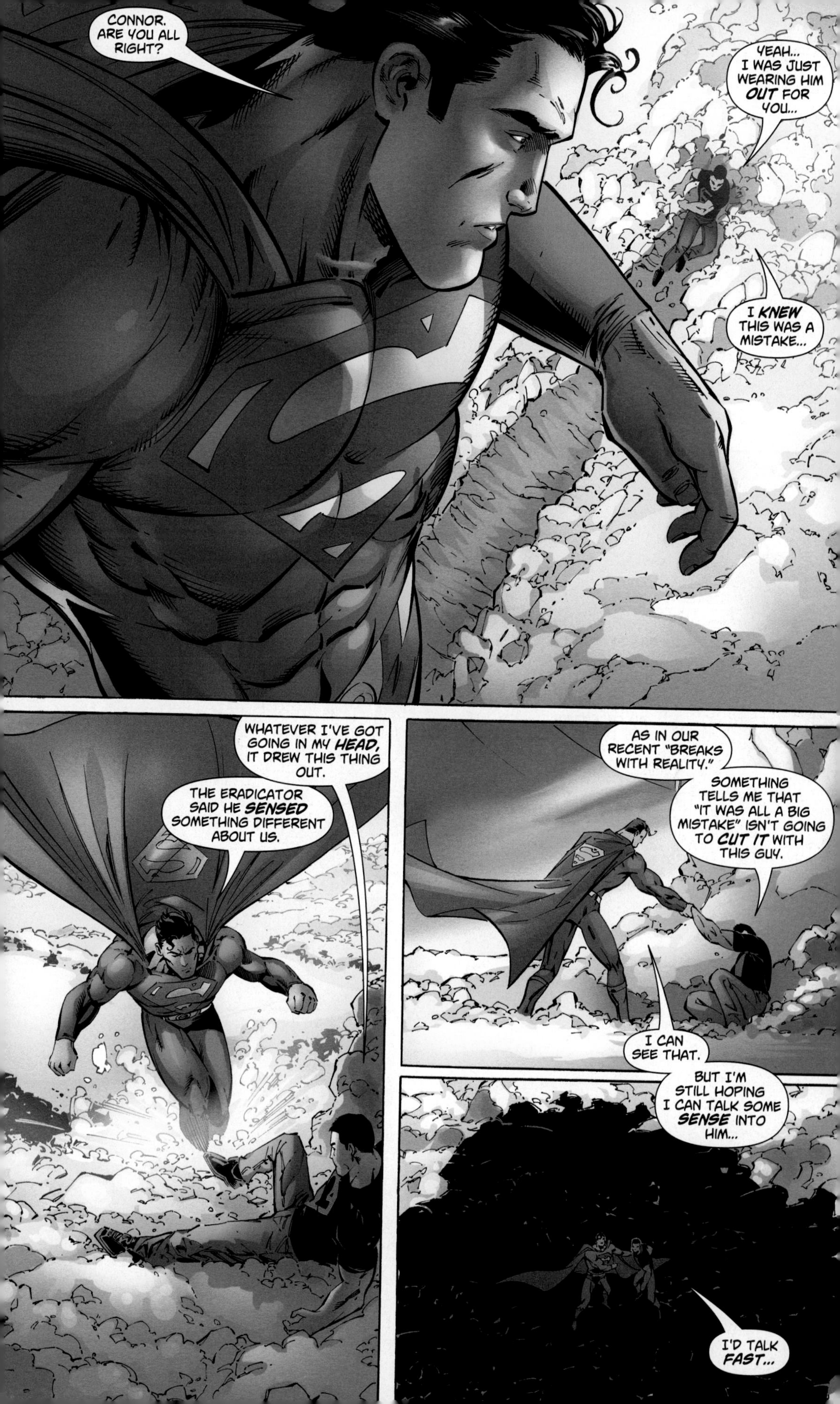
CONNOR. ARE YOU ALL RIGHT?
YEAH... I WAS JUST WEARING HIM OUT FOR YOU...
I KNEW THIS WAS A MISTAKE...
WHATEVER I'VE GOT GOING IN MY HEAD, IT DREW THIS THING OUT.
THE ERADICATOR SAID HE SENSED SOMETHING DIFFERENT ABOUT US.
AS IN OUR RECENT "BREAKS WITH REALITY."
SOMETHING TELLS ME THAT "IT WAS ALL A BIG MISTAKE" ISN'T GOING TO CUT IT WITH THIS GUY.
I CAN SEE THAT.
BUT I'M STILL HOPING I CAN TALK SOME SENSE INTO HIM...
I'D TALK FAST...

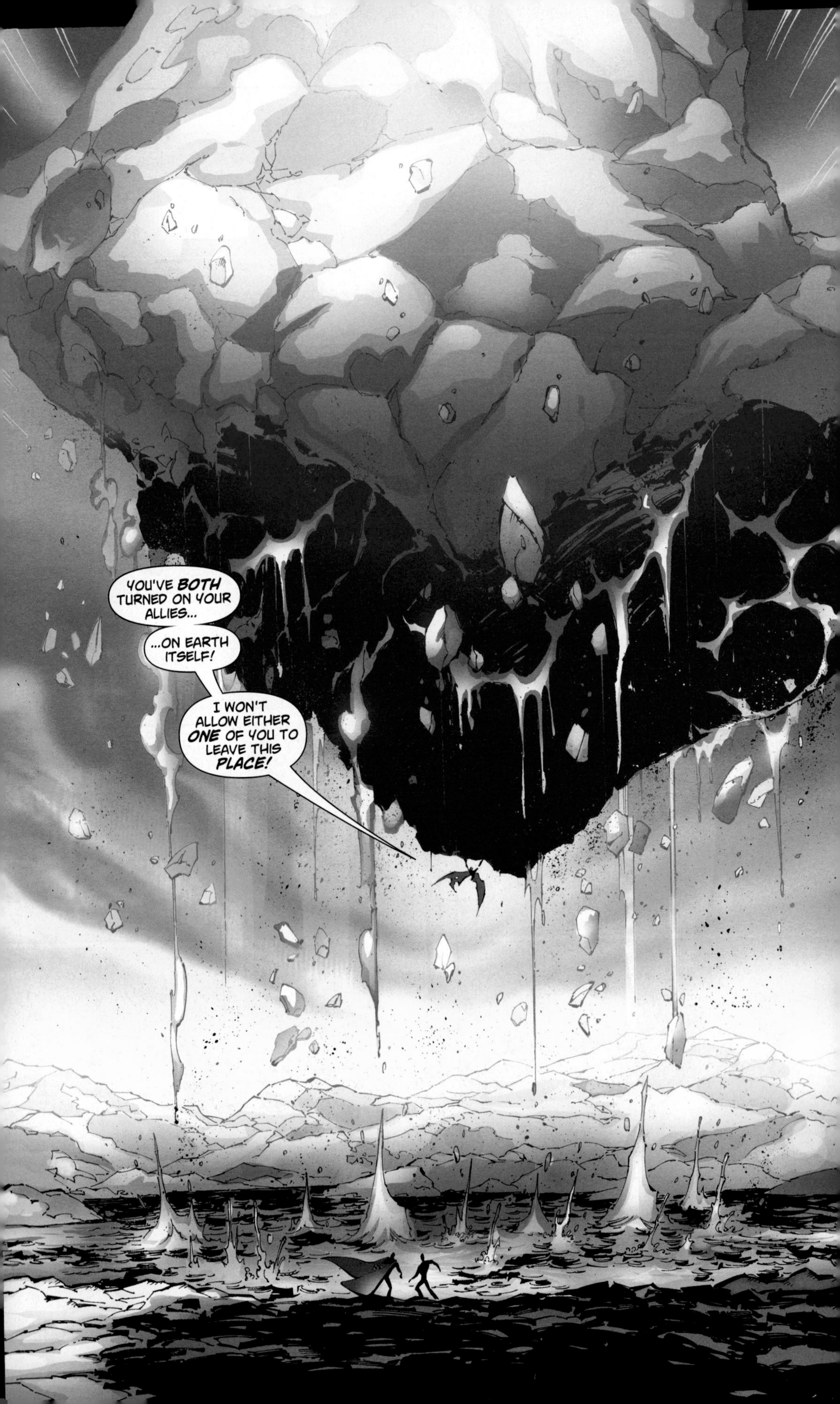
YOU'VE BOTH TURNED ON YOUR ALLIES...
...ON EARTH ITSELF!
I WON'T ALLOW EITHER ONE OF YOU TO LEAVE THIS PLACE!

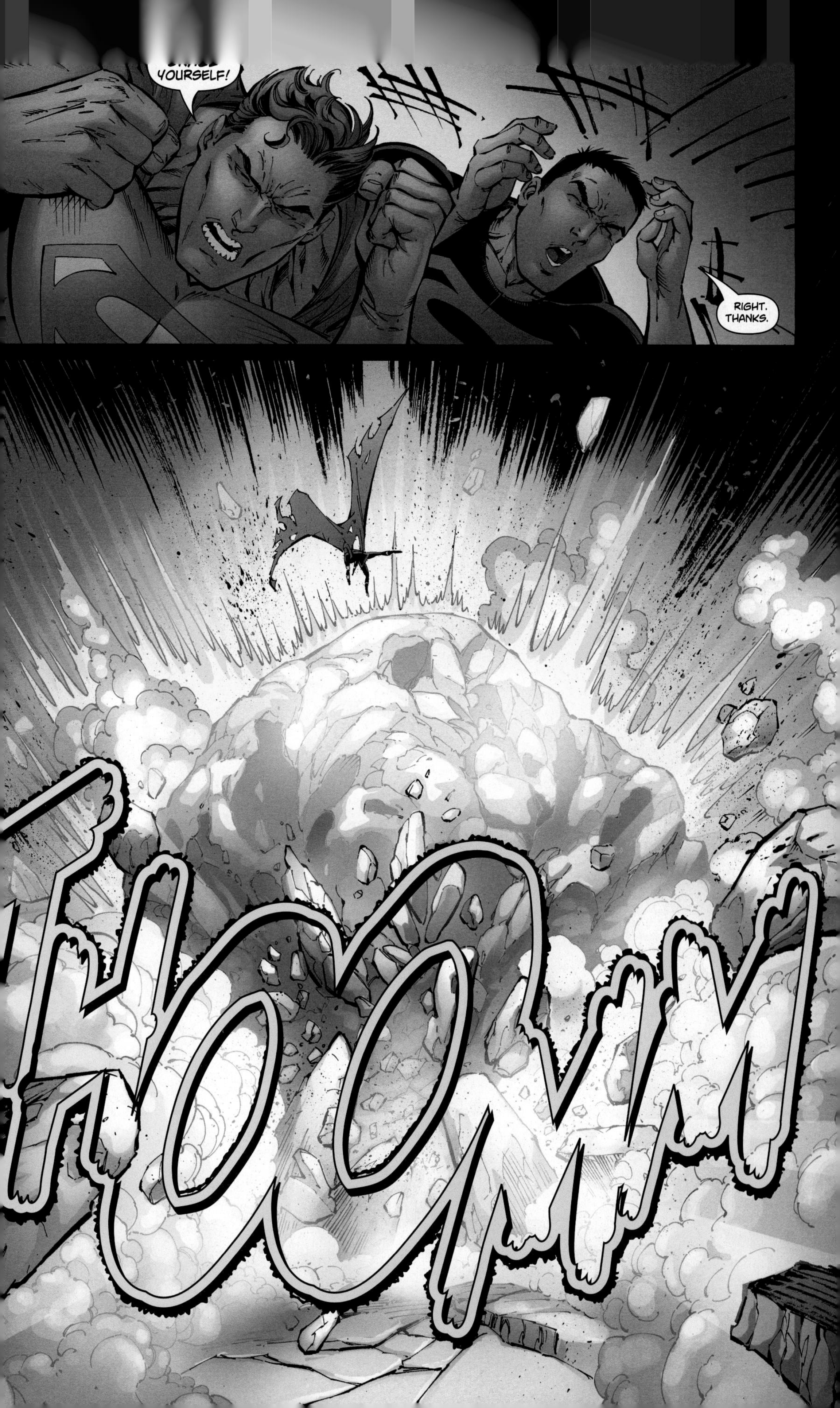
YOURSELF!
RIGHT. THANKS.

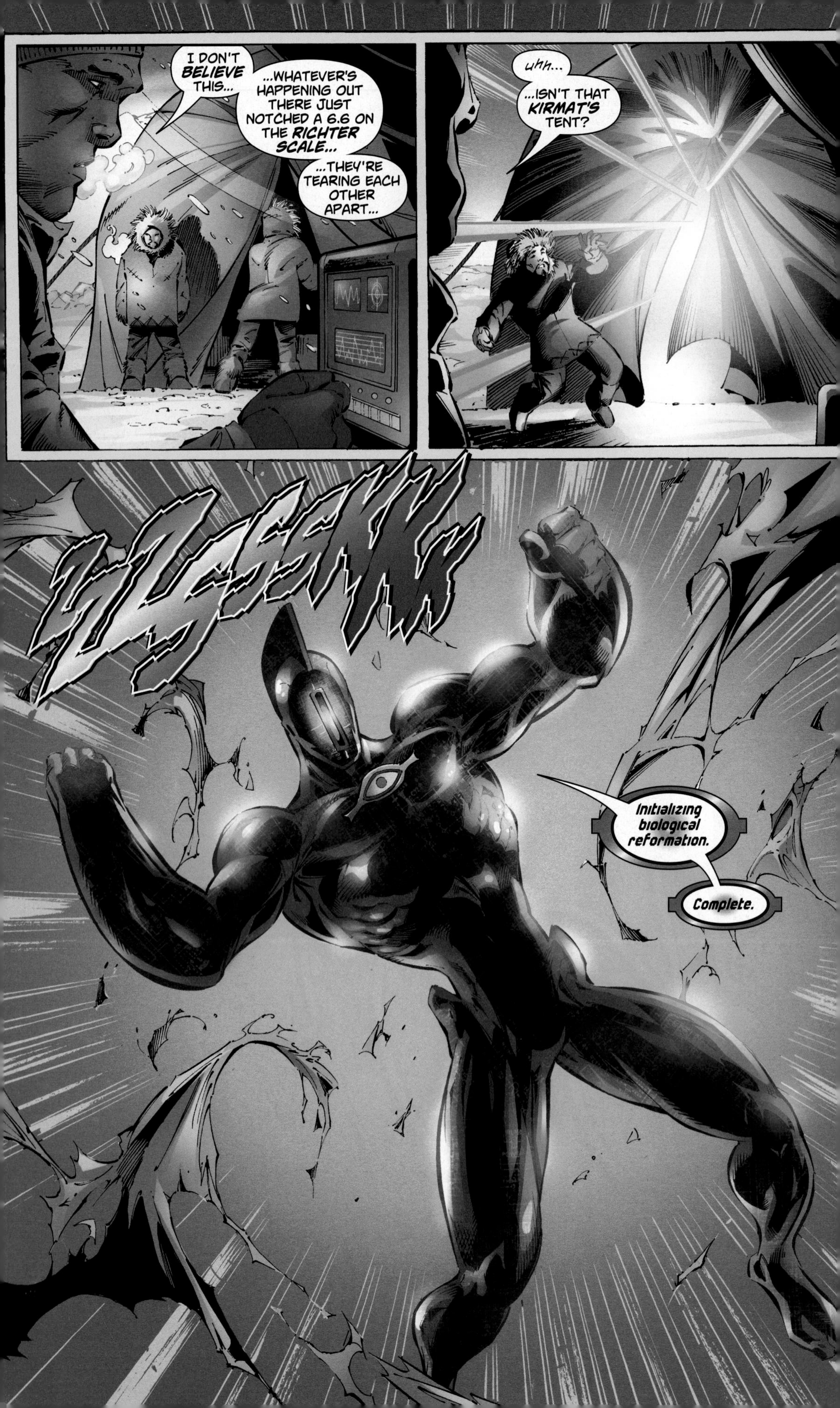
I DON'T BELIEVE THIS...
...WHATEVER'S HAPPENING OUT THERE JUST NOTCHED A 6.6 ON THE RICHTER SCALE...
...THEY'RE TEARING EACH OTHER APART...
uhh...
...ISN'T THAT KIRMAT'S TENT?
Initializing biological reformation.
Complete.

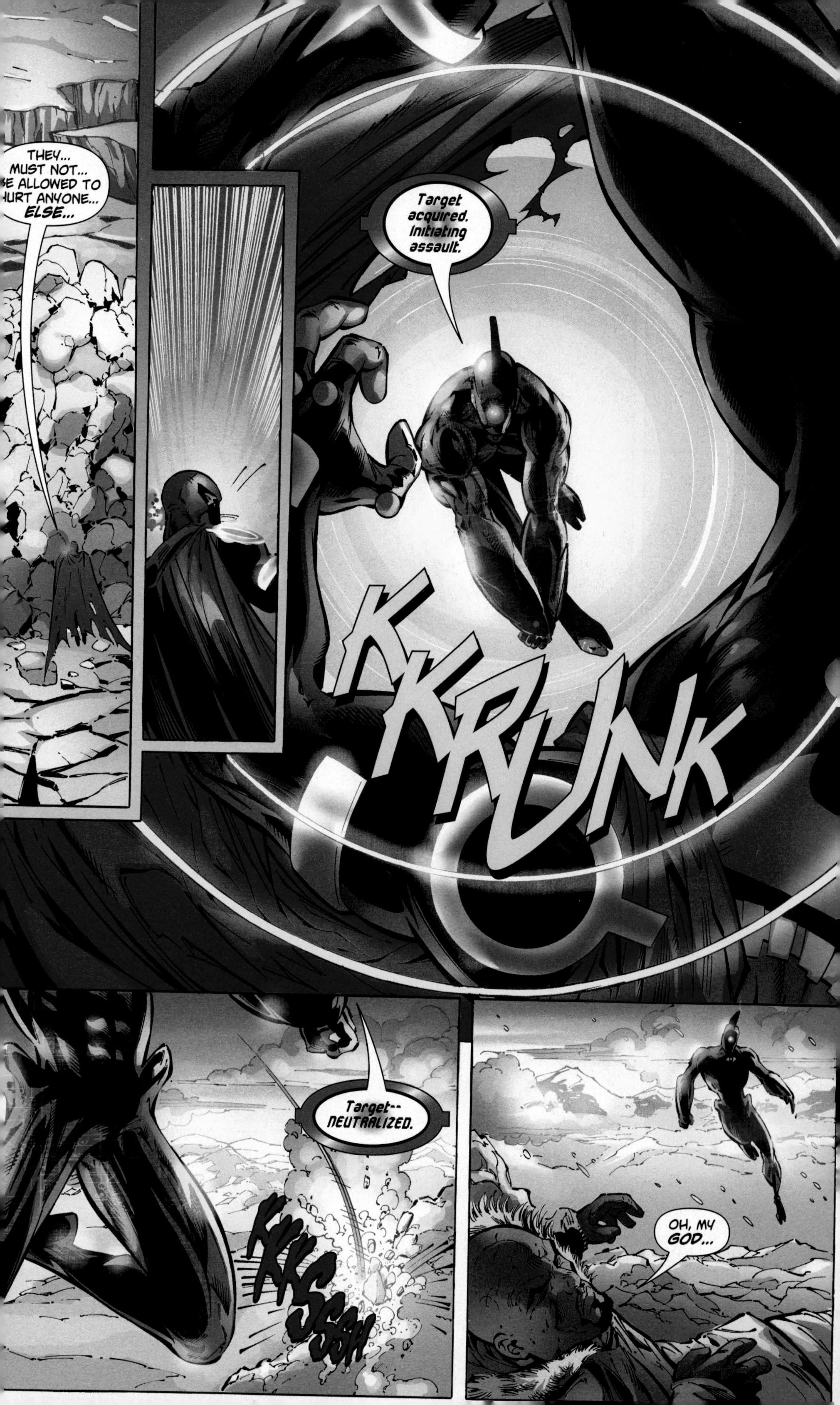

THEY... MUST NOT... BE ALLOWED TO HURT ANYONE... ELSE...
Target acquired. Initiating assault.
KKRUNK
Target-- NEUTRALIZED.
KKSSSH
OH, MY GOD...

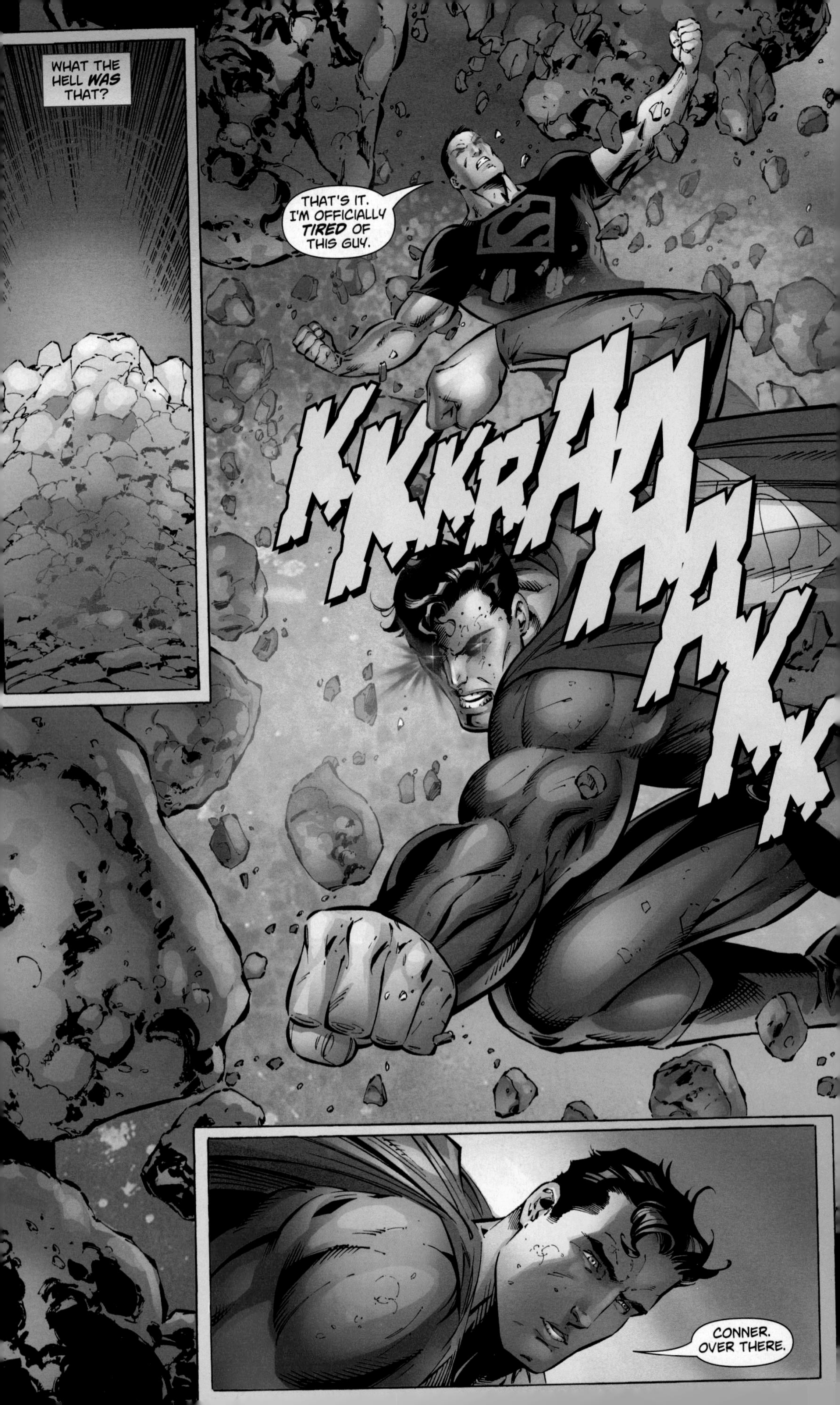

WHAT THE HELL *WAS* THAT?
THAT'S IT. I'M OFFICIALLY *TIRED* OF THIS GUY.
KKKRAAAAKK
CONNER. OVER THERE.

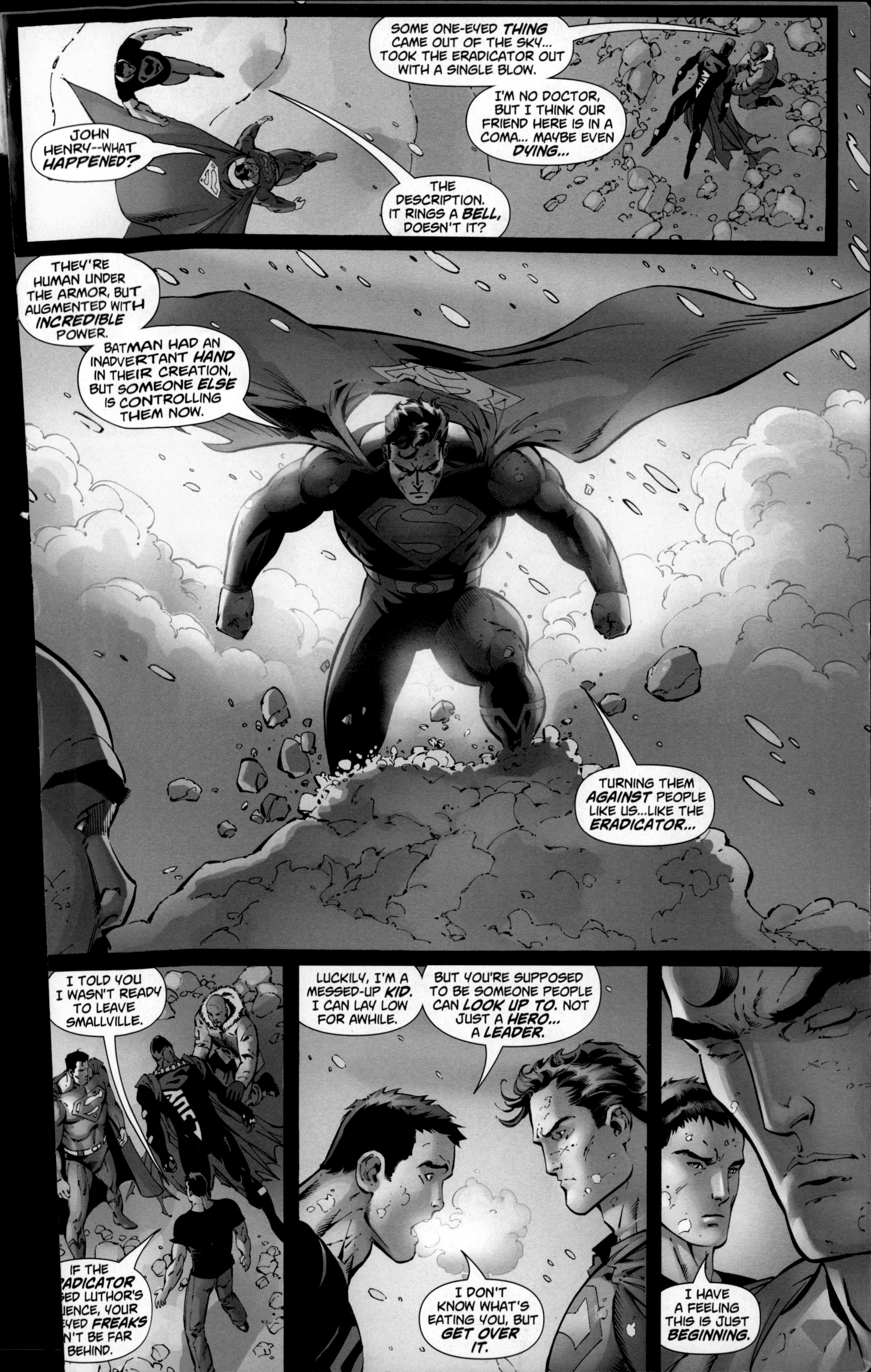

JOHN HENRY--WHAT HAPPENED?
SOME ONE-EYED THING CAME OUT OF THE SKY... TOOK THE ERADICATOR OUT WITH A SINGLE BLOW.
I'M NO DOCTOR, BUT I THINK OUR FRIEND HERE IS IN A COMA... MAYBE EVEN DYING...
THE DESCRIPTION. IT RINGS A BELL, DOESN'T IT?
THEY'RE HUMAN UNDER THE ARMOR, BUT AUGMENTED WITH INCREDIBLE POWER.
BATMAN HAD AN INADVERTANT HAND IN THEIR CREATION, BUT SOMEONE ELSE IS CONTROLLING THEM NOW.
TURNING THEM AGAINST PEOPLE LIKE US...LIKE THE ERADICATOR...
I TOLD YOU I WASN'T READY TO LEAVE SMALLVILLE.
IF THE RADICATOR GED LUTHOR'S IENCE, YOUR EYED FREAKS N'T BE FAR BEHIND.
LUCKILY, I'M A MESSED-UP KID. I CAN LAY LOW FOR AWHILE.
BUT YOU'RE SUPPOSED TO BE SOMEONE PEOPLE CAN LOOK UP TO. NOT JUST A HERO... A LEADER.
I DON'T KNOW WHAT'S EATING YOU, BUT GET OVER IT.
I HAVE A FEELING THIS IS JUST BEGINNING.

DC COMICS™

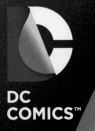

"Writer Geoff Johns and artist Jim Lee toss you–and their heroes–into the action from the very start and don't put on the brakes. DC's über-creative team craft an inviting world for those who are trying out a comic for the first time. Lee's art is stunning."—USA TODAY

"A fun ride."—IGN

START AT THE BEGINNING!

JUSTICE LEAGUE VOLUME 1: ORIGIN

GEOFF JOHNS and JIM LEE

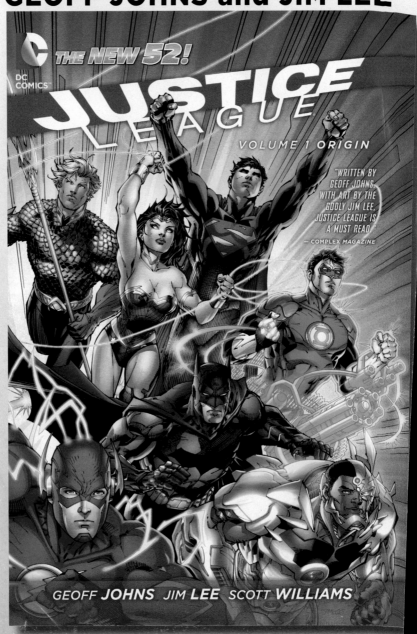

THE NEW 52!
DC COMICS
JUSTICE LEAGUE
VOLUME 1 ORIGIN
"WRITTEN BY GEOFF JOHNS, WITH ART BY THE GODLY JIM LEE, JUSTICE LEAGUE IS A MUST READ."
— COMPLEX MAGAZINE
GEOFF JOHNS JIM LEE SCOTT WILLIAMS

JUSTICE LEAGUE VOL. 2: THE VILLAIN'S JOURNEY

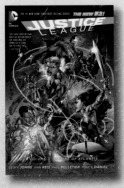

THE NEW 52!
JUSTICE LEAGUE
GEOFF JOHNS JIM LEE SCOTT WILLIAMS

JUSTICE LEAGUE VOL. 3: THRONE OF ATLANTIS

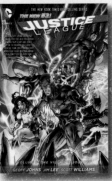

THE NEW 52!
JUSTICE LEAGUE
THRONE OF ATLANTIS
GEOFF JOHNS IVAN REIS PAUL PELLETIER TONY S. DANIEL

JUSTICE LEAGUE OF AMERICA VOL. 1: WORLD'S MOST DANGEROUS

JUSTICE LEAGUE OF AMERICA
WORLD'S MOST DANGEROUS
GEOFF JOHNS DAVID FINCH BRETT BOOTH DOUG MAHNKE

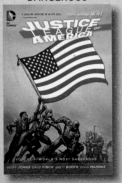